Han Civilization

汉英对照

汉代考古学概说

王仲殊 著　张光直等 译

外语教学与研究出版社
FOREIGN LANGUAGE TEACHING AND RESEARCH PRESS
北京 BEIJING

U0670455

图书在版编目 (CIP) 数据

汉代考古学概说：汉英对照 / 王仲殊著；张光直等译. — 北京：外语教学与研究出版社，2014.12
ISBN 978-7-5135-5375-9

I. ①汉⋯ II. ①王⋯ ②张⋯ III. ①秦汉考古－汉、英 IV. ①K871.41

中国版本图书馆 CIP 数据核字 (2014) 第 293629 号

地图审图号：GS (2014) 2888 号

出 版 人　蔡剑峰
系列策划　吴　浩
责任编辑　刘　佳　蒲　瑶
装帧设计　视觉共振设计工作室
出版发行　外语教学与研究出版社
社　　址　北京市西三环北路 19 号（100089）
网　　址　http://www.fltrp.com
印　　刷　中国农业出版社印刷厂
开　　本　650×980　1/16
印　　张　26
版　　次　2014 年 12 月第 1 版　2014 年 12 月第 1 次印刷
书　　号　ISBN 978-7-5135-5375-9
定　　价　50.00 元

购书咨询：（010）88819929　电子邮箱：club@fltrp.com
外研书店：http://www.fltrpstore.com
凡印刷、装订质量问题，请联系我社印制部
联系电话：（010）61207896　电子邮箱：zhijian@fltrp.com
凡侵权、盗版书籍线索，请联系我社法律事务部
举报电话：（010）88817519　电子邮箱：banquan@fltrp.com
法律顾问：立方律师事务所　刘旭东律师
　　　　　中咨律师事务所　殷　斌律师
物料号：253750001

"博雅双语名家名作"出版说明

　　1840 年鸦片战争以降，在深重的民族危机面前，中华民族精英"放眼看世界"，向世界寻求古老中国走向现代、走向世界的灵丹妙药，涌现出一大批中国主题的经典著述。我们今天阅读这些中文著述的时候，仍然深为字里行间所蕴藏的缜密的考据、深刻的学理、世界的视野和济世的情怀所感动，但往往会忽略：这些著述最初是用英文写就，我们耳熟能详的中文文本是原初英文文本的译本，这些英文作品在海外学术界和文化界同样享有崇高的声誉。

　　比如，林语堂的 *My Country and My People*（《吾国与吾民》）以幽默风趣的笔调和睿智流畅的语言，将中国人的道德精神、生活情趣和中国社会文化的方方面面娓娓道来，在美国引起巨大反响——林语堂也以其中国主题系列作品赢得世界文坛的尊重，并获得诺贝尔文学奖的提名。再比如，梁思成在抗战的烽火中写就的英文版《图像中国建筑史》文稿（*A Pictorial History of Chinese Architecture*），经其挚友费慰梅女士（Wilma C. Fairbank）等人多年的奔走和努力，于 1984 年由麻省理工学院出版社（MIT Press）出版，并获得美国出版联合会颁发的"专业暨学术书籍金奖"。又比如，1939 年，费孝通在伦敦政治经济学院的博士论文以 *Peasant Life in China—A Field Study of Country Life in the Yangtze Valley* 为名在英国劳特利奇书局（Routledge）出版，后以《江村经济》作为中译本书名——《江村经济》使得靠桑蚕为生的"开弦弓村"获得了世界性的声誉，成为国际社会学界研究中国农村的首选之地。

　　此外，一些中国主题的经典人文社科作品经海外汉学家和中国学者的如椽译笔，在英语世界也深受读者喜爱。比如，艾恺（Guy S. Alitto）将他 1980 年用中文访问梁漱溟的《这个世界会好吗——梁漱溟晚年口述》一书译成英文（*Has Man a Future? —Dialogues with the Last Confucian*），备受海内外读者关注；

此类作品还有徐中约英译的梁启超著作《清代学术概论》（*Intellectual Trends in the Ch'ing Period*）、狄百瑞（W. T. de Bary）英译的黄宗羲著作《明夷待访录》（*Waiting for the Dawn: A Plan for the Prince*），等等。

有鉴于此，外语教学与研究出版社推出"博雅双语名家名作"系列。

博雅，乃是该系列的出版立意。博雅教育（Liberal Education）早在古希腊时代就得以提倡，旨在培养具有广博知识和优雅气质的人，提高人文素质，培养健康人格，中国儒家六艺"礼、乐、射、御、书、数"亦有此功用。

双语，乃是该系列的出版形式。英汉双语对照的形式，既同时满足了英语学习者和汉语学习者通过阅读中国主题博雅读物提高英语和汉语能力的需求，又以中英双语思维、构架和写作的形式予后世学人以启迪——维特根斯坦有云："语言的边界，乃是世界的边界"，诚哉斯言。

名家，乃是该系列的作者群体。涵盖文学、史学、哲学、政治学、经济学、考古学、人类学、建筑学等领域，皆海内外名家一时之选。

名作，乃是该系列的入选标准。系列中的各部作品都是经过时间的积淀、市场的检验和读者的鉴别而呈现的经典，正如卡尔维诺对"经典"的定义：经典并非你正在读的书，而是你正在重读的书。

胡适在《新思潮的意义》（1919 年 12 月 1 日，《新青年》第 7 卷第 1 号）一文中提出了"研究问题、输入学理、整理国故、再造文明"的范式。秉着"记载人类文明、沟通世界文化"的出版理念，我们推出"博雅双语名家名作"系列，既希望能够在中国人创作的和以中国为主题的博雅英文文献领域"整理国故"，亦希望在和平发展、改革开放的新时代为"再造文明"、为"向世界说明中国"略尽绵薄之力。

外语教学与研究出版社
人文社科出版分社

1979 年，王仲殊（左）在美国哈佛大学讲学，张光直（右）翻译

List of Figures 图录

83. Pottery model of pigsty and privy, unearthed from a Han tomb in Luoyang
洛阳汉墓出土的陶猪圈及厕所模型
84. Taro harvesting depicted on pictorial brick unearthed in Pengxian, Sichuan
四川彭县出土的画像砖上的采芋图
85. Picking mulberry tree leaves depicted on pictorial stone at the Wu Liang Family Shrine in Jiaxiang, Shandong 山东嘉祥武梁祠画像石上的采桑图
86. Picking mulberry bush leaves depicted on pictorial brick unearthed in Chengdu, Sichuan
四川成都出土的画像砖上的采桑图
87. "Granary Records of Zheng Village"—inscribed bamboo slips (partial) unearthed from tomb number 10 at Fenghuangshan in Jiangling 江陵凤凰山十号墓出土的"郑里廪簿"（部分）
88. A manor depicted in a wall painting in the Han tomb at Holingor in Inner Mongolia (copy)
内蒙古和林格尔汉墓壁画中的庄园图（摹本）
89. Grazing horses depicted in wall painting in the Han tomb at Holingor in Inner Mongolia
内蒙古和林格尔汉墓出土的牧马图
90. Grazing cattle depicted in wall painting in the Han tomb at Holingor in Inner Mongolia
内蒙古和林格尔汉墓出土的牧牛图
91. Fortress and watchtower depicted in wall painting in the Han tomb at Holingor in Inner Mongolia
内蒙古和林格尔汉墓壁画中的堡垒和望楼
92. Clay figurine of farmer holding spade and wearing large knife, unearthed from a Han tomb at Tianhuishan in Chengdu, Sichuan 四川成都天廻山汉墓出土的持铲佩刀农夫俑
93. A military barracks in a wall painting in a Wei-Jin period tomb at Jiayuguan, Gansu
甘肃嘉峪关魏晋墓壁画·营垒图
94. A soldiers' farm in a wall painting in a Wei-Jin period tomb at Jiayuguan, Gansu
甘肃嘉峪关魏晋墓壁画·屯垦图

4 146 – 153

95. Lacquered *ding*-tripod unearthed from Han tomb number 1 at Mawangdui, Changsha
长沙马王堆汉墓一号墓出土的漆鼎
96. Lacquered box from Mawangdui Han tomb number 1 马王堆汉墓一号墓出土的漆盒
97. Lacquered boxes for toilet articles from Mawangdui Han tomb number 1
马王堆汉墓一号墓出土的漆奁
98. Lacquered tray and plates from Mawangdui Han tomb number 1
马王堆汉墓一号墓出土的漆案和漆盘
99. Lacquered plate with fabric core from Mawangdui Han tomb number 1
马王堆汉墓一号墓出土的夹纻胎漆盘
100. Lacquered ladles with bamboo cores from Mawangdui Han tomb number 1
马王堆汉墓一号墓出土的竹胎漆勺
101. Lacquered *hu* from Mawangdui Han tomb number 1 马王堆汉墓一号墓出土的漆壶
102. Lacquered *fang*-vessel from Mawangdui Han tomb number 1 马王堆汉墓一号墓出土的漆钫
103. Designs of silver sheets attached to lacquerware unearthed from a Han tomb in Lianyungang, Jiangsu
江苏连云港汉墓出土漆器的贴银箔花纹
104. Animal designs on lacquerware unearthed from a Han tomb near Pyongyang, Korea
朝鲜平壤出土漆器的动物图案
105. Fish designs on lacquerware unearthed from a Han tomb at Fenghuangshan in Jiangling
江陵凤凰山汉墓出土漆器的鱼纹
106. Lacquerware design depicting human figures in a story, unearthed from Shi Qi Yao's tomb from the Western Han period in Haizhou, Jiangsu 江苏海州侍其繇墓出土漆器的人物故事图
107. Lacquerware design depicting human figures in a story unearthed from Shi Qi Yao's tomb from the Western Han period in Haizhou, Jiangsu 江苏海州侍其繇墓出土漆器的人物故事图

5 *174 – 187*

186. Round-based pottery urn unearthed from the Western Han tomb in Guanghua, Hubei
湖北光化西汉墓出土的圆底陶瓮
187. "Duck-egg jar" unearthed from the Han tomb in Xinxiang, Henan　河南新乡汉墓出土的彩绘"鸭蛋壶"
188. Hard pottery jar with impressed designs, unearthed from the Han tomb in Mawangdui, Changsha
长沙马王堆汉墓出土的印纹硬陶罐
189. Hard pottery jar with impressed designs, unearthed from the Han tomb in Shaoxing, Zhejiang
浙江绍兴汉墓出土的印纹硬陶罐
190. Hard pottery jar with impressed designs, unearthed from the Han tomb in Shaoxing, Zhejiang
浙江绍兴汉墓出土的印纹硬陶罐
191. Hard pottery jar with impressed designs, unearthed from the Han tomb in Shaoxing, Zhejiang
浙江绍兴汉墓出土的印纹硬陶罐
192. Gourd-shaped jar unearthed from the Han tomb in Guangzhou　广州汉墓出土的匏壶
193. Jar with four interconnecting parts, unearthed from the Han tomb in Guangzhou
广州汉墓出土的四联罐
194. Pottery jar with three legs, unearthed from the Han tomb in Guangzhou　广州汉墓出土的三足陶罐
195. Pottery jar with green glaze of the Han dynasty, in the collection of the Palace Museum
汉绿釉陶壶（故宫博物院藏）
196. Pottery model of granary with green glaze, unearthed from the Han tomb in Lingbao, Henan
河南灵宝汉墓出土的绿釉陶仓
197. Pottery model of storied building with green glaze, unearthed from the Han tomb in Shaanxi
陕西汉墓出土的绿釉陶楼
198. Hard pottery jar with green glaze and purple core, unearthed from the Han tomb in Changsha
长沙汉墓出土的绿釉紫胎硬陶壶
199. Same as fig. 198, from Luoyang　洛阳出土的绿釉紫胎硬陶壶
200. Pottery lamp unearthed from the Han tomb in Luoyang　洛阳汉墓出土的陶灯
201. Pottery incense burner unearthed from the Han tomb in Luoyang　洛阳汉墓出土的陶薰炉
202. Pottery money jar unearthed from the Han tomb in Luoyang　洛阳汉墓出土的陶扑满
203. Pottery human figure on horseback, unearthed from the Han tomb at Yangjiawan in Xianyang,
Shaanxi　陕西咸阳杨家湾西汉墓中的骑马陶俑
204. Pottery dog unearthed from the Han tomb at Baiquan in Huixian, Henan
河南辉县百泉村汉墓中的陶狗
205. Pottery sheep from the same site as fig. 204　河南辉县百泉村汉墓中的陶羊
206. The names "He ting" and "He shi" stamped on pottery unearthed from the site of the Han town of
Henanxian in Luoyang　洛阳河南县汉墓出土陶器上的"河亭"、"河市"戳记
207. The name "Shan ting" stamped on pottery unearthed from the Han tomb in Shanxian, Henan
河南陕县汉墓出土陶器上的"陕亭"戳记
208. The name "Shan shi" stamped on pottery unearthed from the Han tomb in Shanxian, Henan
河南陕县汉墓出土陶器上的"陕市"戳记
209. The name "Han ting" stamped on pottery unearthed from a Han dynasty site in Handan, Hebei
河北邯郸汉代遗址出土陶器上的"邯亭"戳记
210. The name "An ting" stamped on pottery unearthed from a Han dynasty site in Xiaxian, Shanxi
山西夏县汉城遗址出土陶器上的"安亭"戳记
211. Clay seal impressed with the inscription "An cheng tao wei"　"安城陶尉"封泥
212. Hollow bricks of the Han dynasty, unearthed in Henan　河南出土的汉代空心砖
213. Small, rectangular brick of the Han dynasty, unearthed from a Han tomb in Luoyang
洛阳汉墓出土的小型长方砖
214. Square bricks unearthed at the site of the Han city of Chang'an in Xi'an
汉长安城遗址出土的正方砖
215. Granary built with small, rectangular bricks, excavated at the site of the Han town of Henanxian in
Luoyang　洛阳汉河南县城遗址发掘出的小型长方砖砌筑的粮仓

8   *282 – 303*

300. Bronze horses buried in the Han tomb at Leitai in Wuwei, Gansu　甘肃武威雷台汉墓中的铜马
301. Clay coins unearthed from Han tomb number 1 at Mawangdui, Changsha
长沙马王堆一号汉墓出土的泥钱
302. Silk book unearthed from Han tomb number 1 at Mawangdui, Changsha (*Laozi*, version A, in part)
长沙马王堆一号汉墓出土的帛书（《老子》，甲本，部分）
303. Silk book unearthed from Han tomb number 3 at Mawangdui, Changsha (*Laozi*, version B, in part)
长沙马王堆三号墓出土的帛书（《老子》，乙本，部分）
304. Bamboo slips of *Sun Bin bing fa* (in part), unearthed from the Han tomb at Yinqueshan, Linyi,
Shandong　山东临沂银雀山汉墓出土的竹书（《孙膑兵法，部分》）
305. Wooden slips of *Yi li*, unearthed from the Han tomb at Mozuizi, Wuwei, Gansu (reproductions)
甘肃武威磨咀子汉墓中木书（《仪礼》，复制品）
306. Seals with the inscriptions "Seal of Marquis Dai," "The Chengxiang of Changsha," and "Li Cang,"
unearthed from the Han tomb number 2 at Mawangdui, Changsha
长沙马王堆二号墓出土的印有"轪侯之印"、"长沙丞相"和"利苍"的印章
307. Bronze seals with the inscriptions "Don Wan" and "Dou Jun Xu," unearthed from Han tomb number 2
in Mancheng　满城二号汉墓出土的刻有"窦绾"、"窦君须"字样的铜印
308. "Tomb security jar" (dated the third year of Chu Ping), unearthed from a Han tomb in Luoyang
洛阳汉墓出土的初平三年镇墓瓶
309. Husband-and-wife burial in a Western Han tomb in Luoyang　洛阳西汉墓中的夫妇合葬
310. Husband-and-wife burial in an Eastern Han tomb in Luoyang　洛阳东汉墓中的夫妇合葬
311. Earthen mound of the mausoleum of Emperor Wu Di ("Mao Ling") in Xingpingxian, Shaanxi
陕西兴平的汉武帝陵（茂陵）
312. Cemetery of prisoner-laborers of Eastern Han, excavated at Xidajiaocun, Yanshixian, Henan
河南偃师西大郊村出土的东汉刑徒墓地
313. Tombs of prisoner-laborers of Eastern Han, excavated at Xidajiaocun, Yanshixian, Henan
河南偃师西大郊村的东汉刑徒墓地
314. Skeletons and inscribed bricks in the tombs of prisoner-laborers of Eastern Han, excavated at
Xidajiaocun, Yanshixian, Henan
河南偃师西大郊村的东汉刑徒墓地中的尸骨和刻有文字的砖
315. Prisoner-laborer brick inscribed with the designation "Kun qian," unearthed from a prisoner laborer
tomb at Xidajiaocun, Yanshixian, Henan
河南偃师西大郊村刑徒墓地中刻有"髡钳"字样的砖
316. Prisoner-laborer brick inscribed with "Wan cheng dan," unearthed from prisoner-laborer grave at
Xidajiaocun, Yanshixian, Henan　河南偃师西大郊村刑徒墓地中刻有"完城旦"字样的砖
317. Prisoner-laborer brick inscribed with "Gui xin," unearthed from prisoner-laborer grave at Xidajiaocun,
Yanshixian, Henan　河南偃师西大郊村刑徒墓地中刻有"鬼薪"字样的砖
318. Prisoner-laborer brick inscribed with "Si kou," unearthed from prisoner-laborer grave at Xidajiaocun,
Yanshixian, Henan　河南偃师西大郊村刑徒墓地中刻有"司寇"字样的砖
319. Commoner's grave of the Han dynasty, unearthed in Luoyang　洛阳汉代平民墓
320. Commoner's grave of the Han dynasty, unearthed in Luoyang　洛阳汉代平民墓

PREFACE

In the beginning of 1979, soon after China and the U.S. established diplomatic relations, five scholars from the Chinese Academy of Social Sciences (CASS) were invited to visit and lecture in the U.S. This was done as a part of an agreement between the China Association for Science and Technology and the Committee on Scholarly Communication with China (CSCC). The five people invited were Sun Yefang and Xu Dixin from the Institute of Economics, Xia Nai and Wang Zhongshu from the Institute of Archaeology, and Luo Ergang from the Institute of Modern History. After some deliberations, CASS sent only Xu Dixin and Wang Zhongshu from their respective institutions. Luo was unable to go due to health reasons.

Although the host institute in the U.S. was CSCC, the person directly responsible for receiving my team was Professor Kwang-Chih Chang of Harvard University. We agreed that I would stay three months in the U.S., spending more than one month at Harvard University in Cambridge, Mass., and then stay at University of Washington in Seattle and University of California at Berkeley for four weeks each. During the trip, aside from sightseeing and research, I would devote most of my energy to lecturing about Chinese archaeology of the Han period at these three universities.

In preparation, beginning in April 1979, I started writing my lecture manuscripts. I chose nine topics for the lectures. They were: "Chang'an: The Capital City of Western Han," "Luoyang: The Capital City of Eastern Han," "Han Dynasty Agriculture," "Lacquerware," "Bronzes," "Iron Implements," "Ceramics," "Tombs—I," and "Tombs—II." Two months before I left for the U.S. in early October of that year, I had finished all lecture preparations (including making hundreds of projector slides), and sent the materials to Professor Chang. He invited Sinologists in the U.S. to translate "Luoyang," "Han Dynasty Agriculture," "Lacquerware," "Bronzes," "Iron Implements," and "Ceramics" into English. He himself took on the translation of "Chang'an," "Tombs—I" and "Tombs—II." When I was in the U.S., besides lecturing all the nine topics at the three universities mentioned above, I also delivered speeches "Luoyang" at Columbia University and University of California at Los Angeles, and "Tombs—I, II" at the United States National Academy of Sciences and Stanford University.

In the 1960s and 1970s, it was popular for Western scholars in countries like the U.S. and U.K. to publish papers regarding the origin of civilizations. Professor Chang recognized this boom in international

前言

1979 年年初，在中美两国建立外交关系之后不久，按照中国科学技术协会与美中学术交流委员会的协议，美国方面邀请中国社会科学院的五名学者前去访问、讲学，他们是经济研究所的孙冶方、许涤新，考古研究所的夏鼐、王仲殊和近代史研究所的罗尔纲。经商议，社会科学院决定经济所的二人中去许涤新一人，考古所的二人中去王仲殊一人，近代史所的罗尔纲因健康欠佳，不能应邀。

美方的接待单位为美中学术交流委员会，但对我的接待主要是由哈佛大学教授张光直担当的。他与我约定在美国访问的时间为三个月，其中在剑桥城的哈佛大学一个多月，在西雅图的华盛顿大学和加利福尼亚大学伯克利分校各约四个星期。访问期间除参观、考察等活动以外，主要任务是在上述三个大学作学术讲演，主题为中国汉代考古学。

为此，从 1979 年 4 月开始，我便着手撰写讲演的文稿。我选了九个专题，作为讲演的题目。它们是：《西汉的都城——长安》、《东汉的都城——雒阳》、《汉代的农业》、《汉代的漆器》、《汉代的铜器》、《汉代的铁器》、《汉代的陶器》、《汉代的墓葬（上）》、《汉代的墓葬（下）》。在同年 10 月初动身赴美国之前约两个多月，我结束了全部讲演稿的撰写（并制作了数百枚供讲演时放映的幻灯片），将稿件邮送给张光直教授。张光直约请几位美国的汉学家分别用英文翻译《雒阳》、《农业》、《漆器》、《铜器》、《铁器》、《陶器》各专题的讲演稿，他本人则担任《长安》、《墓葬（上）》、《墓葬（下）》三个专题文稿的翻译。到了美国以后，除了在上述三个大学各作九个专题的全部讲演以外，我还分别在哥伦比亚大学和加利福尼亚大学洛杉矶分校讲《雒阳》，在美国国家科学院和斯坦福大学讲《墓葬（上）》和《墓葬（下）》。

在 20 世纪六七十年代，文明起源为一项时兴的课题，美、英等西方国家的学者们发表了不少相关的论著。张光直教授趁这股国际上的

academia, and initiated the publication of a series of books on early Chinese civilization. This was a collective effort to popularize the study of ancient China. Chang himself wrote *Shang Civilization*, while professor Cho-yun Hsü at the University of Pittsburgh co-authored *Western Chou Civilization*. Later, Li Xueqin at the Institute of History of CASS published *Eastern Zhou and Qin Civilizations*. The series of the nine lectures was compiled by Chang into a book entitled "Han Civilization," and published in 1982 by Yale University Press. Chang himself contributed the foreword, and Yu Ying-shih of Yale University revised the manuscript.

Xia Nai, who had been in charge of the Institute of Archaeology of CASS for long, was my mentor in my youth. After seeing my lecture manuscripts translated and published in the U.S., he suggested that the original text should also be organized into a book and published in China. I did as he suggested, and brought the nine lectures together to produce the Chinese edition, whose name literally means "A Brief Examination of Han Dynasty Archaeology." This book was published by the Zhonghua Book Company in Beijing in 1984.

By coincidence, Professor Xia was also invited to visit the U.S. in 1981, and gave lectures on "Jade and Silk of Han China." His lecture manuscripts were translated into English and published in book form in the U.S. Some American scholars thought that *Han Civilization* and Professor Xia's book were coherent in content, calling them "sister works." I find this comparison a great honor, and feel very happy.

Now, Foreign Language Teaching and Research Press plans to include both Professor Xia's *Jade and Silk of Han China* and my *Han Civilization* in the "Bilingual Series of Liberal Arts Masterpieces," so I take this occasion to write this foreword, explaining how these books came into being. I hope readers would like them.

Wang Zhongshu
February 25, 2013
(Translated by Qi Chen at Columbia University)

学术热潮，从弘扬中国古代文明的立场出发，筹划了一套中国古代早期文明研究丛书的编撰出版。他自己写了《商文明》，在美国匹兹堡大学任教授的许倬云写了《西周文明》，以后又有中国社会科学院历史研究所的李学勤写《东周与秦代文明》。我的关于汉代考古学的九个专题讲演稿由张光直编译成一本新书，书名定为"Han Civilization"（《汉代文明》）。他为《汉代文明》写了序言，并请美国耶鲁大学教授余英时审核书稿而于1982年由耶鲁大学出版社出版。

当时，长期任考古研究所所长的夏鼐先生是我青年时代的导师。夏先生看到我在美国的九个专题讲演稿已由张光直及其他美国学者译为英文，并编辑成书在美国出版，他主张我的中文原稿亦应编成一本专书，在中国国内出版。我遵从夏鼐先生的意旨，将九个专题的中文原稿编成一本名为《汉代考古学概说》的书，由北京的中华书局于1984年出版。

事有巧合，夏鼐先生也于1981年应邀访问美国，在美国的大学作题为《汉代的玉器和丝绸》的学术讲演。美国方面将夏鼐先生的原稿译为英文，并编成专书而在美国出版。美国学者称夏先生的《汉代的玉器和丝绸》与我的《汉代文明》（《汉代考古学概说》）属内容连贯、关系密切的姐妹卷，使我深感荣幸，十分欣喜。

最近，外语教学与研究出版社决定要将夏鼐先生的《汉代的玉器和丝绸》和我的《汉代文明》（《汉代考古学概说》）列入其所编"博雅双语名家名作"，找便写了这篇"序言"，以叙明当初的事情、缘由，供读者参考。

王仲殊
2013年2月25日

FOREWORD TO THE ENGLISH EDITION (1982)

Of all the historical dynasties of imperial China, the Han is without question the most archaeologically dependent. On the one hand, because of the Han custom of richly furnishing the brick- and stone-constructed graves, archaeologists have been particularly amply rewarded with Han remains, including many written documents. On the other, because of Han's antiquity, its traditional literary documentation is glaringly incomplete. Therefore, a book on Han archaeology has long been awaited by not only Han scholars but also students interested in Chinese history, art, and archaeology.

The present volume, in which Wang Zhongshu masterfully summarizes the important archaeological data pertaining to the Han civilization, is that long-awaited book. In it the latest data are carefully synthesized and presented by one of China's principal archaeologists of the Han civilization. Wang Zhongshu, research fellow and deputy director of the Institute of Archaeology, Chinese Academy of Social Sciences, has not only participated in many excavations at Han sites, but also was the director of the excavations of the site of Chang'an in the 1950s and early 1960s.

In October 1979 Wang Zhongshu gave a series of nine lectures on Han dynasty archaeology at Harvard University. He came under the auspices of a senior lectureship program arranged between the Committee on Scholarly Communication with China (Washington, D.C.) and the China Association for Science and Technology (Beijing). After speaking at Harvard, Wang delivered some of the same lectures at the University of Washington (Seattle) and the University of California (Berkeley) before returning to China. At Harvard, Wang's visit was sponsored by the American School of Prehistoric Research at the Peabody Museum of Archaeology and Ethnology, and his lectures were delivered at the departments of Anthropology, East Asian Languages and Civilizations, and Fine Arts.

Soon after their arrival in Cambridge, Wang and his assistant, Xu

Pingfang, who is a senior archaeologist best known for his work at Yuan Dadu, raised with me the possibility of publishing his lectures in this country. Having received the Chinese texts of his forthcoming lectures beforehand, I was familiar with their rich content and superb quality, and I reacted enthusiastically to the idea. Soon they decided to entrust me with the task that has resulted in the volume that appears before you.

1982 年英文版序言

在中国的历朝历代中，汉代无疑是最依赖考古研究的一个。一方面，汉代厚葬的风俗使考古学家在砖石结构的墓室中发现了大量包括文字资料在内的汉代遗迹；另一方面，由于汉代年代久远，很多传统文献已残缺不全。因此，无论是汉学家，还是对中国历史、艺术、考古感兴趣的学生都对有关汉代考古研究的著作期待已久。

《汉代考古学概说》正是这样一部让人期待已久的著作。作者娴熟地总结了与汉文明相关的考古资料，将其经过审慎的整合后在书中呈现。王仲殊是中国社会科学院考古研究所的副所长和研究员，曾参与众多汉代遗址的发掘工作，并于 19 世纪 50 年代至 60 年代初期主持了长安城遗址的发掘，是中国汉代考古的主要研究者之一。

1979 年 10 月，在美中学术交流委员会（华盛顿特区）和中国科学技术协会（北京）联合举办的高级讲师项目支持下，王仲殊以汉代考古学为主题在哈佛大学、华盛顿大学（西雅图）和加州大学（伯克利）分别进行了数场讲座。在哈佛，王仲殊的访问得到了皮博迪考古与民族学博物馆美国史前研究院的赞助，讲座分别在人类学系、东亚语言与文明系以及艺术系举办。

到达剑桥后不久，王仲殊和他的助手——以元大都研究而著称的资深考古学家徐苹芳，问我是否有可能在美国出版这一系列讲座内容。讲座之前我就收到了中文讲稿，深知稿件内容丰富，且质量极高，因此，我积极地回应了这一提议。随后他们将此书的出版工作委托于我，成果便是大家眼前的这部著作。

The book could not have been prepared without two sources of generous support. The first is the National Endowment for the Humanities, which awarded me a grant to help prepare the manuscript for publication. I am grateful to the Endowment, which, of course, will not be held responsible for any of the views expressed herein.

The other source of support comes from my Harvard colleagues who served as interpreters during Wang's lectures, given in Chinese, and generously placed at my disposal the English translations of the various chapters they had prepared. They are Professor Ronald Egan of the Department of East Asian Languages and Civilizations, who translated chapters 2 and 3; Dr. Loh Wai-fong, of the same department, chapters 5 and 6; Mr. Robert Mowry, of the Fogg Museum (now curator of the Asia House Gallery in New York), chapter 7; and Ms. Jenny So, of the Department of Fine Arts, chapter 4. (Chapters 1, 8, and 9 were translated by me.) Mr. Thatcher Deane of the University of Washington provided me with his own translation of chapter 6, a particularly difficult chapter to translate, and I frequently consulted it in preparing the final manuscript. I thank all of them for their excellent work and herein acknowledge their respective contributions. As editor, however, I alone am responsible for any errors of translation. Most of the illustrations in this volume appeared previously either in publications of the Chinese Academy of Social Sciences or in the journal *Wenwu*. In each case, the appearance is noted in the endnotes. The author and editor acknowledge their gratitude to the Academy and *Wenwu* for allowing them to be published here. The footnotes and the captions for illustrations were translated by me, and I prepared the appendix.

Figures 2, 28, 29, 30, 37, and 42, and the frontispiece have been redrawn by Mrs. Nancy Lambert Brown.

Harvard University   K. C. Chang
                                                        September 1, 1980

本书的出版有赖于两方面的大力支持。首先，非常感谢美国人文基金会，他们为本书的出版提供了经费。当然，本书观点与基金会无关。

另一方面的支持来自哈佛大学的同事们，他们曾在王仲殊先生讲座期间承担口译工作，又慷慨地将他们准备的各章节的英文译稿提供给我。东亚语言与文明系的艾朗诺教授和陆惠风教授分别翻译了第2、3章和第5、6章；福格艺术博物馆的罗伯特·莫里先生（现纽约亚洲博物馆馆长）翻译了第7章；艺术系的苏芳淑女士翻译了第4章；我翻译了第1、8、9章。华盛顿大学的杜泰池先生向我提供了他自己翻译的第6章，这一章极难翻译，我在准备终稿时曾多次查阅他的译文。在此，我要对所有人的出色工作致以敬意，对他们的贡献表示感谢。译本中若出现任何错误，我作为编者将承担全部责任。书中大部分插图之前都曾出现在中国社会科学院的出版物或者《文物》杂志上，上述情况都在尾注中作了说明，在此本书作者和编者对社科院及《文物》杂志表示感谢。此外，我翻译了脚注及图说，并编写了附录。（按：不同译者对同一专有名词的译法略有出入，根据作者意见，本版不作改动。）

图2、28、29、30、37、42以及卷首插图由南希·兰伯特·布朗女士重新绘制。

张光直
哈佛大学
1980年9月1日

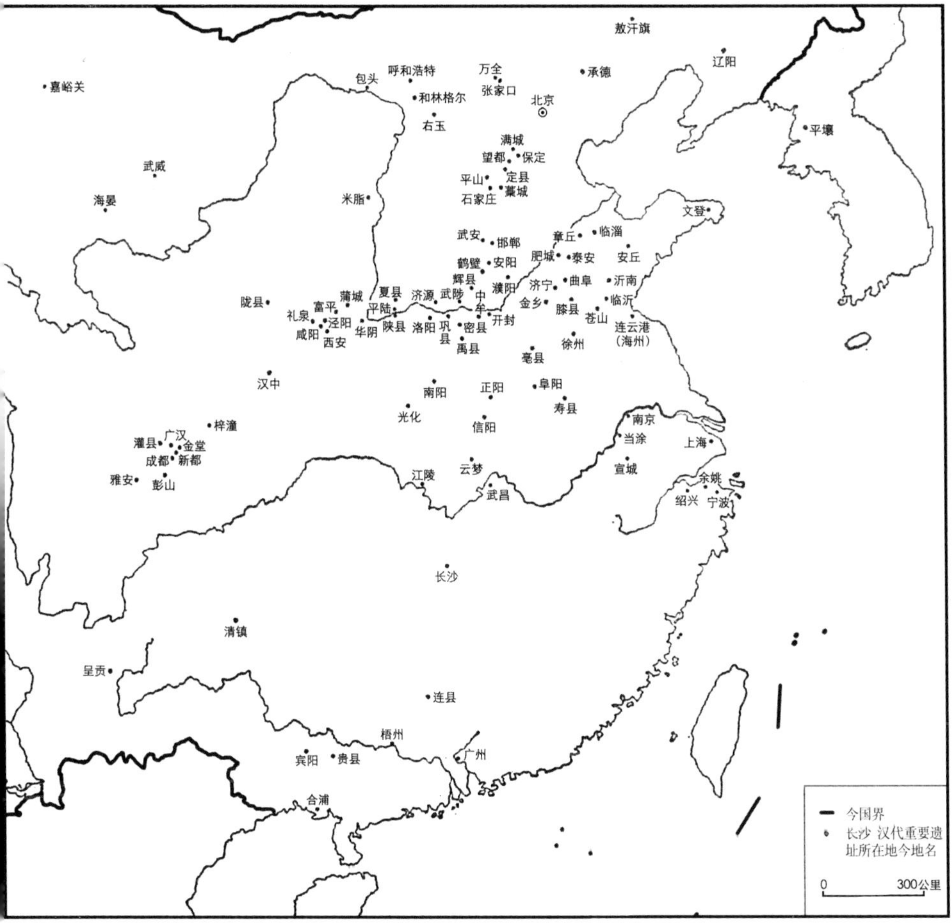

嘉峪关

武威

海晏

陇县

礼泉 富平
咸阳 泾阳
西安 华阴

汉中

雅安 彭山
成都 新都
灌县 广汉 金堂
梓潼

呈贡

清镇

宾阳 贵县
梧州
合浦

包头 呼和浩特 万全
和林格尔 张家口
右玉

米脂

敖汗旗

承德

北京

辽阳

平壤

文登

满城
望都 保定
平山 定县
石家庄 藁城

武安 邯郸 章丘 临淄
鹤壁 安阳 肥丝 泰安 安丘
夏县 济源 辉县 濮阳 曲阜 沂南
蒲城 武陟 济宁 临沂
平陆 中牟 金乡 滕县 苍山
陕县 巩县 开封 连云港
洛阳 密县 亳县 徐州 (海州)
禹县

南阳 正阳 阜阳
光化 信阳 寿县

江陵 云梦
武昌

南京
当涂 上海
宣城 余姚
绍兴 宁波

长沙

连县

广州

今国界

长沙 汉代重要遗
址所在地今地名

0   300公里

Map of China showing locations of major Han dynasty sites 汉代重要考古遗迹分布图

CHAPTER 1   CHANG'AN: THE CAPITAL CITY OF WESTERN HAN

The ruins of Chang'an, the capital city of Western Han, are located about 3 km northwest of the present Xi'an city, Shaanxi Province, and 2 km south of the Weishui River. Seeing the remnants of its city walls (fig. 1) and the scattered tiles there, one can imagine the magnificent scale and the prosperity of Chang'an in the past. The Qin capital city of Xianyang is north of the Weishui River. Probably the Han dynasty capital was built south of the river because the land here was more level and wider and because the south-of-the-river region had better access to the vast areas east of the Hangu Gate.

The building of the city of Chang'an was accomplished in three stages during the Han dynasty. (1) Under Emperor Gao Zu, the Changlegong Palace was an expansion of Xinglegong, a Qin dynasty resort palace. In addition, the Weiyanggong Palace was constructed to the west of Changlegong, and an armory was built between the two palaces. (2) Under Emperor Hui Di, the city wall was constructed. The building of the wall probably began at the northwestern corner: the west wall was the first to be erected, next the south wall, then the east wall, and finally the north wall. (3) Under Emperor Wu Di, the Mingguanggong Palace was built north of Changlegong; the Guigong and Beigong palaces were built north of Weiyanggong; and the Jianzhanggong Palace was constructed to the west, outside the city. In addition, the Shanglinyuan Park was expanded and the artificial lake called Kunmingchi was opened. At that point, the capital city was basically complete.

City Wall   The plan of the city is basically square, with the city oriented according to the cardinal directions. However, the city wall was constructed after completion of the Changlegong and Weiyanggong palaces and adjusting its course to the locations of these two palaces caused the south wall to zigzag. The north wall also zigzagged, due to topography and the course of the river. The book *San fu huang tu* (*A Guide to the Three Military Districts of the Capital*) claims that the southern part of the city was shaped like the Southern Dipper and the northern part, like the Big Dipper. It appears that these so-called dipper shapes are a later speculation and were not represented in the original design. Neither Ban Gu nor Zhang Heng, in their famous poems about Chang'an, *Xi du fu* and *Xi jing fu*, used the dipper analogy.

When archaeologists investigated the Chang'an ruins, they found that most of the wall was still exposed above ground. Many wall sections

🏛 西汉的都城——长安

西汉的首都长安城遗址，在今陕西省西安市西北约三公里，北距渭水南岸约二公里。在遗址上，但见残存的城墙绵亘起伏，重重叠叠的瓦片遍地皆是，昔日宏大的规模和繁华的景象于此可以想见（图1）。秦代首都咸阳城，在渭水北岸。汉代将都城建在渭水之南，可能是出于地形方面的选择。特别是从加强首都与函谷关以东广大地区的联系来考虑，这里的交通条件要比渭北便利得多。

长安城的建设，大体上可以分为三个阶段。汉高祖时，将秦代的离宫兴乐宫改建为长乐宫，在长乐宫的西面兴建未央宫，又在长乐、未央两宫之间建武库。汉惠帝时筑城墙（其进程大概是从城的西北方起，先筑西墙，再筑南墙，又筑东墙，最后筑北墙），并建东市和西市。汉武帝时，在长乐宫的北面建明光宫，在未央宫的北面建桂宫、修北宫，在西面城外建建章宫，并扩建上林苑，开凿昆明池，都城的规模至此大备。

长安城的平面形状，基本上呈方形，正方向，经纬相等。但是，由于城墙的建筑是在长乐宫和未央宫已经建成之后，必须迁就两宫的位置，所以南面城墙有多处曲折。北面城墙因地势的关系，主要是由于河道的限制，更有许多曲折、偏斜之处。《三辅黄图》说："城南为南斗形，城北为北斗形。"其实，所谓南斗形和北斗形是出于后世的附会，并非筑城时有意模仿。班固《西都赋》和张衡《西京赋》在叙述长安城的形制时都没有提到南斗形和北斗形，也足以说明这一问题。考古工作者在长安城遗址勘察时，大部分城墙犹高出地面，虽然有不少断缺之处，但仍有墙基

collapsed, but underground the foundations still remained. According to the two surveys of 1957 and 1962, the east wall was 6,000 m long, the south wall 7,600 m, the west wall 4,900 m, and the north wall 7,200 m. The total length of the four walls was 25,700 m, which corresponds to a little over 62 *li** according to the Han system of measurement. This basically conforms to the recorded 63 *li* in *Han jiu yi.* The total area was about 36 km^2 (fig. 2).[1]

The city wall was built of rammed yellow earth. Its height was over 12 m, and the width at base was 12 to 16 m. The description of the wall's dimensions in *San fu huang tu* (3.5 *zhang* tall, 1.5 *zhang* wide at base, and 9 *chi* at top) is not accurate. Despite its construction of earth, without bricks or stones, the wall has proved to be unexpectedly strong (figs. 3, 4). According to *Hanshu* ("Hui Di ji"), the wall was built by conscript labor provided by farmers who lived within a 600-*li* radius of Chang'an and by prisoners sent in by the feudal lords and princes. One wall section required a whole month of work by 145,000 or 146,000 laborers. The completion of all four city walls probably took five years. Outside the city wall was a moat, but 8 m wide and 3 m deep. The excavations in 1962 of the area outside the Zhangchengmen Gate clarified the shape of the moat outside the city gate and also proved that wooden bridges were built over the moat (fig. 5).[2]

City Gates   There were twelve city gates, three to each wall. The gates along the east wall, from north to south, were known as Xuanpingmen, Qingmingmen, and Bachengmen; the south wall gates, from east to west, were called Fu'angmen, Anmen, and Xi'anmen; the west wall gates, from south to north, were Zhangchengmen, Zhichengmen, and Yongmen, along the north wall, the gates, from west to east, were Hengmen, Chuchengmen and Luochengmen. (See fig. 2) Of these, the Xuanpingmen, Bachengmen, Xi'anmen, and Zhichengmen gates were excavated in 1957.

The city gates followed strict designs. Each gate had three gateways, and each gateway was 6 m wide. The width of the gateway corresponded exactly to four times the width of a carriage (figs. 6, 7). This fact had been clearly stated in *San fu jue lu*, *Xi jing fu*, and the commentary on *Xi jing fu* by Xue Zong.[3] The distance between each two gateways was 4 m for the Xuanpingmen Gate and Zhichengmen Gate, but it was 14 m

遗留于地下。经 1957 年和 1962 年两次实测，东面城墙长约 6000 米，南面城墙长约 7600 米，西面城墙长约 4900 米，北面城墙长约 7200 米；四面城墙总长约 25700 米，合汉代六十二里强，基本上与《史记·吕后本纪》索引及《续汉书·郡国志》注引《汉旧仪》长安城周围六十三里的记载相符。全城总面积约 36 平方公里（图 2）。[1]

城墙全部用黄土夯筑而成。其高度在 12 米以上，下部宽度为 12—16 米。《三辅黄图》说"城高三丈五尺，下阔一丈五尺，上阔九尺"，与实际不符。虽然是土筑的城墙，没有使用砖和石料，但其坚固的程度超出了人们的想象（图 3、4）。据《汉书·惠帝纪》记载，当时是征调长安六百里内的农民和各地诸侯王、列侯的徒隶来筑城墙的。十四万五六千人，劳动一个月，只能建成一面城墙。四面城墙的建成，大概经历了五年的时间。在城墙的外侧，有壕沟围绕。经勘探、发掘，壕沟宽约 8 米，深约 3 米，与《三辅黄图》"广三丈，深二丈"的记载近似。1962 年在章城门外的发掘，究明了城门前面壕沟的形制，可以判断当时在壕沟上架有木桥，以便出入（图 5）。[2]

全城共有十二个城门，半均分布在东南西北四面，每面各三个城门。东面的城门自北而南为宣平门、清明门、霸城门，南面的城门自东而西为复盎门、安门，西安门，西面的城门自南而北为章城门、直城门、雍门，北面的城门自西而东为横门、厨城门、洛城门。（见图 2）其中，宣平门、霸城门、西安门、直城门于 1957 年经过发掘。

城门的设计，按照严格的规制。每个城门都有三个门道，每个门道的实际宽度都为 6 米，恰好相当于四个车轨（图 6、7）。这就是《三辅决录》的所谓"三涂洞开"和《西京赋》的所谓"三途夷庭，方轨十二"。三国时薛综注《西京赋》说："一面三门，门三道，故云三途，途容四轨，故方十二轨。"[3] 这是对长安城城门形制最具体的说明。宣平门和直城门，门道之间的间隔为 4 米；霸城门和

for the Bachengmen Gate and Xi'anmen Gate. The greater the distance between gateways, the wider the whole city gate, of course, and the more majestic it looked. This greater distance in the latter case was possibly because the Bachengmen Gate lay directly opposite the east entrance to the Changlegong Palace and the Xi'anmen Gate lay across the southern entrance to Weiyanggong.[4]

Street Grid   The street system within Chang'an was made clear through surveys and excavations in 1961-1962. No large avenues were built inside the four gates that were close to Changlegong and Weiyanggong (i.e., Bachengmen, Fu'angmen, Xi'anmen, and Zhangchengmen). All the other eight gates led into long avenues extending into the city. Therefore, although there were twelve city gates in Chang'an, the city had only eight major avenues within its walls, just as described in *Han jiu yi* and *San fu jiu shi*. These avenues were straight, running north-south or east-west, forming many T-intersections and cross-sections. The longest was the Anmen Gate Avenue, 5,500 m long, followed by the Xuanpingmen Gate Avenue, 3,800 m long. The shortest was the Luochengmen Gate Avenue, 850 m long. The length of each of the other avenues was about 3,000 m, and each had its own name. For example, the Anmen Gate Avenue was probably called Zhangtai Jie; the Zhichengmen Gate Avenue was probably Gao Jie; the Qingmingmen Gate Avenue was probably Xiangshi Jie; and the Hengmen Gate Avenue probably Huayang Jie.[5]

Although their lengths varied, the eight avenues were of equal width; that is, about 45 m. Their width was obviously the result of uniform planning. It is noteworthy that each avenue was divided into three parallel lanes, which were separated by two drainage ditches, each about 90 cm wide and 45 cm deep. The ditches were semicircular in cross-section. The central lane was the widest, about 20 m, and the two on the outside were each about 12 m wide (fig. 8). According to textual records, the central lane was called "Chi dao" and was meant exclusively for the emperor. Even imperial princes were not permitted to use it, let alone mere commoners and officials. These three-lane avenues are referred to in *Xi du fu* in the following line: "[It is] covered with wide avenues with three lanes." The layout of the avenues also explains why each gate had three gateways. The central one was for use of the emperor, and the two lateral gateways, for commoners' use.[6]

西安门，门道之间的间隔为 14 米。门道之间的间隔愈大，整个城门也就显得愈为广阔、雄伟。这可能是由于霸城门和西安门分别对着长乐宫的东门和未央宫的南门之故。[4]

1961 年至 1962 年的钻探和发掘工作，究明了长安城内街道的形制。除了霸城门、复盎门、西安门、章城门因入门不远便是长乐宫和未央宫而外，其余八个城门都各有一条大街通入城内，延伸甚长。这就是说，长安城虽有十二个城门，但城内主要的大街是八条，正与《汉旧仪》《三辅旧事》等的记载相符。这些大街，或作南北向，或作东西向，全街成一直线，毫无曲折。它们互相交错、接合，形成了许多"丁字路口"和"十字路口"。最长的是安门大街，计 5500 米；其次是宣平门大街，计 3800 米；最短的是洛城门大街，计 850 米。其余的大街，长度多为 3000 米左右。在当时，各条大街都有专门的名称。从文献记载结合实际勘察的情况来看，安门大街可能是章台街，直城门大街可能是稟街，清明门大街可能是香室街，横门大街可能是华阳街。[5]

八条大街的长度虽各有差别，但它们的宽度却完全相同，都在 45 米左右。这显然是出于统一的规划。值得注意的是，每一大街都分成三条并行的道路，其间有两条宽约 90 厘米、深约 45 厘米的排水沟。这两条排水沟，形状很规整，断面成半圆形，它们固然是为了排除雨水而设，但也起了使大街一分为三的作用。中间的一条道路宽度较大，计 20 米；两侧的两条道路宽度较小，各为 12 米左右（图 8）。据文献记载，中间的一条道路称"驰道"，是专供皇帝行走的；平民和官吏都不得行"驰道"，皇太子亦不例外。《西都赋》所说"披三条之广路"，就是指长安城内的大街都分为三条并行的道路而言的。这也说明了每个城门为什么都要有三个门道（中间的一个门道为皇帝所专用，一般吏民的出入是经左右的两个门道）。[6]

Drainage   A drainage system is of obvious importance for a city surrounded by gigantic walls. At Chang'an water was drained mainly through large drainholes buried under the city gates. Finds from beneath the Zhichengmen and Xi'anmen gates indicate that the drainholes were 1.2 and 1.6 m wide, respectively, and 1.4 m deep, built with bricks and rocks, with the top part constructed of brick and forming an arc (fig. 9). Water that accumulated inside the city was carried away through the ditches alongside the avenues and then let out into the moat through the drainholes underneath the gates. *Hanshu* (the "Biography of Liu Qumao") describes a battle in which tens of thousands were killed and blood flowed into the ditches. These must have been the ditches built alongside the roads. In addition, at some locations, when the wall was built, pottery waterpipes, pentagonal or round in cross-section, were buried under the foundation, to drain water away (fig. 10).[7]

Palaces, Armory, and Market   Research was undertaken in the areas of the Changlegong and Weiyanggong palaces in 1961-62. Changlegong was located in the southeastern portion of Chang'an, surrounded itself by an enclosure. Changlegong and Weiyanggong were built before the city wall was constructed, and they themselves were enclosed by ramparts over 20 m wide at the base, for defense. Changlegong was an expansion of a resort palace of the Qin dynasty, not according to a separate plan, and therefore it was of irregular shape. From the foundation remains, it can be seen that the enclosure of Changlegong was in toto 10,000 m long, or over 20 *li* according to the Han system of measurement. The total area of Changlegong was about 6 km^2, which is about one-sixth of the total area of the city.[8] According to historical texts, Changlegong had four doors on four sides, the eastern and the western doors being the main ones. Outside the door on the east was a towering monument called *dong que* (East Que), and on the west, one called *xi que* (West Que). *Xi que* was immediately close to the Anmen Gate Avenue.

Located in the southwestern portion of Chang'an, Weiyanggong was not quite in symmetry with Changlegong to its east. Built entirely during the Han dynasty, it had a regular, square shape. The lengths of the enclosures are: 2,150 m for both east wall and west wall, and 2,250 m for south and north walls, with a perimeter of 8,800 m (or 21 *li* according to the Han measurement system) and an area of 5 km², about

对于四周筑有高大城墙的都市来说，排水设施是十分重要的。长安城的排水设施，主要是在城门的地下埋筑宽大的涵洞。据在直城门和西安门发掘所见，涵洞的宽度各约 1.2 米和 1.6 米，高约 1.4 米左右，系用砖和石块砌筑，顶部都用砖发券（图 9）。城内的积水，通过大街两旁的水沟，从城门地下的涵洞排入城外的壕沟。《汉书·刘屈氂传》说："太子驱四市人，凡数万众，至长乐西阙下，逢丞相军，合战数日，死者数万人，血流入沟中。"此处所说的沟，就是指安门大街两旁的排水沟。此外，在建筑城墙时，还预先有计划地将一些断面成五角形或圆形的陶制水管埋入墙基，也起了排水的作用（图 10）。[7] 城内许多重要建筑物的地下排水系统，也是普遍使用这种陶制的水管来敷设的。

1961 年至 1962 年，对长乐宫和未央宫的范围进行了勘探。长乐宫在城的东南部，所以又称东宫。宫的周围筑有围墙。由于兴建长乐宫和未央宫时，长安城还没有城墙，为了防卫，两宫的围墙都很宽阔，基部宽在二十米以上。可能是因为长乐宫系由秦代的离宫改建而成，缺乏系统的规划，所以全宫的平面形状不很规整。从埋存在地下的断断续续的墙基看来，长乐宫的围墙全长在 10,000 米左右，合汉代二十余里；宫的全部面积约 6 平方公里，占长安城总面积约六分之一。[8] 据文献记载，长乐宫四面各有一门，称"司马门"。其中东面和西面的司马门是主要的，门外有阙，称东阙和西阙，后者紧临安门大街。

未央宫在长安城的西南部，当时也称西宫。但是，经勘察，它的位置和东面的长乐宫不很对称。因为完全是汉代新建的，所以和长乐宫相反，它的规划十分整齐，全宫平面为一规整的方形。四周围墙的长度，东墙和西墙各为 2150 米，南墙和北墙各为 2250 米，周围全长 8800 米，合汉代二十一里；全宫面积约 5 平方公里，

one-seventh the size of Chang'an. The walls are mostly gone, with only the foundations left, but a small section of the west wall 11 m high still stands. The famous *qian dian*, or Anterior Hall (the Audience Hall), is in fact located at the center of the Weiyanggong Palace, its foundation still standing. Its length north-south is 350 m, its width east-west 200 m, and the highest northern end, located on a natural hill, is about 15 m above ground (fig. 11). The palace was indeed grandiose. No wonder Emperor Gao Zu accusingly questioned Xiao He, who built the palace: "All under heaven is chaotic, and battles are still raging on after several years, their results uncertain. Why are palaces constructed so much beyond their proper limits?" According to *San fu huang tu*, the palace had doors on all four sides. The main ones were apparently the east and the north doors. Two gate towers (*que*) were built outside these two doors: the East Que and the North Que. When feudal lords came in for an audience, they would use the East Que, but the people would use the North Que for petitions. On the west and south sides, no gate towers were built outside the doors. Actually, the south and west walls of the Weiyanggong Palace were so close to the ramparts of Chang'an that in fact no room was left for *que* to be built.[9]

Hanshu ("Gao Di ji") says, "Xiao He build the Weiyanggong, erected the East Que, the North Que, the Anterior Hall, the Armory, and the Grand Storehouse." *San fu huang tu* places the Armory (*wu ku*) at the Weiyanggong, but according to *Shiji* ("Chulizi zhuan") and other records, the Armory was in fact located between the Weiyanggong and the Changlegong. The *Zizhitongjian* commentary quoted *Yuanhe junxian zhi* as saying that the two palaces were one *li* apart. This information has proved through actual surveying at the site to be incorrect. The western wall of Changlegong and the eastern wall of Weiyanggong were separated by a distance of 950 m, which corresponds to over 2 *li* in the Han system. The Armory was located in this area.

Extensive excavations since 1975 have disclosed the areal scope, form, and structure of the Armory. Walls enclosed a rectangular area, 320 m on the east and west and 800 m on the north and south sides. A partition wall separates the Armory into two courtyards. The eastern courtyard had in it four houses and the western courtyard had three houses (fig. 12). Some of these houses provided shelters for the officials, but most served as warehouses for the storage of weapons. The largest of the warehouses was 230 m long, 46 m wide, and incorporated four storage areas, each about 1,500 m^2 in area (fig. 13). Within the storage area,

占长安城总面积约七分之一。围墙虽已夷平，仅存地下的墙基，但西墙尚有一小段遗留在地面上，其高度竟达11米。有名的未央宫前殿，基本上居全宫的正中，其基址至今犹高耸在地面上，南北长约350米，东西宽约200米，北端最高处高在15米以上，是利用龙首山的丘陵造成的（图11）。萧何营建未央宫，其规模如此宏伟，无怪汉高祖要责问："天下匈匈，苦战数岁，成败未可知，是何治宫室过度也？"据记载，未央宫四面各有一"司马门"，而以东面和北面的"司马门"为重要，门外有阙，称为"东阙"和"北阙"。诸侯来朝，入自东阙；士民上书，则诣北阙。至于西南两面，则有门无阙。从实际情况看来，未央宫的南墙和西墙距长安城的城墙都很近，亦无立阙的余地。[9]

《汉书·高帝纪》说："萧何治未央宫，立东阙、北阙、前殿、武库、太仓。"《三辅黄图》说："武库在未央宫。"但是，从《史记·樗里子传》和其他许多有关的记载来看，武库不在未央宫内，而在未央宫与长乐宫之间。《资治通鉴》注引《元和郡县志》谓未央宫与长乐宫相隔一里，其实不然。根据实际的勘探，长乐宫的西墙与未央宫的东墙相距为950米，合汉代二里有余，武库的位置便在这一地段上。

1975年以来，对武库进行了全面的发掘，究明了它的范围、形制和结构。它的四周都筑有围墙，整个平面成一规整的长方形，东墙和西墙各长320米，南墙和北墙各长约800米。在内部有一道隔墙，将整个武库划分为两个院落。东院有四个仓库，西院有三个仓库，共计七个仓库（图12）。其中最大的一个仓库，长约230米，宽约46米，包含着四个库房，每一库房的面积在1500平方米以上（图13）。

weapons racks were densely arranged. The wooden racks have long been rotted, but their stone bases still remain, fully testifying to the description of such weapons racks in the *Xi jing fu* (fig. 14). According to the excavated remains, the Armory, like the other structures within Chang'an, was destroyed during the war at the end of the Wang Mang period. Although most of the weapons that were stored here had been removed, a few remained, including iron armor, *ji*-halberds, spears, swords, knives, and arrowheads as well as bronze arrowheads and *ge*-halberds (figs. 15-18).[10]

According to historical records, the Guigong Palace was north of Weiyanggong, and near Jianzhanggong on the other side (to the west) of the city wall. Accordingly, its location should be north of the Zhichengmen Gate Avenue, west of the Hengmen Gate Avenue, and south of the Yongmen Gate Avenue. Test diggings in 1962 in this area indeed disclose the enclosure of Guigong, which was 1,800 m long on the east and west, 880 m long on the north and south, with a total perimeter of 5,300 m, or about 13 *li* in the Han system. The plan of the palace was rectangular, and its area was 1.6 km^2. As for Beigong and Mingguanggong, we are told by historical records that the former was north of Weiyanggong and east of Guigong and that the latter was north of Changlegong, but these palaces have not yet been located on the ground. Finally, Jianzhanggong outside the western ramparts was identified through test diggings in 1962, but only further excavations will disclose additional details.[11] North of Jianzhanggong was Taiyechi, or the Lake Taiye; its remains are vaguely recognizable. In 1973, a massive fish-shaped stone sculpture, almost 5 m long, was found to the north of the lake site (fig. 19), substantiating various records about stone fishes on the north shore of the Lake Taiye at the time.[12]

According to historical records, there were nine markets within Chang'an, three of them "to the east of the avenue" and six "to the west." These were collectively referred to as Dong Shi (the Eastern Markets) and Xi Shi (the Western Markets). Because the southern and the central portions of Chang'an were all palace areas, the nine markets could only be located in the northern part of the city area. According to *San fu jiu shi* the nine markets were located near the Tumen Gate (also called the Yongmen Gate) and on both sides of the Heng Bridge Avenue (also called the Hengmen Gate Avenue), and we can further narrow the location of the markets down to the northwestern portion of the city. On the surface in this area archaeologists have collected many pottery figurines and

在库房中，紧密地排列着放置各种兵器的木架。木架本身虽已朽坏无存，而木架的础石犹一一可数，充分显示了《西京赋》所说"武库禁兵，设在兰锜"的情形（图 14）。发掘工作说明，和长安城中其他许多建筑物一样，武库毁于新莽末年的战火。所藏武器虽然多已被取走，但仍有一些残余，其种类包括铁制的甲、戟、矛、剑、刀、镞和铜制的戈和镞等，完全足以说明它是武库（图 15—18）。[10]

据文献记载，桂宫在未央宫之北，西面隔城与建章宫相近。因此，它的位置应在直城门大街之北，横门大街之西，雍门大街之南。1962 年，通过钻探，在这一范围内发现了桂宫的围墙，计东墙和西墙各长约 1800 米，南墙和北墙各长约 880 米，四面围墙总长约 5300 米，约合汉代十三里；全宫平面呈长方形，面积约 1.6 平方公里。至于北宫和明光宫，迄今尚未究明它们的范围，只是根据文献记载，认为前者的位置应在未央宫之北、桂宫之东，后者的位置应在长乐宫之北而已。西面城外的建章宫，经 1962 年的勘探，大致究明了它的位置和范围，但还待进一步考察才能确定。[11] 建章宫北有太液池，其遗迹尚大致可寻。1973 年在池址的北侧发现了一件巨型的鱼形石雕，长近 5 米，证实了各种文献关于太液池北岸当时置有石鱼的记载（图 19）。[12]

综合各种文献记载，可以肯定长安城内有九市。三市在街道之东，称东市；六市在街道之西，称西市。由于长安城的南部和中部都属宫殿区，九市只能是在城的北部。《三辅旧事》记述九市的位置在突门（雍门）附近、横桥大道（应即横门大街）的两侧，因而可以进一步判断它们是在城的西北部。在城的西北部一带，有的地方

molds for coins, suggesting that this northwestern area had handicraft workshops, which may be regarded as a corroboration of the above judgment.[13] According to *Hanshu* ("Hui Di ji"), "the Western Markets of Chang'an were built in the sixth year [or 189 B.C.]," suggesting that the location of the market was chosen even prior to the building of the city wall.

Zhouli kaogongji describes the ideal city plan of the Zhou dynasty as follows: "Its area is 9 *li* square; it has three gates on each side; within the city are nine longitudinal lines and nine latitudinal lines; the longitudinal avenues each are nine carriage tracks wide; the ancestral temple is located on the left and the earth altar on the right; the audience hall faces south; and the market is in the north." In actuality, practical considerations have to enter into the planning of a city; and, as the imperial capital, Chang'an was of a scope far greater than the prototype of the *Kaogongji*. But it is evident that Chang'an's planning does conform with the *Kaogongji* ideal. The enclosure was basically square; there were twelve gates, three to each side; each gate had three openings, which were measured according to carriage tracks; all avenues leading from the gates were each divided into three lanes; the principal palaces were located in the south; the markets were in the north. In short, the city of Chang'an built at the beginning of Western Han, like other early Western Han institutions, still retained the supposed Zhou tradition.

The palaces probably occupied more than half the area of the southern and central parts of the city. A few mansions of the nobility were located near the North Que of Weiyanggong, referred to as the "Bei Que Jia Di." Otherwise, the ordinary people, including most officials, resided in the northern part of the city, especially in the northeastern part, the area near the Xuanpingmen Gate. Yu Xin's *Ai jiang nan fu* has the following lines: "Perform rituals at Changle, in the sight of the noble residences at Xuanping." These lines suggest that the Xuanpingmen Gate area was indeed a residential district. In the central and southern parts of the city, because of their extensive occupation by palaces, most of the gates were used exclusively for access to the palaces, and consequently the Hengmen Gate in the northwest and the Xuanpingmen Gate in the northeast were the gates that were used the most often. The Hengmen Gate in fact controlled the communication in the northwestern direction. Not far

曾发现地面上散布着许多陶俑和钱范，说明这里是手工业作坊的所在，也可以作为上述判断的一种依据。[13]《汉书·惠帝纪》说："（惠帝）六年（公元前 189 年），起长安西市。"由此可见，市的位置早在筑城之初已经选定。

《考工记》说："匠人营国，方九里，旁三门，国中九经九纬，经涂九轨，左祖右社，面朝后市，市朝一夫。"这是中国古代都城的一种理想化的规划。据考证，《考工记》为东周时所作，但就调查发掘所知，东周列国都城的形制多与《考工记》不符。然而，综上所述，长安城的规划却的确有与《考工记》符合之处。这主要表现在：城的平面形状虽然不很规整，但基本上呈方形，经纬相等；十二个城门平均分布在四面，每面三个城门；每个城门各有三个门道，其宽度按车轨计算；经由城门的主要大街，都各分为并行的三条道路；长乐宫和未央宫在城的南部，东市和西市在城的北部。这可能是由于《考工记》在汉初受到重视，因而在设计长安城时被充分参照，相反，也可能是由于汉儒从长安城的实际情况出发，增改了《考工记》的"匠人营国"部分的关系。

长安城内的宫殿，仅长乐、未央两宫就占了全城总面积的三分之一，再加上桂宫、北宫和明光宫，宫殿所占的面积可能在全城总面积的二分之一以上。由于宫殿集中在城的南部和中部，所以，除了少数权贵人物的邸宅在未央宫北阙附近，即所谓"北阙甲第"而外，一般的居民，包括官吏在内，就只能居住在城的北部，特别是在城的东北部，靠近宣平门的地区。庾信《哀江南赋》有"践长乐之神皋，望宣平之贵里"之句，也说明了宣平门附近一带是汉代的重要住宅区。由于长乐宫和未央宫等宫殿的存在，霸城门、复盎门、安门、西安门、章城门、直城门等城门实际上成为宫廷所专用。因此，西北面的横门和东北面的宣平门就成了长安城中吏民出入最频繁的城门。横门主要是管西北方的交通，门外不远，便是

outside the gate was the famous bridge Zhong Wei Qiao, also called Heng Qiao or Hengmen Qiao, which spanned the Weishui River, with Xianyang on the other bank of the river. The Xuanpingmen Gate, on the other hand, controlled the communication in the southeastern direction. Coming out of this gateway, one traveled along the southern bank of the Weishui River to Hanguguan. Therefore, the Xuanpingmen Gate (also known as the Dongdumen Gate or Dumen Gate) was the most important of the Chang'an gateways and the one most mentioned in *Hanshu* and *Hou Hanshu*.

History of the Xuanpingmen Gate Archaeological excavations have shown that many structures in Chang'an—including the Bachengmen Gate, Xi'anmen Gate, and Zhichengmen Gate—were destroyed during the warfare at the end of the Wang Mang period (fig. 20). The Xuanpingmen Gate suffered the same fate. The two walls of the gateways had been burned to a red color, and parts had collapsed. From the debris under the gateways were found coins of the Western Han dynasty and the Wang Mang period, especially the *huo bu* and the *huo quan* of the latter period, which accurately date the burning of the gateway.[14] Evidence at the Bachengmen Gate and Xi'anmen Gate shows that after they were destroyed the debris was never cleared away, indicating that these gateways were no longer in use during the Eastern Han, Wei, Jin, and the Six Dynasties periods (fig. 21). At a few other gates, such as Zhichengmen, we find that one of the openings was cleared of debris for reuse on a reduced scale. On the other hand, although the Xuanpingmen Gate was destroyed at the same time, it was subsequently cleared of debris and repaired.

There have been at least two repairs of the Xuanpingmen Gate since Eastern Han. The first took place during the early part of Eastern Han, involving rebuilding of new walls of rammed earth at the northern and the southern openings (fig. 22). *Hou Hanshu* ("Du Du zhuan") states that in the nineteenth year of Jian Wu (A.D. 43) the Dongduchengmen (the Eastern Capital City Gate) was repaired in Chang'an. This historical evidence not only confirms judgments formed in the course of archaeological excavations, it also precisely dates the repair. Thenceforth, the Xuanpingmen Gate continued to be used until the end of Eastern Han. From the later years of the dynasty we have many records pertaining to this gate.[15] They indicate that the gate was still in use when Emperor Xian Di was at Chang'an at the end of the dynasty and that it was complete with a gate tower. In the debris under

有名的中渭桥，又称横桥或横门桥，横跨渭水，过桥即至咸阳。与此相反，宣平门主要是管东南方面的交通，出门沿渭水南岸东行，出函谷关而达关东广大地区，其重要性更在横门之上。根据各种文献记载，宣平门又称东都门，或称都门，由于位置重要，出入频繁，《汉书》、《后汉书》中有关此门的记载也最多。

发掘工作证明，长安城的许多建筑物，其中包括霸城门、西安门、直城门等城门，都是在新莽末年的战火中被焚毁的（图20）。宣平门亦不例外，门道的两壁都被烧得发赤，并大量崩塌。在门道的堆积层中，发现了西汉和新莽的铜钱，尤以新莽的货布和货泉为多，这就具体地说明了城门焚毁的确实年代。[14]霸城门和西安门，被毁以后，一任崩塌的乱土、碎瓦和灰烬等堆塞在门道中而未加清除，说明了它们在此后的东汉、魏晋、五胡十六国时期和西魏、北周是废弃不用的（图21）；有的城门如直城门，则只修理了三个门道中的一个，以供出入。与此相反，宣平门虽然也在同一时期被焚毁，但堆塞在门道中的乱土和灰烬完全被清除，门道两壁有着显著的修补遗迹。可以断定，自东汉以来，宣平门至少重建过两次。

第一次重建是在东汉初期，重建的遗迹是在北门道和南门道的旧壁上另用夯土补筑，形成了新壁（图22）。《后汉书·杜笃传》说："（建武十九年，即公元43年）于长安修理东都城门。"这不仅证实了发掘工作中的判断，而且进一步说明重建的具体年份。重建后的宣平门，一直使用到东汉末年，所以东汉末年有着许多关于宣平门的记载。[15]《后汉书·献帝纪》说："（初平二年，即公元191年）三月，宣平门外屋无故自坏。"《三国志·董卓传》说："司徒王允挟天子上宣平城门避兵。"《后汉书·董卓传》说："王允奉天子保宣平城门楼上。"这些记载都说明直到东汉末年献帝居长安时，宣平门仍然存在，而且是一个筑有门楼的完整的城门。在门道的堆积层

the gateways we have found Eastern Han *wu zhu* coins and some small and poorly manufactured coins possibly of the Dong Zhuo period.[16]

The second repair of the Xuanpingmen Gate consisted of the construction of new wall surfaces in the central and the southern openings, using fired and sundried bricks (fig. 23). Some of the bricks bear the inscription "Shi An" (figs. 24, 25). According to *Weishu* ("Dixingzhi"), Shi An was the name of a county under the Xianyang Prefecture, established by Shi Le of the Later Zhao. This evidence suggests that the new repair took place in the middle of the fourth century. Several texts mention that during the Later Zhao reign of Shi Hu, the city of Chang'an was rebuilt on a rather large scale, and the repair of the Xuanpingmen Gate was probably part of the rebuilding.[17]

As shown from the excavated remains, no major rebuilding occurred after the Later Zhao, but throughout the Sixteen States period and the Northern Dynasties (fourth through sixth centuries), it continued to be used as a principal gateway. Its name, however, had been changed to Qingmen, as we see in the text *Han gongdian ming*. When Liu Yu of Eastern Jin was attacking Chang'an, Yao Hong of Later Qin had planned to come out of Qingmen to surrender himself. During the Northern Zhou dynasty, Qingmen was still an important gate; the *wu xing da bu* coins of the Northern Zhou have been found in later debris under the gateway. The gateway continued into Sui: wheel tracks have been found under it, and *wu zhu* coins of the Sui dynasty suggest that the gateway was in use then.[18] During the Tang dynasty, the three gateways were finally blocked forever.

In short, although Chang'an was badly damaged by war during the final years of the Wang Mang period, it continued to be an important city throughout the Eastern Han, Wei, Jin, Sixteen States, Western Wei, Northern Zhou, and early Sui dynasties, and many of these dynasties even used it as their capital. The Xuanpingmen Gate excavations have, thus, disclosed a cross-section of the whole history of Chang'an.

Royal Parks The Shanglinyuan royal parks were built by the Qin dynasty within its capital city in Xianyang, and they were abandoned at the beginning of the Han dynasty. Emperor Wu Di incorporated

中发现的一些东汉的五铢钱和可能是董卓时所铸的粗制滥造的小铜钱，都是很好的物证。[16]

宣平门的第二次重建的遗迹，主要是在中门道和南门道用砖和土坯砌筑新壁（图 23）。值得注意的是，所用的砖往往印有"石安"字样（图 24、25）。据《魏书·地形志》记载，咸阳郡的石安县为后赵石勒所置，这就说明了这次改建的年代是在后赵（公元 4 世纪中叶）。《晋书·石季龙载记》说："（石虎）以石苞代镇长安，发雍、洛、秦、并州十六万人城长安未央宫。"《十六国春秋·后赵录》也说："（后赵石虎建武）十一年（公元 345 年），发雍、梁十六万人城长安未央宫。"由此可见，后赵石虎时曾大规模地修建过长安城，其中也包括了宣平门。[17]

从发掘出来的遗迹来看，自后赵以后，宣平门未有重大的改建，但在整个五胡十六国时期和北朝（公元 4 世纪至 6 世纪），它一直作为一个重要的城门被使用着。当时宣平门已改名为青门，这可以从《后汉书·逢萌传》注引《汉宫殿名》的记载中得到证明。东晋刘裕攻长安，后秦姚泓曾打算从青门出降。到了北周，青门仍然是一个重要的城门。《周书·宣帝纪》说"（大象元年，公元 579 年）帝亲擐甲胄，入自青门"，便是最好的说明。在门道的晚期堆积层中发现了北周的"五行大布"铜钱，证明了文献记载的正确。发掘工作还证明，这个城门甚至在隋代还继续被使用着，在门道地面上清楚地遗留着隋代的车辙，而所发现的隋代五铢钱则有力地说明了它们的年代。[18]到了唐代，城门的三个门道才被用夯土全部填塞。

总之，长安城虽然在新莽末年的战火中受到严重的破坏，但它在此后的东汉、魏、晋、五胡十六国时期、西魏、北周以迄隋初，一直是一个重要的城市，不少朝代仍在此建都。从宣平门遗址的发掘工作中，可以看出自西汉直到隋初的长安城全部历史的一个缩影。

上林苑为秦都咸阳时所置，汉初荒废。汉武帝时收上林苑为

Shanglinyuan into the palace parks and expanded them. The vast area southeast to southwest of Chang'an, more than 200 *li* in perimeter, was roped in as a result. In the parks were placed birds and animals for the imperial hunt, and several dozen resort palaces were built. A great number of eaves tiles impressed with the name Shanglin are the most conspicuous remains of these palaces. In 1961, at Gaoyaocun in Sanqiaozhen about 2 km southwest of Chang'an, an architectural site was found consisting of several house floors, the largest being about 340 m long by 65 m wide, probably the remains of an important palatial building within the Shanglinyuan parks.[19] A storage pit was discovered near the house floor, containing more than twenty bronze vessels such as basins, *ding*-tripods, *fang*-jars, and cooking pots. Inscriptions incised on the vessels (fig. 26) indicate that these were used within the Shanglinyuan parks; likely they were intentionally buried during the fighting at the end of the Wang Mang period.[20]

In the third year of Emperor Wu Di's reign period Yuan Shou (120 B.C.), the artificial lake called Kunmingchi was excavated between the rivers Feng and Jue to the southwest of Chang'an, for the purpose of training a water-bound fighting force (in preparation for war with the state of Kunming) and to help alleviate the water shortage in the capital. After two thousand years the remains of the lake are still vaguely recognizable. The lake site now is a depression more than 10 km^2 in area. An elevated ground in the northern part appears to have been an island within the lake, possibly the site of the Yuzhang Hall described in the *Xi jing fu*. In describing the Kunming Lake, both *Xi du fu* and *Xi jing fu* refer to "the Niu Lang [or Cow Boy] on the left and the Zhi Nü [or Weaving Lady] on the right." A pair of sculptured stone human figures still stand today near Doumenzhen; their style is highly archaistic, apparently dating from the Western Han period.[21] The stone sculpture on the eastern side of the lake is that of a male, presumably the Cow Boy (fig. 27, left), and the one on the western side that of a female, presumably the Weaving Lady (fig. 27, right), completely conforming with their descriptions in the two poems by Ban Gu and Zhang Heng.[22] The floors of many houses were brought to light around the ancient lake site, yielding a few stone foundations and a large number of tiles. These could be the remains that are described in ancient texts of the Xuanqugong, Baiyanggong, and Xiliugong palaces within the Shanglinyuan parks (fig. 28).[23]

宫苑，并大事扩充，长安城东南面至西南面的广大地区都在它的范围之中，周围至二百多里。苑内放养禽兽，供皇帝射猎，并筑离宫别馆数十处，许多印有"上林"字样的瓦当便是它们最明显的遗物。1961 年在长安城址西南面约二公里的三桥镇高窑村发现了一处建筑遗址，由好几座房基组成，较大的一座房基长约 340 米，宽约 65 米，当为上林苑中重要宫观的遗址。[19] 在房基附近发现了一个窖穴，内有铜鉴、铜鼎、铜钫和铜锅共二十余件，器上所刻铭文（图 26）表明它们是上林苑中所用之物，大概是因新莽末年的战乱而被有意埋藏起来的。[20]

　　元狩三年（公元前 120 年），为了准备与昆明国作战而训练水军，并解决首都水源不足的问题，在长安城西南面沣水和滈水之间开凿昆明池。两千多年后的今日，昆明池的遗迹犹依稀可辨。它是一片面积约十多平方公里的洼地，北部的一处高地像是当时池中的岛屿，应该便是《西京赋》所说的"揭焉中峙"的豫章馆的所在。《西都赋》在叙述昆明池及豫章馆时说"左牵牛而右织女"，《西京赋》说"牵牛立其左，织女处其右"。今斗门镇附近尚遗存石雕人像一对，一东一西，遥遥相对，它们的作风古朴，显然是西汉的作品。[21] 东面的石雕是男像，应系牵牛（图 27，左），西面的石雕是女像，当为织女（图 27，右），前者位于豫章馆所在岛屿的东部，后者位于昆明池址的西侧，与班张两赋的记述完全相符。[22] 在池址的周围，发现许多建筑物的基址，遗留着一些石础和大量的瓦片，对照有关文献的记载，它们可能便是上林苑中的宣曲宫、白杨宫、细柳宫等的遗迹（图 28）。[23]

Ritual Structures   Emperor Wu Di paid great attention to Confucian rituals, and some of his Confucian officials had proposed to him that a new Ming Tang (a ritual hall where the emperor pronounced the new year, officiated at festivities, performed rituals, and received the feudal lords) be built. However, it was not. (It should be mentioned that there was a Ming Tang at that time, located on the Taishan Mountains). Under the reign of Emperor Cheng Di, officials suggested that a "Pi Yong" (a place where the emperor performed rituals and music and promulgated virtuous principles) be built in the south of Chang'an, but again it was not done at that time. At the end of Western Han, when Wang Mang became regent, he had Ming Tang, Pi Yong, Ling Tai (the spiritual terrace), and Tai Xue (the imperial academy) built in Chang'an. After he enthroned himself, Wang Mang went even further, building his Jiu Miao, or "Nine Temples." These "mysterious" buildings, full of religious color, were designed in accordance with both traditional Confucian regulations and Taoist *yin yang* and *wu xing* (Five Elements) principles; they were of large scale and quite complex. The sites of these buildings, which the archaeologists refer to as ritual structures, were first excavated in 1956, and since then more than ten such structures have come to light (fig. 29).[24]

A ritual structure excavated in 1956, located south-southeast of the Anmen Gate, consisted of a square building surrounded by a square composed of four walls, each 235 m long. Through each of the four walls was a door. At each corner, within the enclosure and close to the wall, were built elbow-shaped houses (fig. 30). At the center of the courtyard was a square hall (with side rooms on four sides) built on a round platform 60 m across (fig. 31). Outside the courtyard was a large circle 360 m long, formed by a ditch 2 m wide. In short, a peculiar architectural plan characterized this building: a square was placed within a circle, and within the square was another circle. These principles are consistent with the textual characterizations of Ming Tang and Pi Yong, such as "circular above and square below," or "circular outside and square inside." What is more, the records all characterize the Pi Yong as a structure surrounded by water on all sides, and as circular as a jade ring. It looks as if the excavated structure was indeed the Pi Yong (fig. 32).[25]

All the other ritual structures are clustered in the area south-southwest of the Anmen Gate. Their shapes are similar to the Pi Yong above, but they were not surrounded by ditches, and their central halls were not built on round platforms. Thus, they were probably neither the

汉武帝崇尚儒术，儒臣们向他建议在长安城南立"明堂"，但未能付诸实施（当时的"明堂"在泰山）。成帝时，大臣们议立"辟雍"于长安城南，亦未成事实。到了西汉末年，王莽执政，才在长安建立"明堂"、"辟雍"，同时兴建"灵台"和"太学"。当了皇帝以后，王莽又大兴土木，建造他的宗庙，即所谓"九庙"。这些神秘的、充满宗教色彩的建筑物，是按照儒家的传统礼制和当时流行的阴阳五行学说设计的，规模宏大，结构复杂。它们的遗址，自 1956 年以来，在汉长安城安门和西安门外的南郊陆续被发现，达十余座之多，有的已经过发掘。考古学家们统称之为"礼制建筑"（图 29 ）。[24]

1956 年发掘的一座"礼制建筑"，位置在安门南面偏东处。它是一个平面呈正方形的大庭院，四面的围墙各长 235 米，每面设一门，四面共四门。在院内的四隅，紧靠着围墙，都筑有平面成曲尺形的房屋（图 30 ）。院内的中央，则是这个建筑物的主体所在，它是一个在直径为 60 米的圆形台基上建立起来的厅堂，平面呈正方形，四面附有配室，互相对称（图 31 ）。在庭院的外面，由宽约 2 米的水沟围绕成一个直径达 360 米的大圆圈。总之，这个建筑物的特点，表现在它的整个平面图上，是圆形之中有方形，方形之中又有圆形，正与"明堂"、"辟雍"的所谓"上圆下方"或"外圆内方"的形制相符。由于各种记载中都说"辟雍"是"四面周水，圜如璧"，所以它很可能便是"辟雍"的遗迹（图 32 ）。[25]

其余的许多"礼制建筑"，都集中在安门的南面偏西处。它们的形制虽与上述的"辟雍"有相似之处，但周围没有水沟环绕，中央的厅堂也不是建筑在圆形的台基之上，所以不像是"辟雍"或"明堂"。

Ming Tang nor the Pi Yong. Artifactual remains found here date from the Wang Mang period, and consequently most archaeologists believe them to be the Nine Temples. It is noteworthy that the eaves tiles used above the four doors of the temple were decorated with designs representing the Four Deities: eaves tiles with Green Dragon designs, over the east gate; White Tiger eaves tiles, over the west gate; Red Bird tiles, over the south gate; and Black Turtle tiles, over the north gate. This usage is consistent with the principle that "the Four Deities were in charge of the Four Directions" (figs. 33-36).[26] All of these ritual structures were destroyed at the end of the Wang Mang period, too, and they were never rebuilt.

由于出土的遗物明确地表明它们是新莽时所建，所以考古学家们多认为它们可能便是王莽的九庙。值得注意的是，庙的四门所用瓦当的图纹多属"四神"（图33—36），而青龙瓦当用于东门，白虎瓦当用于西门，朱雀瓦当用于南门，玄武瓦当用于北门，正与"四神分司四方"的说法相符。[26] 发掘工作证明，所有这些"礼制建筑"，包括"辟雍"和"九庙"，都和长安城的城门、宫殿一样，是在新莽末年的战火中被毁的，此后一直未曾经过重建。

1. Remains of city wall of Chang'an of the Han dynasty (southeastern corner) 汉长安城的城墙遗迹（东南角）

2. City plan of Chang'an of the Han dynasty 汉长安城遗址平面示意图

3. Remains of city wall of the Han Chang'an (stamped earth layers seen on collapsed section) 城墙断面上所见的夯土层次

4. Han Chang'an city wall near the Bachengmen Gate 霸城门附近的城墙

5. Plan of the Han Chang'an's Zhangchengmen Gate and a section of moat outside the gate 章城门及门外城壕平面示意图

6. Remains of the Xuanpingmen Gate 汉长安城宣平门遗迹

7. The southern gateway and remains of carriage tracks at the Bachengmen Gate 霸城门南门道及车辙遗迹

8. Cross-section of street at the Anmen Gate Avenue　安门大街横截面示意图

9. Brick drainhole buried under the Xi'anmen Gate　西安门地下的砖筑涵洞

10. Ceramic water main pipes buried under the city wall 城墙基部所埋的陶制水管

11. Remains of the Anterior Hall of the Weiyanggong Palace (aerial photo) 未央宫前殿遗址鸟瞰

12. Plan of the Armory site　武库遗址平面示意图

13. Remains of house number 7 of the Armory　武库第七号房址鸟瞰

14. Remains of house number 1 of the Armory and foundation stones of weapons racks　武库第一号房址及其所遗兵器架的础石

15. Iron armor plates unearthed at the Armory　武库出土的铁甲片

ji-halberds unearthed at the Armory 武库出土的铁戟

17. Iron sword, knife, and spears unearthed at the Armory 武库出土的铁制的剑、刀和矛

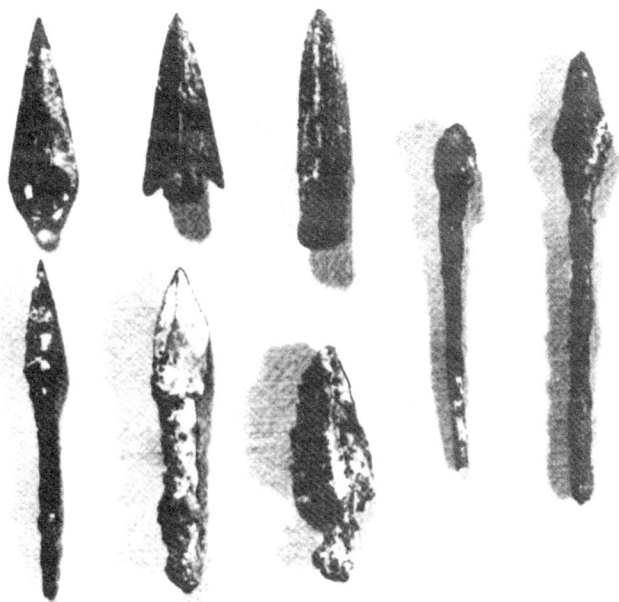

18. Iron and bronze arrowheads unearthed at the Armory 武库出土的铁制和铜制的镞

19. Fish-shaped stone sculpture found at the site of the Lake Taiye 太液池遗址出土的石鱼

20. Burned timber posts at the southern gateway of the Bachengmen Gate 霸城门南门道被烧毁的木柱遗迹

21. Ashes and other deposits at the southern gateway of the Bachengmen Gate　霸城门南门道的灰烬和沉积物

22. Stamped earthen wall rebuilt during the Eastern Han period at the northern gateway of the Xuanpingmen Gate (The carriage tracks were left during the Sui dynasty.)
宣平门北门道东汉补筑的夯土壁（车辙为隋代遗迹）

23. Brick wall built during the Sixteen States period at the central gateway of the Xuanpingmen Gate　宣平门中门道十六国时期用砖砌筑的墙壁

24. Brick (inscribed with "Cao Chu of Shi An") used for rebuilding during the Sixteen States period at the Xuanpingmen Gate
宣平门遗址出土的后赵砖块（"石安曹处"）

25. Brick (inscribed with "Song Li of Shi An") used for rebuilding during the Sixteen States period at the Xuanpingmen Gate
宣平门遗址出土的后赵砖块（"石安宋利"）

26. Inscriptions on bronze vessels in use at the Shanglinyuan royal park unearthed at Sanqiaozhen in Xi'an
西安三桥镇出土，上林苑所用铜器上的铭文

27. Stone statues of the Cow Boy (left) and the Weaving Lady (right) at the site of the Kunming Lake
左牵牛石像，右织女石像

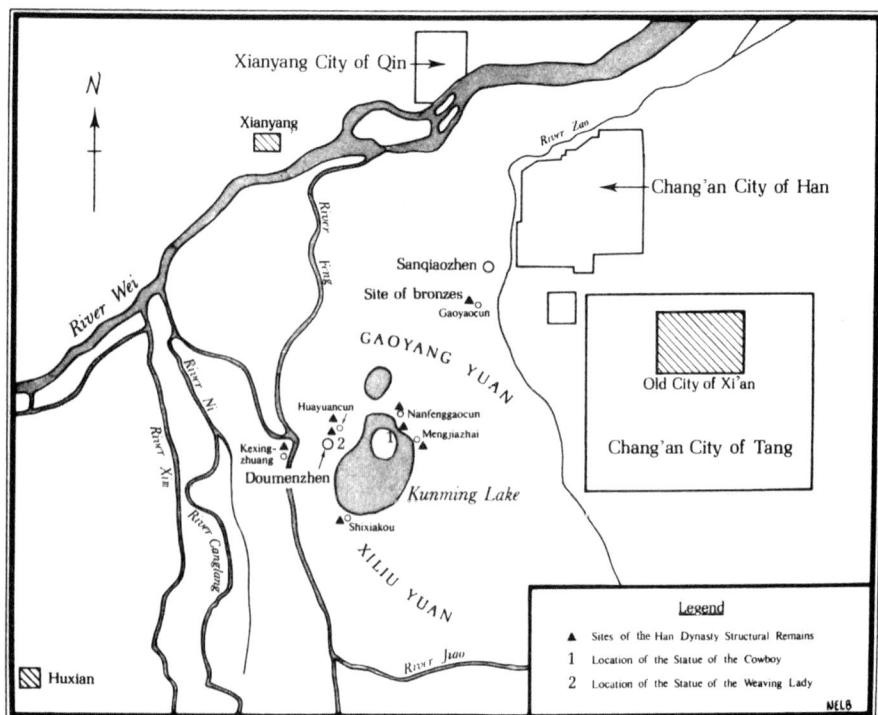

28. Map of the Shanglinyuan royal park and the Kunming Lake 上林苑遗址分布示意图

29. Distribution of sites of ritual structures in the southern suburb of the Han Chang'an
汉代长安南郊"礼制建筑"分布图

30. Plan of the site of Pi Yong "辟雍"遗址平面示意图

31. Reconstruction of the main central building of Pi Yong　汉长安南郊礼制建筑复原图

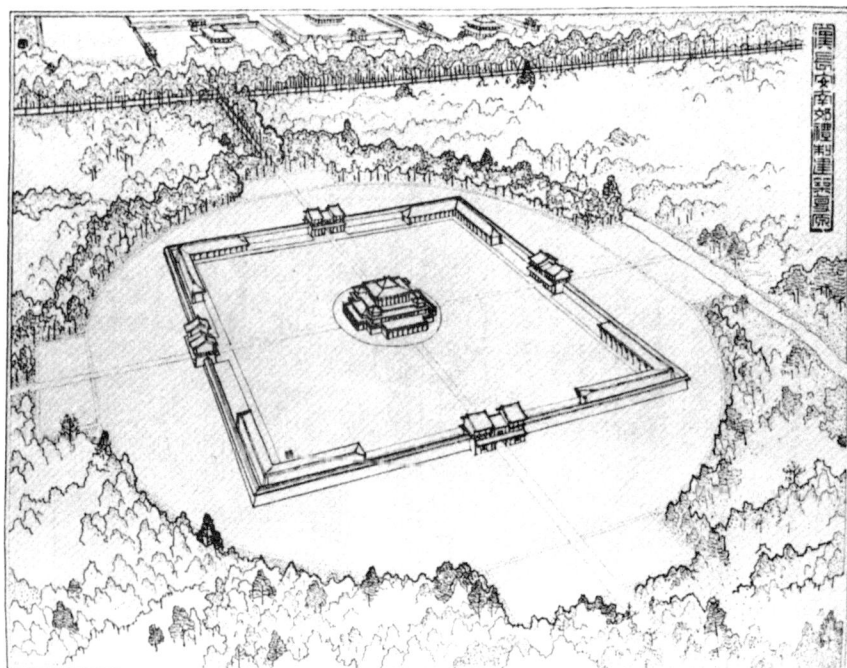

32. Reconstruction of the structure of Pi Yong　汉长安南郊礼制建筑复原图

An eaves tile with a Green Dragon design (unearthed at the site of the ritual structures in the southern suburb of the Han Chang'an)
青龙瓦当（出土于汉代长安南郊"礼制建筑"遗址）

34. An eaves tile with a White Tiger design (unearthed at the same site as fig. 33)
白虎瓦当（出土地同图 33 中文物）

35. An eaves tile with a Red Bird design (unearthed at the same site as fig. 33)
朱雀瓦当（出土地同图 33 中文物）

36. An eaves tile with a Black Turtle design (unearthed at the same site as fig. 33)
玄武瓦当（出土地同图 33 中文物）

CHAPTER 2   LUOYANG: THE CAPITAL CITY OF EASTERN HAN

The remains of the capital of the Eastern Han dynasty, Luoyang, are situated approximately 15 km east of the present-day city of Luoyang in Henan. Since the site is bordered on the north by the Mangshan Mountains and overlooks the Luo River to the south, it has protective natural barriers and is also at an important junction for transportation and communication (fig. 37). For these reasons, as early as the Western Zhou dynasty a major city, Chengzhou, was constructed there. Chengzhou lasted through the Eastern Zhou times. Subsequently, the Western Han city of Luoyang was built on the same site. In other words, the Eastern Han capital of Luoyang was located not only on the site of the Western Han Luoyang but also on that of the Zhou city of Chengzhou.

Architectural traces of Chengzhou are difficult to find now. However, a cluster of Zhou dynasty tombs, which were originally north of the Zhou city, still exists today. The famous Jincun tombs discovered in 1928 are part of this cluster.[1] From the location of these tombs we can speculate that the area within the boundaries of Chengzhou was much smaller than that of the Eastern Han Luoyang. The Zhou city was closer to the present course of the Luo River and farther removed from the Mangshan Mountains on the north. As for the location and boundaries of the Western Han Luoyang, we can estimate that they must have been roughly the same as those of the earlier Zhou dynasty city. Among the Western Han city's palaces, Nangong, or the South Palace, was the most important. When Emperor Guang Wu Di, the founder of Eastern Han, decided to establish his capital at Luoyang in the first year of his reign period Jian Wu (A.D. 25), he first took up residence in the South Palace. Then he embarked on a project to build a new city wall, expanding the boundaries of the old city and enclosing the site of the Zhou dynasty graveyard within the northern section of the new city. Remains that can still be seen today thus confirm the statement from *Diwang shiji* quoted in the commentary on the "Treatise on Commanderies and Kingdoms" in

Xu Hanshu that in the northeastern part of Luoyang of Eastern Han there was a graveyard from the Yin (Shang) dynasty as well as the tomb of King Jing of the Zhou dynasty.

City Wall   Today, above ground we still find remains of the eastern, western, and northern walls of the Eastern Han city of Luoyang. When archaeologists went to inspect the site in 1962, there were still walls that stood over 7 m high (fig. 38). As for the southern wall of the city, it was destroyed by water long ago when the Luo River changed its course, so that today no traces of it remain. Fortunately remains of Ming Tang and Ling Tai, which were located in the southern suburb of the Eastern

贰 东汉的都城——雒阳

　　东汉首都雒阳城的遗址，在今河南省洛阳市以东约十五公里。这里北靠邙山，南临洛河，不仅有天然的屏障，而且是交通的要冲（图 37 ）。所以，早在西周时，便选择在这里建立成周城，一直延续到东周。因在洛河之北，战国时改称雒阳。西汉时的雒阳城，基本上是成周城的旧址，东汉的雒阳城是在西汉的雒阳城的基础上扩建的，新的城墙和城门大约建成于光武帝建武十四年（公元 38 年）前后。

　　成周城的建筑遗迹，已经很难找到了。但是，城址北面的周代墓群却遗留至今，1928 年发现的著名的金村大墓便是其中的一部分。[1] 西汉雒阳城的位置和范围，估计大概与成周城差不多，其中的南宫是当时雒阳城中的主要宫殿。东汉光武帝于建武元年（公元 25 年）定都雒阳，先居住在南宫，以后全面建筑城墙，扩大城的范围，把成周城北面的周代墓地也包括在都城之内。《续汉书·郡国志》注引《帝王世纪》说，东汉雒阳城内的东北部有“殷之墓地”及“周景王塚”，总的说来，是与实际情况相符的。

　　东汉雒阳城的东面、西面和北面的城墙，至今犹残留在地面上，1962 年考古工作者前往勘察时，有的地段上的城墙犹高达 7 米多（图 38 ）。至于南面的城墙，则早因洛河改道而被冲毁，已无遗迹可寻。幸好当时在城的南郊所建的“明堂”和“灵台”的遗迹

Han Luoyang, can still be seen. According to *Han guanyi* and *Luoyang ji*, the distance from these two structures to the southern city wall was approximately 2 or 3 *li*. Therefore, we can conclude that the southern wall was located in what is now the middle of the Luo River. As in Chang'an, the Western Han capital, in Luoyang the city wall was constructed out of rammed yellow earth and was extremely sturdy (fig. 39). The thickness of the wall at the base was determined by our test diggings to be about 14 m for the eastern wall, about 20 m for the western wall, and about 25 m for the northern wall—all different. The thickness of the western and northern walls may have been increased for defense purposes during the subsequent Wei and Jin dynasties. Measurements show that the remains of the eastern wall are 3,900 m long, those of the western wall 3,400 m long, and those of the northern wall 2,700 m long. Though the southern wall no longer exists, if we calculate the distance between the southern tips of the eastern and western walls, we can determine that it must have been 2,460 m long.[2] Since the southern wall was in the middle of what is today the Luo River, we must add approximately 300 m to the length of both the eastern and western walls to determine their full length. Once we do this, then we can calculate that the total length of the four city walls of the Eastern Han Luoyang must have been approximately 13,000 m, or about 31 Han dynasty *li*. *Diwang shiji*, as quoted by the commentary on the "Treatise on Commanderies and Kingdoms" in *Xu Hanshu*, says "From east to west the city is 6 *li* and 10 *bu*; from north to south it is 9 *li* and 100 *bu*." Also, *Jin Yuankang didao ji* notes that "From north to south the city is 9 *li* and 70 *bu*, while from east to west it is 6 *li* and 10 *bu*." All these figures coincide with our own measurements. Although none of the existing walls is perfectly straight and both the eastern and northern walls have substantial sections that are curved, the basic shape of the city was rectangular (See fig. 37). Since its length, measured north to south, was approximately 9 *li* and its width, measured east to west, was approximately 6 *li*, it was known as the "nine-six city." The layout of the Western Han capital of Chang'an was square, while the layout of the Eastern Han capital of Luoyang was rectangular; this was but one of many differences between the two capitals.

City Gates　According to *Luoyang ji, Luoyang qielan ji,* and other documentary sources, Luoyang of Eastern Han had twelve city gates. Although the number of gates was thus the same as in the Western Han capital of Chang'an, there was an important difference in their location: the Luoyang gates were not equally distributed along the four sides of the city.

仍然存在，据《后汉书·光武帝纪》注引《汉官仪》和《文选·闲居赋》注引《洛阳记》记载，它们与雒阳城的南面城墙相距为二里或三里，可以由此判定南面城墙的位置大约在今洛河河道的中央。与西汉的长安城一样，这里的城墙亦系用黄土夯筑而成，十分坚固（图39）。经钻探了解，城墙的基部厚度，东墙约为14米，西墙约为20米，北墙约为25米，各不相等。这可能是由于魏晋时为了加强防御，增加了西墙和北墙的厚度的缘故。经实测，东面城墙残长约3900米，西面城墙残长约3400米，北面城墙全长约2700米；南面城墙已不存存，其长度若按现存东墙和西墙在南端的距离计算，应约为2460米。[2] 假定南面城墙的位置在今洛河河道的中央，则东墙和西墙的长度应在现存的长度之上各增加约300米。这样，四面城墙的总长度应约为13000米，合汉代约三十一里。《续汉书·郡国志》注引《帝王世纪》说"城东西六里一十步，南北九里一百步"，又引《晋元康地道记》说"城内南北九里七十步，东西六里十步"，是符合实际情况的。虽然现存的三面城墙都不成直线，特别是东面城墙和北面城墙各有一处较大的曲折，但全城的平面形状基本上呈长方形（见图37）。由于自南至北的长度约九里，自东至西的宽度约六里，所以这个都城被称为"九六城"。西汉长安城平面形状基本上呈正方形，东汉雒阳城平面形状基本上呈长方形，这是两汉都城形制的许多相异处之一。

　　据文献记载，东汉雒阳城有十二个城门。城门的数目虽与西汉长安城相等，但与长安城不同的是，它们不是平均分布在城的四面，

Instead, the eastern and western sides each had three gates, while there were four gates in the south and only two in the north. The three city gates on the east, from north to south, were the Shangdongmen Gate, Zhongdongmen Gate, and Maomen Gate. The three western gates, from south to north, were the Guangyangmen Gate, Yongmen Gate, and Shangximen Gate. The two northern gates, from west to east, were the Xiamen Gate and Gumen Gate. And the four southern gates, from east to west, were the Kaiyangmen Gate, Pingchengmen Gate, Xiaoyuanmen Gate, and Jinmen Gate. During the 1962 survey, clear traces were found of all eight gates on the east, west, and north.[3] Even though the four southern gates have been washed away by the Luo River so that no traces can be found, we can still determine their location from the four large avenues that run north to south through the city, which were found during the same survey. From the city plan, as determined by actual measurements, we can see that the Shangdongmen Gate and Maomen Gate on the east were directly opposite the Shangximen Gate and Guangyangmen Gate on the west. Moreover, the Kaiyangmen Gate, Pingchengmen Gate, Xiaoyuanmen Gate, and Jinmen Gate were more or less equidistantly spaced. This arrangement shows a high degree of planning when the city was constructed. Since we have not done excavation, we are not certain about the precise shape and structure of the gates. But the Xiamen Gate at the western part of the northern wall is unusually well preserved. From what can be seen we can conclude that, just as in the case of the gates of Chang'an, this gate had three separate openings,[4] a fact corroborated by entries found in *Luoyang ji* and other historical records.

City Streets   During our survey, traces of many streets were also found. Most of these streets date from the Northern Wei dynasty.[5] However, we can infer that the layout of streets in the Eastern Han capital was basically the same as that of the Northern Wei city. In other words, the streets of the Northern Wei city followed those of the Eastern Han capital, the only changes being those made to accommodate the relocation of certain palaces and city gates. Therefore, using the remains of the streets found during our survey as a basis, and taking into account what we know about the location of the city gates and the palaces in the Eastern Han city, we can derive the following description of the layout of streets and avenues in the Eastern Han Luoyang.

There were five avenues that ran north to south. The first, which we could call the Kaiyangmen Gate Avenue, ran north from the Kaiyangmen Gate and was 2,800 m long. The second, which we could call the Pingchengmen

而是东面和西面各三个城门，南面四个城门，北面二个城门。东面的三个城门，自北而南为"上东门"、"中东门"、"旄门"；西面的三个城门，自南而北为"广阳门"、"雍门"、"上西门"；北面的二个城门，自西而东为"夏门"、"谷门"；南面的四个城门，自东而西为"开阳门"、"平城门"、"小苑门"、"津门"。在 1962 年的勘探工作中，发现了东面、西面和北面的八个城门，它们都有很明显的遗迹存在。[3] 南面的四个城门，虽然都已被洛河冲毁，无遗迹可寻，但可以根据勘察工作中所发现的城内的四条南北向的大街分别确定它们的位置。从实测的城的平面图上可以看出，东面的上东门和旄门分别与西面的上西门和广阳门对直，而南面的开阳门、平城门、小苑门和津门的位置也相当均称，这说明了筑城时的计划性较强。由于没有经过发掘，城门的形制和结构不甚清楚。但是，北面西头的夏门，遗迹保存得特别好，可以根据钻探所得的情况，判断它和西汉长安城的城门一样，有三个门道。[4] 这与文献的记载是相符的。

在钻探工作中，发现了许多街道的遗迹，它们主要是属于以后的北魏时期的。[5] 但是，可以认为，东汉时的街道分布情况，基本上与北魏时的街道分布情况相似；换言之，北魏时的街道，主要是沿用东汉以来的街道，只是因宫殿和个别城门位置的改变而有所增筑或改修而已。因此，可以以钻探出来的街道遗迹为主要根据，并参照东汉时期的宫殿范围和城门的位置，来判断东汉雒阳城内街道的分布情形。

南北纵行的大街，共有五条：第一条可称"开阳门大街"，自开阳门往北，全长约 2800 米。第二条可称"平城门大街"，自平城门

Gate Avenue, ran north from the Pingchengmen Gate and stopped at the southern gate of the South Palace, a distance of 700 m. The third, which we could call Xiaoyuanmen Gate Avenue, ran north from the Xiaoyuanmen Gate and stopped at the southern gate of the North Palace, a distance of 2,000 m. The fourth, which we could call the Jinmen Gate Avenue, ran north from the Jinmen Gate and was approximately 2,800 m long. The fifth, which we could call the Gumen Gate Avenue, ran south from the Gumen Gate, turned eastward when it met the northern wall of the North Palace, then turned southward again, covering 2,400 m. The street that ran south from the Xiamen Gate stopped 100 m inside the city wall where it met the northern wall of the North Palace, hence we cannot consider it an avenue. There were also five avenues that ran east to west. The first one, which we could call the Shangdongmen Gate Avenue, ran west from the Shangdongmen Gate and stopped at the eastern wall of the North Palace, a distance of 600 m. The second, which we could call the Zhongdongmen Gate Avenue, ran west from the Zhongdongmen Gate, passing between the South Palace and the North Palace, covering approximately 2,200 m. The third, which we could call the Shangximen Gate Avenue, ran east from the Shangximen Gate and stopped at the western wall of the North Palace, a distance of 500 m. The fourth, which we could call the Yongmen Gate Avenue, ran east from the Yongmen Gate and stopped at the Jinmen Gate Avenue, a distance of about 500 m. The fifth, which we could call Maomen-Gate-to-Guangyangmen-Gate Avenue, crossed the entire width of the city between those two gates, a distance of 2,460 m. These various avenues formed a network of crossroads and T-shaped intersections. If we count the number of avenue segments marked off by the intersections we come up with a total of twenty-four segments. *Hanyi*, as quoted by the commentary on the "Treatise on the Bureaucracy" in *Xu Hanshu*, says that Luoyang had twenty-four "streets" (*jie*); it is probably these avenue segments that the statement refers to. Except for some of the smaller avenues that were 20 m wide, most of the avenues measured 40 m across. Without excavations we cannot have a complete understanding of how they were constructed. But according to *Luoyang ji*: "The large avenues within the city and those running through the palace gates all have three lanes. The middle lane is the imperial by-way and is bordered on either side by a mud wall that stands over 4 *chi* high. Only the noblemen and high officials are allowed to use this middle lane. Pedestrians must use the side lanes, the left-hand one for entering and the right-hand one for exiting." This passage indicates that the avenues of Luoyang, with their three parallel lanes, were just like those of the Western Han capital of Chang'an.[6]

往北, 遇南宫的南门而止, 长约 700 米。第三条可称 "小苑门大街", 自小苑门往北, 至北宫的南门而止, 全长约 2000 米。第四条可称 "津门大街", 自津门往北, 全长约 2800 米。第五条可称 "谷门大街", 自谷门往南, 遇北宫的北墙而东折, 然后再折而向南, 全长约 2400 米。至于自夏门南行的街道, 因入城不到 100 米即遇北宫的北墙而止, 所以实际上算不了一条大街。东西向横行的大街, 亦有五条: 第一条可称 "上东门大街", 自上东门往西, 遇北宫的东墙而止, 长约 600 米。第二条可称 "中东门大街", 自中东门往西, 穿南宫与北宫之间而过, 全长约 2200 米。第三条称 "上西门大街", 自上西门往东, 遇北宫的西墙而止, 长约 500 米。第四条称 "雍门大街", 自雍门往东, 遇 "津门大街" 而止, 长约 500 米。第五条可称 "旄门——广阳门大街", 自旄门至广阳门, 横贯全城, 全长 2460 米。以上各条大街, 互相交叉结合, 形成许多十字路口和丁字路口, 若以每二个路口之间为一段, 则共有二十四段。《续汉书·百官志》注引《汉仪》说 "洛阳二十四街, 每街一亭", 可能是指此而言。除个别大街宽约 20 米以外, 一般的大街宽在 40 米左右。由于没有经过发掘, 街道的形制不能得到明确的了解。但是,《太平御览》引《洛阳记》说: "宫门及城中大道皆分作三, 中央御道, 两边筑土墙高四尺余外分之, 唯公卿、尚书章服从中道, 凡行人皆行左右。" 这说明了雒阳城内的大街也是由三条并行的道路组成, 与西汉长安城的街道相似。[6]

Palaces   Among the palaces of Luoyang, the most important were Nangong, or the South Palace, and Beigong, or the North Palace. They already existed during the Western Han dynasty, but then they were much smaller than during Eastern Han. Nevertheless, the South Palace was already famous during Western Han and is often referred to in the historical records. The "Annals of Emperor Gao Zu" in *Hanshu* says that in the fifth year of that emperor's reign (202 B.C.), "The emperor held a banquet in Luoyang's South Palace." Again, the "Biography of Wang Mang" in *Hanshu* records that in A.D. 22, "The chancellor, Wang Xun, led more than ten thousand troops to camp at Luoyang; he occupied the South Palace." We can thus deduce that from the beginning to the end of the Western Han dynasty, the South Palace was the major palace in Luoyang. In 1961, a bronze *zhong*-jar was found in the ruins of the Western Han Chang'an with the words "South Palace *zhong*"[7] inscribed on it. It must have come from the South Palace of Luoyang of Western Han (fig. 40).[8] In the first year of the reign period Jian Wu of Eastern Han (A.D. 25), Emperor Guang Wu Di decided to establish his capital at Luoyang and took up residence in the Quefei Hall of the South Palace. The Quefei Hall must have been part of the legacy of the Western Han Luoyang. Subsequently, with continuous construction, the South Palace grew steadily until A.D. 38, when its most important structure, the Anterior Hall, was completed.

Since there has not been thorough excavation, remains of the South Palace have not yet been uncovered. But, as mentioned above, we already have some knowledge of the layout of Luoyang's gates and avenues. Based on this, we can make certain general statements about the location of the South Palace and its boundaries. From a map based on our measurements, we can tell that in the southern section of Luoyang—that is, south of the Zhongdongmen Gate Avenue, north of the Maomen-Gate-to-Guangyangmen-Gate Avenue, west of the Kaiyangmen Gate Avenue, and east of the Xiaoyuanmen Gate Avenue—there was a large rectangular space, which was approximately 1,300 m north to south and 1,000 m east to west. This must have been the location of the South Palace. According to the "Treatise on the Five Phases" in *Xu Hanshu*, the Pingchengmen Gate was the city gate that faced directly south and also the one that provided access to the South Palace. When the suburban sacrifices were held, the emperor's carriage came out from this gate; it was the most important of the city gates. During our test diggings, we found that the Pingchengmen Gate Avenue led directly from the southern suburb into the city and continued on into the space we described above, which according to our estimate must have been the location of the South Palace. The path of this avenue confirms the accuracy of our estimate.[9]

　　东汉雒阳城内的宫殿，主要是南宫和北宫。它们在西汉时即已存在，但规模不如东汉。西汉时的南宫是很有名的，常在文献记载中被提到。《汉书·高帝纪》说，"（高帝五年，公元前 202 年）帝置酒雒阳南宫"，《汉书·王莽传》说，"（地皇三年，公元 22 年）司徒王寻将十余万屯雒阳，填南宫"，可见从西汉初年到西汉末年，南宫一直是雒阳城中主要的宫殿。1961 年在西安西汉长安城外上林苑遗址发现的一件铜钟，刻有"南宫鍾"字样，[7] 应系当时雒阳南宫中所用之物，后来才被征调到长安的（图 40）。[8] 建武元年（公元 25 年），光武帝定都雒阳，居住在南宫的却非殿，它可能是西汉遗留的旧建筑。以后，由于不断进行扩建，南宫的规模日益增大，建武十四年（公元 38 年）终于在南宫中建成最重要的"前殿"。

　　由于还没有经过全面的发掘，南宫的遗迹迄今未被揭露出来。但是，如前所述，东汉雒阳城的城门和街道的分布情形已经究明，所以对于南宫的位置和范围也就可以据此作大概的判断。从实测图中可以看出，在雒阳城的南部，"中东门大街"之南，"旄门——广阳门大街"之北，"开阳门大街"之西，"小苑门大街"之东，有一片范围广大的长方形的区域，南北长约 1300 米，东西宽约 1000 米，应该便是南宫之所在。《续汉书·五行志》说，平城门是"正阳之门"，与南宫相连，举行郊祀的典礼时，皇帝的车驾从此门而出，是最重要的城门。在钻探工作中发现的"平城门大街"，由南郊向北通入城内，直达上述南宫所在的范围，这就证明了以上的判断是正确的。[9]

The South Palace was the most important construction project undertaken by Emperor Guang Wu Di. Under the next emperor (Emperor Ming
Di), the North Palace was rebuilt; this rebuilding lasted from A.D. 60 to
A.D. 65. Within the North Palace, the Deyang Hall was the most important
palace building. It held ten thousand people and stood atop a twenty-*chi*-
high flight of steps, and the Zhuque Que in front of the hall was high into
the clouds, allegedly visible 40 *li* away. During our survey, we could not
definitely determine the boundaries of the North Palace. But from the
layout of the avenues, we could determine that the North Palace must have
been situated north of the Zhongdongmen Gate Avenue, east of the Jinmen
Gate Avenue, and west of the Gumen Gate Avenue. This last avenue, the
Gumen Gate, which ran south from that gate, turned eastward after a
short distance; this bend must have been made in order to circumvent the
northern wall of the North Palace. If this is so, then we could conclude that
the northern wall of the North Palace was very close to the northern city
wall. The North Palace was probably even larger than the South Palace, and
its location was not only north but also slightly to the west. According to
textual records, the distance between the South Palace and North Palace
was 7 *li*; this figure, however, could not be confirmed by our survey work.
Possibly the correct figure was 1 *li*, which later became corrupted into 7 *li*.
Between the two palaces there were covered passageways, built to provide
security for the emperor as he moved back and forth.

In the Western Han capital of Chang'an, the two major palaces, Changlegong and Weiyanggong, were both located in the southern part of the
city, side by side. In the Eastern Han capital of Luoyang, however, the two
major palaces were located in the northern and the southern parts of the
city, respectively, and had connecting passageways between them. This is
another distinct difference in the design of the two Han capitals. Yet from
another point of view, the capitals were similar in the respect that their
palaces, wherever they were located, occupied over half the entire area
of each city. In addition to the South Palace and North Palace, Luoyang

also had the Yong'angong Palace, situated northeast of the North Palace, near the Shangdongmen Gate. Furthermore, in the northwestern part of the capital there was Zhuolongyuan, an imperial park. Southeast of the South Palace, near the Maomen Gate and Kaiyangmen Gate, stood the ministries of the grand commandant (*taiwei*), the imperial secretary (*sikong*), and the chancellor (*situ*). These were the highest administrative bodies of the empire. Northeast of the North Palace, right next to the northeastern corner of the city wall, stood the Grand Storehouse (*taicang*) and the Armory (*wuku*). The residential districts of the high officials and aristocrats, such as the Buguang and Yonghe precincts, were mostly located near the Shangdongmen Gate.

　　光武帝在位时，主要是修建南宫。到了明帝时，又营建北宫，自永平三年（公元60年）开始，历时五年，至永平八年（公元65年）才全部建成。北宫中的"德阳殿"，是最重要的宫殿，"周旋容万人，陛高二丈"，殿前的朱雀阙高耸入云，据说从四十多里以外就可以望见。在勘察工作中，尚未明确究明北宫的遗迹。但是，可以根据街道分布的情形，判断北宫应在"中东门大街"之北，"津门大街"之东，"谷门大街"之西；由于"谷门大街"入城后南行不远便折而向东，这显然是由于遇到了北宫的北墙，从而可以认为北宫的北墙离雒阳城的北面城墙很近。和南宫比较起来，北宫的范围可能更大，它的位置在南宫之北，而略为偏西。据文献记载，南北两宫相去七里，但从上述实际的勘察工作看来，七里恐系一里之讹。两宫之间有复道相连，以保证皇帝往来时的安全。

　　西汉长安城中的长乐宫和未央宫，都在城的南部，左右并列；东汉雒阳城中的南宫和北宫则各在城的南部和北部，前后相接。这是两汉都城在形制和布局上的又一重大的不同之处。但是，从另一方面来看，都城中将近一半的面积都为宫殿所占，则是长安城和雒阳城所共同的。除了南宫和北宫之外，雒阳城中还有永安宫，其位置在北宫的东北，靠近上东门处。在城的西北部，则有濯龙园，也是皇家的宫苑。在南宫的东南，靠近旄门和开阳门，则有太尉府、司空府和司徒府，是全国最高的行政机构。在北宫的东北方，紧靠城的东北角，则是太仓和武库之所在。达官贵族的居住区，如步广里、

The residence of Dong Zhuo, for example, was in the Yonghe Precinct.[10] As for the common people, they lived outside the city, just beyond the city gates. The residential areas of the commoners were mostly outside the city wall immediately by the gates, similar to those of the Western Han Chang'an. As for industrial and commercial centers, there were three markets: Nanshi (the South Market), Mashi (the Horse Market), and Jinshi (the Gold Market). The South Market and Horse Market were both located outside the city, the former in the southern suburb and the latter in the eastern suburb. The Gold Market was located inside the city, northeast of the Yongmen Gate, southwest of the North Palace and northwest of the South Palace.

In A.D. 25, Emperor Guang Wu Di established his capital at Luoyang. One hundred and sixty-five years later, in 190, the rebel Dong Zhuo forced Emperor Xian Di to flee from the city and seek refuge in Chang'an. We read that Dong Zhuo "burned the palaces, temples, and houses of Luoyang," and "the fire lasted more than three days, until the city of Luoyang was reduced to ruins." In this way, the prosperous Luoyang was totally destroyed. In 196, when Emperor Xian Di returned to Luoyang, we read "the palaces were completely burned, and the officials had to clear away brambles and seek shelter between tumbled walls." There was no building left in which Emperor Xian Di could reside; he had no choice but to bow to Cao Cao's wish and move his capital to Xuxian.

Luoyang in Wei and Jin Dynasties   Nevertheless, because of Luoyang's strategic location the capital was reestablished there during the succeeding Wei dynasty, ruled by the Cao clan. Emperor Wen Di of the Wei (Cao Pi) rebuilt parts of the North Palace. Then, in the year 235, under the direction of Emperor Ming Di (Cao Rui), a major reconstruction was undertaken. The Taiji Hall, Zhaoyang Hall, and other buildings were constructed on top of the old foundations of the Chongde Hall in the South Palace of Eastern Han. At the same time, several parks, including

Fanglinyuan, were restored and expanded. Since the destruction at the end of Eastern Han had been so severe, it was an enormous feat to rebuild the capital on top of the ruins. According to the "Biography of Gao Tanglong" in *Weizhi*: "There were tens of thousands involved in the labor. Everybody from ministers of state to students joined in the task. The emperor himself led the others, taking part in the digging." It is safe to assume that the size of Luoyang during the Wei dynasty did not exceed that of the Eastern Han Luoyang. The Western Jin dynasty, which followed Wei, continued to construct new buildings, but did not make any major changes in the design of the city.

永和里，多在上东门内，董卓的住宅即在永和里。[10] 至于一般的人民，则多居住在城外，尤其是靠近城门的地区，与西汉长安城的情况相似。工商业区有南市、马市和金市。南市和马市都在城外，前者在南郊，后者在东郊。金市在城内，其位置在北宫的西南，南宫的西北。

从建武元年汉光武帝定都雒阳以来，经历了一百六十五年，到初平元年（公元190年），董卓胁迫汉献帝迁都长安，"焚洛阳宫庙及人家"，"火三日不绝，京都为丘墟矣"。繁华的雒阳城，遭到了彻底的破坏。建安元年（公元196年），汉献帝自长安回到雒阳时，这个都城已是"宫室烧尽，百官披荆棘，依墙壁间"，连可供居住的地方都没有了，所以只好在曹操的挟持下，迁都于许县。

但是，由于洛阳在地理上的重要性，曹魏继东汉之后，仍然选择在这里建都。魏文帝曹丕时，主要是修复了北宫的一部分建筑物。到魏明帝曹叡青龙三年（公元235年），才大兴土木，在东汉南宫崇德殿的旧基上建太极、昭阳诸殿，同时又增饰芳林园等。由于东汉末年的破坏太严重了，在废墟上重建都城，工程艰巨。据《魏志·高堂隆传》记载，当时的情形是"百役繁兴，作者万数，公卿以下，至于学生，莫不展力，帝乃躬自掘土以率之"。看来曹魏时洛阳城中的建设，不会超过东汉的规模。西晋都洛阳，继续有所兴建，但在城的形制和布局上也并没有什么大的变化。

However, it should be mentioned that Emperor Ming Di (Cao Rui) of the Wei dynasty built the Jinyongcheng Fortress at the northwestern corner of the city. (He was following the example of his grandfather, Cao Cao, who had built three defense towers, Tongquetai, Bingjingtai, and Jinhutai, at the northwestern corner of his stronghold, Yecheng.) The Jinyongcheng Fortress was built for military purposes. Its walls and ramparts were particularly strong. And because it stood against the Mangshan Mountains and was situated on high ground that commanded a view of all of Luoyang, it was of critical military importance. In the final years of the Western Jin dynasty, that is, during the rebellions of the Yong Jia period (307-313), this fortress was fought over intensely by those who were contending for control of Luoyang. At that time, it was known as the Luoyang Rampart. In the survey done in 1962, it was determined that the Jinyongcheng Fortress measured 1,080 m from north to south and 250 m from east to west. The fortress consisted of three separate fortifications, whose walls were 13 m thick. The northern fortification and the middle one were outside the Luoyang city wall; the southern fortification was just inside it. These fortifications had connecting doors and ramps.[11] It is also noteworthy that along the walls of the Jinyongcheng Fortress there were projecting bastions at intervals of 60 or 70 m. These bastions were about 15 m long and 8 m wide (fig. 41). Similar bastions were found on the northern and western city walls of Luoyang, where they were about 18 m long and 8 m wide, and they were constructed at about 120 m intervals. These bastions, like the Jinyongcheng Fortress itself, were apparently constructed during the Wei or possibly the Western Jin dynasty.[12] No other examples of such bastions built on the outer edges of city walls have been found from any remains dating from the Han to the Sui-Tang period, except for those on the fortress walls built in border regions. Such bastions were used again in the Northern Song dynasty capital of Bianliang. In the Song dynasty, they were called "Horse Faces" and were used to supplement the city's defenses, ensuring that enemy forces who approached or scaled the city wall would be attacked from three sides. The appearance of these bastions on the city walls of Luoyang during the Wei and Jin dynasties is indicative of constant fighting during that period. They were an innovation made in response to special military needs.

During the year 311, the Xiongnu chieftain, Liu Cong, led his army to invade Luoyang. In the intense battle that ensued, most of its palaces, temples, government offices, and houses were burned down. The Luoyang which had been slowly rebuilt over a seventy-year period during the Wei and Jin dynasties was again reduced to ashes.

但是，应该特别提出来的是，魏明帝曹叡，仿效他祖父曹操在邺城的西北角筑铜雀台、冰井台和金虎台等"三台"的经验，在洛阳城的西北角也建筑了金墉城。它实际上是一种军事性的城堡，壁垒坚固，由于紧靠邙山，地势高亢，可以由此俯瞰洛阳全城，在军事上具有制高点的作用，在西晋末年"永嘉之乱"的洛阳争夺战中是交战双方的必争之地，当时称为"洛阳垒"。1962 年的勘查工作，究明了金墉城南北长约 1080 米，东西宽约 250 米，系由三个城堡组成，墙垣厚达 13 米。北面的一个城堡和中间的一个城堡筑在洛阳城的城墙之外，南面的一个城堡筑在城墙之内，三者互相连接，有门道相通。**11** 值得注意的是，在金墉城的城壁上，每隔六七十米，就设有一个墩台，长约 15 米，宽约 8 米（图 41）。同样的墩台，还见于洛阳城的西面和北面的城墙上，长约 18 米，宽约 8 米，相互之间的距离约 120 米，它们和金墉城一样，显然是魏晋时所增设的。**12** 这种设在城墙外壁的墩台，除了边塞的城鄣以外，在从两汉以迄隋唐的城墙上是没有类例的，直到北宋建汴梁城时才开始被普遍采用，当时称为"马面"，其作用在于加强防守，使攻城者在接近或扳登城墙时三面受敌，攻势受阻。它们在魏晋洛阳城的城墙上出现，充分说明了当时战乱频仍，出于军事上的需要，乃有这种特殊的发明。

西晋永嘉五年（公元 311 年），匈奴族的刘聪率军攻入洛阳，在激烈的战争中，城内的宫庙、官署和住宅多被焚毁。在东汉末年的废墟上经魏晋两朝七十余年的经营才重建起来的洛阳城，再一次化为灰烬。

Luoyang in the Northern Wei Dynasty   One hundred eighty years later, in 493, the Northern Wei dynasty established its capital at Luoyang, the last dynasty to do so. Emperor Xiao Wen Di of Northern Wei decided to shift his capital from Pingcheng to Luoyang that year. Subsequently, after many years of development and reconstruction, Luoyang not only became a prosperous city once again, but also was given a new layout that made it, as the Northern Wei capital, different in many respects from the Luoyang of earlier dynasties. Since Northern Wei was the last dynasty to make Luoyang its capital and afterward the site was abandoned, the remains are quite well preserved. After our survey, we were able to make a relatively accurate and reliable plan of the city (fig. 42).

The most important change in the Northern Wei Luoyang was the abolition of the custom of having two palaces, the South and the North palaces, which had existed since Eastern Han. Instead, a single, walled palace was built. This palace was in the northern part of the city, slightly off to the west, built on the foundation of the North Palace of the Han and Wei dynasties. It had a neat rectangular plan, enclosed by four walls. The eastern and western walls each measured 1,400 m, and the northern and southern walls were 660 m. The palace occupied approximately one-tenth of the area of the entire city. Near the west end of the southern wall of the palace, the remains of an enormous gate have been found. This was the Changhemen Gate, the main palace gate.[13]

The names of the twelve city gates of the Eastern Han Luoyang were all changed by now, with the exception of the Kaiyangmen Gate at the east end of the southern city wall. Actually, some of the gate names had already been changed during the Wei and Jin dynasties, some were not changed until Northern Wei, while still others were changed twice. The former Shangdongmen Gate was now the Jianchunmen Gate, the Zhongdongmen Gate was now the Dongyangmen Gate, the Maomen Gate was now the Qingyangmen Gate, the Pingchengmen Gate was now the Pingchangmen Gate, the Xiaoyuanmen Gate was now the Xuanyangmen Gate, the Jinmen Gate was now the Jinyangmen Gate, the Guangyangmen Gate was now the Ximingmen Gate, the Yongmen Gate was now the Xiyangmen Gate, the Shangximen Gate was now the Changhemen Gate, the Xiamen Gate was now the Daxiamen Gate, and the Gumen Gate was now the Guangmomen Gate. All twelve gates were rebuilt, eleven of them on their former Han and Wei dynasty sites. But the Xiyangmen Gate on the western wall was moved from the old site of the Yongmen Gate 500 m to the north, so that it was now directly opposite the Dongyangmen Gate on the eastern wall. Furthermore, when Emperor Xiao Wen Di first arrived at

　　从这以后，过了一百八十余年，最后在这里建都的朝代是北魏。北魏的孝文帝于太和十七年（公元 493 年）自平城迁都到此，经过多年的经营，不仅使洛阳重新成为繁华的城市，而且在都城的形制和布局上改变了汉和魏晋的旧制，出现了许多新的变革，由于北魏的洛阳城年代最晚，废弃以后，不再有别的朝代在这里建都，所以它的遗迹保存较好，经过勘察以后，能够绘制出一幅比较明确可靠的城的平面图（图 42）。

　　和前代比较起来，北魏洛阳城最重要的改变，是在宫殿方面废除了东汉以来分为南北两宫的制度，建立了单一的宫城。宫城的位置在全城的北部而略为偏西，是在汉和魏晋的北宫的基础上兴建的。它的平面成一规整的长方形，四面筑围墙，计东墙和西墙各长约 1400 米，南墙和北墙各长约 660 米，其面积约占全城的十分之一。在宫城的南墙近西端处，发现了一处巨大的门址，它便是宫城的正门——阊阖门。[13]

　　东汉以来的十二个城门，除南面东头的开阳门以外，都改变了名称。有的是魏晋时就改名的，有的是北魏时才改名的，也有的是魏晋改名以后，北魏又改名。上东门改称建春门，中东门改称东阳门，旄门改称青阳门，平城门改称平昌门，小苑门改称宣阳门，津门改称津阳门，广阳门改称西明门，雍门改称西阳门，上西门改称阊阖门，夏门改称大夏门，谷门改称广莫门。十二个城门，都经过重建，其中十一个城门仍然建立在汉和魏晋的旧址上，但西面的西阳门却从汉代的雍门旧址北移约 500 米，使得它恰好与东面的东阳门对直。此外，孝文帝初到洛阳时，因宫室未就，暂居金墉城，

Luoyang, the palaces were not ready, and so he resided temporarily in the Jinyongcheng Fortress. While there, he created a new city gate near the fortress at the north side of the west wall of the city. This new gate was called the Chengmingmen Gate (fig. 43), thus now Luoyang had thirteen city gates.[14]

Since the boundaries of the palaces and the location of some of the city gates had been changed, the streets within the city also underwent changes. For example, because the South Palace had been totally demolished, it now became possible for an avenue to span the length of the entire city, north to south, from the Guangmomen Gate to the Pingchangmen Gate. Since the Yongmen Gate of Eastern Han no longer existed, the Yongmen Gate Avenue was probably also done away with. Due to the opening of the Chengmingmen Gate, there was now a new avenue leading from that gate eastward into the city. It should be pointed out that now there was also an avenue that cut across the city in an east-west direction from the Jianchunmen Gate to the Changhemen Gate. This avenue cut across the walled palace, running through the palace's own east and west gates, dividing it in two halves, north and south. The southern half was used for palace audiences, while the northern half was the site of the imperial residence. More important, since the newly constructed Xiyangmen Gate was directly opposite the Dongyangmen Gate, the Zhongdongmen Gate Avenue of Eastern Han was extended to cross the entire city. This was thus a second avenue that cut across the entire city, east to west. This avenue passed by the southern wall of the walled palace and formed a kind of interior boundary within the city. North were the imperial palaces and parks; south were the government offices, temples, and houses of the aristocrats. Last, we should note that since the walled palace was in the north of the city, slightly west of center, and its southern gate, the Changhemen Palace Gate, directly faced the Xuanyangmen Gate on the southern city wall, the avenue that connected the two gates, the Tongtuo (Bronze Camel) Avenue, became a kind of major artery, just as the Pingchengmen Gate Avenue had been during Eastern Han.[15] All the high officials' offices, all the temples and ancestral halls, as well as the other important buildings were arrayed along the two sides of the Tongtuo Avenue (figs. 44-46).[16] The famous Yongning Temple was on the west side of the avenue, where its remains are still preserved today and have recently undergone excavation (fig. 47).[17] So it was that the Xuanyangmen Gate became the most important city gate in the Northern Wei Luoyang, as the Pingchengmen Gate had been during Eastern Han.

As mentioned above, when Northern Wei rebuilt the Eastern Han city of Luoyang, it gave the city a new appearance and design. But this

为了出入方便，在西面北头紧靠金墉城处新开了一个城门，称为承明门（图43），使得洛阳城有了十三个城门。[14]

由于宫城的范围和个别城门位置的改变，城内的街道也在东汉以来的基础上有许多变更。例如：南宫已经被彻底废弃，所以在广莫门和平昌门之间有了一条纵贯全城的南北向大街。东汉的雍门已经废绝，所以东汉以来的"雍门大街"可能已不再存在。由于新辟了承明门，所以增添了由承明门往东通入城内的大街，其北即为华林园。值得注意的是，建春门和阊阖门之间有了一条横贯全城的东西向大街，它从宫城的东门和西门穿过，将宫城分为南北两半，南半部是朝会之处，北半部为寝宫所在。更重要的是，由于新建的西阳门正好与东阳门对直，所以东汉以来的中东门大街被延长而贯通于西阳门和东阳门之间，成为又一条横贯全城的东西向大街，它在宫城南墙外通过，是全城的一条分界线。它的北面主要是皇家的宫殿和园囿，它的南面则分布着官署、佛寺和贵族的邸宅。最后，特别要提出来的是，由于宫城的位置在全城的北部而略为偏西，它的南门——阊阖门与南面城墙上的宣阳门对直，所以自阊阖门至宣阳门的南北向大街——铜驼街就成了全城的中轴线，代替了东汉时的平城门大街。[15]当时的司徒府、太尉府等高级官署和宗庙、社稷等重要建筑物，就分布在铜驼街的两侧（图44—46）。[16]有名的永宁寺在街的西侧，其塔基遗迹至今犹保留在地面上，最近已经过发掘（图47）。[17]这样一来，宣阳门也就代替了东汉时的平城门，成为北魏洛阳城的最重要的城门。

如上所述，东汉以来的洛阳旧城，经过重建，面貌一新。但是，

new Luoyang we have been describing so far was actually only the inner city of the Northern Wei Luoyang. Far beyond the old city wall, another wall was erected, known as the outer city wall, enclosing a much larger area. According to *Luoyang qielan ji*, the outer city wall was 20 *li* long from east to west and 15 *li* long from north to south—very long indeed. The city within was divided into 320 wards, each of which was square and enclosed by walls. These ward walls were 300 *bu* on a side, about one *li* by contemporary reckoning. The city had a very exact and neat layout. According to the "Annals of Emperor Shi Zong" in *Weishu*, the construction of this outer city began in 501, during the reign of Emperor Xuan Wu Di, eight years after Emperor Xiao Wen Di moved to Luoyang and made it the site of his new capital, and the actual construction required tens of thousands of laborers. The wards outside the inner city were occupied by the common people, who were kept under strict control and regulation. The markets—that is, the centers of industry and commerce—were also located in the outer city. Dashi (the Big Market) was in the western part of the city, west of the inner city. Xiaoshi (the Small Market) was east of the inner city. Sitongshi (the Four-Way Access Market) was south of the inner city, just outside the Xuanyangmen Gate. Jinshi (the Gold Market), which had been inside the Luoyang of the Han and Jin dynasties, was demolished and a Buddhist temple was constructed on its former site. These changes thus ended the Eastern Han tradition of having a market just north of the main palace.[18] In summary, we can say that the structure and layout of the Northern Wei Luoyang, when compared to that of the two Han capitals, shows epoch-making changes, and established a precedent later adopted for the Sui capital of Daxing and the two Tang capitals of Chang'an and Luoyang.

Ritual Structures According to the "Annals of Emperor Guang Wu Di" in *Hou Hanshu*, the Pi Yong (Hall of Learning), Ming Tang (Ritual Hall), and Ling Tai (Spirit Terrace) were all built in A.D. 56. All documentary references indicate that the three structures were located just south of the Eastern

Han Luoyang, outside the Kaiyangmen Gate and Pingchengmen Gate. This location has been confirmed by archaeological excavations.[19]

The Pi Yong was situated on the eastern side of the large road outside the Kaiyangmen Gate. The remains show that the ground plan was square and that it was surrounded by a wall that was 170 m on each side. Within this large square enclosure there were four clusters of buildings evenly spaced apart. Each cluster consisted of three structures.[20] According to *Han guanyi*, the Pi Yong was surrounded on all sides by a moat, over which there were bridges. However, archaeological excavation has not

随着都市建设的进一步发展，它在北魏的整个洛阳城中，只是作为内城而存在，在它的外围还筑有郭城，即外城。据《洛阳伽蓝记》记载，外郭城"东西二十里，南北十五里"，范围极其广大，在全城的范围内，划分为三百二十坊，每个坊都呈正方形，四周筑围墙，每边长三百步，即当时的一里，规划十分严密而整齐。据《魏书·世宗纪》记载，它们都是在宣武帝景明二年（公元 501 年），即孝文帝迁都洛阳以后的第九年，发动数万人夫兴建起来的。在内城以外的各个坊内，居住着一般的人民，他们受到严格的管理和控制。作为工商业区的"市"，也设置在内城之外的郭城中。其中的"大市"在内城以西的西郭，"小市"在内城以东的东郭，"四通市"在内城以南、宣阳门外的南郭，三市的方位都在宫城以南，而汉和魏晋以来建在城内的金市则废为佛寺，从而完全改变了西汉以来在宫城北面设市的所谓"面朝后市"的老传统。[18] 总之，北魏洛阳城的形制和布局，和两汉以来的都城相比，出现了划时代的变革，而为此后隋代的大兴城、唐代的长安城和隋唐的洛阳城开创了先例。

据《后汉书·光武帝纪》记载，东汉的辟雍、明堂和灵台都建于建武中元元年（公元 56 年）。各种记载都说明它们的位置在雒阳城南，在开阳门和平城门外，这已得到了考古发掘工作的证实。[19]

辟雍在开阳门外大路的东侧。遗址平面呈正方形，四面筑有围墙，每面长约 170 米。在这正方形的大院内，均称地配置着四组建筑物，每组各由三座房屋组成。[20] 据《后汉书·光武帝纪》注引《汉官仪》记载，辟雍四面都设沟堑，其上架桥，东、南、西三面堑中

yet turned up any remnants of such of a moat. During the Wei dynasty and the Western Jin dynasty, the Pi Yong was rebuilt, probably on the site of the Eastern Han Pi Yong. In 1930, a stele was discovered on the site commemorating three visits to the Pi Yong by Emperor Wu Di of the Jin dynasty (reigning from A.D. 265 to 290) (fig. 48), and in recent years the base of this stele has likewise been found. This discovery proves beyond a doubt that the ruins on this site are those of the Pi Yong of the Han and Wei dynasties.[21] During the Northern Wei dynasty, reconstruction of the Pi Yong was undertaken, but it was never completed.

The Ming Tang was located on the western side of the large road outside the Kaiyangmen Gate, and was 150 m west of the Pi Yong. The remains show that the ground plan was square and that the building was surrounded on all sides by a wall which was 400 m on a side. Within this large square enclosure there was a round terrace, 62 m in diameter, that was the site of the main structure. Thus, the remains have some correspondence with the description in *Shuijingzhu*, which states that the design of the Ming Tang was circular at the top and square at the bottom.[22] During both the Western Jin and the Northern Wei dynasties, the Ming Tang was reconstructed on the same site.

The Ling Tai was on the western side of the large road outside the Pingchengmen Gate, 80 m west of the Ming Tang. The remains indicate that the Ling Tai also had a square ground plan and a wall around it. The walls on the east and west sides were each 220 m long, while those on the north and south were 200 m long. Within this large square enclosure there was a high terrace that had a square ground plan. Its base was approximately 50 m on a side, and it was the site of the main structure (fig. 49). What remains today of this terrace stands 8 m high. The top has been destroyed. According to historical records, the terrace was flat and had no superstructure on top (fig. 50). Other buildings or structures flanked the terrace on all sides, mainly on two levels. The upper level was 1.86 m higher than the lower level and was approachable by ramps. The structures on the lower level in reality were verandas, whose banks or aprons were covered with oval river stones (fig. 51). The structures on the higher level on each side of the central terrace consisted of five rooms. The floors of these rooms were lined with rectangular tiles and the walls were painted various colors. The eastern rooms were painted green, the western ones white, the southern ones red, and the northern ones black. Obviously, these colors were related to the Four Deities that the structures represented (i.e., the Green Dragon, the White Tiger, the Red Bird, and the Black Turtle). It is noteworthy that the five rooms on the western side had dark inner chambers that were sunk below the

有水。曹魏和西晋时重建辟雍，应系在东汉的旧址上。1930 年曾出土晋武帝三临辟雍的纪念碑（图48），近年又发现了它的碑座，可证此遗址为汉和魏晋的辟雍无疑。[21] 北魏虽曾修辟雍，但未完成。

明堂在开阳门外大路的西侧，平城门外大路的东侧，东距辟雍约150 米，遗址平面呈正方形，四面筑有围墙，每面长约 400 米。在这正方形的大院的正中，有一直径为 62 米的圆形台基，即系主体建筑之所在，与《水经注》所说"寻其基构，卜圆下方"的情形不无相符之处。[22] 西晋和北魏时，都曾重建明堂，当系在东汉明堂的旧址上。

灵台在平城门外大路的西侧，东距明堂约 80 米。遗址的总平面基本上亦呈正方形，四面筑有围墙，东墙和西墙各长 220 米，南墙和北墙各长 200 米。在这正方形的大院的正中，有一座平面成正方形的高台，其基部约为 50 米见方，是主体建筑之所在。（图49）高台残存高度约 8 米，顶部已塌毁，据记载，当时是"上平无屋"（图 50）。房屋筑在高台的四周，可分上下两层，上层比下层高出1.86 米，有坡道可以升登。下层的房屋实际上是回廊，廊外有用河卵石铺成的"散水"（图 51）。上层房屋每面各五间，屋内地面用长方砖铺砌，墙壁上涂有色彩。东面房屋所涂为青色，西面房屋所涂为白色，南面房屋所涂为红色，北面房屋所涂为黑色，显然是按照"四神"——青龙、白虎、朱雀、玄武分别代表四方的学说设计的。值得注意的是，西面的五间房屋，都设有深入于土台之中的暗室，

central terrace. In these dark inner chambers the door was lined with square tiles (fig. 52). According to the "Treatise on Astronomy" in *Jinshu*, Zhang Pingzi (Zhang Heng, A.D. 78-139) constructed a bronze armillary sphere in a sealed room; it is perhaps these chambers that the text refers to. During the Wei and Western Jin dynasties, the Eastern Han Ling Tai continued to be used. But since it suffered severe damage during the fighting of the last years of Western Jin, it was abandoned during Northern Wei and a Buddhist pagoda was built on top of the terrace. The Buddhist images carved on bricks which were found during our excavation date from Northern Wei.[23]

Academies   The Tai Xue (Imperial Academy) occupied a very large area. Because of the pilfering of stone classics from the Tai Xue site before the founding of the People's Republic of China, the remains have been severely damaged. But our reconnaissance and excavations showed that it consisted of two distinct sections. The first section was north of the Pi Yong. Its ground plan was rectangular, the eastern and western sides being approximately 200 m long, and the northern and southern sides 100 m long. In the past, fragments of stone classics were mostly dug up just north of this section. Hence, we can assume that this was the most important part of the Eastern Han Tai Xue. The second section was approximately 100 m northeast of the first section, and its remains are very well preserved. Its ground plan was also rectangular. The northern and southern sides were approximately 200 m long; the eastern and western sides 150 m long. It was surrounded by a wall.[24] The construction of the Tai Xue began in A.D. 29. Later, the Tai Xue was expanded several times and it did not reach its completed form until A.D. 132. At that time, the number of students enrolled in the Tai Xue occasionally exceeded 30,000. In 175, Emperor Ling Di had the Confucian classics cut on stone at the Tai Xue; hence, these works are referred to as the "Xi Ping Stone Classics," taking their name from Emperor Ling Di's reign period (fig. 53). So many people were eager to look at and copy from the stone classics that more than a thousand carriages arrived at the Tai Xue every day, jamming the streets nearby. At the end of Eastern Han, when Dong Zhuo burned the palaces and temples of Luoyang, the Tai Xue was also damaged. In 224, Emperor Wen Di of the Wei dynasty rebuilt the Tai Xue on its former site. Sometime between 240 and 249, another set of stone classics was cut in three calligraphic styles (fig. 54). At the beginning of the Western Jin dynasty, the Tai Xue was established in accordance with the Han and Wei precedents. In 276, the Guo Zi Xue (National Academy) was established to exist side by side with the Tai Xue. Therefore, in his "Xianju fu," Pan Yue says, "The two academies stand side by side, identical in appearance. The right-hand one is for the descendants of the imperial clan,

室内用正方砖铺地（图 52）。《晋书·天文志》说"张平子（张衡）既作铜浑天仪于密室中"，也许就是指此而言的。曹魏和西晋，都沿用东汉的灵台。由于在西晋末年的战乱中灵台受到严重的毁坏，所以北魏时就废弃不用，而在台上筑佛塔。在发掘工作中发现的一些砖雕的佛像，便是北魏的遗物。[23]

太学的范围很大。由于新中国成立前在这里盗掘石经，遗址遭到严重的破坏。经过勘探和试掘，可以确认其主要遗迹可分为两部分。一部分在辟雍之北，其范围略呈长方形，东西长约 200 米，南北宽约 100 米，过去许多石经碎片大多是在这里的北面附近出土的，从而可以认为是东汉太学的主要部分之所在。另一部分在它的东北约 100 米处，遗迹保存较好，其范围亦成长方形，南北长约 200 米，东西宽约 150 米，四周筑有围墙。[24]东汉的太学始建于光武帝建武五年（公元 29 年），以后屡经扩建，至顺帝阳嘉元年（公元 132 年）才全部完竣，当时太学生多达三万余人。灵帝熹平四年（公元 175 年）立石经于太学，称"熹平石经"（图 53），观摹者"车乘日千余辆，填塞街陌"。汉末董卓烧洛阳宫庙，太学亦遭殃及。魏文帝黄初五年（公元 224 年）在东汉的旧址上重建太学，正始（公元 240 至 249 年）中又立三体石经（图 54）。西晋初年，依汉魏之制兴太学，而咸宁二年（公元 276 年）又另立国子学，与太学并存。所以，潘岳《闲居赋》有"两学齐列，双宇如一，右延国胄，

and the left-hand one for talented common people."
Moreover, according to *Shuzhengji*, the Tai Xue stood
200 *bu* east of the Guo Zi Xue. Therefore, we can
deduce that the Tai Xue of Western Jin occupied the
northeastern part of the grounds occupied by the
Tai Xue during the Han and Wei dynasties. And the
southwestern part of the Han and Wei Tai Xue was
converted into the Guo Zi Xue.

左纳良逸" 之句。据《述征记》记载，
"太学在国子学东二百步"。因此，推测
西晋的太学在汉魏太学的东北部分，而
将汉魏太学的西南部分改设国子学。

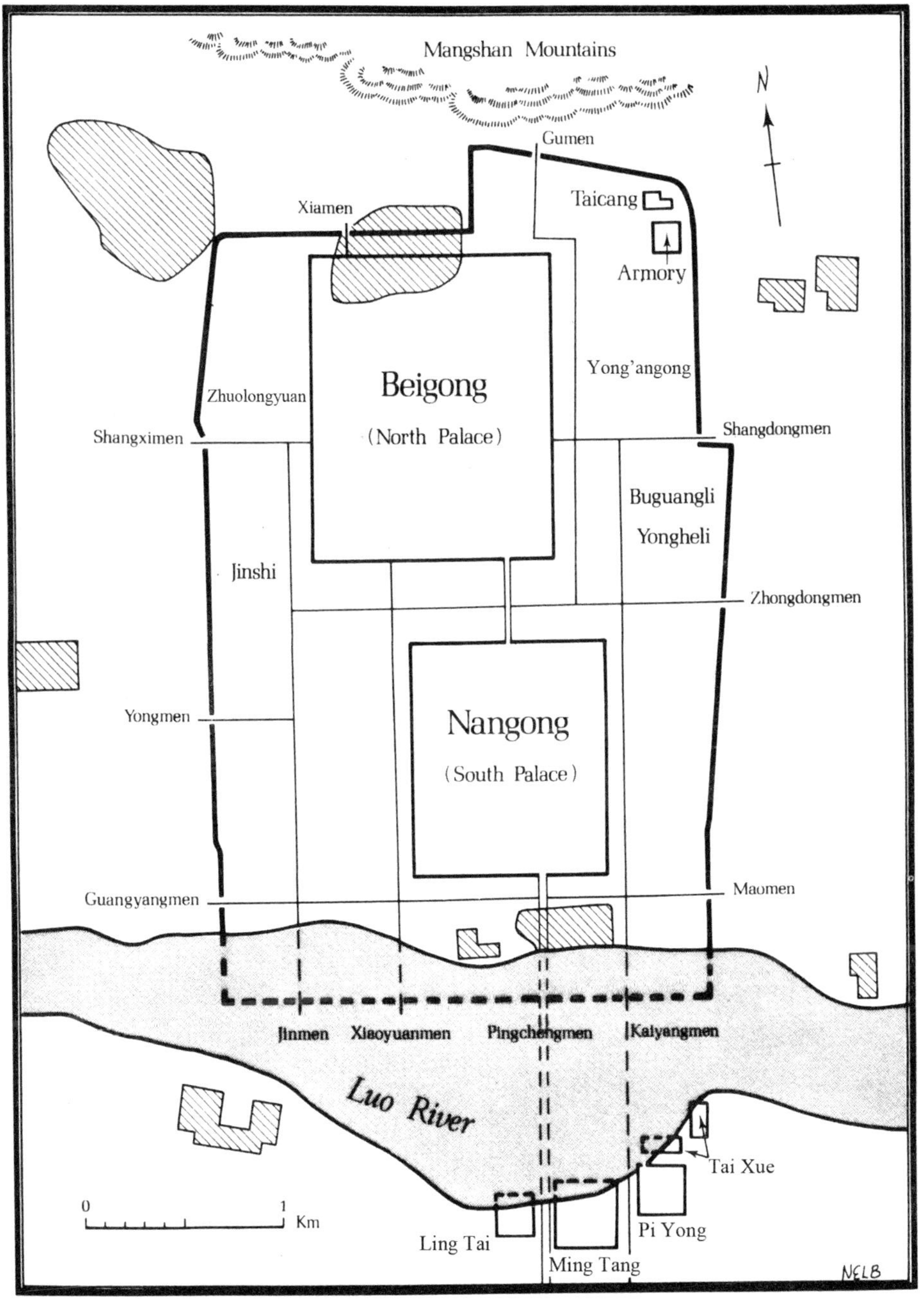

Mangshan Mountains

Gumen

Xiamen

Taicang

Armory

Zhuolongyuan

Beigong

（North Palace）

Yong'angong

Shangximen

Shangdongmen

Buguangli

Yongheli

Jinshi

Zhongdongmen

Yongmen

Nangong

（South Palace）

Guangyangmen

Maomen

Jinmen   Xiaoyuanmen   Pingchengmen   Kaiyangmen

Luo River

Tai Xue

0   1

Km

Ling Tai

Pi Yong

Ming Tang

NELB

37. Plan of the Eastern Han city of Luoyang 东汉雒阳城平面示意图

69

38. Remains of a section of the northern wall of the Eastern Han Luoyang 东汉雒阳城城墙遗迹

39. Stamped earth layers on a section of the eastern wall of the Eastern Han Luoyang 东汉雒阳城墙上的夯土层次

40. "Nangong *zhong*," a *zhong*-vessel of the South Palace of Luoyang, unearthed at Sanqiaozhen, Xi'an
"南宫鐘"，西安三桥镇出土

41. Western wall of the Jinyongcheng of Luoyang and a bastion (the so-called "Horse Face") 洛阳金墉城城墙及墩台（所谓"马面"）

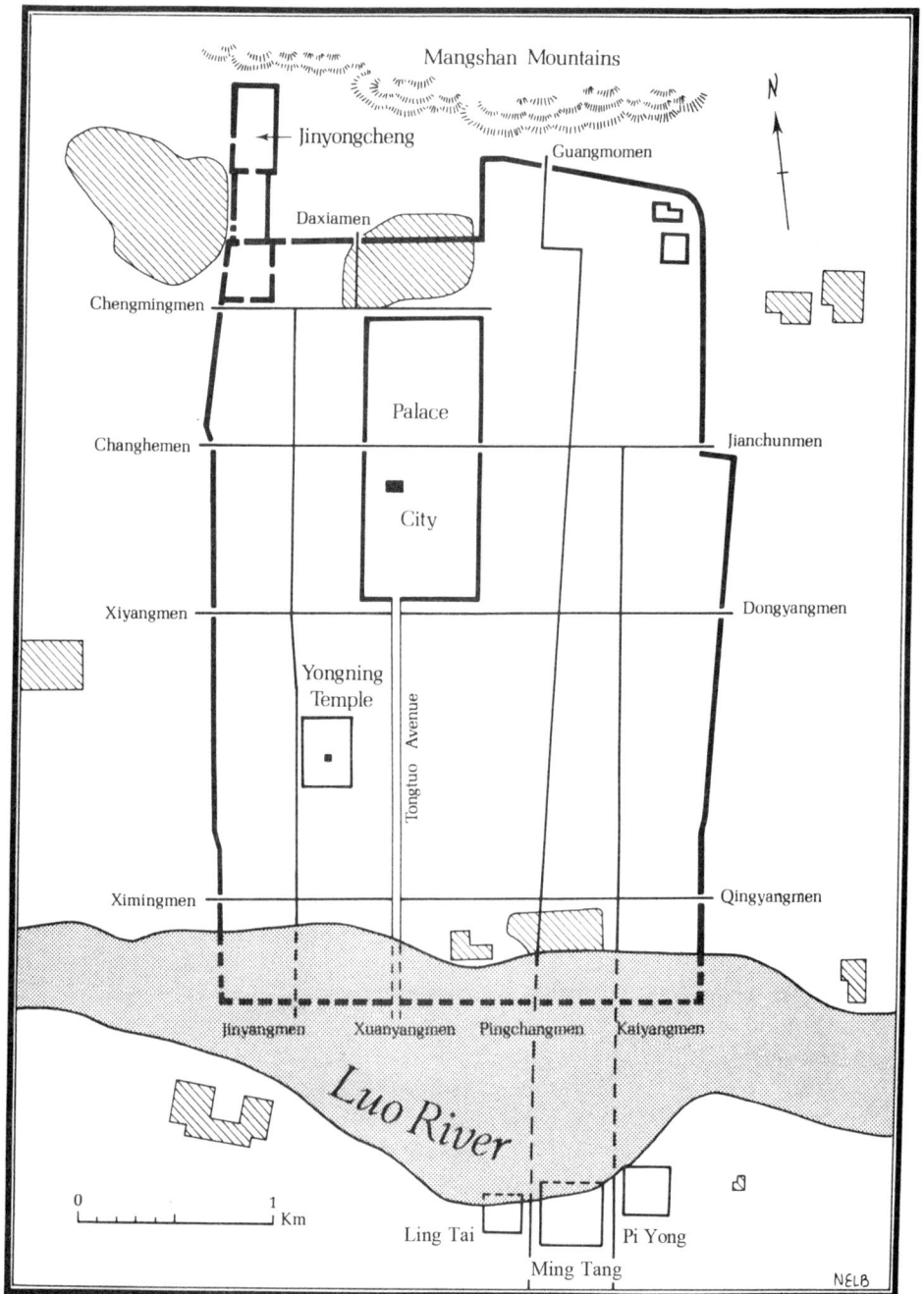

Mangshan Mountains

Jinyongcheng

Guangmomen

Daxiamen

Chengmingmen

Palace

Changhemen

Jianchunmen

City

Xiyangmen

Dongyangmen

Yongning
Temple

Tongtuo Avenue

Ximingmen

Qingyangrnen

Jinyangmen   Xuanyangmen   Pingchangmen   Kaiyangmen

Luo River

0   1
⊢——┴——┴——┴——┴——┤ Km

Ling Tai   Pi Yong

Ming Tang

NELB

42. Plan of the city of Luoyang during the Northern Wei dynasty (The Jinyongcheng at the northwestern corner was first built during the Cao Wei period.)
北魏洛阳城平面示意图（西北角的金墉城为曹魏时期首次修建）

43. Remains of the Chengmingmen Gate of Luoyang during the Northern Wei dynasty　北魏洛阳城承明门遗址

44. Structural remains on the east side of the Tongtuo Avenue in the Northern Wei city of Luoyang (possibly a portion of the Zongzheng administrative building or the royal ancestral temple)　铜驼街东侧的建筑遗址（或为宗正署或宫庙局部）

45. Eaves tiles unearthed at the structural site on the east side of the Tongtuo Avenue in the Northern Wei Luoyang　铜驼街东侧建筑遗址出土的瓦当

46. Brick engraved with animal face unearthed at the structural site on the east side of the Tongtuo Avenue in the Northern Wei Luoyang
　　铜驼街东侧建筑遗址出土的兽面砖

47. Remains of the base of a pagoda in Yongning Temple in the Northern Wei Luoyang　北魏洛阳城永宁寺塔基遗迹

48. Portion of the inscribed monument commemorating the three visits to Pi Yong by Emperor Wu Di of Jin　晋武帝三临辟雍碑

49. Plan and cross-section of the site of Ling Tai of the Eastern Han Luoyang　东汉雒阳灵台遗址示意图及截面图

50. Main structure of Ling Tai in the Eastern Han Luoyang　东汉雒阳灵台遗迹全景

51. Remains of the stairs on the northern side of the main structure of Ling Tai and of the stone-covered banks of the verandas
灵台北面坡道和"散水"遗迹

52. Brick-paved floor of the "dark room" in the west of the main structure of Ling Tai in the Eastern Han Luoyang
东汉雒阳灵台主体建筑西面暗室的砖铺地面

53. Fragment of the Stone Classics engraved during the Xi Ping reign of Han
汉熹平石经残石

54. Fragment of the Stone Classics engraved during the Zheng Shi reign of Wei
魏正始石经残石

CHAPTER 3   HAN DYNASTY AGRICULTURE

Agricultural Products   We begin our discussion of Han dynasty agriculture by talking about the agricultural products of the period evidenced by archaeological finds.

Remains of agricultural products have been discovered in many tombs dating from Western Han and Eastern Han, including tombs found in Xianyang in Shaanxi, Luoyang in Henan, Jiangling and Guanghua in Hubei, Changsha in Hunan, Xuzhou and Haizhou in Jiangsu, Guixian in Guangxi, and Guangzhou in Guangdong.[1] The tombs that contain the largest variety of agricultural products and the most well preserved products are the Mawangdui tombs in Changsha. Moreover, the pottery models of granaries found in the Shaogou tombs in Luoyang and the bamboo slips contained in the Mawangdui tomb have the names of various agricultural products written on them (fig. 55). To summarize, the most important food products of the Han dynasty were grains such as foxtail millet, rice, wheat, barley, panic millet, and beans. The rices included short-grain, long-grain, and glutinous rice. The beans included soybeans and red beans. In the Yellow River region of the North, the primary products were foxtail millet and wheat. A scene of a farmer tilling the soil with an ox-drawn plow found on a pictorial stone in the Mizhi district of Shaanxi has engraved on it a picture of full-grown foxtail millet, which must have been an important grain in that area (fig. 56).[2] We have also found remains of foxtail millet in the tombs in Xianyang, Luoyang, Jiangling, Guanghua, Changsha, Xuzhou, and Guangdong. These finds indicate that the cultivation of foxtail millet was very widespread. Wheat and barley were also cultivated in the Yangtze River region as well as in the Yellow River region. Remains of these were found in the Han Mawangdui tomb. Similarly, rice was cultivated in the Yellow River region (in addition to the South); a grain found in a Han Luoyang tomb has been identified as short-grain rice.[3] Furthermore, the word *shudao* written on the pottery found in that tomb must stand for glutinous rice.[4] In the Yangtze River region and other southern areas, rice was of course the most important grain. It has been determined that, the rice found in the Han tomb excavated at Guangzhou was long-grain rice, whereas the rice found in the Mawangdui tomb in Changsha included all three varieties, short-grain, long-grain, and glutinous; references on the bamboo slips of the same tomb corroborate the physical reclaim.[5] In a Fenghuangshan tomb of Jiangling, we found four very well preserved sheaves of rice in a pottery granary. The ears measured 18.5 cm, and every ear had on the average fifty-one grains of rice. They have been identified as a kind of short-grain rice (fig. 57).[6] In addition, it has been

叁 汉代的农业

在谈到汉代的农业时，首先要根据考古工作中的发现，说一说当时有哪些农产品。

在陕西省的咸阳，河南省的洛阳，湖北省的江陵、光化，湖南省的长沙，江苏省的徐州、海州，广西壮族自治区的贵县，广东省的广州等地的西汉和东汉的墓中，都发现了当时农产品的遗留[1]，其中以长沙马王堆汉墓出土的种类最多，保存最好。洛阳烧沟汉墓的陶仓和长沙马王堆汉墓的竹简上，还书写着各种农产品的名称（图55）。归纳起来，在汉代作为食物的农产品中，粟（小米）、稻、小麦、大麦、黍（黄米）、豆等谷物是最重要的。稻有粳、籼、糯等品种，豆有大豆和赤豆等。在黄河流域和北方地区，以种植粟和小麦为主。陕西米脂画像石的牛耕图中，刻绘着成熟的粟，可见它是当地主要的谷物（图56）。[2] 由于在咸阳、洛阳、江陵、光化、长沙、徐州、广东等地也发现了粟，可见它的种植是很普遍的。除了黄河流域以外，长江流域也种小麦和大麦，马王堆汉墓中即发现了它们的遗品。黄河流域也种稻，洛阳汉墓出土的稻谷经鉴定为粳稻[3]，而墓中陶器上所书的"秝稻"则应系糯稻[4]。长江流域和南方地区，稻是主要的谷物。经鉴定，广州汉墓出土的稻谷为籼稻；长沙马王堆汉墓出土的稻谷，从竹简上的文字，并从实物的鉴定看来，有籼稻，也有粳稻和糯稻。[5] 江陵凤凰山汉墓发现有稻穗四束，放在一个陶仓中，保存得很好，稻穗长约18.5厘米，每穗平均有51粒，经鉴定，是一种粳稻（图57）。[6] 此外，据报道，

reported that remains of sorghum have been unearthed from Han tombs in Xianyang, Luoyang and Guangzhou as well as from a Han village site at Sandaohao in Liaoyang,[7] but they have not been scientifically examined. Besides these grains, there were of course other agricultural food products, including job's tears, taro, mallow, mustard green, sweet melon, bottle gourd, bamboo shoot, lotus root, and ginger (fig. 58). Among the fruits were the chestnut, Chinese jujube, pear, peach, plum, apricot, Chinese plum, red bayberry and olive. For weaving cloth, there was hemp, already quite common. In the Shaogou tombs in Henan, a pottery granary had the words "ten thousand piculs of hemp" written on it; and actual remains of hemp seeds have been found in the Han tombs at Changsha Mawangdui and at Luobowan in Guixian.

Agricultural Implements One of the distinguishing characteristics of Han agriculture was the widespread use of iron agricultural implements. They have been found throughout the nation; that is, not only in the Central Plains area but also on the frontiers. Archaeological excavations have turned up a variety of types of iron agricultural implements, from such distant places as Inner Mongolia and Liaoning in the northeast to Yunnan and Guizhou in the southwest; from Guangdong and Fujian in the southeast to Gansu in the northwest.[8] The types of implements include the spade, shovel, pick, and plow, all used for tillage; the hoe, used for weeding; and the sickle, used for harvesting (figs. 59, 60). Furthermore, two- and three-toothed rakes, used for loosening the soil (fig. 61), have been found in Liaoyang in Liaoning, Mancheng and Baoding in Hebei, and Xuzhou in Jiangsu.[9]

The plowshares attached to Han plows were commonly made entirely of iron. They were a vast improvement over the wooden plowshares dating from the Warring States period, whose only iron part was the blade. The Han plowshares varied according to the soil type. Some were small and light, suitable for cultivated soil. Some were sharp and heavy, as would be needed to open uncultivated land. There was also a kind of giant plowshare, found in Sandaohao in Liaoyang, Liaoning, as well as in the village of Changcheng in Tengxian, Shandong, and the village of Donggangtou of Shijiazhuang, Hebei. Their length and width exceed 40 cm.[10] The famous Han tomb at Mancheng also contained one of these giant plowshares (fig. 62).[11] Because it was so heavy an enormous amount of power must have been required to move it and it would not have been suitable for normal land conditions. Therefore, some people have speculated that these giant plowshares were used in irrigation projects, in other words, used to dig ditches. However, the "Treatise on Irrigation"

咸阳、洛阳、广州等地的汉墓和辽阳三道壕的汉代村落遗址中都曾发现高粱的残迹[7]，只是还没有经过正式的鉴定。除了上述的谷物以外，作为食物的农产品还有薏苡、芋、葵（冬苋菜）、芥菜、甜瓜、葫芦、笋、藕、生姜等类（图58），果品方面则有栗、枣、梨、桃、李、杏、梅、杨梅、橄榄，等等。作为主要纺织材料的大麻，已普遍种植，洛阳烧沟汉墓中有写着"麻万石"字样的陶仓，长沙马王堆和贵县罗泊湾汉墓更发现了大麻子的实物。

汉代农业生产的特点之一，是铁农具的普遍使用。当时的铁农具，不仅在中原一带，而且在边远地区广泛使用，普及全国。在考古调查发掘工作中，从东北的辽宁、内蒙古到西南的云南、贵州，从东南的广东、福建到西北的甘肃，都发现了汉代的各种铁农具。[8] 它们的种类，包括翻土用的锸、铲、镬、犁，除草用的锄，收割用的镰，等等（图59、60）。在辽宁省的辽阳、河北省的保定和满城、江苏省的徐州等地，还发现了一种三齿耙和双齿耙，用于耙地松土（图61）。[9]

安在犁上的铧，一般都系"全铁制"，比之战国时代套在木铧上的"铁口铧"显然要进步得多。铁铧因耕作对象的不同而有各种类型。有的小而轻巧，适用于翻耕熟地。有的锐利而厚重，适用于开垦生地。也有一种巨型铧，如在辽宁辽阳三道壕、山东滕县长城村、河北石家庄东岗头村等处出土的，长度和宽度都在四十厘米以上[10]；在有名的满城汉墓中，也发现了这种巨型的铁铧（图62）[11]。由于形制特别厚重，牵引极费力，不适于翻耕一般的农田，所以颇有人认为这种巨型铧大概是适应水利工程的需要，用于开沟

in *Hanshu* says that the *cha* serves to produce "clouds," and that ditches serve to produce "rain." In Yan Shigu's commentary he states, "the *cha* is a spade, to open irrigation ditches"; thus the plow does not seem to have been an important implement in irrigation projects. In excavations in Pucheng, Liquan, Xi'an, and Longxian, all in modern Shaanxi, we have found evidence of a technique of using a plowshare crown—that is, of attaching a crown at the leading end of the plowshare to prevent damage to the plowshare itself (fig. 63).[12] Since this crown was narrow and fit only onto the blade part of the plowshare, it must have been relatively inexpensive to make and readily replaceable once worn down.

The use of the moldboard had already begun in the Han dynasty. Moldboards of the Han dynasty date have been found in Anqiu of Shandong, Zhongmu and Hebi of Henan, and in Chang'an, Liquan, Xi'an, Xianyang, and Longxian in Shaanxi.[13] Moldboards (*libi*, also called *lijing*) were attached on top of the plowshare and used in combination with the plowshare to turn the soil (fig. 64). Among the moldboards found in Shaanxi Province were ones with only a single leaf, used to turn the earth on a single side, as well as ones with double leaves, forming a saddle shape, which were used to turn the soil on both sides. From this evidence we can see that the design of moldboards during that period had already reached a high degree of sophistication.[14]

In the Han dynasty, the use of oxen as draft animals was also widespread. The wooden model of ox and plow dating from the last years of Western Han, found in Mozuizi in Wuwei, Gansu (fig. 65); that depicted in the mural of the Wang Mang period found in the Shanxi village of Zaoyuancun in Pinglu; that on the engraved stone of Eastern Han found at Shuanggou in Suining, Jiangsu (fig. 66); that on the engraved stone of Eastern Han found at Hongdaoyuan in Tengxian, Shandong; that on the engraved stone of Eastern Han found in Mizhi, Shaanxi; and that in the mural depicting soil tillage of Eastern Han found in Holingor, Inner Mongolia—all these are valuable sources for the study of the use of oxen as draft animals.**¹⁵** In the pictures on the stamped bricks and in the murals, we usually see two oxen pulling a plow. The oxen bear a yoke that draws a plow with a long shaft, which a single farmer holds as he drives the oxen. This is the most common way oxen were used during the Han dynasty. The passage in *Hanshu*'s "Treatise on Food and Money" which says, "in the use of the double harness plow, there are two oxen and three men," has been interpreted in several different ways. Yet the archaeological material now available to us leaves no doubt that the so-called "double harness plow" refers to a plow drawn by two oxen. At the

作渠的。但是,《汉书·沟洫志》说"举锸为云,决渠为雨",颜师古注"锸,锹也,所以开渠者也",可见汉代开渠主要还是用锸而不用犁。如在陕西省的蒲城、礼泉、西安、陇县等地的发掘工作中所见,为了防止铁铧的口刃部分被磨损,往往采取在铧的前端套接"铧冠"的方法(图 63)。[12]"铧冠"也系铁制,甚锐利,但它实际上只相当于铧的口刃部分,形体较狭,所以铸造比较节省,损坏后易于更换。

在汉代,犁壁的使用也已经开始了。在山东的安丘,河南的中牟、鹤壁,陕西的长安、礼泉、西安、咸阳、陇县等地,都发现了汉代的犁壁。[13]犁壁又称犁镜,它安装在犁铧的上边,是铧的一种复合装置,其效用在于翻土起垄(图 64)。在陕西省各地发现的犁壁,有向一侧翻土的单叶壁,有向左右两侧翻土的马鞍形双叶壁,说明当时对于犁壁的设计和使用已经达到相当的水平。[14]

在汉代,牛耕已经相当普遍。甘肃武威磨咀子西汉末年的木牛和木犁模型(图 65)、山西平陆枣园村新莽时期的壁画、江苏睢宁双沟的东汉画像石(图 66)、山东滕县宏道院的东汉画像石、陕西米脂的东汉画像石及内蒙古和林格尔的东汉壁画中的牛耕图,都是研究当时牛耕的珍贵资料。[15]画像石和壁画中的牛耕图,大多数是所谓"二牛抬杠"。两头牛抬着犁衡,牵引着一张长辕的犁,一人扶犁并驱牛,这是汉代牛耕的最通常的形式。对于《汉书·食货志》"用耦犁,二牛三人"的记载,迄今有许多不同的解释。但是,从上述的考古资料看来,所谓"耦犁",是指二牛牵引一犁,大概是

end of Eastern Han, and especially during the Wei and Jin dynasties, technology involving the use of oxen in plowing improved. In Gansu's Jiayuguan, a mural has been found that shows a single ox pulling a plow.[16]

Another noteworthy matter is the use during the Han dynasty of the seed plow for seeding. In the Wang Mang period mural mentioned above, found in Pinglu, Shanxi, in addition to the scenes of tillage there are also scenes showing the use of a seeder (fig. 67).[17] Since the mural has become faint, the depictions are unclear. The seeder seems to have three legs, but the body is not clearly shown. There is, however, no question that the implement pictured is a seeder. The mural confirms references to such an implement found in entries about sowing in the "Treatise on Food and Money" in *Hanshu* and in Cui Shi's *Zhenglun*. Although this is our only archaeological evidence of the use of the seeder during the Han dynasty, there is a feeling among archaeologists that what had seemed to be a small version of an iron plowshare found in the Han sites at Sandaohao, Liaoyang, and in the town of Qinghe, Beijing, and in Fuping, Shaanxi, might actually have been the legs for seeders; if so, these implements could be called "seeder-shares" (fig. 68).[18] In contrast to plows drawn by two oxen, the seeder depicted in the Han mural is drawn by a single ox. Obviously, the power needed to draw a seeder was far less than that required to draw a plow. With a three-legged seeder, three rows of seeds could be planted simultaneously. This method was of course much more efficient than sowing seeds by hand, and the results were also superior.

In the Wei and Jin period murals found in Jiayuguan, Gansu, there were also scenes of harrowing and leveling. Both the harrow and the leveler were drawn by oxen. The farmer stood on the implements as they moved, to increase the downward pressure (figs. 69, 70).[19] These murals supply us with our earliest pictorial information concerning the two implements. After the earth was tilled by a plow, the resultant lumps of earth had to be broken up by big harrows with teeth on them. After sowing, the seeds had to be covered; the leveler used in this stage of the process helped to make the soil even more fine while it also pressed and leveled the ground, protecting the soil against erosion. The use of the leveler was confined to the dry fields of the North. The harrow was used not only in the dry northern fields but also in the wet fields of the South. We find this fact attested by the pottery models of plowed and harrowed fields in the Western Jin tombs excavated at Lianxian, Guangdong.[20] In historical records, the use of harrows and levelers is first mentioned in *Qimin yaoshu*, a text dating from Northern Wei of the sixth

没有疑问的。到了东汉后期，特别是魏晋时期，犁耕的技术有了改进。甘肃嘉峪关魏晋时期壁画中的牛耕图有只用一牛牵犁的，便是例证。[16]

　　一个值得注意的问题是，汉代已经开始用耧车播种。在前面提到的山西平陆枣园村的新莽时期的壁画中，除了牛耕图以外，还有耧播图（图67）。[17]壁画已经漫漶，不甚清晰。耧车似为三足，耧斗表现得不清楚。但是，壁画所绘系耧车，则是没有疑问的，从而证明了《汉书·食货志》和崔寔《政论》关于耧播的记载。关于汉代的耧车，在考古资料方面虽然只有上述的一个孤例，但考古学家们认为，在辽阳三道壕、北京清河镇、陕西的富平等地的汉代遗址里发现的一种小型铁铧可能便是安装在耧车的足上的，可称之为耧铧（图68）。[18]1930年在内蒙古居延西汉遗址中发现的一件木制的农具，它的尖端应附有小型的铁铧，应该便是耧车的足。与耕犁用二牛牵引不同，壁画中的耧车只用一牛牵引，这显然是由于牵引耧车所需的力远比牵引耕犁所需的力为小之故。用三足的耧车播种，一耧可播三行，比之人工撒播，效率大大提高，效果也较好。

　　在甘肃嘉峪关魏晋时期的壁画中，还有耙田图和耱田图，耙和耱都用牛牵引，农夫站在它们的上面，以增加重量（图69、70）。[19]这是迄今发现的关于操作这两种农具的最早的形象资料。田地经耕犁翻起后，用带有排齿的大耙将土块切碎，使田地平整，播种以后，用土覆盖，又用不带齿的耱进一步将土块压碎、压平，以达到保墒的效果。耱的使用，限于北方的旱地。耙则不仅限于北方的旱田，而且也适用于南方的水田。广东连县西晋墓出土的犁田和耙田的陶制模型，便是例证。[20]关于耙和耱的使用，始见于北魏时的《齐民要术》

century; the implements are not referred to in Han or Jin writings. But since archaeological evidence shows that their use was already extensive during the Wei and Jin (they have been found even on the distant frontiers), it does not seem impossible that they were first used as early as Eastern Han.

Irrigation   The widespread use of iron implements also permitted developments in irrigation. Large-scale irrigation projects were sponsored and managed by the government. One early example is the Zhengguo Canal built during the Qin dynasty in the Guanzhong area. During Western Han this canal was renovated and maintained, and a branch canal, the Bai Canal, was added to it. In 1973, archaeologists found remains of the Zhengguo Canal and the Bai Canal in Jingyangxian, Shaanxi. At the head of the Bai Canal, they discovered a "well canal" section, over 300 m long. The well canal was a new development in canal technology during Han (fig. 71).[21] The Dujiang Weir built during the Qin dynasty in Guanxian of modern Sichuan was also renovated and maintained during Han. In 1974, a stone statue of Li Bing, sculpted by an Eastern Han official in charge of local irrigation in A.D. 168, was found at the bottom of the Dujiang Weir. The statue stands almost 3 m high. It was placed in the middle of the water not only to commemorate Li Bing's deeds but also to serve as a gauge of the water level (fig. 72).[22]

The use of a crossbar and ropes to pull water out of river or well to irrigate farming fields was a common practice during Han, and it is depicted in engraved stones in tombs.[23] Use of wells for irrigation was extensive in the Yellow River valley and other northern areas. Pottery models showing wells have been found in many places, and in some of them it is clear that the wells were for irrigation. For example, a pottery well excavated from a Han tomb at Luoyang has a well frame complete with winches; two buckets were used alternatively to draw water. Alongside the well there is a long water trough. This model seems to indicate that after water was drawn from the well it flowed through the trough into canals to irrigate the fields (fig. 73). In the Yangtze River

valley and other parts of southern China, in addition to the extensive
use of river water, artificial ponds with embankments were also built to
hold water for irrigating rice fields. In the tombs of the Han and the Wei
and Jin periods located at Shaanxi's Hanzhong, and Sichuan's Chengdu
and Pengshan, Yunnan's Chenggong, and Guangdong's Lianxian, we
have found pottery models of ponds with embankments which are
connected to rice paddies.[24] Such ponds were artificial reservoirs,
which were equipped with sluice-gates in order to regulate the amount

（公元 6 世纪），汉和魏晋文献上并没有这方面的记载。但是，由于魏
晋时使用得相当普遍，而且已普及到边远地区，所以认为东汉时已
经开始有了这种耕作技术，这也并不是完全没有可能的。

　　铁工具的广泛使用，使水利建设具备了优越的条件。大规模的
水利工程，是由当时的政府主持的。例如，秦代在关中地区兴建的
郑国渠，西汉时又经维修和改建，并增设了一条支渠，称为白渠。
1973 年，考古工作者在陕西省泾阳县调查了郑国渠和白渠的渠首遗
址，发现白渠的渠首长约三百余米的一段是"井渠"，这是汉代开
凿水渠的一种新技术（图 71）。[21] 秦代在四川灌县修建的都江堰水利
工程，汉代也继续维修和改进。1974 年，在都江堰的江底发现了东
汉建宁元年（公元 168 年）当地主管水利的官吏所建的李冰石像，
高近三米，它被置立在江水中，不仅表示对李冰的纪念，而且实际
上起了测量水位的作用（图 72）。[22]

　　利用桔槔汲取河水或井水以灌溉农田，在汉代是相当普遍的，
它们的具体形状可以在画像石中见到。[23] 在黄河流域和北方地区，大
量利用水井灌溉。水井的陶制模型，在各地汉墓中被发现，有的显
然是灌溉用井。例如，洛阳汉墓出土的陶井，设有辘轳井架，用两
个汲水桶交替汲水，井旁附设长条状的水槽，表示从井中汲出的水
经水槽流入沟渠，灌溉农田（图 73）。在长江流域和华南地区，除
了充分利用河流以外，还多筑陂塘，塘中蓄水，灌溉稻田。在陕西
的汉中、四川的成都和彭山、云南的呈贡、广东的连县等处的汉和
魏晋时期的墓中，发现了陶制的陂塘模型，往往与水田相连。[24]
这是一种人工开凿的蓄水池，设有闸门，表示可以调节水流，灌溉

of water needed to irrigate the nearby fields (figs. 74, 75). The Shao Embankment built in Lujiangjun (modern Lujiang, Anhui) in the early years of Western Han was renovated during Eastern Han. It was a large-scale irrigation project. The Anfeng Pond in Shouxian, Anhui, is the old site of this Shao Embankment. In 1959, archaeologists also found a weir on that location dating from Eastern Han. Iron implements used in the construction of the weir were found nearby; among them was an iron hammer incised with the words *Dushuiguan* ("Water Conservancy Official"), indicating that the irrigation project was carried out under government supervision.[25]

Harvesting and Food Processing   To harvest grains, iron sickles were widely used. A pictorial brick of the Eastern Han period excavated from Yangzishan of Chengdu, Sichuan, depicts a rice-harvesting scene. The picture shows very clearly how rice was harvested.[26] First the ears were cut off, then a long-handle, hooked scythe was used to cut the straw (fig. 76).

After grains were harvested, threshing and winnowing had to be done; these are also featured on certain pictorial bricks and murals. It is noteworthy that in the Han tombs in Luoyang and Jiyuan of Henan we have also found pottery models of winnowing machines (figs. 77, 78).[27] Generally speaking, millet and wheat were planted in the North, and the threshing process was necessary to separate out the chaff; whereas in the South, where rice was cultivated, the winnowing machine was needed to separate out the husks. However, from the Han tombs excavated at Luoyang and Jiyuan, we see that some winnowing machines were also used in the northern Central Plains area.

To process grains, a *jiandui* (treadle-operated tilt hammer) was commonly used. It was a simple machine operated by foot whose purpose was to pound grain. Pictures of this machine appear on pictorial stones and bricks as well as in pottery models found in many places (figs. 79, 80). From historical records we know that during the Wei and Jin dynasties there was also widespread use of water-powered tilt hammers. Mills, consisting of two rotating stone slabs, were also common during Han. Actual mills as well as pottery models of them have been discovered at many Han archaeological sites and tombs (fig. 81). The earliest stone mill was found in a Han tomb in Mancheng. Underneath the mill there was a large bronze bowl, used to catch the flour ground out by the mill (fig. 82).[28] A pottery model of a similar mill has been found in a Han tomb in Yinqueshan in Linyi, Shandong, which is even older than the actual mill found in Mancheng and probably predates the reign of Emperor Wu Di

附近的稻田（图 74、75）。西汉初年在庐江郡（今安徽庐江）开凿的芍陂，东汉时加以修复，是一项大规模的水利工程。安徽省寿县的安丰塘，便是当时芍陂的旧址，1959 年考古工作者在这里发现了东汉时期的水堰。在附近发现的修筑堰坝的铁工具中，有一件刻有"都水官"铭文的铁锤，说明了这一水利工程是由官府主管的。[25]

收割成熟的谷物，已经普遍使用了铁镰。四川成都扬子山出土的东汉画像砖上，有一幅水稻收割图，形象、生动地说明水稻的收割情形。[26] 从这画像上可以看出，当时收割水稻，是先割取稻穗，然后再用长柄的钩形镰刀刈割稻草（图 76）。

谷物收获后，要经过打场、扬场，其情形可以在画像石和壁画中看到。值得注意的是，河南省洛阳和济源的汉墓中，发现了陶制的风车箱模型（图 77、78）。[27] 一般说来，北方多种粟和小麦，所以往往在场地上用扬弃的方法去除草秕。南方多种稻谷，需要用风车箱扇去秕糠。洛阳和济源汉墓中的发现，说明了风车箱不仅在南方，而且在中原地区也被使用。

谷物的加工，已普遍使用"践碓"。这是一种简单的机械装置，用人力践踏，以舂捣谷物。它们的具体形象，可以在各地发现的画像石、画像砖和陶质模型中看到（图 79、80）。据文献记载，到了魏晋时期，还普遍应用了利用水力的水碓。石制的转盘式的双扇磨盘，在汉代也已普遍使用。它们的实物和陶质模型，在汉代的遗址和坟墓中多有发现（图 81）。年代最早的石磨实物，是在满城汉墓中发现的，石磨下面置一大铜盘，以承受磨出来的粉（图 82）。[28] 山东临沂银雀山汉墓出土的，是上述石磨的陶质模型，其年代比满城汉墓还

of Han.[29] The widespread use and manufacture of such large, rotary stone mills must have been closely tied to the development of iron implements. In the pottery models found in various Eastern Han tombs, we often see the treadle-operated tilt hammer and the mill placed together in a single room to facilitate grain processing.

Domestication of Animals and Silkworms   During the Han dynasty, there were also many other, supplementary kinds of food production. The most common was raising domestic fowl and animals. From archaeological evidence we know that the types of domestic fowl that were kept included chickens, ducks, and geese; among domestic animals there were horses, cows, sheep, pigs, and dogs. In pottery models found in Han tombs, pigpens are often connected to the privies, the arrangement indicating that pig excrement was used to fertilize the fields (fig. 83). In addition to these domestic animals, camels were also domesticated in the North to help in transportation. The archaeological evidence for the camel includes, in addition to the camel-shaped handles of some seals, a funerary statue of a man riding a camel, found in 1969 in Dingxian, Hebei, in the tomb of Prince Mu of Zhongshan (Liu Chang), who lived at the end of Eastern Han, and also images of camels on Eastern Han pictorial bricks found in 1978 in Xinduxian of Sichuan Province.[30] At that time hunting also served to supplement agriculture. Wild rabbit and sika deer were among the food found in the Mawangdui Han tomb of Changsha; the fowls found there included turtledove, wild goose, owl, bamboo partridge, magpie, ringed pheasant, and crane.[31] Hunting scenes have been found on pictorial stones and bricks recovered from many sites, and a pictorial brick from Yangzishan in Chengdu, Sichuan, shows hunting of birds;[32] this is the kind of material that throws much light on contemporary practices. In addition to the fish and other water animals caught from rivers and lakes, fish and turtles were also obtained from artificial ponds. This practice is evidenced by pottery models of ponds found in Hanzhong, Shaanxi.[33] Archaeological evidence has also been found of the consumption of various kinds of aquatic plants such as lotus root and water chestnut (fig. 84).

The cultivation of mulberries and silkworms was also an important supplementary industry in agricultural villages. As early as the Warring States period, two kinds of mulberry trees are found depicted on bronze vessels. The taller kind we could call "mulberry trees," and the shorter kind we could call "mulberry bushes." The latter were not only easier to pick but also juicier and more tender, hence more suitable for feeding the silkworm. These two different types of mulberries have also

要早一些，可能在汉武帝时期之前。[29] 这种转盘式的大型石磨的普遍制作与使用，显然是与铁工具的发达分不开的。在各地东汉墓中出土的陶质模型中，往往可以看到践碓与磨盘同时装置在一个碓房中，以进行谷物的加工。

汉代的农副业是多种多样的，豢养家禽与家畜是其中最普遍的一项。从各种考古资料来看，家禽是鸡、鸭和鹅，家畜则有马、牛、羊、猪、狗等。汉墓中出土的陶制猪圈，往往与厕所相连，说明了当时已经注意养猪积肥，以粪肥田（图 83）。在北方和西北地区，还饲养骆驼，以供运输之用。在河北省定县发掘的东汉后期中山穆王刘畅的墓中曾发现骑骆驼的陶俑，在四川省新都县发现的东汉画像砖上也有骆驼的图像。[30] 射猎也是一种农副业。长沙马王堆汉墓随葬的肉食品中，走兽有野兔、梅花鹿等，飞禽有斑鸠、雁、鸮、竹鸡、喜鹊、雉、鹤等。[31] 各地画像石和画像砖中有狩猎图，四川成都扬子山画像砖上还有弋射图[32]，都是很能说明问题的资料。除了在河流、湖泊中捕捞鱼类和其他水产动物以外，在人工开凿的陂池中也养殖鱼、鳖之类，以供食用，陕西汉中出土的陶制陂池模型很生动地说明了这种情形。[33] 利用各种水面，种植荷藕、菱角之类，采取以供食用的情形，也可以在有关的考古资料中看到（图 84）。

植桑养蚕，也是农村的一项重要副业。至少在战国时代，据铜器上的图纹所见，桑树已有两种。一种可称为"树桑"，甚高大；一种可称为"地桑"，较低矮。后者不仅便于采摘，而且叶多而嫩润，比前者更宜于饲蚕。汉代的桑树，据在画像石和画像砖上所见，

been found on pictorial stones and bricks of the Han period (figs. 85, 86). According to the section on methods for improving the mulberry in *Fan Shengzhi shu*, mulberry bushes were artificially developed.[34] During the Han dynasty, the cultivation of mulberries and silkworms spread from the Yellow River region to the frontiers. Needless to say, there was abundant production of silk in the area of modern Sichuan. According to the "Treatise on Geography" in *Hanshu*, the region of modern Guangxi and Guangdong also had a silk industry as early as Western Han. From the "Biography of Wei Sa" in *Hou Hanshu*, we can see that there was mulberry and silkworm cultivation in the Guiyang Prefecture of modern Hunan in the early part of Eastern Han. The mural in the Holingor Han tomb shows that toward the end of Eastern Han at the latest Dingxiang Prefecture (with its seat in the north of modern Shanxi, transferred there from Inner Mongolia) also had mulberry cultivation.[35]

Population and Economy   Tomb number 10 excavated in 1973 at Fenghuangshan in Jiangling, Hubei, was occupied by a certain Zhang Yan, who was buried in A.D. 153. He was a landowner and a local official in his hometown of Jianglingxian. His duty was to collect government taxes from the farmers. His tomb contained many bamboo and wooden slips which were the official records of the local government administration. Among them was a group of bamboo slips called "Granary Records of Zheng Village," which were local government receipts for grain seeds loaned to twenty-five families of farmers of Zheng village. These receipts record the amount of farmed land and the population of Zheng village (fig. 87).[36] According to these records, the twenty-five families of Zheng village consisted of 105 persons; sixty-nine of them were capable of agricultural labor. The village had a total of 617 *mu* of land. Thus, there was on the average 24.6 *mu* per family, or less than 6 *mu* per person (with each *mu* equivalent to 456 m^2).[37] From these figures we can see that even in the first part of the Western Han period, the average independent farmer was quite limited in the amount of land he farmed. The "Zhushuxun" chapter of *Huainanzi* says that for middle-quality fields, the grain produced in a year did not exceed four *dan* (piculs) per *mu*. According to the "Biography of Zhong Changtong" in *Hou Hanshu*: "The harvest from the highest quality fields is about three *hu* per *mu* [a *hu* being equivalent to a *dan* (picul)]." We can determine, therefore, that the average farmland during the Han dynasty produced three to four piculs per *mu*. Therefore, 6 *mu* of land (the average per person) could only produce about 20 piculs (each

亦有"树桑"与"地桑"两种（图 85、86），而《氾胜之书》有关改进栽桑方法的记载则说明了低矮的"地桑"正是用改进了的方法培植出来的。[34] 在汉代，植桑养蚕已从黄河流域推广到边远地区。四川省境内，盛产丝绸，自不待言。据《汉书·地理志》记载，广东、广西一带，早在西汉时便有蚕桑之业。《后汉书·卫飒传》则记载东汉初期，湖南省南部的桂阳郡一带亦已开始种桑养蚕。据和林格尔汉墓壁画所见，至迟在东汉后期，山西北部和内蒙古境内的定襄郡（其治所西汉时在今内蒙古和林格尔，东汉时在山西省右玉）也有了蚕桑。[35]

1973 年发掘的湖北省江陵凤凰山十号墓，墓主人名为张偃，葬于西汉景帝四年（公元前 153 年）。他是一个地主，在当时江陵县他的家乡任乡吏，替政府向农民征收赋税。在他的墓里，随葬着许多竹简和木牍，是乡里行政机构的文书和簿册。其中有一组竹简称为"郑里廪簿"，是乡里行政机构向"郑里"这个农村的二十五户农民放贷种子的账簿，记录了农户的人口和土地数量（图 87）。[36] 据这本账簿的记录，郑里农民 25 户，105 人，能从事生产劳动的 69 人，共有土地 617 亩，平均每户 24.6 亩，每人不到 6 亩（每亩合今约 456 平方米）。[37] 由此可见，即使在西汉前期，一般的自耕农也只能有少量的土地。《淮南子·主术训》说"中田之获，卒岁之收，不过亩四石"，《后汉书·仲长统传》说"今通肥饶之率，计稼穑之入，令亩收三斛"。由此可见，汉代一般农田的产量大约为每亩三石至四石，六亩田只能产粮二十石左右（每石合今约 20 公升）。

picul being equivalent to approximately 20 liters). If we estimate that a person's daily food requirement is about 5 *sheng* (or roughly one liter), then the annual requirement should be 18 piculs. We can thus see that the harvest realized from a whole year of the farmer's hard labor left him with little surplus in addition to what was needed to fill his stomach. According to the receipts, there was a certain farmer named Ye whose family consisted of eight people, and yet he only had 15 *mu* of land. This averages out to less than 2 *mu* per person, which would have made living conditions harsh indeed.

Furthermore, the farmers were responsible for taxes and corvée labor. According to the records found in tomb number 10 at Fenghuangshan, these taxes and corvée labor requirements were quite heavy. Under such circumstances, some farmers were forced into bankruptcy. Then, the big landowners would take advantage of the opportunity to buy up the farmland of the bankrupt farmers. In order to live, the bankrupt farmers had to become tenant farmers or hired laborers of the landowners; some even had to sell themselves as slaves. In time, these conditions became more and more severe. Because of this process of land aggrandizement, we read that toward the end of Western Han, "the wealthy families owned huge numbers of formerly independent farms." Therefore, there is the emergence at this time of many privately owned manors.

In Eastern Han, due to the lenient policies of the court, the land aggrandizement problem became more severe and the influence of the powerful landowners increased; manors became both more numerous and larger. Agricultural production on the manors was carried out by the landowners' slaves and others who were personally dependent upon them, that is, the so-called bond-servants. The salient point about the economy of the manors was diversification. Agriculture was still primary, but it was supplemented by related activities and various crafts. The manors became self-sufficient. And one step beyond self-sufficiency was the landowners' involvement in commercial enterprises, that is, the marketing of a portion of their manors' products.

As mentioned several times before, a tomb in Holingor, Inner Mongolia, was excavated in 1972, the occupant of which had risen to the post of colonel of the Wuhuan army. He was an important official and landowner. Many murals were found in this tomb, among which, on the south wall of the posterior room, was one that depicts in a lively and concrete fashion the activities of the tomb occupant's manor (fig. 88).[38] In the center of the mural are the manor's houses. Far in the northeast corner there is a large field. Farmers hold plows and drive oxen, tilling

每人每天的食量以五升（合今 1 公升）计算，一年就需粮十八石，这就是说，农民们辛勤劳动一年的收获，除了勉强糊口之外，就没有什么剩余。至于账簿里所记一个名叫"野"的农民，全家八口，只有十五亩土地，平均每人不到二亩，那就更难于生活了。

而且，农民们还必须负担国家的赋税和徭役。从凤凰山十号墓出土的文书和簿册的记录也可以看出，当时的赋税和徭役是相当繁重的。在这种情况下，有的农民就不免破产。于是，大地主们就趁机收买破产农民的土地，而破产农民为了维持生活，就不得不成为大地主的雇农和佃户，有的甚至卖身为奴。随着时代的推移，这种情况愈来愈严重。到了西汉后期，由于土地兼并，结果，"富者田连阡陌"，就出现了许多私人占有的大庄园。

到了东汉，由于朝廷的纵容，土地兼并愈益激烈，豪强地主的势力愈益强大，庄园也愈来愈多，愈来愈大。豪强地主们使用他们的奴婢和与他们有人身依附关系的农民，即所谓"徒附"，在庄园中进行各种生产活动。庄园经济的特点，是从事多种经营，以农业生产为主，同时也包括各种农副业和手工业，从而能够做到"自给自足"。自足有余，庄园主也搞商业活动，将一部分产品出售。

如前面已经多次提到过的，1972 年在内蒙古和林格尔发掘了一座东汉后期的墓，墓主人官至"护乌丸校尉"，是一个大官僚兼大地主。墓中有大量的壁画，其中后室南壁的一大幅壁画是庄园图，生动而形象地描绘了当时庄园的各种情形（图 88 ）。[38] 在画面的中部，是庄园的房舍。在它的东北方远处，是大片的原野，农夫们

the land. Closer to the dwellings there are vegetable gardens where two farmers are working intently with hoes. Walls surround the vegetable garden to prevent the fowl and other animals from straying in. Near the dwellings there are stables and pens for oxen and sheep. The presence of young as well as full-grown animals gives evidence of continuous breeding. Outside the pens, there are scattered groups of chickens and pigs. Nearby the dwellings there is a mulberry grove where four women appear, holding ropes, hooks, and nets, picking mulberry leaves. Close by, there are bamboo baskets and screens used in silkworm cultivation. On the far west side, there are three pools in which bundles of hemp are placed. Workers stand beside the pools, netting the hemp. Nearby, there is also a structure to house vehicles. In addition to this mural on the south wall, murals in the front room of the tomb likewise depict piles of harvested foods, oxcarts used in transporting the food, grain bins for storing the food, and people in the process of hulling the grain with tilt hammers. On the mural found in the middle room, brewing is also shown. This indicates that not only was food processed on the manor, wine and vinegar were also made there. There are also several murals in the front room depicting the pasturing of horses, cattle, and sheep. These show that aside from agriculture the manors engaged in animal husbandry. This tomb is located in the northern grasslands, where animal husbandry must have been especially widespread (figs. 89, 90).[39]

It is noteworthy that in the center of the mural on the south wall in the rear room of the Han tomb at Holingor there is a watchtower situated beside the dwellings. Similarly, in the upper corner of the mural that depicts sheepherding in the front room there is a walled fort. At the rear of the fort is a tall watchtower at a corner (fig. 91). Hence we can see that the manor's buildings included those used for military or defensive purposes. The farmers who worked on the estate were not only the wards of the powerful landlord, they were also members of his private militia. Many of the historical records corroborate this fact, indicating that especially in the last years of Eastern Han the men who were attached to powerful landlords had military as well as agricultural duties. From a late Eastern Han tomb at Tianhuishan in Chengdu, Sichuan, archaeologists found clay figures of farmers and soldiers; they not only are wearing the same kind of clothes, the farmers are also shown wearing large battle knives. This evidence further corroborates the military roles of the farmers at that time (fig. 92).[40]

扶着犁，驱赶着牛，正在耕地。在房舍的附近，则另有园圃，以种植蔬菜之类，两个农夫手执锄头，正在精耕细作；为了防止家禽、家畜的侵扰，园圃四周还筑有围墙。房舍附近还有马厩、牛圈和羊圈，其中既有壮畜，也有幼畜，表示牲畜不断繁殖。在圈栏之外，还有一些散放着的鸡群和猪群。在房舍的周围，有一片桑林，四个女子拿着绳索、长钩和网子，正在采桑，旁边还有一些筐箔之类，以表明庄园中有蚕桑之业。在西面较远处，则有三个方形的池坑，里面堆放着麻，有人正在池坑旁边进行着沤麻的操作。在附近，还有一个车库，存放着一些备用的车辆。除了南壁这一大幅庄园图以外，在墓的前室壁画中还可以看到收获下来的成堆的粮食、运粮的牛车、存贮粮食的囤囷，以及人们正在利用"践碓"舂捣谷物。在中室的壁画中，则有酿造图，表示庄园中自行加工谷物，而且还自制酒、醋之类。在前室的另几幅壁画中，则又有牧马、牧牛、牧羊图，表示庄园中除了农业以外，还从事畜牧业，特别是因为这里是北方草原地带，所以牧畜业尤其兴盛（图89、90）。[39]

　　值得注意的是，在和林格尔汉墓后室南壁庄园图中部的房屋旁边有一座望楼。在前室牧羊图的上方，则有四面筑有围墙的堡垒，在堡垒后部的一角也建有一座高大的望楼（图91）。这些都显示了庄园中的建筑物是带有军事防御性的。在庄园中从事生产劳动的农夫，也就成了豪强地主的部曲，即他们的私人武装部队。在许多文献记载中，也都说明在东汉，特别是在东汉的后期，豪强地主的部曲是具有亦农亦兵的性质的。四川成都天迥山东汉晚期墓出土的农夫俑和武士俑，衣著完全相同，而且前者和后者一样，也佩有作战用的大刀，正生动而形象地说明了这一问题（图92）。[40]

At the end of Eastern Han when Cao Cao seized control of the government he curbed the power of the landlords, prohibited land aggrandizement, and established the *tuntian* ("agriculture colony") system. There were two kinds of *tuntian*, the commoners' and the soldiers'. In the first, common farmers who did not have their own land or oxen were recruited to farm government land under the direction of various agriculture officials. Fifty to sixty percent of their harvest had to be turned over to the government. In the second kind of *tuntian*, soldiers were organized to engage in agricultural production and the harvest was used by the military. In the tomb mentioned above dating from the Wei and Jin periods found in the Jiayuguan district of Gansu, there are two extremely precious wall murals depicting a military *tuntian* colony.[41] The first mural shows the military camp. In the middle there is a large tent occupied by a military official, which has guards stationed outside. The guard on the right holds a banner and seems to be the runner. On the right of the tent there are six serrated banners implanted in the ground in two rows. They evidently mark the entrance to the headquarters tent. On the remaining three sides many smaller tents are arrayed in rows. In front of each tent, *ji*-halberds and shields stand in the ground (fig. 93). The second mural depicts the cultivation of land by the military. In the center a military officer gallops about on horseback; on each side there is a platoon of foot soldiers marching with *ji*-halberds and shields. Beside each platoon there are two men driving oxen and tilling the land. One of them wears a hat and looks like a member of the Han race. The other, with untied hair, wears the clothes of one of the minority ethnic groups (fig. 94). These two murals, viewed together, provide us with a realistic picture of the military cultivation of land west of the Yellow River during the Wei and Jin dynasties. During the Wei dynasty, military cultivation of land was also widely practiced in the Central Plains area. However, we have not yet uncovered archaeological evidence of it.

东汉末年曹操掌握政权后，抑制豪强地主，严禁土地兼并，实行屯田制。屯田制分民屯与军屯两种。前者是招募无地或无牛的农民，在各级典农官统率下耕种官田，将收获的五成或六成交纳给官府；后者则是组织士兵从事农业生产，以其所获供军用。在前面多次提到的甘肃嘉峪关魏晋时期的墓中，有两幅关于当时军屯的壁画，是十分珍贵的材料。[41] 一幅可称为"营垒图"，正中绘一大军帐，帐中坐一军官，帐外左右两侧各立一军士，右立者手执一旗，似为传令官。大军帐的右方，树牙旗六面，分为两列，似为营门之所在；其余三方则排列着许多较小的军帐，重重叠叠，帐前立戟与盾牌（图93）。另一幅可称为"屯垦图"，其中部画着一个骑马驰驱的武将，两侧各有一队荷戟持盾的步兵在行进。在兵队的旁边，则有二人正在驱牛耕地，一人戴帽似汉人模样，一人披发作少数民族装束（图94）。"营垒图"和"屯垦图"结合起来，正是当时河西地区军队屯田的真实写照。曹魏的屯田制，在中原地区也广泛推行，只是有关的考古资料迄今还付之阙如。

55. Names of agricultural products inscribed on pottery granaries unearthed from Han tombs in Luoyang
洛阳烧沟汉墓出土陶仓上写的农产品名称

56. Ox-drawn plow and millet plants on a pictorial stone unearthed in Mizhi, Shaanxi
陕西米脂出土画像石上的牛耕图和粟

57. Rice ears from a pottery granary unearthed from a Han tomb at Fenghuangshan, Jiangling
江陵凤凰山汉墓出土的陶仓中的稻穗

58. Remains of job's tears from a pottery jar unearthed from a Han tomb in Luoyang
洛阳烧沟汉墓出土的陶壶及薏苡

59. Iron spade with wooden handle unearthed from the Han tomb at Mawangdui in Changsha 长沙马王堆汉墓出土的木柄铁锸

60. Stone human figure holding a spade, unearthed in Pixian, Sichuan 四川郫县出土的手握铲的石像

61. Iron rake with two teeth, unearthed from the Han tomb in Mancheng 满城汉墓出土的双齿铁耙

62. Large iron plowshare unearthed from the Han tomb in Mancheng 满城汉墓出土的巨型铁铧

63. Iron plowshare and its crown, unearthed in Longxian in Shaanxi
陕西陇县出土的铁铧和铧冠

64. Iron plowshare and moldboard unearthed in Chang'anxian, Shaanxi
陕西长安县出土的铁犁铧和犁壁

65. Wooden models of ox and plow unearthed from the Western Han tomb at Mozuizi in Wuwei, Gansu
甘肃武威磨咀子西汉墓出土的木牛和木犁模型

66. Plowing with oxen in the pictorial stone art unearthed at Shuanggou, Suiningxian, Jiangsu　江苏睢宁双沟出土的画像石中的牛耕图

67. Use of a seeder depicted in the wall painting of a Han tomb at Zaoyuancun in Pinglu, Shanxi　山西平陆枣园村汉墓壁画中的耧播图

68. Iron blade of a seeder unearthed in Fuping, Shaanxi 陕西富平出土的铁耧铧

69. A harrowing scene depicted (in the lower part) on a pictorial brick in a Wei-Jin period tomb at Jiayuguan in Gansu
甘肃嘉峪关魏晋时期壁画中的耙田图（下）

70. A soil-leveling scene depicted on a pictorial brick in a Wei-Jin period tomb at Jiayuguan in Gansu　甘肃嘉峪关魏晋时期壁画中的耱田图

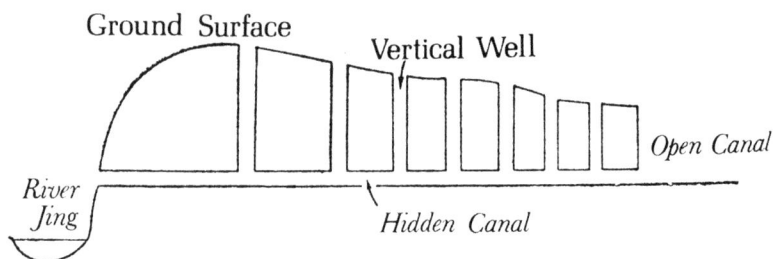

71. Well canal at the head of the Bai Canal in Jingyangxian, Shaanxi　陕西省泾阳县白渠渠首的井渠

72. Stone statue of Li Bing and its inscription, unearthed at the Dujiang Weir in Guanxian, Sichuan
四川灌县都江堰出土的李冰石像和铭文

73. Pottery models of a well and water trough unearthed from a Han tomb in Luoyang 洛阳烧沟汉墓出土的陶井与水槽模型

74. Pottery model of a pond unearthed from a Han tomb in Hanzhongxian, Shaanxi 陕西汉中汉墓出土的陶陂塘模型

75. Pottery model of a pond unearthed from a Han tomb in Chengdu, Sichuan　四川成都汉墓出土的陶陂塘模型

76. Fishing, hunting, and harvesting depicted in a pictorial brick unearthed from a Han tomb at Yangzishan in Chengdu, Sichuan
四川成都扬子山汉墓出土的画像砖上的弋射收获图

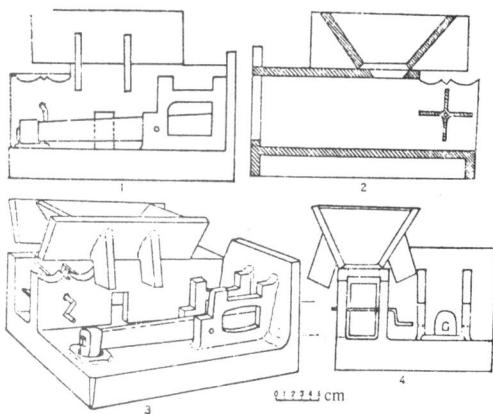

77. Pottery models of winnowing machine and treadle-operated tilt hammer unearthed from Han tomb in Luoyang
洛阳汉墓出土的陶制风车箱模型和践碓

78. Reconstructive drawing of fig. 77 图 77 的重构图

79. Treadle-operated tilt hammer as depicted in pictorial brick unearthed from the Han tomb in Pengxian, Sichuan
四川彭县汉墓出土的画像砖上的践碓图

80. Pottery model of treadle-operated tilt hammer unearthed from the Han tomb in Shanxian, Henan　河南陕县汉墓出土的陶践碓模型

81. Stone quern unearthed at the site of the Han city of Chang'an 汉长安城遗址出土的石磨

82. Stone quern and bronze receptacle unearthed from the Han tomb in Mancheng　满城汉墓出土的石磨及铜承盘

83. Pottery model of pigsty and privy, unearthed from a Han tomb in Luoyang　洛阳汉墓出土的陶猪圈及厕所模型

84. Taro harvesting depicted on pictorial brick unearthed in Pengxian, Sichuan　四川彭县出土的画像砖上的采芋图

85. Picking mulberry tree leaves depicted on pictorial stone at the Wu Liang Family Shrine in Jiaxiang, Shandong
　　山东嘉祥武梁祠画像石上的采桑图

86. Picking mulberry bush leaves depicted on pictorial brick unearthed in Chengdu, Sichuan 四川成都出土的画像砖上的采桑图

87. "Granary Records of Zheng Village"–inscribed bamboo slips (partial) unearthed from tomb number 10 at Fenghuangshan in Jiangling 江陵凤凰山十号墓出土的"郑里廪簿"（部分）

88. A manor depicted in a wall painting in the Han tomb at Holingor in Inner Mongolia (copy) 内蒙古和林格尔汉墓壁画中的庄园图（摹本）

89. Grazing horses depicted in wall painting in the Han tomb at Holingor in Inner Mongolia 内蒙古和林格尔汉墓出土的牧马图

90. Grazing cattle depicted in wall painting in the Han tomb at Holingor in Inner Mongolia
内蒙古和林格尔汉墓出土的牧牛图

91. Fortress and watchtower depicted in wall painting in the Han tomb at Holingor in Inner Mongolia
内蒙古和林格尔汉墓壁画中的堡垒和望楼

92. Clay figurine of farmer holding spade and
wearing large knife, unearthed from a Han
tomb at Tianhuishan in Chengdu, Sichuan
四川成都天廻山汉墓出土的持
铲佩刀农夫俑

93. A military barracks in a wall painting in a Wei-Jin period tomb at Jiayuguan, Gansu　甘肃嘉峪关魏晋墓壁画·营垒图

94. A soldiers' farm in a wall painting in a Wei-Jin period tomb at Jiayuguan, Gansu 甘肃嘉峪关魏晋墓壁画·屯垦图

CHAPTER 4 LACQUERWARE

Lacquerware Before the Han Dynasty Archaeology tells us that lacquered wares existed in China probably as early as the Neolithic period. In 1978, many wooden objects were found at the site of Hemudu, Yuyaoxian, Zhejiang Province. One of the wooden bowls is covered both inside and out with a bright red pigment that appears to be a lacquerlike substance.[1] The Hemudu site has been dated by radiocarbon to about 7,000 B.P. If the pigment on the bowl proves to be lacquer, then it will be the earliest known lacquered vessel in China.

By the Shang period, the decoration on lacquered vessels was already quite accomplished. Many fragments of lacquered vessels, which included types like basins and boxes, were found in 1973 at a middle Shang site at Taixicun, in Gaochengxian, Hebei Province. The designs were in black against a red background, and included *taotie*, leaf, thunder-cloud, and dragon motifs, all closely comparable to bronze motifs. Some fragments were even decorated with turquoise inlays or gold sheets. Fragments of lacquered vessels have also been frequently found at Yinxu at Xiaotun in Anyang, Henan, the site of the late Shang dynasty capital, but they are so poorly preserved that neither the vessel shape nor the decoration can be distinguished clearly.[2]

It is, in any event, certain that the production of lacquer wares was quite advanced in the Shang period. As a result of the far-ranging influence of Shang civilization, lacquered vessels were also found in distant regions. For example, a burial belonging to the Lower Xiajiadian culture excavated in 1977 at Dadianzi, Aohan Banner, in Liaoning Province, yielded two well preserved red lacquered vessels, somewhat like the Shang bronze *gu* in shape.[3] Radiocarbon dates place the site at Dadianzi at about 3,500 B.P. These two *gu*-shaped lacquered vessels may be regarded as the earliest well preserved examples of lacquered vessels.

Lacquer vessels are also known from excavated sites of the Western Zhou period. For example, they have been found in the early Western

Zhou tombs at Pangjiagou, at Luoyang, Henan, excavated in 1964, and at the late Western Zhou to early Eastern Zhou burials of the Guo state at Shangcunling in western Henan, excavated in 1956. The vessels from both sites are decorated with inlaid shell discs. The early Western Zhou burials excavated in 1953 at Puducun, Chang'anxian, in Shaanxi Province, also contained lacquered fragments with what appears to be shell disc inlays.[4]

🈚 汉代的漆器

考古发掘工作说明，早在新石器时代，中国可能已经有了漆器。1978 年，在浙江省余姚县的河姆渡遗址中发现了许多木器。其中有一件木碗，里外施朱红色涂料，色泽鲜艳，其物理性能与漆相同。[1]经放射性碳素测定，河姆渡遗址的年代距今约七千年。上述的木碗，其涂料如果的确是漆，那末它便是中国迄今发现的最早的漆器。

到了商代，漆器上的花纹和装饰已经相当精致。1973 年，在河北省藁城县台西村的商代中期遗址里，发现了许多漆器的残片，可以辨认的器形有盘、盒之类，它们是朱红色地，黑色花纹，纹样有饕餮纹、焦叶纹、云雷纹、夔纹等，与铜器上的花纹相似，有的还镶嵌着绿松石，有的则贴金箔，作为装饰。在商代后期都城遗址——河南省安阳市小屯村的殷墟，也常常发现漆器的残迹，可惜由于保存情况不好，器形和纹饰已不清楚。[2]总之，可以肯定的是，商代的漆器已经相当发达。在商文化的影响下，边远地区也出现了漆器。例如，1977 年在辽宁省敖汉旗大甸子的夏家店下层文化的墓葬中也发现了二件朱红色的漆器，外形保存得比较完好，有些像商代的觚。[3]经放射性碳素测定，大甸子遗址的年代距今约三千五百年。上述的二件觚形的漆器，可以说是迄今发现的年代最早的器形保持比较完整的漆器。

属于西周时代的漆器，在考古发掘工作中也有发现。例如，1964 年在河南省洛阳庞家沟发掘的西周早期墓和 1956 年在同省陕县上村岭发掘的西周晚期或东周早期的虢国墓里，都发现了漆器。它们的共同的特点是用蚌壳制成的圆泡镶嵌，作为装饰。1953 年在陕西省长安县普渡村发掘的西周早期墓中，也发现过类似的镶有蚌泡的漆器的残迹。[4]

Rapid and astounding advances in the development of the lacquer industry were made only with the beginning of the Warring States period. Large numbers of well preserved lacquered vessels were found before the founding of the P.R.C. in sites in Changsha, Hunan, and in Luoyang, Henan; and, after the founding of the P.R.C., in Changsha, Hunan, in Jiangling and Suixian, Hubei, in Xinyang, Henan, and in Chengdu, Sichuan.[5] In addition to lacquered vessels, these finds included various types of lacquered home furnishings, grave goods, musical instruments, and weapon accessories, indicating that lacquered items were widely used for various aspects of social life. Considering only lacquered vessels, for example, most early Warring States vessels have wood cores, which tend to make them heavy and bulky.

From the mid-Warring States period on, vessel cores made with thin wooden sheets or fabric began to appear. By the late Warring States period, inlaid bronze discs (gold or silver gilded) were added to thin-cored lacquered vessels, making them sturdier as well as more elaborate and beautiful. The painted designs on these are also very rich and elegant. In short, Warring States lacquerware had reached very high standards in every respect. Han period lacquerware represents a further development from the foundations laid in the Warring States period.

Han Lacquer Wares Han lacquerware has been discovered at many localities; only the most notable finds will be mentioned here. Finds before 1949 include the large numbers of well preserved vessels from Pyongyang in Korea and Noin Ula in Mongolia.[6] Many of these are dated by inscription and are extremely valuable for research. Since the establishment of New China, lacquer vessels in various states of preservation have come from Han burial sites in Luoyang in Henan; Wendeng in Shandong; Yancheng and Lianyungang in Jiangsu; Ningbo in Zhejiang; Changsha in Hunan; Guangzhou in Guangdong; Qingzhen in Guizhou; and Wuwei in Gansu.[7] The lacquer vessels from Qingzhen and Wuwei also carry detailed inscriptions with dates like those from

Pyongyang. In the past ten years or so, finds of Han lacquerwork have been virtually innumerable: at Hepu and Guixian in Guangxi, Haizhou in Jiangsu, Linyi in Shandong, Mancheng in Hebei, and Fuyang in Anhui, to name only a few.[8] Particularly notable are the rich finds from the Han tombs at Mawangdui in Changsha, Fenghuangshan in Jiangling, and Dafentou in Yunmeng, which yielded large numbers and varieties of

　　漆器制造业的进一步迅速发展，突飞猛进，是在战国时代。新中国成立前在湖南省的长沙和河南省的洛阳，新中国成立后在湖南省的长沙、湖北省的江陵和随县、河南省的信阳、四川省的成都等地的战国墓中都发现了大量的漆器，保存情况良好。[5] 它们的种类，除了器皿以外，还包括各种家具、丧葬用具、乐器以及兵器上的附件等等，说明了漆器已被广泛应用于社会生活的各个方面。就器皿来说，战国初期的漆器多系木胎，厚重有余，轻巧不足。从战国中期以后，漆器的胎壁有系用薄木片制成的，而且开始有了夹纻胎。到了战国晚期，有时在薄胎的漆器上镶铜扣，其上镀金银，不仅加强了器物的牢固，而且增进了它们的精致和美观。漆器上的花纹，也绘描得十分富丽和精美。总之，无论从哪一方面来说，战国时代的漆器已经达到了很高的水平。汉代的漆器，便是在战国时代的基础上进一步发展起来的。

　　汉代的漆器，发现地点甚多。举其主要者而言，新中国成立前在朝鲜的平壤、蒙古的诺音乌拉发现的漆器，数量多，保存好，且多有纪年的铭文，研究价值很高。[6] 新中国成立以后，在河南省的洛阳、山东省的文登、江苏省的盐城和连云港、浙江省的宁波、湖南省的长沙、广东省的广州、贵州省的清镇、甘肃省的武威等地的汉墓中，都有漆器出土，有的已经朽坏，有的保存尚好，[7] 而清镇和武威的漆器有详细的纪年铭文，可以与朝鲜境内发现的漆器相比较。最近十多年来，各地汉墓出土漆器，更是不胜枚举：广西壮族自治区的合浦和贵县、江苏省的海州、山东省的临沂、河北省的满城、安徽省的阜阳等地的汉墓中都发现了许多漆器。[8] 特别要提出来的是，长沙马王堆、江陵凤凰山、云梦大坟头汉墓中随葬的漆器，

lacquered vessels in pristine condition, all of which are valuable new material for the study of Han lacquerware (figs. 95-98).[9]

The core materials used in Han lacquerware are mainly wood and fabric (fig. 99); bomboo cores were also used, but only rarely (fig. 100). The method of constructing the cores has been learned by both observing the excavated examples and experimenting.[10] Wood cores were made in three ways. (1) For circular-shaped objects, a round shape would first be carved with the help of a turntable and then the interior would be hollowed out. This method is generally used to make *ding* (tripods), boxes, *hu* (wine vessels), and *yu* (basins) (fig. 101). (2) For more regularly shaped vessels, the core would still be carved from a single piece of wood, but without using a turntable. Ear-cups (that is, cups with earlike handles), spouted *yi* vessels, and square wine vessels (*fang*), low tables, and other noncircular objects would be made by this method (fig. 102). (3) The core would be formed with thin pieces of wood, curved and fitted to each other with wooden nails to form a thin cylinder, with the bottom of the vessel attached as a separate sheet. Cylindrical vessels with straight walls like *zun* or *lian* were made in this way. This method requires a covering of hemp cloth to be spread over the thin wood core before lacquering to cover the seams. In fabric-cored vessels, numerous layers of hemp or silk cloth would be built over a model of the vessel constructed of wood or clay. After the layers of fabric had dried and hardened, the inner wood or mud core would be removed, leaving only the fabric armature. This is known traditionally as *tuotai*. Generally speaking, the majority of lacquer vessels of the early Western Han period were wood-cored. Among the twenty-odd lacquered vessels from the Han tombs at Fuyang, Anhui, almost half had fabric cores, but among the over 180 lacquer vessels from the early Western Han tomb number one at Mawangdui, Changsha, only a few vessels like *zhi* and *lian* had fabric cores.

From mid-Western Han on, in the lacquered remains from sites such as Changsha, Mancheng, Qingzhen, and Pyongyang, for example, fabric cores were increasingly used for vessels like ear-cups, trays, *zhi*, boxes, and *lian*, although wood-cored lacquer vessels were still common.

Decoration was applied on lacquerware in the following ways. (1) Painting with lacquer: the most common method, which involves the mixing of pigments with the semitranslucent lacquer and applying this mixture to the lacquered surface of the vessel. The colors thus applied are brilliant and durable. (2) Painting with oil: here, pigments were mixed with oil (possibly tung oil) and applied to the lacquered surface of the vessel. The oil and pigment mixture deteriorates with age, and the

数量大，种类多，保存极好，往往完美如新，为研究汉代漆器提供了新的珍贵的材料（图 95—98 ）。[9]

汉代漆器的胎质，主要有木胎与夹纻胎二种（图 99 ）。另外也有竹胎的，但很少（图 100 ）。根据对出土实物的观察，并作了一些模拟试验，了解了器胎的制作方法。[10] 木胎的制法大概有三种：一种是用轮旋刮削的方法制成器物的外壁，然后再剜空其内部，鼎、盒、壶、盂等圆形器物多用此法（图 101 ）。一种是用割削、剜凿的方法制成，而未经轮旋，杯、匣、钫、案等非圆形器物用此法（图 102 ）。另一种是用几块薄木片卷曲成弧形的器壁，用木钉拼接成一个圆筒，另接器底；有些直壁的圆筒状器如樽、奁等即用此法。用后一种方法制成的木胎，要用麻布裱起来，然后再涂漆，使得不露接缝。夹纻胎是先用木头或泥土制成器型，作为内模，然后用多层麻布或缯帛附于内模上，干实以后，去掉内模，便剩下麻布或缯帛的夹纻胎，这便是所谓"脱胎"。一般说来，西汉前期以木胎漆器为多。安徽阜阳双古堆汉墓中的二十余件漆器，夹纻胎的虽然将近半数，但长沙马王堆一号汉墓中共有一百八十多件漆器，夹纻胎的仅有少数卮、奁等器而已。西汉中期以后，如长沙、满城、清镇、平壤等处的遗品所见，木胎漆器虽然仍不少，但杯、盘、卮、盒、奁等器物用夹纻胎的颇有增多。

在漆器上施花纹，有下列几种方法：一种是漆绘，用生漆制成半透明的漆液，加上各种颜料，绘描于已经涂漆的器物上，色泽光亮，不易脱落，大多数漆器的花纹都用此法绘描。一种是油彩，

decoration painted in this way is not very durable and rubs off easily.[11] (3) Incising: decoration is incised into the lacquered surface of the vessel with a pointed needlelike instrument. Bamboo slips from tomb number 3 at Mawangdui, Changsha, record that this method was known as *zhuihua*.[12] On two lacquered *zhi*-vessels unearthed at a Han tomb at Guanghua in Hubei, the incised tiger, hare, bird, and other animals and cloud-scroll designs were filled in with gold so that they resembled the gold- and silver-inlaid decorations on bronzes.[13] (4) Finally, individual motifs were cut out from thin sheets of gold or silver and attached to the lacquered surface of the vessel, resembling what was later known as *pingtuo* (fig. 103).[14] The most common designs found on Han lacquerware include conventionalized dragon, bird, "scrolling cloud" (*juanyun*), floral, and geometric motifs, as well as more realistic animal, bird, and fish motifs (figs. 104, 105). In general, these designs are all delicate and flowing. The designs on early Western Han lacquer vessels are rich and complex; those on Eastern Han vessels appear simpler. The isolated finds of vessels from Pyongyang decorated with scenes from mythology and stories of filial piety are unusual themes,[15] but they nevertheless are representative of a new trend, or a trend which had existed as early as the middle and late Western Han period as shown by the finds from the tomb of Shi Qi Yao in Haizhou, Jiangsu (figs. 106, 107).[16] Gold and silver sheet motifs on lacquerware from places such as Changsha, Hepu, and Lianyungang include a colorful variety of birds, animals, horses and carriages, human figures, and various geometric patterns.[17]

From the late Warring States period on, and especially since mid-Western Han, gilt or silvered bronze mountings were often added to the rims of lacquered *pan*-basins, *zun*-vessels, boxes, and cosmetic boxes; also, gilded buttons were inlaid onto the handles of lacquered cups. These are the so-called "silver rims and yellow handles" referred to in *Yan tie lun* (*Discourses on Salt and Iron*) or the "button objects" referred to in the "Biography of He Xi Empress Deng" in *Hou Hanshu*. In the Eastern Han period, lacquered cosmetic boxes from Luoyang and Pyongyang carried quatrefoil decorations in bronze, and were even inlaid with crystal or glass beads (fig. 108).[18]

The durability of lacquered wares is illustrated by the discovery of Western Han lacquered vessels in the Eastern Han tombs at Qingzhen in

用油汁（可能是桐油）调颜料，绘描于已经涂漆的器物上，所绘花纹往往因油脂年久老化，易于脱落。[11] 一种是针刻，用针尖在已经涂漆的器物上刺刻花纹，长沙马王堆三号墓出土的竹简记录着这种技法在当时称为"锥画"。[12] 值得注意的是，湖北省光化汉墓中的二件漆卮有针刻的虎、兔、鸟等动物纹及流云纹的纹样，在刺刻出来的线条内填入金彩，产生了类似铜器上金银错的花纹的效果。[13] 此外，还有一种方法是用金、银箔制成各种图纹，贴在器物的漆面上，呈现了类似"金银平脱"的效果（图 103 ）。[14]

汉代漆器上所描花纹的纹样，最常见的有图案化的龙凤纹、云气纹、花草纹，也有各种几何形纹，以及许多近于写实的兽类、鸟类和鱼类的图纹（图 104、105 ）。总的说来，纹样的特点是细致而流利。西汉前期的漆器，花纹富丽而复杂；东汉的漆器，其花纹则显得比较简单。朝鲜平壤附近出土的个别东汉的漆器有神仙及孝子等人物故事画[15]，虽系很少见的特殊的例子，却代表了一种新的作风，而江苏海州侍其繇墓的发现则又说明这种以人物故事为题材的漆器图纹早在西汉中晚期即已存在（图 106、107 ）。[16] 金银箔贴的纹样，如长沙、合浦、连云港等处的遗品所见，有飞禽、走兽、车马、人物及各种几何图案，可以说是丰富多彩。[17]

从战国晚期以来，特别是西汉中期以后，在盘、樽、盒、奁等漆器的口沿上镶有镀金或镀银的铜箍，在漆杯的双耳上镶有镀金的铜壳。这就是《盐铁论》中的所谓"银口黄耳"，也就是《后汉书·和熹邓皇后纪》中的所谓"扣器"。东汉时，有些漆器如盒和奁的盖上附有柿蒂形铜饰，同时镶嵌水晶或琉璃珠，在洛阳和平壤曾发现过这样的遗物（图 108 ）。[18]

漆器的耐用程度相当高。在贵州省的清镇，西汉时制作的漆

Guizhou Province. In the Western Han tombs at Shiyanli at Pyongyang, lacquered ear-cups dated 85 B.C. and A.D. 3 were found together,[19] clearly indicating that such vessels can last for at least eighty years or more.

In other words, the high level of workmanship, beautiful colors, exquisite designs, and durability of Han lacquer vessels made them the most valuable vessels of the period, and needless to say, the price of Han lacquerware was accordingly high. Hence it was recorded in the *Yan tie lun* that the price of one lacquered cup equaled that of ten bronze ones, and that it required a hundred workmen to make one lacquered cup and the effort of a thousand workmen to make one lacquered screen.

Because lacquer goods were so valuable, Han nobles and high-ranking officials often inscribed them with their clan names or official titles as signs of ownership. For example, the lacquer cups from tombs of Wang Xu and Wang Guang at Pyongyang are inscribed with the characters "Li Wang" and "Wang Shi Lao."[20] The lacquered cup in the tomb of Geng Ying in Yanggao, Shanxi Province, was inscribed with the character "Geng."[21] The characters "Yang zhu jia pan" were inscribed on the lacquered *pan* found in the tomb of Liu Jiao in Changsha, Hunan.[22] The lacquered *pan* found from a tomb at Yangjiashan in Changsha, traditionally alleged to be the grave of a queen, was inscribed with the following phrase: "Yang zhu jia pan, jin Changsha Wang hou jia pan."[23] Lacquer pieces from the tombs of the Marquis of Dai, his wife and son, buried in tombs number 1, 2, and 3 at Mawangdui, Changsha, are inscribed with "Dai Hou Jia," etc. (fig. 109).[24] Some lacquer items are inscribed with the characters "Shang Lin" (fig. 110), signifying that they were used in the Shang Lin Palace.[25] Some are inscribed "Da Guan" or "Tang Guan," indicating that they were used in the royal kitchens.[26] Some lacquer vessels carry inscriptions dealing with their actual func-tions. For example, many ear-cups and *pan* basins from Mawangdui are inscribed with such auspicious phrases as "Jun xing jiu" ("Auspicious Drinking") and "Jun xing shi" ("Auspicious Banqueting") (figs. 111, 112), and lacquered ear-cups from Han tombs in Ningbo carry "Yi jiu" ("Desirable Wine") inscriptions.

The eating and drinking vessels of the Han ruling class were often decorated with gold and silver mounts. A passage in the "Biography of Gong Yu" in *Hanshu* says: "I once followed His Majesty to the Eastern Palace [Changlegong] and was given cups and tables, all adorned with gold and silver." A passage in the "San bu zu" section of *Yan tie lun* notes: "The wealthy today possess *shu* cups with silver rims, gold handles, and

器在东汉的墓中出土，便说明了这一问题。在平壤石岩里的一座西汉墓中，始元二年（公元前 85 年）的漆杯与元始三年（公元 3 年）的漆杯共存[19]，说明了前者至少被保存达八十余年之久。

总之，汉代的漆器制作精巧，色彩鲜艳，花纹优美，装饰精致，而又相当耐用，是当时最珍贵的日用器物，而其价值之高昂也就不言而喻。所以，《盐铁论》说"一文杯得铜杯十"，又说"一杯棬用百人之力，一屏风就万人之功"。

由于漆器珍贵，所以当时的贵族和官僚们往往在漆器上书写姓氏或官爵之类的文字，作为所有权的标志。例如：朝鲜平壤王盱墓和王光墓中的漆杯有"利王"和"王氏牢"字样[20]，山西省阳高耿婴墓中的漆杯有"耿"字[21]，湖南省长沙刘骄墓中的漆盘有"杨主家般"字样[22]，长沙杨家山传"王后家"出土的漆盘有"杨主家般、今长沙王后家般"字样[23]，长沙马王堆轪侯利苍家属墓中的许多漆器都有"轪侯家"字样（图 109）[24]，等等。有些漆器书写"上林"字样（图 110），说明它们曾是上林苑宫观中所用之物[25]；有的漆器则刻有"大官"、"汤官"字样，说明它们本是少府属官中主管皇家膳食的官署所藏之器[26]。有些漆器上还书写着有关器物的用途的文字，如马王堆汉墓出土的许多杯、盘等器都书有"君幸酒"、"君幸食"（图 111、112），宁波汉墓中的漆杯也有"宜酒"的字样，它们都兼有祝福吉祥的意思。

汉代统治阶级日常所用的饮食器皿，往往是带有金银装饰的漆器。《汉书·贡禹传》说："尝从之东宫（长乐宫），见赐杯案，尽文画金银饰。"《盐铁论·散不足》说："今富者银口黄耳，金错蜀杯。"

inlays of gold." Another in *Han jiu yi* says, "Gold-mounted wares are used by the highest officials, and silver-mounted wares by the middle level and the imperial household officials." These texts indicate that not only were lacquer vessels widely used in royal and noble households, they were also exquisitely beautiful. Two lacquered *pan* dating to the Wang Mang inter-regnum (beginning of first century A.D.) from Pyongyang are inscribed, stating that they belonged with *pan* Nos. 1,450-4,000[27] and 2,173-3,000[28] respectively. Hence there must have been thousands of *pan*-vessels alone in use in the royal kitchens in the Changlegong, not to mention other vessel types (fig. 113). The astounding number of lacquered vessels in the royal household illustrates the extravagance and luxury of the lives of the Han ruling elite, as well as the advanced state of the lacquer-manufacturing industry in the Han period.

Lacquerware Industry in the Han Dynasty   In the Han period, lacquer articles were manufactured in many regions. It is important to note that many of these lacquer workshops were government managed. Lacquer wares found in an early Western Han tomb at Shitougang in Xicun, Guangzhou, were fire-branded with the characters "Pan yu" (fig. 114).[29] Fire-branded characters "Bu shan" and "Shi fu" were found on lacquer wares from the early Western Han tomb at Luobowan in Guixian, Guangxi.[30] Lacquer wares from the early Western Han tomb at Yinqueshan in Linyi, Shandong, were fire-branded with the names "Ju shi" and "Shi fu" (fig. 115).[31] Fire-branded characters "Cheng shi" and "Shi fu" appear on lacquer items from the early Western Han tombs at Mawangdui, Changsha and Fenghuangshan, Jiangling.[32] These characters indicate that these lacquer wares were manufactured at Panyu in what was then Nanhai Prefecture (now Guangzhou), at Bushan in Yulin Prefecture (now Guiping in Guangxi), in Juxian in Chengyang Principality (now Juxian, Shandong), and in Chengdu in Shu Prefecture (now Chengdu). These were all administrative seats of prefectures or principalities. They also indicate that these early Western

Han lacquer goods were manufactured under the supervision of the Shi Fu, that is, the local department of commerce and handicraft. As the lacquer industry of Sichuan was especially prosperous, large numbers of lacquer goods from Chengdu were sold as far away as Changsha and Jiangling.

Among the numerous lacquer wares unearthed in 1977 from the early Western Han tomb of the Marquis of Ruyin at Shuanggudui in Fuyangxian, Anhui Province, many carry incised inscriptions.[33] For

《汉旧仪》说：＂大官令尚食，用黄金扣器；中官长、私官长尚食，用白银扣器。＂以上说明，当时宫廷和贵族所用的器皿，主要是漆器，而漆器的制作又是如何的精致。朝鲜平壤附近出土的二件新莽时期的漆盘，在底部分别刻有＂常乐大官，始建国元年正月受，第千四百五十至四千＂[27] 和＂常乐大官，始建国元年正月受，第二千一百七十三至三千＂[28] 字样，说明在当时的长乐宫（新莽时改称＂常乐室＂）中主管皇家膳食的官署中所用的漆器，仅漆盘一种，即达数千件，其数量之多到了惊人的程度（图 113）。这说明了统治阶级的奢侈和铺张，同时也说明漆器制造业的发达。

在汉代，许多地方都出产漆器。值得注意的是，制造漆器的手工业作坊有很多是官营的。广州西村石头冈西汉初年墓中的漆器有＂番禺＂的烙印（图 114）[29]，广西贵县罗泊湾西汉初期墓中的漆器有＂布山＂、＂市府＂的烙印[30]，山东临沂银雀山西汉前期墓中的漆器有＂莒市＂、＂市府＂等烙印（图 115）[31]，长沙马王堆和江陵凤凰山西汉前期墓中的漆器有＂成市＂、＂市府＂等烙印[32]。这说明了这些漆器是分别在南海郡的番禺（今广州）、郁林郡的布山（今广西桂平）、城阳国的莒县（今山东莒县）和蜀郡的成都（今成都）制造的，它们都是郡国的治所所在地；同时也说明了在西汉前期，漆器是由这些城市中主管商业和手工业的官府——＂市府＂经管的。由于四川的漆器制造业特别兴盛，所以成都的产品大量地远销到长沙和江陵。

1977 年在安徽省阜阳县双古堆发掘的西汉初年的汝阴侯墓中出土了许多漆器，其中有不少器物刻有铭文。[33] 例如：有一件

example, a lacquered *zhi* is inscribed *"Zhi* belonging to the Marquis of Ruyin, capacity 5 *sheng*; made in the third year by the Ku official of Ruyin, named Ji, and the workman Nian." An inscription on a lacquered *pan* says, "Flat, fabric-cored *pan* belonging to the Marquis of Ruyin, diameter one [Chinese] foot three inches; made in the seventh year by the officer Hui and the workman Su." Some vessels are branded with "Ruyin" shopmarks, clearly indicating that they were made locally. References to the same officials and workshops on an inscribed bronze lamp from the same tomb at Fuyang indicate that as early as the beginning of Western Han, local lords often established their own workshops for the production of lacquered and other wares. Since their power extended over rather limited territories one workshop often served to produce all types of wares, and the same officials were put in charge of the production of different types of wares.

According to the "Treatise on Geography" in *Hanshu*, handicraft officials were established in modern-day Luoyang, Wuzhi, Yuxian, and Nanyang in Henan Province, in Zhangqiu and Tai'an in Shandong, in Chengdu and Zitong in Sichuan, and these were directly controlled by the central government. Government-controlled industries were probably founded during the reign of Emperor Jing Di and the early part of Emperor Wu Di's reign. *Hanshu* ("Biography of Gong Yu") also records that the workshops in Shu and Guanghan prefectures of Sichuan manufactured both lacquered and gold and silver vessels. Most of the mid-Western Han to early Eastern Han lacquer goods found in Pyongyang, Noin Ula, and Qingzhen are inscribed with the names of the Shu and Guanghan workshops of Sichuan, confirming the textual records. Many of these also carry gilt or silvered bronze mounts, clearly illustrating what was maintained by *Hanshu*. The workshop of the prefecture of Shu was located in Chengdu and that of Guanghan was in Zitong, which was renamed Zitong during the Wang Mang Interregnum. Hence, lacquer goods made in these two workshops during the interregnum were inscribed with "Chengdu Jun" and "Zitong Jun."[34]

As previously mentioned, the burials in Mawangdui (Changsha) and in Fenghuangshan (Jiangling) date from the early Western Han period, and many of the lacquer wares from these burials carry Chengdu

漆卮，其铭文为"女（汝）阴侯卮容五升，三年女阴库己、工年造"。又有一件漆盘，其铭文为"女阴侯布平盘，径尺三寸，七年吏讳、工速造"。铭文中的"库己"、"吏讳"是汝阴侯国中掌管财务和器材的官吏，"己"、"讳"是他们的名字；"工年"、"工速"是制器的工人，"年"、"速"是他们的名字。有些器物还烙有"女阴"字样的戳记，表明它们的制作地点便在汝阴（今安徽阜阳）。汝阴侯墓中还出土许多铜器，其中的一件铜灯有铭文，表明它也是"库己"和"工年"所造。由此可见，在西汉初期，分封在各地的诸侯王和列侯也有自设手工业作坊以制造各种器物的，其中包括漆器。侯国规模不大，所以它的手工业作坊是综合性的，有关的官员同时管理着漆器和铜器等其他器物的制造。

据《汉书·地理志》记载，汉朝在河南郡（治所在今洛阳）、河内郡的怀县（今河南武陟）、颍川郡的阳翟县（今河南禹县）、南阳郡的宛县（今河南南阳）、济南郡的东平陵县（今山东章丘）、泰山郡及其属县奉高（今山东泰安）、蜀郡的成都县（今成都）、广汉郡（治所在今四川梓潼）及其所属雒县（今四川广汉）设有工官，由中央政府直接控制。这些工官的设置，大概是在景帝至武帝的前期。《汉书·贡禹传》说："蜀、广汉主金银器，岁各用五百万。"如淳注："地理志，河内怀、蜀郡成都、广汉皆有工官，工官主作漆物者也。"可见蜀郡和广汉郡的工官制造金银器，同时也制造漆器。在平壤、诺音乌拉、清镇发现的西汉中期至东汉前期的大多数漆器，都在铭文中记明它们是蜀郡和广汉郡工官的产品，从而证实了上述史书的记载。漆器上多镶有镀金或镀银的铜扣，正说明蜀郡、广汉郡的工官也制作金银器。蜀郡的治所在成都，广汉郡的治所在梓潼（新莽时改为子同），所以在新莽时期的漆器铭文中称蜀郡工官为"成都郡工官"、称广汉郡工官为"子同郡工官"。[34]

前面曾经说过，长沙马王堆汉墓和江陵凤凰山汉墓的年代属西汉前期，墓中随葬的漆器有许多烙有"成市"、"市府"的戳记，说明

workshop marks such as "Cheng shi" and "Shi fu." This evidence suggests that the locally controlled workshops at Chengdu had, by the mid-Western Han period, already passed under the direct control of the central government. These government-controlled workshops at Shu and Guanghan in Sichuan were mainly responsible for the supply of lacquer goods to the royal court and high officials' households; those lacquer goods inscribed with "Cheng yu" were used specifically by the emperor. The discovery of these lacquer wares as far away as Qingzhen, Pyongyang, and Noin Ula probably indicates they were imperial gifts to officials guarding the frontiers, to the leaders of minority groups, or to foreigners.

The lacquer wares from Qingzhen, Noin Ula, and Pyongyang all carry detailed and dated inscriptions. The earliest is dated 85 B.C., the latest, A.D. 102. These inscriptions mention the year of manufacture, the name of the workshop, the type of vessel and its capacity, and the names of officials and workmen involved; thus, they provide detailed information on the organization of the two largest lacquer workshops at Shu and Guanghan and on the actual processes of production. The inscription on a lacquered cup unearthed in Qingzhen in Guizhou may be given as an example:

> In the third year of reign period Yuan Shi [of Emperor Ping Di, A.D. 3], the Guanghan Prefecture official workshop manufactured this Cheng yu lacquered, incised, painted, wood-cored, yellow ear-cup, with a capacity of one *sheng*, sixteen *yue*. It was manufactured by Sugong Chang, Xiugong Li, Shanggong Jie, Tong'erhuangtugong Chang, Huagong Fang, Diaogong Ping, Qinggong Kuang, Zaogong Zhong, under the supervision of Hugongzushi Yun, Shou Chang Yin, Cheng Feng, Yuan Lin, Shoulingshi Tan.

From the list of craftsmen named, we can see that there was detailed division of labor between the various workmen and the different stages of lacquer production. First comes the "Sugong," who made the wood core (he would not be mentioned if a fabric core was used); then the "Xiugong" who applied the lacquer. He is followed by the "Shanggong," who was also responsible for the application of lacquer, but in contrast to the "Xiugong," he applied the final layers. It has been argued that the Shanggong attached bronze parts, but since his name also appeared on lacquer items without bronze parts, this interpretation cannot stand. The Shanggong is followed by the workman responsible for gilding the bronze handles of the plate

它们是成都县市府所属作坊的产品。因此，可以认为，西汉前期由成都市府经管的漆器制造业，到了西汉中期已经归中央政府直接控制了。蜀郡和广汉郡工官所制的漆器，主要是供宫廷中使用；有的漆器在铭文中有"乘舆"字样，正说明它们是皇帝的御用品。这些漆器在清镇、平壤、诺音乌拉等地出土，大概是由于当时的朝廷用它们来赏赐边郡的官吏和少数民族的首领，或赠送给外国。

平壤、诺音乌拉、清镇出土的漆器，有详细的纪年铭文，年代最早的为西汉昭帝始元二年（公元前 85 年），最晚为东汉和帝永元十四年（公元 102 年）。铭文中记录着制作的年份、工官的名称、器物的名称和容量、制器工人和各级官员的名字，由此可以了解蜀郡和广汉郡工官的组织体制和制作漆器的工序。兹举贵州省清镇出土的一件漆杯的铭文为例：

> 元始三年，广汉郡工官造乘舆髹泪画木黄耳杯，容一升十六龠；素工昌、休工立、上工阶、铜耳黄涂工常、画工方、泪工平、清工匡、造工忠造，护工卒史恽、守长音、丞冯、掾林、守令史谭主。

从铭文中可以看出，工人按工作性质不同，分为"素工"、"髹工"、"上工"、"铜耳黄涂工"、"画工"、"泪工"、"清工"、"造工"。"素工"是制木胎的工人；如系夹纻器，则不用"素工"。"髹工"是漆工。"上工"有时作"沕工"，可见也是漆工，它与"髹工"的区别可能在于"髹工"是初步涂漆，"上工"是进一步涂漆。有人认为"上工"是镶嵌铜扣的工人，但不镶铜扣的漆器在铭文中也有"上工"，可见此说不可信。"铜耳黄涂工"的任务是在漆杯所镶的

or pot, the "Tong'erhuangtugong"; then the workman who painted the decoration, called the "Huagong." The job of the "Diaogong" has been greatly disputed, and he has been thought to have been responsible for carving decoration and inscriptions on the lacquers. However, although many lacquer wares from Dafentou in Yunmeng, Hubei, did not have carved inscriptions, the word "diao," was still mentioned in the inventory tablet found in the grave.[35] Hence, it seems likely that his job involved not the carving of decorations or inscriptions but the final polishing and buffing of the lacquered surface to make it shine. He is followed by the "Qinggong" who makes sure it is cleaned—i.e., a kind of product inspector—and, finally, the "Zaogong," the general supervising foreman of the entire workshop. The order presented above suggests that the processes involved were as follows: (1) making of the core; (2) application of the base layers of lacquer; (3) application of top layers of lacquer; (4) attachment of metal parts; (5) painting the surface designs; (6) buffing; (7) final cleaning and inspection. In the earlier lacquer vessels dated to 85 B.C., the only stages named by the inscriptions were, lacquering, painting and buffing, but inscriptions dating from the reign of Cheng Di (late first century B.C.) included also the second lacquering process, the attachment of metal parts, and the final cleaning and inspection. This evidence suggests that the manufacturing process became increasingly more refined.

Among the lacquer wares from Pyongyang and Qingzhen with more complete inscriptions, two were made in A.D. 3 and two in A.D. 4 by the Guanghan workshop, and three were made in A.D. 3 and seven in A.D. 4 by the Shu workshop, as can be seen in table 1 and table 2. Looking at the seven lacquer vessels made by the Shu workshop in the year A.D. 4 alone, we notice that the names of the various workmen are different. Evidently, not only were there different workmen responsible for different stages of lacquer production, but there were also many different workmen trained in a given skill. In general, the largest numbers of workmen were employed in the application of lacquer, followed in number by those in charge of adding bronze parts, painting the designs, and applying the final layers of lacquer. Polishers occupy a relatively small number, probably because the job is relatively simple. There must have been only a few inspectors and foremen, for the same inspector's name, Ping, appeared

铜耳上镀金；如系镶有铜箍的漆盘和漆壶等，则铭文中称"铜扣黄涂工"。"画工"是在器物上画花纹的。"洀工"的性质曾引起许多争论，但看来以系"雕工"的可能性为大，其任务或认为在于雕刻花纹和铭文。但是，有些漆器并无雕刻的花纹，而铭文中仍有"洀工"的名字；湖北省云梦大坟头汉墓中的许多漆器没有雕刻的铭文，但该墓的"赗方"中仍称它们的"髹洀画盂"等等[35]，可见"洀"字的意义不在于雕刻花纹或铭文，可能是指在漆器上精心刮摩，使其发生光泽。"清工"是将制成的漆加以修整、洗净，实际上负有检验产品的责任，也可以说是检验工。"造工"则是工场中的工人主任。各种不同工种的工人名字在铭文中的排列次序，说明了制造漆器的工序先后是制木胎，初步涂漆，进一步涂漆，镶铜耳或铜扣，绘描花纹，刮摩使发光泽，最后加以修整、洗净，经过检验，全部制作过程乃告结束。在年代较早的始元二年（公元前85年）的漆器铭文中，工人只有"髹工"、"画工"和"洀工"，只是在成帝以后的漆器铭文中才增加了"上工"、"黄涂工"与"清工"。这可能是说明起初分工较简单，到后来才越分越细。

在平壤和清镇出土的铭文较完整的漆器中，属于元始三年（公元3年）广汉郡工官制造的共有二件，元始四年（公元4年）广汉郡工官制造的共有二件，元始三年蜀郡西工制造的共有三件，元始四年蜀郡西工制造的共有七件。以同属元始四年蜀郡西工所造的七件漆器为例，各器的髹工、上工、黄涂工、画工的名字各不相同，可见在工场中不仅有着许多不同工种的工人，而且同一工种的工人也各有多人。总的说来，髹工人数最多，这是由于髹漆的任务最为繁重。上工、黄涂工、画工人数亦较多，但次于髹工。洀工人数较少，可能是由于刮摩漆器比较容易之故。值得注意的是，七件漆器

on all seven lacquers, while the same foreman's name, Zong, appeared on five of the seven lacquer pieces. This evidence supports our interpretation of their responsibilities (tables 1, 2).

We should note, however, that although there was a clear division of labor among the workmen, many workmen were capable of different jobs. For instance, workman Tan applied the top layers of lacquer as well as painted in designs; the workman Feng carved wood cores, made bronze mounts, painted designs, and polished; the foreman Zong occasionally also helped with lacquer application. And based on information derived from known dated lacquers, each workman functioned over a considerable length of time. For example, the foreman Zong was in charge for eighteen years from 4 B.C. to A.D. 14; and the workman Feng, responsible for wood-core carving, painting, and polishing, worked for as long as twelve years, from 4 B.C. to A.D. 8.[36]

的清工都是"平",其中五件的造工都是"宗",说明了清工和造工的人数最少,从而也进一步说明了清工是检验工,造工是工人主任(见表一、表二)。

值得注意的是,工场中虽有明确的分工,但工人们却往往兼有各种技能。例如工人谭既能任上工,又能做画工;工人丰既是素工,又兼任黄涂工、画工和泪工;造工宗有时也兼任糅工。从全部有纪年的漆器铭文看来,工人们的任期相当长。例如:造工宗自建平三年(公元前4年)至天凤元年(公元14年),任职达十八年;素工兼画工和泪工丰自建平三年(公元前4年)至居摄三年(公元8年),任职达十二年之久。[36]

Table 1 Titles and Names of Workmen and Officials at the Government Lacquer Workshop at Guanghan Jun in the 3rd and 4th Years of the Reign Yuan Shi (A.D. 3-4) of Emperor Ping Di

Guanghan Jun Workshop	Lacquered cup of A.D. 3 (found in Qingzhen)	Lacquered cup of A.D. 3 (found in Qingzhen)	Lacquered tray of A.D. 4 (found in Qingzhen)	Lacquered cup of A.D. 4 (found in Pyongyang)
Sugong	Chang	Chang		
Xiugong	Li	Long	Ze	Xuan
Shanggong	Jie	Sun	Liang	Hu
Huangtugong	Chang	Hui	Wei	
Huagong	Fang		Yi	Wu
Diaogong	Ping	Ping	Ping	
Qinggong	Kuang	Kuang	Lang	
Zaogong	Zhong	Zhong		Ren
Hugong Zushi	Yun	Yun	Yun	Yun
Zhang	Yin	Yin	Qin	Qin
Cheng	Feng	Feng	Feng	Feng
Yuan	Lin	Lin	Zhong	Zhong
Ling Shi	Tan	Tan	Wan	Wan

表一：元始三年至四年广汉郡工官工人、官员名字表

广汉郡工官	素工	髹工	上工	黄涂工	画工	汩工	清工	造工	护工卒史	长	丞	掾	令史
元始三年漆杯（清镇）	昌	立	阶	常	方	平	匡	忠	恽	音	冯	林	谭
元始三年漆杯（清镇）	昌	隆	孙	惠		平	匡	忠	恽	音	冯	林	谭
元始四年漆盘（清镇）		则	良	伟	谊	平	郎		恽	亲	冯	忠	万
元始四年漆杯（平壤）		玄	护		武			仁	恽	亲	冯	忠	万

Table 2 Titles and Names of Workmen and Officials at the West Workshop of Shu Jun in the 3rd and 4th Years of the Reign Yuan Shi (A.D. 3–4) of Emperor Ping Di

West Workshop of Shu Jun	Lacquered cup of A.D. 3 (found in Qingzhen)	Lacquered cup of A.D. 3 (found in Pyongyang)	Lacquered cup of A.D. 3 (found in Pyongyang)	Lacquered box of A.D. 4 (found in Pyongyang)	Lacquered plate of A.D. 4 (found in Pyongyang)	Lacquered plate of A.D. 4 (found in Pyongyang)	Lacquered cup of A.D. 4 (found in Pyongyang)	Lacquered cup of A.D. 4 (found in Pyongyang)	Lacquered cup of A.D. 4 (found in Pyongyang)	Lacquered cup of A.D. 4 (found in Pyongyang)
Sugong	Feng	Feng	Jin				Yi	Yi	Yi	Yi
Xiugong	Jian	Gan	Ji	Lü	Gong	Shi	Shun	Zong	Li	Bian
Shanggong	Chang	Tan	Qin	Huo	Zhou	Tan	Kuang	Huo	Dang	Kuang
Huangtugong	Wu	Chong	Wu	Gu	Wei	Feng	Gui	Gui	Gu	Gui
Huagong	Dian	Tan	Feng	Qin	Fu	Zhang	Cen	Meng	Ding	Feng
Diaogong	Wan	Rong	Yi	Rong	Feng	Rong	Rong	Feng	Feng	Zhong
Qinggong	Zheng	Zheng	Zheng	Ping	Ping	Ping	Ping	Ping	Ping	Ping
Zaogong	?	Yi	Yi	Zong	Zong	Zong	Zong	Yi	Zong	Yi
Hugong Zushi	Zhang	Zhang	Zhang	Zhang	Zhang	Zhang	Zhang	Zhang	Zhang	Zhang
Zhang	Liang	Liang	Liang	Liang	Liang	Liang	Liang	Liang	Liang	Liang
Cheng	Feng	Feng	Feng	Feng	Feng	Feng	Feng	Feng	Feng	Feng
Yuan	Long	Long	Long	Long	Long	Long	Long	Long	Long	Long
Ling Shi	Kuan	Kuan	Kuan	Bao	Bao	Bao	Bao	Bao	Bao	Bao

表二：元始三年至四年蜀郡西工工人、官员名字表

蜀郡西工	素工	髹工	上工	黄涂工	画工	泪工	清工	造工	护工卒史	长	丞	掾	令史
元始三年漆杯（清镇）	丰	建	常	武	典	万	政	？	章	良	凤	隆	宽
元始三年漆杯（平壤）	丰	赣	谭	充	谭	戎	政	宜	章	良	凤	隆	宽
元始三年漆杯（平壤）	禁	给	钦	武	丰	宜	政	宜	章	良	凤	隆	宽
元始四年漆盒（平壤）		吕	活	古	钦	戎	平	宗	章	良	凤	隆	褒
元始四年漆盘（平壤）		恭	周	威	铺	丰	平	宗	章	良	凤	隆	褒
元始四年漆盘（平壤）		石	谭	丰	张	戎	平	宗	章	良	凤	隆	褒
元始四年漆杯（平壤）	匋	顺	匡	段	岑	戎	平	宗	章	良	凤	隆	褒
元始四年漆杯（平壤）	匋	宗	活	段	孟	丰	平	宜	章	良	凤	隆	褒
元始四年漆杯（平壤）	匋	立	当	古	定	丰	平	宗	章	良	凤	隆	褒
元始四年漆杯（平壤）	匋	便	匡	段	丰	忠	平	宜	章	良	凤	隆	褒

In Han handicraft workshops, the workmen involved in actual production were often from one of three groups. The same division also occurred in the Shu and Guanghan lacquer workshops. They consisted of (1) exiled peasant laborers, (2) convicts, and (3) skilled workmen, discussed in detail above. The first two groups were primarily responsible for all the odd jobs and the dirty work around the workshop. Although the workmen of the third group were distinguished by their special skills, they were nevertheless still slave-laborers, with no personal freedom, and hence were hardly different from the other two groups.

Lacquer inscriptions also tell us that there were five administrative posts attached to the lacquer workshops at Shu and Guanghan. They are: (1) the Zhang, the chief administrator, and (2) the Cheng, his assistant, with positions and salaries comparable to those of district magistrates and assistant magistrates respectively; (3) the Yuan, their subordinate, whose job was to see that orders were carried out properly (i.e., a type of executive officer); (4) the Ling Shi, in charge of paperwork; and (5) the Hugong Zushi, or head supervisor. This last rank was generally used for rather ordinary supervisory posts throughout the Han administrative system, but since he was sent directly by the prefectural government, and answerable only to it, he possessed authority and power even above the chief administrator (Zhang), and his name was therefore usually placed first in the inscriptions.[37] In the inscription dated to 85 B.C., the name of the head supervisor (Hugong Zushi) was listed after those of the chief and assistant administrators; only in inscriptions dated 23 B.C. and later did his name appear at the head of the list, and this order of listing became the rule thereafter. This development suggests that the central government had tightened its grip over the workshops at Shu and Guanghan from the time of Cheng Di on (late first century B.C.).

As shown in the tables, four lacquer items from Pyongyang and Qingzhen were produced by the Guanghan workshop and ten were produced by the Shu workshop between A.D. 3 and 4. We can also see that the names of the five administrators continue to show up, clearly indicating that there was only one person attached to each administrative post. But on lacquer wares made in more widely separated years, different names usually appear, suggesting that, in contrast to the workmen, who worked in the shops for long years, there was higher turnover in the administrative posts. One Zhang is known to have been in office from A.D. 3 to 8—even so, no more than six years—while other administrators were often transferred after one or two years.

　　据铭文所见，蜀郡和广汉郡工官中的官吏职称有"护工卒史"、"长"、"丞"、"掾"、"令史"等。"长"是工官中主要的行政负责官员，"丞"是他的副职，他们的地位和待遇相当于县长和县丞。"掾"是"长"、"丞"之下的办事官吏，"令史"则是掌管文书的官吏。汉代在官营手工业作坊中从事生产劳动的人，往往有卒、徒、工匠三种，蜀郡和广汉郡工官的作坊当亦不在例外。卒是被迫服徭役的民夫，徒是罪犯，他们在工场中都担任粗杂工；工匠即上述的素工、髹工、上工、黄涂工、汩工、清工和造工，他们有专门的技术，但也没有人身自由。"护工卒史"是监督工官的官员，其监视的对象自然也包括人数众多的卒、徒和工匠。但是，就"护工卒史"这一职称来说，"卒史"是一种官吏的名称，"护工"则是他的具体任务。汉代九卿及郡太守的属吏都有"卒史"。被派到工官中担任监督职务的卒史，则称"护工卒史"。一般卒史的秩位不高，但"护工卒史"为少府所派，在工官中居监视、督察的职位，权力很大，所以在漆器铭文中列名于长、丞之前而居于首位。[37] 在始元二年（公元前 85 年）的漆器铭文中，护工卒史名在长、丞之后，只是在阳朔二年（公元前 23 年）的漆器铭文中才开始将护工卒史之名列于首位，以后乃成为定制。这说明了大概从成帝以后，中央政府对蜀郡和广汉郡工官的控制进一步加强了。

　　如前所述，平壤和清镇出土的元始三年和四年广汉郡工官所造的漆器共四件，元始三年和四年蜀郡西工所造的漆器共十件。值得注意的是，各器铭文中所见"护工卒史"、"长"、"丞"、"掾"、"令史"的名字几乎完全相同，这就说明了工官中的各种官吏每职只有一人。但是，在不同年份的漆器铭文中所见的官员名字则往往不相同，从而说明了与工匠们的任期甚长相反，各种官吏是常常更换的，任期很短，任免频繁。任职年限较长的护工卒史章，自元始三年（公元 3 年）至居摄三年（公元 8 年），前后亦不过六年。其他的官员，往往有任职才一二年即被更替的。

Besides the Shu and Guanghan workshops, lacquer wares were also made at the official workshops at the Western Han capital of Chang'an (modern Xi'an). Some of the lacquers found in Wuwei, Gansu, and in Pyongyang, Korea, have inscriptions stating they were made by "Kaogong," "Yougong," or "Gonggong." Kaogong and Yougong were workshops under the Department of Imperial Household Supplies; Gonggong is believed by some to be another name for Kaogong, or it may be another workshop under the same department. These Chang'an workshops manufactured both bronze and lacquer vessels. These lacquer inscriptions contain terms for various workmen specializing in painting, polishing, and gilding, but usually only a single workman's name is given—the name of the workman comparable to the foreman in the Shu and Guanghan workshops. Among the officials at the workshop were "Ling," "You Cheng," "Yuan," "Ling Shi," and "Se Fu." Some of these titles refer to responsible officials, but only You Cheng were in charge of lacquer working. The relatively few finds from Chang'an workshops suggest that they might have not been as productive as the Shu and Guanghan workshops.

A passage in the "Biography of He Xi Empress Deng" in *Hou Hanshu,* relates: "In A.D. 105, the metal-mounted vessels of Shu and Guanghan and the long swords with silken sashes are no longer available." This may indicate that these two famous Sichuan workshops had stopped supplying lacquer wares to the court. As mentioned earlier, the latest inscription on the lacquers found at Pyongyang is dated A.D. 102. This date corresponds well to the *Hou Hanshu* comment. From these data, we may assume that the government-controlled lacquer industry was already in decline from mid-Eastern Han on, its place taken by the privately owned workshops controlled by the local warlords and wealthy landowners.

To summarize, the lacquer industry that began its rapid development only in the Warring States period reached its height in Han. As with all things that have reached their zenith, the lacquer industry's decline was inevitable. There were many different types of lacquered wares, and the superb quality and beauty of the lacquered food and wine vessels had made them more desirable than bronze vessels. But from the time of the late Eastern Han, Wei, and Jin dynasties, celadon wares became increasingly popular and in many instances came to replace lacquer wares. However, lacquer techniques still continued to develop and advance throughout the post-Han periods.

除了蜀郡和广汉郡的工官以外，设在首都长安的工官亦制作漆器；甘肃武威和朝鲜平壤出土的一部分漆器在铭文中记明系"考工"、"右工"、"供工"所制，即是例证。"考工"和"右工"都系少府属下的工官；"供工"可能即系"考工"，也可能是另一工官，但亦应系属少府管辖。这些设在长安的工官，既制造铜器，亦制造漆器。所制漆器的铭文表明，作坊中的工人亦有画工、洀工、涂工等分工，但在铭文中却往往只举一人之名，作为代表，此人即相当于蜀郡和广汉郡工官中的造工。工官中的官员有"令"、"右丞"、"掾"、"令史"、"啬夫"等，"令"和"左丞"、"右丞"是负责的官员，但主管漆器制造的是"右丞"。从考古发现的情形看来，长安工官的产品可能不如蜀郡和广汉郡工官的产品多。

《后汉书·和熹邓皇后纪》："元兴元年（公元105年）……，其蜀汉扣器、九带佩刀，并不复调。"这可能说明，蜀郡和广汉郡工官从此不再为宫廷制造漆器了。前面已经说过，在朝鲜平壤地区发现的大量有纪年铭文的漆器中，年代最晚的为永元十四年（公元102年），这一事实正与上述《后汉书·和熹邓皇后纪》的记载相符。因此，可以推测，到了东汉中期以后，官营的漆器制造业可能已经衰落，代之而起的则是由各地豪强地主经营的私营手工业。

总之，从战国时代开始突飞猛进的漆器制造业，在汉代度过了它的黄金时代。但是，与任何事物一样，漆器制造业也是盛极而衰。漆器种类很多，其中属于饮食器皿的一类漆器曾因它具有一定的优越性而取代了青铜器。但是，到了东汉以后的魏晋时代，青瓷器兴起，漆制的器皿有相当一部分逐渐被瓷器所取代。当然，就制作技术而言，在汉以后的各个时期中，各类漆器仍然不断在发展，不断在进步。

95. Lacquered *ding*-tripod unearthed from Han tomb number 1 at Mawangdui, Changsha 长沙马王堆汉墓一号墓出土的漆鼎

96. Lacquered box from Mawangdui Han tomb number 1 马王堆汉墓一号墓出土的漆盒

97. Lacquered boxes for toilet articles from Mawangdui Han tomb number 1 马王堆汉墓一号墓出土的漆奁

98. Lacquered tray and plates from Mawangdui Han tomb number 1 马王堆汉墓一号墓出土的漆案和漆盘

99. Lacquered plate with fabric core from Mawangdui Han tomb number 1　马王堆汉墓一号墓出土的夹纻胎漆盘

100. Lacquered ladles with bamboo cores from Mawangdui Han tomb number 1　马王堆汉墓一号墓出土的竹胎漆勺

101. Lacquered *hu* from Mawangdui Han tomb number 1
马王堆汉墓一号墓出土的漆壶

102. Lacquered *fang*-vessel from Mawangdui Han tomb number 1
马王堆汉墓一号墓出土的漆钫

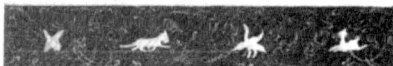

103. Designs of silver sheets attached to lacquerware unearthed from a Han tomb in Lianyungang, Jiangsu 江苏连云港汉墓出土漆器的贴银箔花纹

104. Animal designs on lacquerware unearthed from a Han tomb near Pyongyang, Korea
朝鲜平壤出土漆器的动物图案

105. Fish designs on lacquerware unearthed from a Han tomb at Fenghuangshan
in Jiangling 江陵凤凰山汉墓出土漆器的鱼纹

106. Lacquerware design depicting human figures in a story, unearthed from
Shi Qi Yao's tomb from the Western Han period in Haizhou, Jiangsu
江苏海州侍其繇墓出土漆器的人物故事图

107. Lacquerware design depicting human figures in a story unearthed from Shi Qi Yao's tomb from the Western Han period in Haizhou, Jiangsu 江苏海州侍其繇墓出土漆器的人物故事图

108. Persimmon-butt-shaped bronze decor with inlaid glass beads on a lacquerware unearthed from a Han tomb in Luoyang
洛阳汉墓出土漆器上的柿蒂形铜饰及琉璃珠

109. The inscription "Dai Hou Jia" ("Marquis of Dai's household") on a lacquerware unearthed from Han tomb number 1 at Mawangdui in Changsha
长沙马王堆汉墓一号墓出土漆器上的"轪侯家"字样

110. The inscription "Shang Lin" on a lacquerware unearthed from a Han tomb at Noin Ula in Mongolia　蒙古诺音乌拉汉墓出土漆器上的"上林"字样

111. The inscriptions "Jun xing jiu" on lacquerwares unearthed from Han tomb number 1 at Mawangdui in Changsha
长沙马王堆汉墓一号墓出土漆器上的 "君幸酒" 字样

112. The inscription "Jun xing shi" on a lacquerware unearthed from Han tomb number 1 at Mawangdui in Changsha
长沙马王堆汉墓一号墓出土漆器上的 "君幸食" 字样

113. Inscription on a lacquered tray unearthed from a Han tomb near Pyongyang, Korea
朝鲜平壤汉墓出土漆盘上的铭文

114. The inscription "Pan yu" fire-branded on a lacquerware unearthed from a Western Han tomb in Guangzhou
广州西汉墓出土漆器上的"蕃禺"烙印

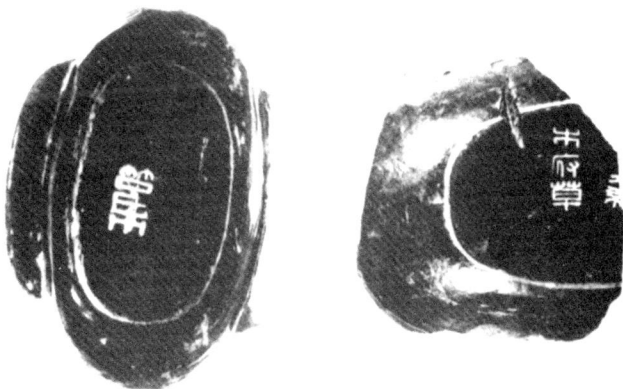

115. "Ju shi" and other inscriptions fire-branded on lacquerwares unearthed from a Western Han tomb at Yinqueshan
in Linyi, Shandong 山东临沂银雀山西汉墓出土漆器上的"莒市"、"市府"烙印

CHAPTER 5 BRONZES

In 1968, in Mancheng, Hebei Province, a large number of valuable bronze vessels were excavated from the tombs of the prince Liu Sheng and his wife Dou Wan of the Western Han period.[1] Among them was a *zhong* inscribed "Chu da guan zao zhong" and gilded with shining gold and silver, with four golden dragons coiled around it and clouds in the background (fig. 116). Another item was the "Changle culinary officer's *zhong*" (*Changle siguan zhong*). On it golden or silver stripes dotted with silver beads formed diamond or triangular shapes in which pieces of green glass were inlaid. It is an extremely colorful and pretty work of art (fig. 117). There were also a pair of *hu* covered with characters in seal script, each character decorated with bird or insect motifs. The characters are decorative, but they also form a literary composition of mysterious content (fig. 118).[2] Another item was a "Bo shan" *lu*, an incense burner. The burner and its lid were made in the form of layers of mountains with trees, animals, and hunters on them. These decorations were patterned with gold threads, some of which were as thin as fine hair. The details of animals, human figures, trees, and hills were delicately depicted with these golden lines (fig. 119). The best-known item among them in the Mancheng find was the Changxin Palace Lamp, gilded with bright gold, in the form of a kneeling palace maid holding the lamp in her hands. Not only was the palace maid beautifully sculptured, the lamp and its cover were cleverly designed so that both the lamp's illuminating power and the direction of its rays were (and still are) adjustable. Since the smoke was absorbed into the body of the maid through her arms, it was in fact an antipollution design (fig. 120). In short, it can be said that the bronzes in the tombs of Liu Sheng and his wife represent the epitome of Han bronze craftsmanship.

The Spring and Autumn-Warring States era was a transitional period for Chinese bronzes. The Warring States bronzes had changed from the solemn, heavy, solid, and archaic style of the Shang and Western Zhou periods to a new style, which was delicate, lively, and full of variation.

The new techniques of gold- and silver-gilding and inlaying with gold, silver, and precious stones made bronzes more colorful and attractive. In the light of the treasures found in the Mancheng Han tombs, we can conclude that the Western Han bronze craft represents a step forward

伍 汉代的铜器

　　1968 年在河北省满城发掘了西汉中山靖王刘胜及其妻窦绾的墓，墓中有着许多珍贵的青铜器。[1] 其中如"楚大官糟锺"，通体镀金银，光彩夺目，主要的花纹是四条金龙，上下蟠绕，其间配置一些云朵，表示龙在云中（图 116）。又如"长乐食官锺"，器身由镀金银的平行的横带和交叉的斜带构成许多菱形和三角形的空格，其中满嵌碧琉璃，在镀金的斜带上又点缀着许多半球状的银珠，彩色缤纷，绮丽异常（图 117）。又有"鸟篆文壶"一对，从壶盖到壶身，全部都用金丝和银丝镶嵌出许多图案化的美术字，这种美术字是在篆体文字上装饰着象征性的鸟，有时也有虫的形象，所以称为"鸟篆文"或"鸟虫书"，它们不仅是壶上的花纹，而且构成了一篇奇妙的文章（图 118）。[2] 还有一件"错金博山炉"，炉身和炉盖的形状铸成层层起伏的山峦，其间有树木、野兽和猎人，花纹用金丝镶嵌，金丝有粗有细，细的有如毫发，用以刻划人物、动物、树木，山峰的细部，制作得极其精致（图 119）。最有名的是一件称为"长信宫灯"的铜灯，通体镀金，灿然发光，它的全体形状是一个跪坐着的宫女用双手执灯，不仅宫女的形象塑造得十分优美，而且灯盘和灯罩的设计也非常巧妙，既可以调节灯光的亮度和照射的方向，又可使蜡烛燃烧时的烟烬通过宫女的手臂纳入其体内（宫女体内是空的），以保持清洁（图 120）。总之，上述刘胜夫妇墓中的铜器，可以说是集中了汉代青铜器工艺的精华。

　　中国古代的青铜器，发展到春秋战国之际，风格为之一变。战国时代的青铜器，在器形和花纹方面，已经摆脱了商代、西周以来那种庄严、厚重、古拙的旧作风，代之而起的则是比较轻巧、生动和多样化的新风貌，而镀金、镀银以及用金银、宝石之类镶嵌花纹的新技术则使得青铜器更加绚丽、美观。从满城汉墓中的珍贵遗品看来，西汉的青铜工艺可以说是在战国的基础上又向前发展了

from that of the Warring States period. Forms became more suitable to the needs of real life and decorations became richer and more handsome.

It should be pointed out that the bronzes found in the tombs of Liu Sheng and Dou Wan were objects available only in palaces or residences of princes. For example, the *Chu da guan zao zhong* was originally owned by the household of the Yuan Prince of Chu, Liu Jiao. In 154 B.C., the grandson of Liu Jiao participated in the rebellion of the seven feudatories and was killed. This *zhong* was confiscated and later given to Liu Sheng by the central court. The same is true for the Changxin Palace Lamp. It originally belonged to the Marquis of Xinyang, Liu Jie. Confiscated in 151 B.C. together with his other property and his title, the lamp was turned over to the Changxin Palace due to an offense committed by the marquis' son. Later the lamp was probably given to Dou Wan by her relative the Empress Dowager Dou.[3] As for the two *hu* vessels with bird-seal inscriptions, although they contained no inscriptions about their owner or the craftsman who made them, because the bird-pattern seal characters were popular in the South during the Spring and Autumn-Warring States periods, it was likely that they were in the collection of the Prince of Wu or that of the Prince of Chu. They were perhaps given to Liu Sheng after being confiscated from their previous owners as a consequence of the latter's participation in the rebellion of the seven feudatories. The bronze known as the Changle culinary officer's *zhong* was originally an item in the imperial palace, and it must have been given to Liu Sheng by the empress dowager. The changing of hands of these items tends to indicate that even in the imperial palace or in the palaces of princes, these beautifully made bronzes were rare, highly valued items. Probably because most of these bronzes were made during or before the reign of Han Wen Di, they preserve a certain likeness in decorative technique to the Warring States bronzes on the one hand, and, on the other, they indicate that new techniques were developed. The similarity in form, pattern, and decorations between the Changle culinary officer's *zhong* and a bronze *hu* found in 1928 in Jincun, Luoyang, in a Warring States tomb is obvious evidence of this transition.[4]

Generally speaking, after mid-Western Han, sophisticated patterns and rich decorations on bronzes gradually became rare; instead, plain bronzes became popular—even the imperial utensils of the palace were no exception. In 1961, twenty-two bronze pieces were found buried in Sanqiaozhen, in the city of Xi'an in Shaanxi Province. They included ten basins, five *ding*-tripods, five *zhong,* one *fang,* and one *juan* (fig. 121).[5]

一步，不仅器物的造型越来越适应现实生活的需要，而且在装饰方面也显得更加丰富多彩。

应该指出的是，刘胜夫妇墓中的这些青铜器，是当时宫廷、王府的专用品。例如，"楚大官糟鍾"原是楚元王刘交家里的器物，景帝前元三年（公元前154年）刘交的孙子参与"七国之乱"败死，此器乃被朝廷抄没，以后转赐刘胜。又如"长信宫灯"，原是信阳侯刘揭家里的器具，景帝前元六年（公元前151年）他的儿子有罪，被削除封爵，撤消封地，此灯亦被朝廷没收，归长信宫中使用，以后可能是由居住在长信宫中的窦太后将它赠送给她的亲族女窦绾的。[3]两件"鸟篆文壶"，虽然没有有关它们的制作和所有主的铭文，但鸟篆义是春秋战国以来流行于南方的美术字，所以它们也很可能本是吴王或楚王府中的藏品，"七国之乱"以后被朝廷没收而转赐刘胜的。至于"长乐飤官鍾"，则本是长乐宫中的御用器物，应该也是由居住在长乐宫中的皇太后赐给刘胜的。以上都说明满城汉墓中的那些青铜器，即使在当时的宫廷、王府之中，也是不可多得的珍品，所以制作得特别精美。另外，可能是由于这些青铜器多系文帝时或文帝以前所制，年代较早，所以在装饰方面保留着战国以来的工艺技术，而且还有所发展。"长乐飤官鍾"的形制、花纹和装饰，与1928年在洛阳金村的战国墓中发现的铜壶极相似，便是最明显的例证。[4]

但是，一般说来，从西汉中期以后，铜器上复杂的花纹和富丽的装饰已经越来越少见了，素面的青铜器则普遍流行，即使是宫廷中的御用品亦不例外。1961年在陕西省西安市三桥镇发现了一批窖藏的铜器，包括铜鉴十件、铜鼎五件、铜鍾五件、铜钫和铜锅各一件，

With only one exception, all have rather detailed inscriptions. They were imperial utensils of the Shanglinyuan imperial park located near the capital city of Chang'an. The characters "Cheng yu" inscribed on one of the five tripods make it clear that it was an imperial vessel (fig. 122). They were made in the middle to late Western Han period (i.e., 97-18 B.C.). Most of them were made in Chang'an, some were from Taishan Prefecture (today's Tai'an district in Shandong), some were from Dong Jun (today's Puyang in Henan) or from the palaces in Luoyang. Some were tributes from the provincial officials of Dong Jun, Yingchuan (today's Yuxian, Henan), or Jiujiang (today's Shouxian, Anhui) (fig. 123).[6] We notice that despite their being used in the palace, they were all plain bronzes, with little pattern or decoration. In fact, except for the very special treasures made in the earlier period, those *zhong* and *fang* that were made during the later years of Liu Sheng's life and those *fang* and *juan* acquired by his palace officials from Hedong (today's Xiaxian, Shanxi) and Luoyang were plain bronzes similar to the ones excavated in Sanqiaozhen in Xi'an (figs. 124, 125). The popular plain Han bronzes have often been considered an indication of a decline in bronze craftsmanship. This plainness, however, may be due to the fact that as the delicate and handsome lacquer wares became more efficient utensils for daily use than bronze vessels, the ruling class began to prefer lacquerware to bronzes. On the other hand, the plain and simple patterns of the bronzes might have been a new fashion of the time.

Despite the simplification of the patterns and decorations of the bronzes, the scale of the Han bronze industry was by no means reduced. On the contrary, it was further developed. The items found in Sanqiaozhen provide very good evidence of this development. According to the inscriptions on the eight basins made by the craftsmen who produced for the Shanglinyuan Palace, we know that during the ninth month in the first year of Yang Shuo (24 B.C.), craftsman Yang Zheng had made ten pieces; as of the fifth month in the fourth year of Yang Shuo (21 B.C.), craftsmen

Li Jun and Zhou Bo had made 240 pieces each; as of the sixth month in the second year of the Hong Jia reign (19 B.C.) craftsmen Yang Fang and Zhou Ba had made 300 pieces each; as of the fourth month in the third year of Hong Jia (18 B.C.) craftsmen Huang Tong and Zhou Bo had made 84 pieces each. Within the seven years from 24 to 18 B.C., 1,258 bronze basins were made, certainly an amazing number (figs. 126, 127). Regarding

共二十二件（图 121）。[5] 除一件铜锺以外，所有的器物都有详细的铭文，说明它们都是首都长安城郊区上林苑的皇家宫馆中所用之物；其中的一件铜鼎，在铭文中还有"乘舆"字样，表明它是皇帝的御用品（图 122）。它们的制作年代，自汉武帝天汉四年（公元前 97 年）至成帝鸿嘉三年（公元前 18 年），属西汉的中晚期。除大部分系在长安铸造之外，有的是从泰山郡（今山东泰安）、东郡（今河南濮阳）和雒阳的宫观中征调来的，有的则为东郡、颍川郡（今河南禹县）和九江郡（今安徽寿县）的地方官所贡献（图 123）。[6] 值得注意的是，这批铜器虽然都是宫廷所用的器物，但却都是素面的，没有什么花纹和装饰。其实，即使就满城汉墓来说，除了那些年代较早的特殊的珍品之外，在刘胜在位的晚期，应中山王府的需要而铸造的铜锺、铜钫以及王府派官员到河东（今山西夏县）、雒阳等地购置的铜钫和铜镟等，正与西安市三桥镇出土的铜锺、铜钫和铜镟一样，也都是素面的（图 124、125）。人们往往将汉代素面青铜器的普遍流行看作是当时青铜工艺的衰落。这可能是由于精巧、美观的漆器，作为日常生活中所用的容器，有时要比青铜容器更具有优越性，从而使统治阶级的爱好从青铜器转向漆器的缘故。但是，从另一方面来说，铜器纹饰的简素，也可能是当时的一种新风尚。

虽然铜器的花纹和装饰变得简素了，但汉代铜器制造业的规模不仅没有衰退，反而有所发展。上述西安市三桥镇出土的铜器，在这一问题上提供了很好的说明。例如，根据三桥镇的八件铜鉴的铭文，就可以知道，仅就上林苑宫馆中所用的铜鉴来说，阳朔元年（公元前 24 年）九月工匠杨政造十件，阳朔四年（公元前 21 年）五月工匠李骏、周博各造二百四十件，鸿嘉二年（公元前 19 年）六月工匠杨放、周霸各造三百件，鸿嘉三年（公元前 18 年）四月工匠黄通、周博又各造八十四件，从阳朔元年到鸿嘉三年的短短七年内共造铜鉴一千二百五十八件，数量之多达到了惊人的程度（图 126、127）。又如铜鼎，甘露三年

ding-tripods, in 51 B.C., craftsman Wang Yi made 116 pieces, and as of the sixth month in 19 B.C., craftsman Zuo Yun made 200.[7] Needless to say, the numbers of other utensils made were also large. Bronzes were used not only in the palaces; they were popular among the nobility, bureaucrats, and even middle and small landowners. Their popularity has been substantiated by the excavation of many Han tombs. It is fair to say that precisely because of the simplification of bronze patterns it was possible to produce large quantities of bronzes, thus making them widely popular during Han.

Compared with bronzes of the previous period, Han bronzes had undergone many changes. The food vessels *fu, gui, dui,* and *dou,* popular in the Zhou dynasty, had already disappeared by Han. Instead, *ding, zhong, hu,* and *fang* were the main vessels used at the time. They inherited the form and style of those of the previous period, with some variation. *Fang* was popular during only Western Han, and had disappeared in Eastern Han. Among other vessels, *juan, xi, mou, zun, pan, zhi, bei, jiao dou, fu,* and *zeng* were the most frequently seen vessels, apart from the four main ones mentioned above. All types bear Han characteristics, and some were first introduced during Han (fig. 128). Lamps, incense burners, tables, irons, stoves, and dripping jars became popular during Han, but had not yet appeared or were rare during the pre-Han period (figs. 129, 130). This evidence indicates that, apart from being used for the serving of drink and food, storage, and cooking, bronzes had also been put to use in other areas of daily life. Among them, in particular, were lamps and incense burners, often elegantly made. In addition to the Changxin Palace Lamp mentioned above, from the Han tombs in Mancheng came the "red bird lamp" (fig. 131), the "sheep lamp" (fig. 132), and the "*danghu* lamp." There were also the "phoenix lamp" found in the Han tomb in Hepu in Guangxi and the "twelve-branch lamp" found in the Leitai Han tomb in Wuwei in Gansu Province (fig. 133).[8] Of clever and innovative design, these were at the same time very efficient utensils.

Although bronze lamps existed during the Warring States period, Han lamps greatly exceeded those of the Warring States in variety, quantity, and popularity.

Although plain bronzes became prevalent after mid-Western Han, gilded bronzes were also quite popular, and some bronzes had patterns composed of thin engraved lines. A *zun* wine jar excavated in a late

〔公元前 51 年〕工匠王意造一百十六件，鸿嘉二年六月工匠左恽造二百件，铸造数量也甚大。[7] 其他各种器物，也有相似的铸造量，当然是无待于言的。除了宫廷中大量使用以外，各地的贵族、官僚，以及一般的中小地主阶级，都相当普遍地使用青铜器，这可以从大量汉墓的发掘工作中得到说明。可以认为，正是因为青铜器的纹饰简素，所以才能得到大量的制作和普遍的使用。

和前代比较起来，汉代铜器在种类和器形上有许多变化。周代流行的簠、簋、敦、豆等食器，到汉代已经不见了。鼎、锺、壶、钫是当时最主要的容器，它们继承了前代的形制而略有改变，其中钫仅流行于西汉，到东汉也就绝迹了。其他的容器，以锅、洗、鍪、樽、盘、卮、杯、镰斗、釜和甑等饮食器皿为炊事用具为最常见，它们在形制上具有汉代的特点，有的是汉代才有的（图 128）。另一方面，汉代又出现了许多新兴的铜器，如灯、博山炉、案、熨斗、炉、漏壶之类，都是前代所未见或少见的（图 129、130），这说明除了供饮食、贮藏、烹饪用的容器以外，青铜器已被推广到日常生活的其他各个方面。在这些新兴的铜器之中，灯和博山炉往往制作得很精致。就铜灯而言，仅以近年来的出土品为例，满城汉墓中除前面说过的"长信宫灯"外，还有"朱雀灯"（图 131）、"羊灯"（图 132）、"当户灯"，广西合浦汉墓有"凤鸟灯"，甘肃武威雷台汉墓有"十二连枝灯"（图 133）[8]，它们都是设计精巧、式样新颖，实用效果也好。战国时代虽然也已经有了铜灯，但汉代铜灯种类之多，制作数量之大，使用之普遍，又大大超过了战国时代。

虽然从西汉中期以后，素面无纹的青铜器已成为主流，但镀金的铜器却相当流行。此外，也还有一些铜器施有花纹，纹样是由镂刻的细线构成的。例如，湖南长沙西汉后期墓中的一件镀金的铜酒樽，

Western Han tomb in Changsha is covered with an elegantly engraved cloud pattern. Its detail and flowing style resemble lacquerware.[9] A *hu* with loop handle, *a pan* with three legs, and other bronzes discovered in the late Western Han tomb in Hepu in Guangxi are all decorated with various types of geometric patterns, as well as phoenixes, deer, or other animals (fig. 134). All patterns were compositions in which thin, engraved lines depict details.[10] A bronze table from an Eastern Han tomb in Wuzhou, Guangxi, is decorated with a similar pattern (fig. 135).[11] This kind of pattern engraved on bronze vessels had first appeared in the Warring States period, it was further developed during Han and was popular mainly in the South. In addition, it should be especially mentioned that in 1962 two gilded bronze goblets were found in Youyuxian in Shanxi Province, both bearing inscriptions testifying that they were made in Western Han in 26 B.C. On the goblets, lively patterns of monkey, camel, ox, rabbit, sheep, deer, tiger, fox, bear, wild goose, crow, goose, duck, and other animals and birds were cast in relief instead of being engraved. This relief casting has not been found among pre-Han bronzes (fig. 136).[12] In short, although the Han bronzes showed signs of decline in pattern and decoration, they nevertheless displayed certain innovations. Nor was the technique of inlaying with gold, silver, and precious stones lost during Han. In recent years, in an Eastern Han tomb in Xuzhou in Jiangsu, we have found an ink-stone box which was inlaid with corals, turquoise, and blue gems (fig. 137).[13] A gilded bronze goblet found in an Eastern Han tomb in Leitai in Wuwei, Gansu, had on it pictures of strange birds and animals with clouds and mist, composed of inlaid silver threads (fig. 138).[14] However, there is no denying that these are extremely rare finds for that period.

Apart from the utensils that were intended for practical use, many bronze models of carriages, horses, and mounted horsemen—which were made particularly for funeral purposes—have been found in Leitai in

Wuwei, Gansu, in 1969. The casting technique reached a highly advanced level (figs. 139, 140). This sophistication is fully demonstrated in the "Flying Horse," now known throughout the world, a running horse with a bird underneath one of its hooves (fig. 141). The date of the Leitai tomb was late Eastern Han. Utilitarian bronzes found in the same tomb include *hu, pan, wan, jian, xi, jiao dou,* iron, as well as the aforementioned

自器身到器盖，全部镂刻着细线流云纹，纹样细致、流畅，很像漆器上的花纹。[9] 广西合浦西汉后期墓中的提梁壶和三足盘等多件铜器，都装饰着由镂刻的细线构成的各种几何图案和凤、鹿等动物的纹样，相当精致（图 134）。[10] 广西梧州东汉墓出土的一件铜案，也有类似的花纹（图 135）。[11] 这种在铜器上镂刻花纹的工艺，在战国时代已经出现，到汉代又得到进一步的发展，但主要流行在南方地区。此外，特别值得提出来的，是 1962 年在山西省右玉县发现的二件镀金的铜酒樽（所刻铭文说明它们的制作年代为西汉河平三年，即公元前 26 年），它们的花纹是铸出来的，纹样有猿、骆驼、牛、兔、羊、鹿、虎、狐狸、熊、雁、鸦、鹅、鸭等各种兽类和禽类，都作浮雕式，形态生动，这在汉以前的铜器花纹中是甚少类例的（图 136）。[12] 总之，汉代的青铜器工艺，虽然在纹饰方面显得衰退，但也不是完全没有创新。而且，在铜器上用金银、宝石之类镶嵌的技术也并没有失传；就近年来的发现为例，江苏徐州东汉墓里的一件镀金的铜砚盒镶嵌着红色的珊瑚、蓝色的绿松石和青金石（图 137）[13]，甘肃武威雷台东汉墓里的一件镀金的铜酒樽用银丝镶嵌出细致的云气纹和各种奇禽异兽的纹样（图 138），便是例证。[14] 但是，像这样的青铜器，当时确实是极少见了，这也是不可否认的事实。

　　除了实用的器物以外，应该提到的是，1969 年发掘的甘肃武威雷台汉墓出土了许多专为随葬而作的铜质的车辆模型、马匹及骑马武士等人物的偶像，它们的铸造技术达到了高度的水平（图 139、140）。特别是其中的一匹足踏飞鸟的奔马，形象逼真，姿态生动，已成为世界闻名的优秀艺术作品（图 141）。雷台汉墓的年代属东汉晚期，而墓中出土的实用的青铜器除上述的灯和酒樽外，还有壶、

lamp and wine goblet; the abundance and diversity of types indicate that bronzes were popular throughout the Han dynasty.[15] It is evident, however, that bronzes declined after the Wei-Jin period. This decline could have been caused by the flourishing of porcelain, which took the place of bronze in daily life.

China is one of the first civilizations to invent the bronze mirror. According to recent excavations, we are now certain that bronze mirrors already existed during the Shang dynasty. By the Warring States period the technique for making mirrors was developing rapidly, and Han mirrors, which had proceeded a step further from those of the Warring States period, became quite widespread. As opposed to ancient Japan, where in Yayoi culture and Tomb culture imported mirrors were considered sacred treasures, in China mirrors have always been mainly utilitarian objects. Because the form and decorations of mirrors changed continuously from one period to another, providing significant chronological data, bronze mirrors have become important objects for archaeological study.

The form and decoration of mirrors of the Warring States period were preserved in those of the early Western Han period. The most common mirror is the type with a *panchi* ("intertwining serpents") design on a ground pattern and with a belt-like knob. The mirrors found in the Han tombs at Mawangdui, Changsha, are of this type (fig. 142).[16] Unlike the mirrors of the Warring States period, mirrors after the beginning of early Western Han began to bear inscriptions. The early Han mirrors, strictly speaking, still belong to the Warring States style. The "Han style" mirror began to appear in mid-Western Han during Wu Di's reign. The earliest type is the so-called grass-leaf pattern mirror, such as those found in the Mancheng tomb (fig. 143).[17] A later style is the so-called star-cloud pattern mirror, also called the "hundred nipple" mirror. The design on this mirror was probably developed from the early Western Han *panchi*-pattern mirror, but the ground pattern had disappeared, as it had in the grass-leaf pattern mirrors (fig. 144). The mirrors most typical of late Western Han were the "*riguang*" mirror and the "*zhaoming*" mirror. They were so named because of their inscriptions. Their designs are characterized by regularity and simplicity. The handle now becomes a hemispheric knob (fig. 145). During the Wang Mang interregnum the Taoist ideology of the *yin yang wu xing* school was reflected in the design

盘、碗、鉴、洗、镰斗和熨斗等等，种类和数量都相当多，说明了青铜器在汉代一直是流行的。[15] 但是，到了魏晋以后，青铜器制造业显然是衰落了。这可能是由于瓷器兴起了，它取代了青铜器在日常生活中所占的地位。

中国是世界上最早发明铜镜的国家之一。根据近年来的考古发掘，可以肯定在殷代已经出现了铜镜。到了战国时代，铜镜的铸造发展得很快，而汉代的铜镜又在战国以来的基础上进一步得到普及。中国的铜镜，始终只是一种日常的生活用具，并不像日本的弥生时代和古坟时代那样把从中国输入的铜镜当作珍宝或神器。只是由于铜镜的形制和花纹随着时代的推移而不断演变，在考古年代学上有较大的意义，所以就成为一种比较重要的研究对象。

在西汉前期，铜镜的形制和花纹保留着战国时代的作风。最常见的是一种带有"地纹"的"蟠螭纹镜"，镜钮呈带状，长沙马王堆汉墓出土的铜镜即属此类（图142）。[16] 与战国铜镜不同的是，从西汉前期开始，有的铜镜上已经有了铭文。由于西汉前期的铜镜保留着战国铜镜的作风，所以严格地说来，它是属于"战国式"的，而不是"汉式"的。到了西汉中叶的汉武帝时期，才出现了真正的"汉式镜"。最初出现的是所谓"草叶纹镜"，满城汉墓中即曾发现过（图143）。[17] 比"草叶纹镜"稍晚，又出现了一种"星云纹镜"（或称"百乳鉴"），它的花纹可能是由西汉前期的"蟠螭纹镜"演变而来，但和"草叶纹镜"一样，完全取消了"地纹"（图144）。西汉后期的铜镜，最典型的是"日光镜"和"昭明镜"，它们都是因铭文的内容而定名的，其花纹的特点是规整而简洁，而镜钮则普遍成为半球状（图145）。到了新莽时期，阴阳五行的思想

of bronze mirrors. A large number of mirrors have as their pattern the Four Deities (Green Dragon, White Tiger, Red Bird, and Black Turtle) and also the duodenary cyclical characters. This type is known as the "*guiju*," or "elbow ruler," mirror (in the West it is sometimes called the TLV mirror). The designs of these mirrors were relatively complicated. They were popular up to the mid-Eastern Han period (fig. 146). Mirrors with dated inscriptions began to appear during the Wang Mang interregnum and became more and more popular in the course of the Eastern Han dynasty. A new style appeared after mid-Eastern Han. The decorative designs of these mirrors were in relief, and they depict either deities and spiritual beasts or human figures and horses and carriages. The former mirrors are referred to as "immortal and animal" mirrors and the latter, as "pictorial" mirrors. Their designs were becoming increasingly lively at the same time that the hemispheric knobs on them were becoming larger and larger (figs. 147, 148). It should be noted that at least since mid-Western Han, the style of bronze mirrors was uniform throughout the empire, but the "immortal and animal" and the "pictorial" mirrors that appeared after mid-Eastern Han were first developed in the Zhejiang area, to the south of the Yangtze River. Thus, in the late Eastern Han and the Three Kingdoms periods, there was a certain degree of difference between the northern and southern mirrors. According to the inscriptions on mirrors excavated in Japan, the craftsmen of Luoyang enjoyed the highest reputation, but those of Kuaiji Jun (modern Shaoxing in Zhejiang) were almost comparable. These inscriptions thus indicate that without question by the late Eastern Han Kuaiji had become a mirror production center.[18]

The inscriptions on mirrors made around the time of Wang Mang often contain a line reading, "good copper produced from Danyang." Danyang Prefecture, with its capital located in today's Xuancheng, Anhui Province, was thus the location of the most famous copper mine during Han. According to the "Treatise on Geography" in *Hanshu,* the

Han government had established the post of copper official in Danyang Prefecture. A mirror of the Wei-Jin period unearthed in Liaoyang of Liaoning and many mirrors excavated in Japan bear a different line reading "copper produced in Xuzhou."[19] Xuzhou was located in present-day southern Shandong and northern Jiangsu, with its capital in modern Xuzhou, Jiangsu, and these inscriptions furnish evidence that it was a well-known copper production center during the Wei-Jin period.

反映到铜镜上，就大量出现一种带有"四神"（青龙、白虎、朱雀、玄武）纹样和"十二辰"（子、丑、寅、卯、辰、巳、午、未、申、酉、戌、亥）文字的所谓"规矩镜"，镜面上的图纹显得比较繁复，这种铜镜一直到东汉中后期仍然流行（图146）。从新莽时期开始，有的铜镜在铭文中有了纪年，东汉时纪年的铜镜越来越多。东汉前期的铜镜，是继承西汉后期和新莽时期的铜镜而有所演变。到了东汉中期以后，铜镜中出现了一种新的型式，它们的花纹是浮雕式的，其题材有的是神仙和灵兽，有的是人物和车马，前者称为"神兽镜"，后者称为"画像镜"，图纹显得很热闹，而半球状的镜钮则变得越来越大（图147、148）。值得注意的是，至少自西汉中期以来，汉代铜镜的样式是全国统一的，但东汉中期以后的"神兽镜"和"画像镜"却首先是在长江流域开始兴起。因此，在东汉后期和此后的三国时期，南方和北方的铜镜存在着一定的区别。根据日本出土的许多铜镜的铭文，当时洛阳的制镜技师是最有名的，但会稽郡（今浙江省绍兴）的技师也可以与洛阳的技师相比。总之，在东汉的中后期，江南的会稽郡无疑也已成为制作铜镜的一个重要的中心了。[18]

新莽时期及其前后的许多铜镜，常常有"善铜出丹阳"的铭文，可见丹阳（今安徽省当涂）是汉代最有名的铜矿所在。据《汉书·地理志》记载，汉朝政府在丹阳郡（其治所在今安徽省宣城）设有铜官。辽宁省辽阳出土的一件魏晋时期的铜镜和日本出土的许多相当于魏晋时期的铜镜，则有"铜出徐州"的铭文。[19]从镜铭来看，到了魏晋时期，徐州（今山东省东南部和江苏省北部，其治所在江苏省徐州市）继丹阳之后成为全国有名的铜矿所在地。但是，

However, in point of fact, no copper mines are actually known in this area and the problem is yet to be solved. To be sure, many copper mines were actually explored during Han; and according to historical records, Sichuan and Yunnan also had rich copper mines.

In 1953 an investigation of a Western Han copper-mine site in Xinglong, Hebei Province, disclosed shafts, ore-selection ground, and smelting workshops. The mine shafts were more than 100 m below the ground surface, and led to spacious mining areas. Iron hammers and pegs found near the shafts were the mining tools. Tunnels were dug around the mining area. Ores were selected near the exits of the tunnels and then taken to four nearby smelting workshops. The furnaces seem to have been round brick structures, according to what is left of them. The finished product was in the form of large disc-shaped ingots, each weighing from 5 to 15 kg. The characters meaning "East 60" or "West 53" were incised on the ingots. "East" and "West" could refer to the location of the workshop, and the numbers might indicate serials. Some ingots bear the characters "Second Year," perhaps indicating that the ingots were made before the reign title system was established by Han Wu Di (fig. 149).[20] In 1955, ten rectangular copper ingots were found at a site near the Han capital Chang'an, each weighing 34 kg, containing 99 percent copper, and all inscribed with weight and serial number. One has a line reading, "Sold by Tian Rong of Wanli in Fubo district in Runan Prefecture." The inscription indicates that the government not only ran copper mines itself but also made purchases from private miners in order to satisfy its demand for bronze manufacturing and cash minting.[21]

The scale of the production of bronze objects under Han-government management was quite large. Government-managed production supplied mainly the palace and other government offices. Two subordinate officials of the Shaofu (Lesser Treasury Ministry) in the central government, the Shangfang *ling* (Shangfang Office) and the Kaogong *ling* (Kaogong Office), were in charge of bronze production for imperial and governmental uses at the capital. The Shangfang Office, according to inscriptions, was by the time of Wu Di's reign already divided into the three offices of Left, Right, and Center, and this division continued into Eastern Han. The Central Shangfang Office had the largest capacity in terms of variety of products. The bronzes it produced included *ding*-tripods, *zhong, hu, jiao dou*, lamps, and so on. The crossbow was an item produced by all three

从实际情况来说，今徐州市及其附近一带自古未闻有铜矿。因此，这便成了一个十分费解的问题，有待进一步探讨。当然，汉代开发的铜矿是比较多的；据文献记载，四川、云南一带的铜矿也相当丰富。

1953 年在河北承德地区调查了一处西汉的铜矿遗址，其中包括矿井、选矿场和冶炼工场等。矿井深达一百多米，有宽广的采矿场。矿井附近发现的铁锤和铁钎，便是当时的采矿工具。采矿场四周有坑道，从坑道运出来的矿石就在井口的附近进行挑选。冶炼工场共发现四处，都在附近不远处。从遗留的炉砖形状来看，炼炉是圆形的。冶炼出来的成品是圆饼状的铸锭，每锭重约五公斤至十五公斤不等。铸锭上面刻有"东六十"、"西五三"等字样，数字是它们的编号，"东"和"西"则可能是指炼铜工场的位置。有的铸锭还刻有"二年"字样，表明它们的制作年代可能在汉武帝建立年号之前（图 149）。[20] 1955 年，在西安汉代首都长安城遗址附近发现了当时的铜锭十块，都作长方形，重各三十四公斤，纯铜率为 99%。铜锭都刻有重量和编号，其中一块刻"汝南（郡）富波（县）宛里田戎卖"的字样，说明当时政府为了铸造铜器和铜钱，除了控制采矿业以外，有时还收购民间的铜材。[21]

汉代官营的铜器制造业，规模很大，其产品主要供宫廷和官府使用。中央政府中少府的属官尚方令和考工令（东汉时属太仆），在首都负责制造御用和官用的铜器。根据铜器上的铭文，在西汉武帝时，尚方已分为左、右、中三部分，至东汉仍然。中尚方所制器物有鼎、锺、壶、镳斗、灯等，种类最多。弩机则为左、右、中

offices. The Kaogong Office which by Eastern Han became subordinate to the Taipu Qing (The Grand Servant) produced more or less the same items as produced by the Central Shangfang Office with the exception of mirrors, which were made only by the Shangfang Office. Another subordinate office of the Lesser Treasury Ministry called the Yougongshi also produced some bronzes. Both the Kaogongshi and the Yougongshi also produced lacquerware.

Bronzes were also produced by some of the workshops run by the prefectural manufacturing offices of the Han central government. For example, the manufacturing offices in Shu and Guanghan prefectures, apart from making lacquerware, were also famous for the bronzes they produced. According to the "Biography of Gong Yu" in *Hanshu*, "Shu and Guanghan produce mainly golden and silver wares." However, archaeological excavations have shown that the manufacturing of golden and silver wares was not that popular in Han. We therefore suspect that what are here referred to as "golden and silver wares" in fact were bronze vessels and utensils gilded with gold or silver. The Palace Museum in Beijing has in its collection a bronze goblet with a saucer. The set was made in A.D. 45 by the Western Manufacturing Office of Shu Jun. Both the goblet and its saucer were gilded with gold. Turquoise and crystal were inlaid on the goblet and on the three bear-shaped legs of the saucer (fig. 150).[22] There is a detailed inscription on the saucer that reads: "In the twenty-first year of the Jian Wu reign, the Western Manufacturing Office of Shu Jun made an imperial goblet with saucer. The saucer is decorated with carved bear-shaped legs. [Both] were inlaid with turquoise. The diameter of the bronze saucer is 2 *chi* 2 *cun*. [The set] was made by these craftsmen: Chong, coppersmith; Ye, carver; Kang, metalsmith; and Ye, artisan; [they were] under the supervision of [the following manufacturing officials]: Yun, craftsman supervisor; Fan, superintendent; Meng, assistant director; Xun, secretary; and Yun, director." The format and the titles of craftsmen and craft officials in this inscription were similar to those on lacquerware. This similarity indicates that the same manufacturing office produced both lacquerware and bronzes.

In 1925, a lacquer cup made in A.D. 52 by the same manufacturing office was excavated in Wang Xu's tomb in Pyongyang in Korea. The inscription on it reads: "In the twenty-eighth year of the Jian Wu reign, the Western Manufacturing Office of Shu Jun made an imperial soup-cup, with a capacity of 2 *sheng* 2 *he*. It was made by craftsmen: Hui, molder; Wu, lacquerman; Wen, polisher; Ting, lacquerman; and Zhong, artisan; [they were] under the supervision of the following manufacturing officials: Han, craftsman supervisor; Fan, superintendent; Geng, assistant

三尚方所共制。考工室所制铜器有鼎、錘、钫、灯、弩机等，其种类与中尚方所制似无多大区别。但是，铜镜则为尚方所制，不由考工制作。曹魏时，制作铜镜的是右尚方。此外，少府属官右工室亦制作铜器。

汉朝政府还在各地设工官，其所属作坊亦有制造铜器的。蜀郡和广汉郡的工官，除制造漆器以外，还以制造铜器而闻名。《汉书·贡禹传》说："蜀、广汉主金银器。"从考古发掘的实际情况来看，汉代的金银器并不发达。所谓"蜀、广汉主金银器"，主要应系指制造镀金或镀银的铜器而言。北京故宫博物院收藏的东汉建武二十一年（公元45年）蜀郡西工所造的一件铜酒樽，附有托盘，通体镀金，并在樽和托盘的三个熊形的足上镶嵌绿松石和水晶，制作极其精致（图150）。[22] 值得注意的是，托盘上有详细的铭文："建武廿一年蜀郡西工造乘舆一斛承旋，雕蹲熊足，青碧闵瑰饰，铜承旋径二尺二寸，铜涂工崇、雕工业、冻工康、造工业造，护工卒史恽、长汜、丞萌、掾巡、令史郎主"。铭文的格式及其所记工官的体制与漆器的铭文完全相同，可见在同一工官中既制造漆器，也制造铜器。

1925年在朝鲜平壤发掘的王盱墓中，有一件建武廿八年（公元52年）蜀郡西工所造的漆杯，其铭文如下："建武廿八年蜀郡西工造乘舆侠纻量二升二合羹杯，素工回、髹工吴、洎工文、汒工廷、

director; Xi, secretary; and Mao, director."[23] Comparing the two inscriptions, we find that the lacquer cup was made seven years later than the bronze; thus, names of many of the manufacturing officials were different. However, the name of the superintendent, Fan, was still found in the later inscription. This evidence indicates that Fan served for quite a long time, at least seven years, and that the same manufacturing officials were in charge of both bronze and lacquerware production.

Private bronze-making workshops were also quite numerous. Inscriptions on some privately produced bronzes mark their prices. Eight hundred and forty copper cash was the price of a bronze *juan* bought from Hedong Prefecture by officials of the Prince of Zhongshan, whose tomb was excavated in Mancheng (fig. 151). Another bronze *fang* produced in Luoyang was also bought by officials of the Prince of Zhongshan. Both are believed to be products of private manufactories.[24] Private mirror producers often made use of mirror inscriptions to advertise the superior quality and elegant design of the mirrors they made. The contents of the inscriptions often claimed that the user of the mirrors "will live long, will continue to enjoy wealth and prestige." To cite some examples: "The substance of this mirror is pure and bright; the rays it radiates could be compared to those of the sun and the moon"; "The mirrors made by the Ye family are handsome and great. They are as bright as the sun and the moon; indeed, they are rare to find!"; "I record here the mirrors I made; they will make the user live longer, likewise his sons and grandsons." It is evident that these mirrors were produced for the market. Many of them, nevertheless, although produced by privately owned workshops, bear inscriptions reading "Made by [the imperial workshop] Shangfang Office," in order to heighten their value. This was probably a customary practice among the private producers.

造工忠，护工卒史旱、长氾、丞庚、掾翕、令史茂主"。[23]
与上述铜酒樽铭文中的各职官吏的名字相比，这件漆杯
由于制作的时间晚了七年，所以护工卒史、丞、掾、令
史等官吏的名字都不相同，但长的名字却没有改变，仍
然是"氾"。这不仅说明了"氾"的任期甚长，至少达
七年之久，而且也说明了在蜀郡的工官中各职官吏既管
漆器的生产，也经管铜器的生产。

　　私营的铜器作坊也很多，其产品有时在铭文中标明
价格。满城汉墓出土的中山王府派官员从雒阳买来的一
件铜钫和从河东买来的一件铜锅，大概也是私营作坊的
产品，铜锅的买价为八百四十钱（图151）。[24] 许多铜镜，
往往在铭文中自夸铜质的优良、制作的精致，使用者可
以长寿富贵，如云"内清质以昭明，光辉象夫日月"，
"叶氏作竟佳且好，明如日月世少有"，"吾作明竟自有
纪，令人长命宜子孙"等等，充分说明了它们是作为商
品而生产的。也有许多铜镜，虽系私营作坊的产品，但
也在铭文中套用"尚方作镜"的字句，这可能已成了一
种习惯，其目的是为了提高产品的声誉。

116. *Zhong*-vessel inscribed with "Chu da guan zao zhong," unearthed from the Han tomb in Mancheng 满城汉墓出土的楚大官糟鍾

117. *Zhong*-vessel inscribed with "Changle siguan zhong," unearthed fro the Han tomb in Mancheng 满城汉墓出土的长乐飤官鍾

118. *Hu*-vessel decorated with bird-seal-script characters, unearthed from the Han tomb in Mancheng 满城汉墓出土的鸟篆文壶

119. "Bo shan" incense burner with gold inlays, unearthed from the Ha tomb in Mancheng 满城汉墓出土的错金博山炉

120. The Changxin Palace Lamp unearthed from the Han tomb in Mancheng
满城汉墓出土的"长信宫灯"

121. Bronze *jian*-basin for use at the Shanglinyuan Park, unearthed at Sanqiaozhen in Xi'an ("Manufactured at Dong Jun in the third year of Chu Yuan") 西安三桥镇出土的上林苑铜鉴 ("初元三年东郡造")

122. Bronze *ding*-tripod with the inscription "Cheng yu," unearthed in Sanqiaozhen, Xi'an　西安三桥镇出土的 "乘舆" 铜鼎

123. Bronze *zhong*-vessel with the inscription "Jiu jiang gong," unearthed in Sanqiaozhen, Xi'an
西安三桥镇出土的上林苑 "九江宫" 铭文铜锺

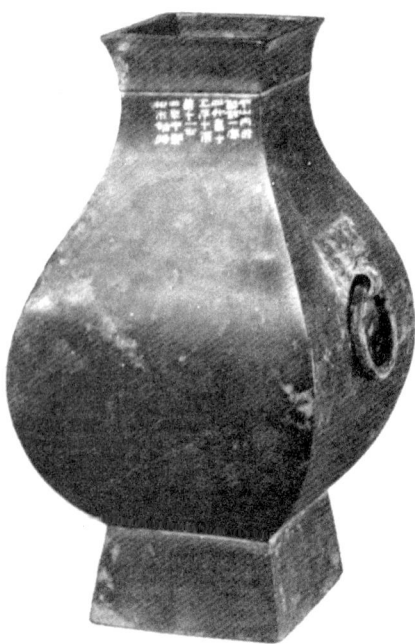

124. Bronze *fang*-vessel unearthed from the Han tomb in Mancheng
满城汉墓出土的铜钫

125. Bronze *juan*-vessel unearthed from the Han tomb in Mancheng 满城汉墓出土的铜镅

126. Inscriptions on Shanglinyuan Park bronze vessels unearthed in Sanqiaozhen, Xi'an
西安三桥镇出土上林苑铜器铭文

178

127. Inscriptions on Shanglinyuan Park bronze vessels unearthed in Sanqiaozhen, Xi'an
西安三桥镇出土上林苑铜器铭文

128. Bronze *mou*-vessel unearthed from a Han tomb in Pingle, Guangxi
广西平乐汉墓出土的铜鍪

129. Square stove of bronze, unearthed in Xi'an ("Manufactured in the second year of Gan Lu") 西安出土的铜方炉（"甘露二年造"）

130. Dripping jar of bronze, unearthed in Yikezhao League in Inner Mongolia
内蒙古伊克昭盟出土的铜漏壶

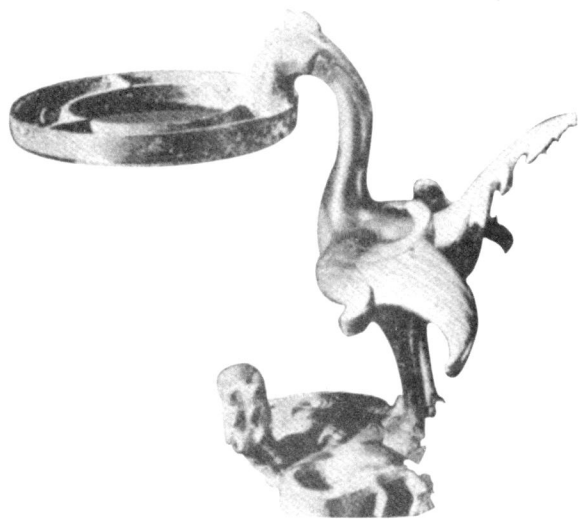

131. Bronze lamp in the shape of the Red Bird, unearthed from the Han tomb in Mancheng
满城汉墓出土的朱雀灯

132. Bronze lamp in the shape of a ram, unearthed from the Han tomb in Mancheng　满城汉墓出土的羊灯

133. Twelve-branch lamp of bronze, unearthed from the Han tomb at Leitai,
in Wuwei, Gansu　甘肃武威雷台汉墓出土的十二连枝灯

134. Incised designs on a bronze tray with three legs, unearthed from a Han tomb in Hepu, Guangxi
广西合浦汉墓出土铜盘上的细线镂刻花纹

135. Incised designs on a bronze table unearthed from a Han tomb in Wuzhou, Guangxi
广西梧州汉墓出土铜案上的细线镂刻花纹

136. Gold-gilded wine *zun*-cup of bronze, unearthed in Youyu, Shanxi 山西右玉出土的镀金铜酒樽

137. Gold-gilded ink-stone box of bronze, unearthed from a Han tomb in Xuzhou, Jiangsu
江苏徐州汉墓出土的镀金铜砚台

138. Gold-gilded wine *zun*-cup of bronze, unearthed from the Han tomb at Leitai in Wuwei, Gansu 甘肃武威雷台汉墓出土的镀金铜酒樽

139. Bronze model of horsedrawn carriage, unearthed from the Han tomb at Leitai in Wuwei, Gansu
甘肃武威雷台汉墓出土的铜质马车模型

140. Bronze figure of warrior on horseback, unearthed from the Han tomb at Leitai in Wuwei, Gansu
甘肃武威雷台汉墓出土的骑马武士

141. The "Flying Horse," bronze galloping horse stepping on a flying bird, unearthed from the Han tomb at Leitai in Wuwei, Gansu
甘肃武威雷台汉墓出土的足踏飞鸟奔马

142. Bronze mirror with designs of intertwining serpents, unearthed from the Han tomb of Mawangdui, Changsha　长沙马王堆汉墓出土的蟠螭纹铜镜

143. Bronze mirror with grass-leaf designs, unearthed from the Han tomb in Mancheng　满城汉墓出土的草叶纹镜

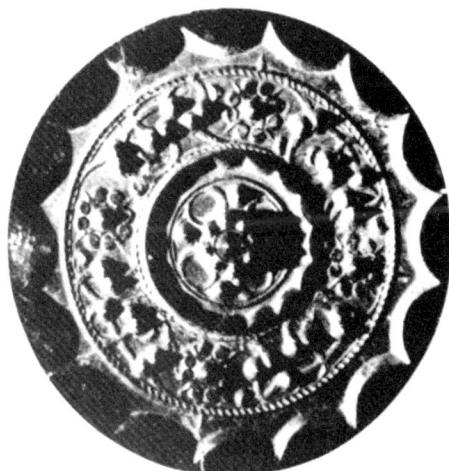

144. Bronze mirror with designs of stars and clouds, unearthed from the Han tomb in Nanchang, Jiangxi　江西南昌汉墓出土的星云纹镜

145. Bronze *zhaoming* mirror unearthed from the Han tomb in Xi'an
西安汉墓出土的昭明镜

146. Bronze mirror with designs in the shape of measuring rules ("elbow ruler"), unearthed from the Han tomb in Xi'an 西安汉墓出土的规矩镜

147. Bronze mirror decorated with design of spiritual beasts, unearthed from the Han tomb in Shaoxing, Zhejiang 浙江绍兴汉墓出土的神兽镜

148. Bronze mirror with pictorial designs, unearthed from the Han tomb in Shaoxing, Zhejiang 浙江绍兴出土的画像镜

149. Bronze ingot of the Han dynasty date, unearthed in Xinglong, Hebei
河北兴隆出土的汉代铜锭

150. Gold-gilded bronze wine *zun*-cup and tray inscribed with manufacturing date (the twenty-first year of Jian Wu), in the collection of the Palace Museum　建武廿一年铭镀金铜酒樽 （故宫博物院藏）

151. Inscription on the bronze *juan*-vessel unearthed from the Han tomb in Mancheng　满城汉墓出土铜钅肙上的铭文

CHAPTER 6   IRON IMPLEMENTS

According to archaeological excavations, Chinese iron metallurgy began in the late Spring and Autumn period. By the Han dynasty, the use and manufacture of iron implements had become common and widespread. It can be said that iron tools became indispensable for every aspect of daily life and production. As we have mentioned earlier, farm tools like the plow, the pickax, the spade, the shovel, the hoe, and the sickle were widely used in all parts of China, and their use caused a noticeable increase in agricultural productivity (fig. 152). According to a historian's estimate, at the end of the Warring States period the total population of the seven major states was about twenty million.[1] It increased drastically after mid-Western Han. According to the "Treatise on Geography" in *Hanshu,* the population reached almost sixty million by the end of the Western Han dynasty. This population growth would have been inconceivable had it not been for the widespread use of iron tools both in farming and in waterworks, the latter having greatly increased productivity of food crops and other farm products.

Craftsman's tools—such as the ax, the adz, the hammer, the chisel, the knife, the saw, the awl, nails, and so on—increasingly raised the efficiency of carpenters, bamboo craftsmen, stonemasons, and earth builders, making possible completion of large-scale construction projects (fig. 153). Concurrent with increasing water transport during the Han dynasty, the shipbuilding industry developed rapidly. In 1975, a shipyard of the late Qin or early Han period was excavated in Guangzhou. The yard comprised three building platforms.[2] These are estimated to have been capable of building large wooden ships 30 m long, 8 m wide, with a weight capacity of 60 metric tons.[3] The discovery offers us a glimpse of the scope of the Han shipbuilding industry, which cannot be separated from the use of iron tools. The rotary quern, a small hand mill for grinding grain, was an important tool that concerned the daily life of everyone. Without iron tools, the widespread use of this particular device would have been impossible. Masterpieces of stone, such as the carved pictorial stones and the gate towers and stone animals often found erected in front of Eastern Han tombs, were also the result of skillful application of fine quality iron tools by artists.

The superior quality of iron became all the more evident when it was used in weapons. By the early Western Han period, long iron swords had completely replaced the short bronze swords of the Warring States period. The length of the Warring States bronze sword was in general

🄴 汉代的铁器

根据考古发掘，中国炼铁的历史开始于春秋晚期。到了汉代，铁器的制造和使用已经很普遍。可以说，在社会生产和生活的各个方面，都离不开铁器。首先，如前面已经讲过的，在农具方面，有犁、镢、锸、铲、锄、镰等，它们在全国范围内被广泛使用，使得当时的农业生产有显著的提高（图 152）。历史学家估计，战国末年，燕、赵、韩、魏、齐、楚、秦七国人口总共二千万左右。[1]西汉中期以来，人口激增，据《汉书·地理志》记载，到西汉末年全国已将近六千万人。如果不是普遍使用铁农具耕作，以及使用铁工具来兴修水利工程，使粮食和其他农作物的产量提高，那是不能想象的。

在工具方面，有斧、锛、锤、凿、刀、锯、锥、钉等，它们使得各种木工、竹工、石工、土工等的效率不断提高，并使大规模的建筑工程得以顺利完成（图 153）。汉代水上交通频繁，造船业突飞猛进。1975 年在广州发掘了一处秦汉之际的造船工场，发现了三个造船台[2]，据估计，可以造长约 30 米、宽约 8 米、载重量可达 60 吨的大木船。[3]汉代造船业的规模于此可见一斑，而这正是与铁工具的使用分不开的。谷物加工用的转盘式的双扇石磨盘，关系着全国人民的最基本的日常生活，如果不是用铁工具来制作，就不可能得到迅速的普及。东汉大墓里常见的石刻画像，以及墓前所立的石阙和石兽之类，正是由于使用了优质的铁工具，才能成为雕刻家们的优秀的艺术作品。

在兵器方面，铁器的优越性更为突出。铁制的长剑在西汉前期就完全取代了战国以来的青铜短剑。战国时代的青铜剑，长度多不足

less than half a meter, whereas the length of the Han iron sword often measured about one meter. The superiority of steel was able to lengthen the sword blade by a hundred percent. In Western Han, a large iron knife with a ring at the end of its handle appeared. Its length was also one meter. This new weapon, unknown to previous periods, became one of the major weapons of the Eastern Han period. Fighting soldiers holding a shield in one hand and this kind of knife in the other are often depicted on pictorial stones. Although the form of bronze *ge*-halberd of the Shang and Zhou periods changed in the course of time, they were still being made and used in Western Han; but before long, they also were completely replaced by iron spears and *ji*-halberds. The length alone of the iron spearheads and *ji*-halberd heads was about half a meter, and the total length of these weapons, including their wooden shafts, could reach more than 2.5 m.[4] While arrowheads were still made of bronze in the Han dynasty, the stem of the arrowhead was made mostly of iron. However, gradually arrowheads made wholly of iron became popular, and finally they came to replace bronze ones. Due to the advancement in iron technology, the quality of armor improved noticeably. Archaeologists have excavated quite a number of specimens of Han iron armor. Among the best-preserved specimens are one excavated at the site of a frontier town in Dingxiang Prefecture (its capital located in present Holingor, Inner Mongolia) (figs. 154, 155) and another found in the tomb of Liu Sheng, the Han Prince Jing of Zhongshan, in Mancheng, Hebei.[5] The latter was an example of so-called fish-scale armor; it was made of more than 2,800 small iron plates. As a defensive device, large numbers of barbed iron balls were made to be placed on the ground outside the city walls. The thorny iron balls were so devised that no matter how each piece was placed, there was always one sharp thorn pointing upward. Their function was to deter marching soldiers and horses (fig. 156).[6] It was precisely these sorts of superior iron weapons that made it possible to deal with the powerful horsemen from the northern tribes. When

Chao Cuo analyzed the military situation between the Han and the Xiong Nu during the reign of Emperor Jing Di of Western Han, he pointed out that one of the advantages the Han had over the Xiong Nu was superior weaponry. The fact that the Han dynasty, following Qin, was able to establish a united empire over such a vast area was, in addition to social, economic, and other factors, also closely related to the application of superior iron weaponry in military affairs.

半米，而汉代的铁剑则往往长达一米左右，钢铁的优越性使剑的长度增加了一倍。柄首成环状的大铁刀，在西汉时就出现，长度亦多达一米；它完全是一种新兴的武器，为前代所未见，到了东汉就成为最主要的武器之一，在石刻画像上常可见到士兵们一手执盾，一手持刀，正在进行战斗的情形。殷周以来的铜戈，其形制随着时代而改变，直到西汉时还有被制作、使用的，但不久也被铁制的矛和戟所完全代替。汉代的铁戟和铁矛，仅戟头和矛头就有长近半米的，加上它们的木柄，全长可达两米半以上。[4] 汉代的矢镞，虽然仍有不少是铜质的，但其铤部已多改为铁制，而铁镞也开始盛行，到后来终于代替了铜镞。由于制铁技术的发展，铠甲的质量和性能有了显著的提高。在考古发掘工作中，已经发现了不少汉代铁甲的实物，其中以内蒙古呼和浩特附近汉定襄郡（治所在今内蒙古和林格尔）的边境城镇遗址出土的一件（图 154、155）和河北满城中山靖王刘胜墓内出土的一件为最完整[5]，它们的制作都很完备，特别是后者，是由二千八百多片细小的铁片编成的鱼鳞甲，尤为精致、完善。为了防止敌兵来袭，大量的铁蒺藜被散布在城墙以外的广大地段上，它们的设计很巧妙，系由四个方位均称的锐刺组成，无论怎样放置，总有一个尖刺是向上的，从而可使人足和马足受创（图 156）。[6] 正是由于掌握了各种先进的铁兵器，所以才能对付北方民族强大的骑兵。西汉景帝时，晁错分析汉朝与匈奴作战的军事形势，就指出汉朝优越的武器是克敌制胜的有利条件之一。继秦代之后，汉代建立统一的大帝国，它的版图达到了空前的规模，除了政治、经济等多方面的原因而外，这也是与军事装备上充分利用铁器的优越性分不开的。

Let us now turn to household utensils. Iron also played an important role in everyday life. Iron provided material for making *ding*-tripods, stoves, cooking pots, belt buckles, tweezers, fire tongs, scissors, kitchen knives, fishhooks, and needles (figs. 157, 158). The widespread use of iron cooking pots greatly facilitated household cooking. A huge iron pot, with a diameter measuring about 2 m, was found in Wafangzhuang, Nanyang, Henan Province; it was possibly used for boiling salt.[7] The kitchen knife—especially made to meet culinary needs—become differentiated from other knives. The Han scissors, like primitive scissors of other civilizations, were made of a bent iron rod with its two sharpened ends facing each other. The resilient nature of steel makes them operable. The convenience offered by scissors in cutting cloth and hair cannot be overemphasized. The iron needle was an indispensable item in the daily life of the Han people. Unfortunately, due to their small size and propensity to rust, needles are difficult to find. Up until today, the needle found in tomb number 167 at Fenghuangshan in Jiangling, Hubei Province, is the only example we have of Han needles. It was this kind of iron needle that was used in sewing and embroidering.[8] Rulers for measuring also were often made of iron. The marks and decorative patterns on an iron ruler found in the Mancheng Han tomb were inlaid with gold threads.[9] In Eastern Han, iron lamps were as popular as bronze lamps. An iron "twelve-branch lamp" found in a Han tomb in Luoyang exhibits the clever and elegant style of the artisan (fig. 159).[10] Even iron mirrors are often found in late Eastern Han tombs. Unfortunately, because of their tendency to rust, they have received much less attention than bronze mirrors. In fact, some of their decorative patterns are quite attractive. For example, through X rays we found that the decoration on the iron mirror discovered in the Han tomb at Leitai in Wuwei, Gansu, was elegantly inlaid with gold and silver threads in a phoenix design (figs. 160, 161).[11] It should not surprise us that when Cao Cao presented gifts to the emperor, he preferred iron mirrors to bronze.

In short, during the Han dynasty iron implements were closely related to national defense, on the one hand, and to economic life of the country, on the other. Therefore, the iron-manufacturing industry came to be an increasingly important sector of the economy, over which the ruling class found it essential to have control. According to the records in the "History of the Southern Yue" in *Shiji* and in the "Biography of the King of South Yue" in *Hanshu,* in early Western Han when the prince Zhao Tuo of

在生活用具方面，铁器也占重要的地位，从鼎、炉、釜等容器、炊具到带钩、镊子、火钳、剪刀、厨刀，以及钓鱼钩和缝衣针之类，无不应有尽有（图157、158）。铁釜的广泛使用，为炊事提供了方便；河南省南阳瓦房庄发现的一件大铁锅，直径达二米左右，可能是煮盐用的。[7] 厨刀从别的各种刀类中分化出来，专门按庖厨的需要而制造。汉代的剪刀，虽然和世界各地的初期剪刀一样，是用一根两端具有锋刃的铁条弯曲而成，利用钢铁的弹性而操作，但它在裁剪布帛乃至剪除须发等生活方面所提供的方便也是不可低估的。在汉代，铁制的缝衣针是日常生活中不可或缺的，但由于极其细小，锈蚀之余，难于发现，因而湖北江陵凤凰山一六七号墓出土的缝衣针就成为迄今唯一保存完好的遗品；当时缝制各种衣物以及在丝织品上刺绣美丽的花纹，用的就是这种铁针。[8] 1975 年在陕西省咸阳市发掘的一座西汉后期墓中，发现了一件漆盒，内有铁针七八枚，放在针筒里，但多已锈蚀断缺。度量用的尺子，也有许多是铁制的；满城汉墓出土的铁尺，其刻度和花纹系用金丝镶嵌。[9] 汉代虽盛行铜灯，但东汉时铁灯也很流行，洛阳等地汉墓中出土的"十二枝灯"等（图159），制作得相当精巧。[10] 甚至是镜子，也有不少是铁制的，往往在东汉后期的墓中被发现，只是由于已经锈蚀，有时不被人们所重视，其实它们的花纹是相当优美的。例如，甘肃武威雷台汉墓中的一枚铁镜，经 X 光透视，可以看出是用金丝和银丝镶嵌成夔凤纹，十分精致（图160、161）。[11] 这就无怪汉末的曹操要用许多铁镜，而不是铜镜，来赠送给皇帝。

总之，当时的铁器，关系到军备国防，关系到国计民生，所以制铁业就越来越成为特别重要的经济部门，统治阶级必须加以控制。据《史记·南越列传》和《汉书·南粤王传》记载，西汉初年，

the Southern Yue advocated separatism and independence, Empress Dowager Lü Hou ordered that shipment of iron implements to that area be banned. The court's punitive move brought on a drastic reaction from Zhao Tuo: he led an army and marched toward Changsha, threatening the central government. This incident demonstrates the importance of iron at that time. In early Western Han, the iron industry was sometimes controlled by the central government and sometimes by provincial lords and principalities. Each lord or prince installed his own iron officials to control iron manufacturing. For example, in the Linzi area of Shandong Province, seals have been found with such inscriptions as "Seal of Qi Iron Office," "Qi Iron Officer," "Qi Iron Office Deputy," and "Iron Deputy of Linzi" (figs. 162-65).[12] In addition, rich merchants, in an attempt to increase their wealth, ran privately owned iron manufactories. Thus, strong competition for control over the iron industry existed between the central government, the principalities, and the wealthy merchants. The strength of the central government greatly increased after the rebellion of the seven states in the Wu and Chu area was crushed by Emperor Jing Di. Eventually, in Wu Di's reign, the central government was able to monopolize the iron industry completely. Like salt, iron implements were manufactured and distributed by government offices.

According to the "Treatise on Geography" in *Hanshu*, more than forty iron offices were established, and they were located as far as Shandong and Jiangsu in the east, Gansu in the west, Liaoning in the northeast, and Sichuan and Yunnan in the southwest, covering a vast area. Inscriptions sometimes can be found on the objects made by the official manufactories. To mention some examples from the excavated finds, those made in the manufactories of the Henan Prefecture (present Luoyang) have the inscriptions "He 1," "He 2," "He 3"; those from the Nanyang Prefecture bear the characters "Yang 1," "Yang 2"; those from the Hedong Prefecture (present Xiaxian, Shanxi Province) have "Dong 2," "Dong 3." The characters "He," "Yang," and "Dong" represent names of prefectures, while the numbers "1," "2," and "3" designate the particular manufactory or workshop of that prefecture (fig. 166).[13]

Extensive investigations carried out since the founding of New China have uncovered many iron foundry sites in Qinghezhen in Beijing, Tengxian in Shandong, and Liguoyi in Xuzhou in Jiangsu.[14] Especially in Henan Province in the Central Plains area, more than a dozen such workshops and foundries have been found. Of these, large-scale excavations were carried out in the site located at Tieshenggou in Gongxian and the one at

南越赵佗搞分裂割据，闹独立，吕后就下令实行铁器禁运，以作为制裁，引起赵佗的强烈反应，甚至出兵进犯长沙，威胁朝廷，从这里也可以看出铁器的重要性。西汉初年，冶铁业有的控制在中央政府手里，有的却被控制在各地的诸侯王手里。诸侯王自设铁官，经营冶铁业，在山东临淄一带就有"齐铁官印"、"齐铁官长"、"齐铁官丞"和"临淄铁丞"等封泥流传下来，便是例证（图162—165）。[12]也有一些大商人，为了谋求巨富，私自经营冶铁业。因此，中央政府和各地诸侯王及富商大贾们互相争夺对冶铁业的控制权，相当激烈。汉景帝击败了吴楚七国的叛乱以后，中央政府的权力大大增强，终于在汉武帝时完全垄断了全国的冶铁业。铁器和食盐一样，由政府设铁官经营，实行官卖政策。

据《汉书·地理志》记载，汉代全国设铁官四十余处，其分布东起山东、江苏，西到甘肃，东北到辽宁，西南到四川、云南之间，范围十分广大。铁官所制的铁器，有时有铭文，作为它的标志。例如，根据出土的遗物，河南郡（今洛阳）所制的有"河一"、"河二"、"河三"字样，南阳郡（今河南南阳）所制的有"阳一"、"阳二"字样，河东郡（今山西夏县）所制有"东二"、"东三"字样；"河"、"阳"、"东"等字是郡名的简称，"一"、"二"、"三"等数字则是各郡铁官所属作坊和工场的编号（图166）。[13]

新中国成立以来，经过广泛调查，在北京清河镇、山东滕县、江苏徐州利国驿等许多地点发现了制铁工场的遗址。[14]特别是中原地区的河南省，迄今已发现的制铁工场和作坊的遗址已达十余处之多，其中巩县铁生沟和南阳瓦房庄两处已经过大规模的发掘。[15]

Wafangzhuang in Nanyang.[15] The former is dated from mid-Western Han to the Wang Mang period, the latter, from mid-Western Han to Eastern Han.

Tieshenggou iron foundry is located in a basin at the foot of Mount Song. There were workshops for smelting, casting, and forging. Only a few kilometers away in the mountains was a rich iron mine from which ore was obtained. Thus, this manufactory in fact encompassed facilities for the whole process from mining and smelting to manufacturing. Within the 2,000 m^2 already excavated, we have found an ore-dressing yard, eighteen smelting furnaces, one crucible furnace, and one forging furnace, as well as mixing pools, storage pits, and other auxiliary facilities (figs. 167, 168). From the excavated remains and objects, we can see that the ore was first delivered to the dressing yard, where it was crushed by hammers and screened so that the ore pieces were more or less the same size. After that, a certain proportion of limestone as a flux was mixed with the ore in the mixing pool. The mixture was then put in the smelting furnace, together with the fuel. The eighteen smelting furnaces can be divided into several types according to their different structures and functions. Some could be called "solid reduction furnaces." In this type of furnace the iron ore was reduced at low temperatures into spongelike bloom iron pieces. Others could be called "blast furnaces," where liquid cast iron was produced at high temperatures. There is another type that could be called a "steel puddling furnace." Smelted cast iron was put in this type of furnace. When it melted, the liquid was constantly stirred by the founder. Steel or wrought iron could be produced by this process. Most of the smelting furnaces were semisubterranean with walls made of refractory bricks, and both the bricks and the bottom of the furnace were covered with refractory clay. The smelted iron blooms produced were stored in the storage pit. The function of the "crucible furnace" was to melt cast iron. Various clay molds were found near it. They were used for casting various tools and utensils. Near the "forge furnace," used in tempering bloom iron and making implements, an iron anvil and a quenching pool were found. Three types of fuel were used: wood, coal, and coal cakes. The coal cakes were made of coal powder mixed with clay and quartz.[16] We found at this site many smelting furnaces, but only a few forging and crucible furnaces and casting molds, so we concluded that the main function of this foundry was smelting, and that forging and casting were secondary.[17]

前者的年代约自西汉中期至新莽时期，后者的年代则自西汉中期至东汉。

巩县铁生沟制铁作坊，坐落在嵩山脚下的一个盆地。作坊中有冶炼工场，也有铸造和锻造工场。附近相距仅数公里的山中有丰富的铁矿，所用矿石便是从那里开采的。因此，这个作坊实际上包括了从开矿、冶炼到制造成品的全部生产过程。在已经发掘的两千平方米的范围内，发现了矿石加工场一处、各种炼炉十八座、熔炉和锻炉各一座，并有配料池、储铁坑等附属设施（图167、168）。从发掘出来的遗迹和遗物可以看出，矿石运到矿石加工场，用铁锤击碎，筛子筛过，使其成为大小均匀的颗粒，并配以一定比例的石灰石作为熔剂，在配料池中搅拌后，与燃料一起放入炼炉。十八座炼炉的型式、结构和功效各有不同。有的可称"固态还原炉"，是用低温将铁矿石还原，炼成海绵状的"块炼铁"。有的可称"高炉"，用高温炼出液态的生铁。还有一种可称"炒钢炉"，是将已经炼好的生铁放在炉内，加热熔化时，不断进行搅拌，使生铁"炒"炼成钢或熟铁。各种炼炉多作半地穴式，用耐火砖砌成炉壁，壁上又涂耐火泥，炉底铺耐火土。炼出来的铁块，放在储铁坑内。熔炉一座，是熔化生铁用的，附近有一些泥范，用以铸造各种器物。锻炉一座，用于锻炼块炼铁并将它制作成器，在附近发现了锤打器物用的铁砧和淬火池。作坊中所用的燃料，据说有木柴、煤和煤饼三种，后者是用煤末掺以粘土和石英制成的。[16] 由于发现的炼炉很多，而锻炉、熔炉和铸范却都较少，因而可以认为这个制铁作坊以冶炼铁料为主，锻铸器物为次。[17]

The iron foundry at Wafangzhuang in Nanyang was located in Wanxian, the administrative seat of Nanyang Prefecture.[18] The iron office of Nanyang Prefecture was the most famous of its time. The Wafangzhuang site is probably one of the many foundries under the Nanyang iron office. Because the remnants of the ancient city walls of Wanxian still stand, we know that this foundry was located in the central part of the walled city. Because its location was far from the mines, its main function was to cast and forge, using cast-iron ingots smelted elsewhere or recycling old and worn-out iron utensils. Its main function was to manufacture various implements and utensils, just the opposite of the Tieshenggou foundry. Within the 3,000 m^2 already excavated, seventeen furnaces have been found. Some were crucible furnaces to melt cast iron for casting. At the site a large number of clay molds were found, including molds for vessels, such as *ding*-tripods, pots, and basins; agricultural implements and tools, such as pickaxes, spades, shovels, plowshares, axes, adzes, hammers, and chisels; and such carriage parts as axle-pins and bearings. It is evident that this foundry had a remarkable capacity, casting large numbers of a variety of items. Some furnaces were steel stirring furnaces, in which cast iron was melted and stirred into steel or wrought iron and was then forged into various tools and utensils. A large number of hammers and anvils for forging as well as many finished products like knives, sickles, and spearheads were also found. Unlike the Tieshenggou foundry, the sole fuel used here was wood.[19]

In recent years, excellent results have been achieved by the combined research efforts of archaeologists and metallurgists, especially of metallurgists in analyzing archaeologically excavated iron implements.[20] It has been shown that by the Spring and Autumn period at the latest (late sixth century B.C.) China had already employed the method of reducing iron ore with charcoal at relatively low temperatures (800-1,000°C) to a relatively pure but spongelike iron bloom. This method is called the "low temperature-solid reduction," or "bloom smelting" method. The product is called bloom-smelted iron (commonly known as wrought iron) and it can be forged into implements. A short piece of iron bar found in 1974 in a tomb of the late Spring and Autumn period in Liuhexian in Jiangsu was forged from this type of bloom-smelted iron.[21] By the late Warring States period, ironsmiths already knew how to produce steel out of wrought iron by the method of solid state carburization of the wrought iron. The technique was to heat pure iron in charcoal for an extended period of time at a temperature above 900°C, or to keep heating the iron

南阳瓦房庄制铁作坊,在汉南阳郡的治所宛县城内。[18] 南阳郡的铁官是当时最有名的,瓦房庄作坊当为南阳郡铁官所属的许多作坊之一。宛县的古城墙至今犹有不少遗留在地面上,从而可以判断这个制铁作坊的位置是在城内的中部。由于作坊设在大城市中,远离矿区,所以它的主要业务是利用从别处运来的已经炼好的生铁锭和废旧铁器作原料,在这里进行熔炼,重点在于制造各种器物,这与上述巩县铁生沟的情况恰好相反。在已经发掘的三千平方米的范围内,发现了十七座炉子。其中一部分炉子是熔炉,将生铁熔化,以供铸造。在遗址中发现了大量的泥范,其种类包括鼎、罐、盆等容器,镬、锸、铲、铧、斧、锛、锤、凿等农具和工具,以及惠和轴承等车具,可见所铸器物种类和数量之多。另外一些炉子则为"炒钢炉",将生铁炒炼成钢或熟铁,以锻制各种器物。锻制时所使用的铁锤和铁砧,以及已经锻制成的刀、镰、矛头等器物,在遗址中都有多量的发现。与巩县铁生沟不同,这里所用的燃料只是木柴。[19]

最近几年来,考古研究与冶金史研究相结合,主要是冶金学家们对考古发掘所得的铁器进行分析、研究,取得了很好的成绩。[20] 研究工作证明:至迟在春秋晚期(公元前 6 世纪末),中国已经使用在较低温度(800℃—1000℃)中用木炭还原铁矿石的方法得到比较纯净但质地疏松的铁块。这种炼铁的方法,称为"低温固体还原法",或称"块炼法",其产品称"块炼铁"(一般也称熟铁),可以锻造成器。1974 年江苏省六合县春秋晚期墓中出土的小铁条,便是用这种"块炼铁"锻制的。[21] 到了战国晚期,冶铁工匠们已掌握了把上述的"块炼铁"用固态渗碳的方法制钢,将纯铁于木炭中以 900℃以上的

in charcoal while forging. As a result, when enough carbon was absorbed by the iron, it turned into steel. A late Warring States sword excavated in 1973 in Yanxiadu in Yixian, Hebei, was made of steel produced by this method.[22]

In the two centuries following the late Warring States period, along with accumulated experience, forging technique also improved. The main technique was repeated forging. By means of repeated beating of the heated metal, the carbon content was evenly alloyed with the metal and impurities were reduced, thus greatly improving the quality of the steel. This early technology was known as "hundred-time forged steel." The sword worn by Liu Sheng and later found in his tomb was a product of this technology during its early stage (fig. 169). The new technology of mid-Western Han was developed from the old technique known as the "solid state carburization method" of the late Warring States period. The cast iron and the carbon infiltration method of the Han period were similar to the material and technique of the late Warring States, the difference being that the Han method extended the hammering and heating process. The hammering process not only forged the metal into the desired shape; it also reduced the number and size of impurities and alloyed the carbon evenly with the metal, thus raising the quality of the steel produced. If we compare the Yanxiadu sword from the Warring States period mentioned above and the Han sword found in Liu Sheng's tomb, we find that the raw materials were both solid-state carbon-infiltrated steel, but the former has an unevenly alloyed carbon content and a high content of larger-sized impurities, whereas the latter has an evenly distributed carbon content with fewer and smaller impurities. The main reason for the difference was that the latter had been produced by a repeated hammering and heating process. This is considered a major development in the history of metallurgy occurring between the late Warring States period and mid-Western Han.

In order to increase its sharpness, Liu Sheng's sword had also undergone the processes of "surface carbonization" and blade-edge quenching. Quenching was a technique of dipping heated steel in cold water in order to increase the strength and hardness of the metal. Only the edge of the blade of Liu Sheng's sword was treated with the quenching process. The result is that only the blade edges are hard and sharp while the body of the sword (the middle thicker part) remains relatively elastic and non-brittle. The same idea was applied in the surface carbonization process so that only the outside of the sword was hardened.

温度长时间加热，或锻造时将铁在木炭中反复加热，使碳渗入铁内而成为钢。1973 年河北易县燕下都出土的战国晚期的铁剑，就是用"块炼铁"渗碳成为低碳钢制成的。[22]

　　从战国晚期以后的一二百年中，随着经验的积累，技术的提高，主要是采取越来越多的反复锻打的方法，使钢内碳的均匀性不断改善，夹杂物的含量不断下降，从而使钢的质量有较大的提高，形成了早期"百炼钢"的工艺。满城汉墓中的刘胜佩剑，便是属于当时正在形成的"百炼钢"工艺的早期产品（图 169）。西汉中期的这种处于初级阶段的"百炼钢"，是在上述战国晚期的"块炼渗碳钢"的基础上直接发展而来的。所用的铁料和渗碳的方法都和战国晚期的相同，但增加了反复加热锻打的次数。锻打不仅起着器物加工成型的作用，而且更重要的是使钢铁中的夹杂物减少、减小，使碳分布均匀化，使钢的质量提高。拿上述燕下都的剑和刘胜佩剑相比，它们的原料同属"块炼渗碳钢"，但前者钢里含碳不均匀，杂质较多、较大，而后者则相反，钢内碳的分布均匀，杂质少而小，这主要便是由于后者大大增加了反复折叠锻打的次数。要之，从战国晚期的"块炼渗碳钢"到西汉中期的反复锻炼成钢，这是冶炼技术史上的一个大进展。

　　为了提高剑的锋利程度，刘胜佩剑还经过表面渗碳和刃部淬火。淬火是一种热处理技术，即将加热的钢放入水中，迅速冷却，以提高其强度和硬度。刘胜佩剑只在刃部淬火，所以剑刃坚硬、锋利，而脊部仍保持较好的韧性。表面渗碳，也是为了使作为剑的外层的刃部因渗碳而提高坚硬的程度。

Other weapons such as the knife, the *ji*-halberd, and the short sword excavated from the Han tomb in Mancheng also indicate a higher quality (fig. 170). A beautifully made desk knife inlaid with gold thread was also found there. Its forging process was similar to that of Liu Sheng's sword, only the body of the blade was made of a steel with lower carbon content and thus of lesser hardness. By reducing its hardness, the craftsman was able to carve the knife and inlay it with gold thread. However, since the blade edge had been infiltrated with carbon and quenched, the knife was hardened and the edge could easily be sharpened.[23]

On the other hand, as early as the early Warring States period in the fifth century B.C., shortly after the bloom smelting technique was developed, the Chinese founder invented a technique which produced cast iron that had more than 2 percent carbon content. An early Warring States iron adz excavated in Luoyang in 1975 was determined to be the earliest tool made of this kind of cast iron.[24] This is 1,800 years earlier than the development of similar techniques in other civilizations. The main factor in founding cast iron is high temperature. Because of the long history of bronze technology and improvements made in the bellows systems, it became possible to bring temperatures up to 1,100-1,200°C or more. At this high temperature the charcoal-reduced iron would rapidly absorb carbon, thus greatly lowering its melting point. When the temperature exceeds 1,146°C the iron with more than 2 percent carbon content begins to melt and its speed of carbon absorption increases. When the process accelerates, the result is completely melted cast iron. This kind of cast iron has a lower content of silicon, and no graphite. It is called white iron because its fracture appears white. It is hard but brittle in character.

In order to improve the quality of white iron, the early Warring States artisans treated it with an extended heating process, causing graphite to separate from the carbonized iron. The resulting cast iron, called elastic cast iron, was not brittle. This kind of iron was widely used for farm tools and weapons in the middle and late Warring States period. A great number of these were found in Warring States period sites and tombs in Changsha of Hunan, Daye of Hubei, and Yanxiadu in Yixian of Hebei. Many iron tools found in the Mancheng Han tomb of mid-Western Han were also made of this elastic cast iron.[25]

It is noteworthy that gray iron pieces were also found in the Mancheng Han tombs. These are the earliest gray iron items ever found in China.

　　满城汉墓出土的铁器，除上述佩剑而外，还有其他的兵器如刀、戟、短剑等，它们也都具有较高的质量（图 170）。另外还有一把错金的"书刀"，其制作工艺尤为精湛。它的冶炼过程和佩剑相似，只是刀身用含碳较低的钢锻成，硬度较低，便于刻槽镶嵌金丝，而刃部则渗碳、淬火，使其坚硬、锋利。[23]

　　另一方面，早在战国初年（公元前 5 世纪），即在开始掌握用"块炼法"炼铁之后不久，我国还发明了炼制含碳量在 2% 以上的生铁，用以铸成器具。1975 年洛阳出土的战国早期铁锛，便是经过鉴定的最早的用生铁铸成的工具。[24] 这比世界各国要早出一千八百年。冶炼生铁，主要是依靠高温。由于长期以来青铜冶铸技术的高度发展，鼓风的进一步加强，使冶炼时的温度能达 1100℃—1200℃ 以上。在这样的高温之下，被木炭还原而成的固态铁就迅速吸收碳，因而使它的熔点比纯铁大大降低。当冶炼温度超过 1146℃ 时，含碳量达到 2% 以上的铁就开始局部熔为液体，而它吸收碳的速度也就进一步提高，含碳量越来越高，熔化越来越快，终于全部熔化为生铁。这种生铁，含硅量低，不含石墨，由于断口光亮，故称"白口铁"，其性质脆而且硬。

　　为了改善生铁的性能，在战国初期也就已经掌握了将"白口铁"长时间加热，使碳化铁分解为铁和石墨，克服了"白口铁"性脆的缺点。经过这种柔化处理的生铁，称展性铸铁。这种展性铸铁，在战国中晚期已被广泛应用于制造农具和兵器等，在湖南长沙、湖北大冶和河北易县燕下都等战国遗址和墓葬中都有发现。到了西汉中期，以满城汉墓为例，亦有不少铁器是展性铸铁的制品。[25]

　　值得注意的是，在满城汉墓中还发现了一批"灰口铁"的铸件。这是迄今已发现的我国最早的"灰口铁"制品。所谓"灰口铁"，

The gray iron was produced by raising the heating temperature and speeding up the cooling process. During the treatment, the carbon content in excess of 2 percent would be separated from the cast iron in the form of thin graphite pieces. Gray iron is so named because the color of its fracture is gray. Its hardness is lower than white iron, but it is not as brittle. It stands up to wear and its surface can be smoothened. The pickax in the Han tomb of Mancheng was made of elastic cast iron, while the carriage bearings were made of gray iron, indicating that the characteristics of various kinds of cast iron were understood and utilized accordingly.[26]

The agricultural implements, tools, utensils, and weapons that were described initially can be divided into forged and cast items. Until mid-Western Han, forged items and cast items were invariably made of "bloomery iron" and cast iron, respectively. Cast items became more and more popular as the size of the furnace became larger and the bellowing system improved. However, the brittleness of cast iron greatly limited its use. On the other hand, the carburization method involved a great deal of labor in forging and both productivity and efficiency were low. In this situation, a new technique was invented to induce decarbonization of cast iron in solid state to become steel. An iron chisel excavated from Wafangzhuang in Nanyang has the appearance of a cast item. However, the structure of surface metal of the chisel, according to metallographic analysis, was clearly steel. Another chisel shows a carbon content of 0.6 to 1 percent. At the current technological level, a temperature above 1,500°C could not have been achieved. Moreover, there was no refractory material which could withstand such heat. Therefore this steel could not have been liquid. Hence we concluded that this type of steel must have been produced by decarburization in the solid state by some kind of heat treatment.[27] Because an arrowhead excavated from the Mancheng Han tomb was also made of this type of cast steel, we are quite sure this new technique had been developed by mid-Western Han.[28]

A more important new technique developed in late Western Han was the "puddling" steel method. Cast iron was heated into a semiliquid state. By constant agitation in an oxidizing atmosphere the hot metal could be decarburized. Wrought iron or steel, depending on the level of carbon content, could be produced by this process. Using cast iron, which could be easily produced in large quantities, as material for producing steel was a revolution in metallurgical history. Thus "hundred-time forged steel"

就是通过提高冶炼温度和降低冷却速度，使生铁中超过 2% 的那一部分碳成为片状石墨在凝固时析出，铁的断口呈灰色，所以称"灰口铁"。它具有硬度比"白口铁"低、脆性较小、耐磨、滑润性能良好等特点。满城汉墓出土的铁镬是展性铸铁的制品，而车轴承则为"灰口铁"铸件，这说明了当时已经掌握了不同种类的铸铁的性能特点，而加以具体的应用。[26]

我在讲演开始时就列举汉代在农具、工具、兵器、生活用具等方面的各种各样的铁器，它们有的是锻件，有的是铸件。直到西汉中期以前，锻件和铸件总是分别用块炼铁和生铁作为原料的。随着炼炉的加大，鼓风设施的改进，生铁冶炼技术不断发展，生铁铸件得到了越来越广泛的应用。但是，由于生铁质脆，其用途又不能不受到限制。块炼铁虽然可用以制成渗碳钢，但必须经过反复锤炼，要花费很大工夫，产量和效率是很低的。在这种情况下，遂又发明了一种新的工艺，使铸铁在固体状态下脱碳成钢。例如，南阳瓦房庄出土的一件铁凿，从外形看来无疑是铸件，但表面的金相分析证明它是钢的组织。有的铁凿经分析，其含碳量为约 0.6% 或约 1%。在当时的条件下，不可能有高于 1500℃ 的高温和与此相应的耐火材料，所以不可能是液态铸钢。因此，可以肯定，汉代的这种钢件，是利用热处理使铸铁在固态下脱碳成钢的。[27] 由于满城汉墓出土的铁镞也是属于这种固态脱碳成钢的铸件，可以肯定这种工艺早在西汉中期即已存在。[28]

更为重要的是，到了西汉后期，随着冶炼技术的进一步发展，终于出现了将生铁"炒"炼成钢的新方法。所谓生铁"炒"钢，就是将生铁加热成为半液体状态，加以不断地搅拌，利用空气中的氧使其脱碳，以获得不同含碳量的钢或熟铁。用生产效率很高的生铁作为制钢的原料，这是炼钢史上的一次革命。这样一来，"百炼钢"

could be obtained either by puddling cast iron into wrought iron and then carbonizing and forging it into steel, or by puddling cast iron until the desired carbon content was reached and then forging it into steel implements. A large iron knife excavated in a Han tomb at Cangshan in Shandong in 1974 has a gold-inlaid inscription which reads "thirty-time forged large knife" and is dated the sixth year of Yong Chu (A.D. 112) (fig. 171).[29] Metallurgists who made analyses of this knife concluded that it was made of puddled steel.[30]

From Emperor Wu Di to the end of Western Han, the iron industry was a monopoly of the state. Among those who worked in the government-run industrial mines and foundries, apart from the specialized artisans, were convicted criminals and corvée laborers. The large scale of the Han iron industry is shown by the fact that, according to the records in the "Biography of Gong Yu" in *Hanshu*, more than a hundred thousand miners were mobilized every year to mine copper and iron ores for the purpose of minting coins and smelting iron. In the late Western Han period, ironworkers in Yingchuan Prefecture (with its capital in modern Yuxian, Henan) and Shanyang Prefecture (its seat in today's Jinxiangxian, Shandong) rebelled in protest of repressive measures against them. In the early Eastern Han period, following the Western Han system, the government still monopolized the iron industry. But influential local power-holders often operated private foundries. The government was unable to enforce the law. Finally, in A.D. 88, Emperor He Di gave in and lifted the ban on private iron and salt production. From then on, both the iron and salt industries were gradually further controlled by local powers.

The Shandong Provincial Museum in its collection has a carved pictorial stone that depicts an iron foundry.[31] Among the twelve artisans shown working, four are bellowing the furnace with leather bellows, the rest are hammering and forging (fig. 172).[32] The stone was excavated at Hongdaoyuan in Tengxian, Shangdong, in 1930. Its date indicates it was made after the ban was lifted. It appears that the tomb's occupant, a powerful landlord, was engaged in the iron industry and for that reason had the manufacturing scene carved on the wall of his tomb. This stone not only provides us with a vivid depiction of iron manufacture, it also may furnish evidence that iron industry was then controlled by privately owned enterprises. However, it is also possible that this scene was carved on the walls of the tomb of a former iron official of the state.

既可用生铁"炒"成的熟铁为原料，经过渗碳锻打成钢，又可把生铁"炒"到所需要的含碳量，成为"炒钢"，然后反复加热锻打成为钢制品。1974年在山东苍山汉墓出土一件大铁刀，刀上的错金铭文称此刀为"三十炼大刀"，并记明其制作年代为永初六年（公元112年）（图171）。[29] 冶金学家将此刀进行分析、研究，认为它就是用"炒钢"为原料而制成的。[30]

自汉武帝时由国家垄断冶铁业以来，一直到西汉末年，仍然如此。在官营的工矿作坊中，参加劳动的除一些专门的工匠以外，有许多是被判罪的刑徒和被迫定期服徭役的民工。据《汉书·贡禹传》记载，为了铸钱及冶铁，到矿山开采铜铁所动用的劳动力每年在十万人以上，可见其规模之大。西汉晚年，颍川郡（其治所在今河南省禹县）和山阳郡（其治所在今山东省金乡县）的铁官徒因不堪压迫，曾先后起义。东汉初期，承袭西汉的制度，冶铁业仍由国家专营。但是，当时的豪强地主势力强大，他们往往私设工场，自造铁器，官府不能禁止。章和二年（公元88年），和帝即位，东汉中央政府终于不得不作出让步，宣布盐铁开禁。于是，冶铁业和制盐业一样，就被逐渐进一步控制在各地豪强地主的手中。山东省博物馆珍藏着一块画像石，上面刻绘着一幅冶铁图。[31] 图中有十二个工匠正在工场中操作，其中四人在用皮橐为炼炉鼓风，其余的人则在持锤锻制器物（图172）。[32] 这块画像石是1930年在山东省滕县宏道院出土的，其年代当在东汉盐铁开禁之后。正是由于豪强地主生前经营冶铁业，所以才将冶铁图刻绘在自己的墓壁上。画像不仅描绘了工场中的冶炼的情形，而且说明了制铁业已转入私人手中。当然，就这块画像石来说，也不能排除另一种可能性：一个生前曾任铁官的官僚，为了纪念其生平事迹，所以在墓内刻绘了一幅冶铁图。

208

152. Han dynasty iron implements unearthed in Luoyang, Gongxian, and other localities in Henan 洛阳、巩县及河南其他地区出土的汉代铁器

153. Han dynasty iron implements unearthed in Luoyang, Hebi, and other localities in Henan　洛阳、鹤壁及河南其他地区出土的汉代铁器

154. Iron armor plates unearthed at the Han city site in Huhhot, Inner Mongolia
内蒙古呼和浩特汉城遗址出土的铁铠甲

155. Reconstruction of the iron armor plates unearthed at the Han city site in Huhhot, Inner Mongolia
内蒙古呼和浩特汉城遗址出土的铁铠甲复原图

156. Barbed iron ball unearthed at the site of the Han city of Chang'an in Xi'an 汉长安城遗址出土的铁蒺藜

157. Iron stove and tray unearthed from a Han tomb in Luoyang 洛阳汉墓出土的铁炉

158. Iron cooking pot unearthed from a Han tomb in Luoyang 洛阳汉墓出土的铁釜

159. Iron lamp with twelve branches, unearthed from a Han tomb in Luoyang
洛阳汉墓出土的铁十二枝灯

160. Iron mirror unearthed from the Han tomb at Leitai in Wuwei, Gansu 甘肃武威雷台汉墓出土的铁镜

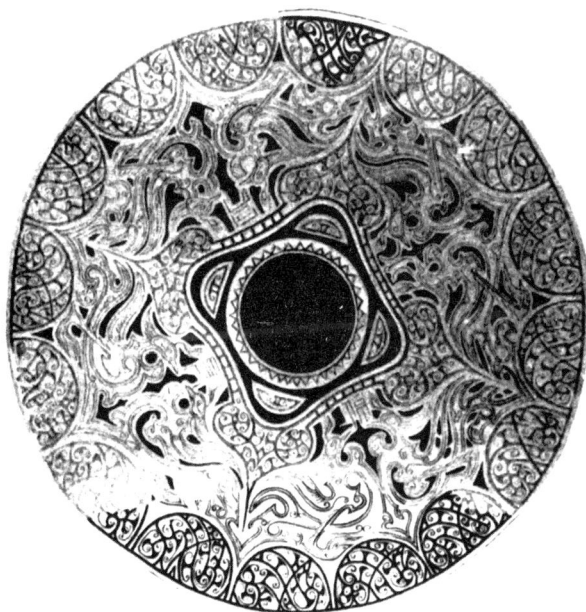

161. Reconstructed decorative designs on the iron mirror unearthed from the Han tomb at Leitai in Wuwei, Gansu
甘肃武威雷台汉墓出土的铁镜花纹复原图

162. Clay seal impressed with the inscription "Seal of Qi Iron Office," unearthed in Linzi, Shandong
山东临淄出土的刻有"齐铁官印"的封泥

163. Clay seal impressed with the inscription "Qi Iron Officer," unearthed in Linzi, Shandong
山东临淄出土的刻有"齐铁官长"的封泥

164. Clay seal impressed with the inscription "Qi Iron Office Deputy," unearthed in Linzi, Shandong
山东临淄出土的刻有"齐铁官丞"的封泥

165. Clay seal impressed with the inscription "Iron Deputy of Linzi," unearthed in Linzi, Shandong
山东临淄出土的刻有"临淄铁丞"的封泥

166. Inscriptions cast on Han dynasty iron implements unearthed in Shaanxi, Henan, Shandong, and other provinces
陕西、河南、山东等省出土的汉代铁器上的铭文

167. Remains of the smelting furnace at the Han dynasty iron foundry at Tieshenggou in Gongxian, Henan
河南巩县铁生沟汉代冶铁遗址中的熔炉

215

168. Remains of the mixing pool at the Han dynasty iron foundry site at Tieshenggou in Gongxian, Henan
河南巩县铁生沟汉代冶铁遗址中的配料池

169. Liu Sheng's personal sword and its accessory jade ornaments, unearthed from the Han tomb in Mancheng 满城汉墓中刘胜的佩剑及玉饰

170. Iron knife with gold inlays, unearthed from the Han tomb in Mancheng
满城汉墓出土的错金铁短剑

171. Iron knife and its gold-inlaid inscription, unearthed from a Han tomb in Cangshan, Shandong
山东苍山汉墓出土的铁刀和刀上的错金铭文

172. Iron founding as depicted in a pictorial stone of the Han dynasty discovered at Hongdaoyuan in Tengxian, Shandong
山东滕县宏道院出土的汉画像石中的冶铁图

217

CHAPTER 7   CERAMICS

Gray Pottery   In the realm of gray pottery, which already had a history stretching back to the Shang and Zhou periods, the Han potters attained an unsurpassed level of quality, basing their work on the achievements of the Warring States period. It is no exaggeration to say that in succeeding periods the techniques of gray pottery manufacture did not advance beyond the level attained by the Han potters. Their improvements in techniques of gray pottery firing are manifest in the pottery's color, which is gray; the firing, which was even and uniform; the firing temperature, which was above 1,000°C; the clay ware, which is hard; as well as in the increase in the number of large vessels. As to the last named—that is, large vessels—this statement is borne out by pottery *weng* from Han tombs in the vicinity of Luoyang, which often stand more than 50 cm in height (figs. 173, 174), and *jiugang* from the Han tombs at Mancheng, which often reach more than 70 cm in height.[1] Such aspects as hardness of ware and greater numbers of large vessels cannot be explained apart from improvements in the kilns. In 1956, more than twenty kilns from the Warring States, Western Han, and Eastern Han periods were excavated at the site of the old city of Wuji in Wu'anxian, Hebei Province; a comparison of these kilns reveals that the Han kiln chambers are larger, their fire tunnels longer, and their chimneys much improved in design (figs. 175-77).[2]

The bodies of all of the rounded Han dynasty gray pottery vessels were turned on the potter's wheel. Vessel shapes are regular and their surfaces are relatively smooth. In general, with the exception of occasional parallel bowstring lines incised on the wheel and some localized incised geometric designs and stamped patterns, the vessels lack decoration and can be called "plain" (figs. 178-80). In the early Western Han period a few vessel types, such as the *weng* and the *guan,* were still occasionally decorated with faint cord patterns;[3] but from the middle Western Han period onward, few vessels have cord marks. Popular for more than three thousand years—from Neolithic times down to early Han—the cord pattern finally died out (except in pottery roof tiles). The decline of the cord pattern must be considered one of the important characteristics of Han ceramics.

In Han tombs of all areas, pottery vessels with decoration painted in colors can be found. These wares also belong to the gray pottery family, the painted decoration having been applied after firing. Several pottery

贰 汉代的陶器

在讲述汉代的制陶业时，首先要提到的是，自商周以来的泥质灰陶系统的陶器，在战国时代的基础上，又向前发展了一步，达到了很高的水平。如果说此后历代的灰陶制作技术基本上是停留在汉代已经达到的水平上，这也并不是过于夸张之辞。汉代灰陶烧制技术的提高，表现在器物都呈青灰色，火候均匀，烧成温度约在摄氏1000度以上，质地坚实，同时也表现在大型器物的普遍增多。关于后者，洛阳等地汉墓中的陶瓮往往高达五十余厘米（图 173、174），满城汉墓中的陶酒缸高达七十余厘米，便是明显的例证。[1] 陶质的坚硬和大型器物的增多，是与陶窑的改进分不开的。1956 年在河北省武安县的午汲古城遗址中发掘了二十余座战国、西汉和东汉的陶窑，可以看出，汉代的窑与战国的窑相比，窑室的体积增大，火道加长，烟道的设计改善，就说明了以上的问题（图 175—177）。[2]

在制坯方面，汉代凡属圆形的灰陶器，无不采用轮制的方法。器物的形状规整，表面比较光滑，除了随着陶轮的旋转而刻划的少许平行的弦纹以及一些局部的几何形划纹和印纹以外，一般都没有什么花纹，基本上可以说是素面的（图 178—180）。西汉前期有少数器物如瓮、罐之类偶而还带有一些不甚明显的绳纹[3]，但到了西汉中期以后，带有绳纹的陶器几乎可以说是不复存在了。自新石器时代以来流行达三千余年之久的绳纹终于绝迹（除瓦以外），这不能不说是汉代陶器的重要特点之一。

在各地汉墓中，往往可以发现一些绘有彩色花纹的陶器。这些陶器也属灰陶，彩色的花纹是在陶器烧成以后才绘描的。例如，洛阳

hu vessels have been discovered in Han tombs in Luoyang and a number of pottery *hu* and *pen* vessels have been recovered from the Han tombs at Mancheng.⁴ The colors are bright and the painting refined; all are handsome works of art (figs. 181, 182). Since the decoration was applied only after the vessels were fired, however, the pigments tend to flake readily. These painted wares have been found only in tombs; not a single one has been recovered from a residential area. Thus, we can surmise that they were made for funerary use only. In addition to the painted wares, there are also gray pottery vessels of the Han period whose surfaces were coated with lacquer, in imitation of (true) lacquerware vessels. A number of gray pottery vessels coated with thick black or brown lacquer have been discovered in Han tombs in Yinqueshan in Linyi, Shandong Province; in Shuanggudui in Fuyang, Anhui Province; and in Dafentou in Yunmeng, Hubei Province.⁵ All of these closely resemble lacquerware (figs. 183-85). A lacquer-coated pottery *hu* from the Han tomb at Dafentou is called a *xiuhua waweng*, or "lacquer-painted pottery vessel," in the inventory tablet of that tomb.

In terms of shape, among the few early Western Han vessels with cord-marked decoration, such as the *weng* and *guan* mentioned above, are ones which have rounded bases (fig. 186).⁶ From the middle Western Han period on, however, almost all of the pottery vessels have flat bottoms, with the exception of three-legged and ring-footed vessels. Already at some time before the advent of the Han dynasty, the pottery *li*—current from the Neolithic through the Shang and Western Zhou periods—had disappeared. The pottery *dou*, which was popular in the Warring States period, was still frequently seen in early Western Han, but not long thereafter it too disappeared. The pottery *fang* did not appear until in the late Warring States period; it was most popular in the Western Han period but is very seldom seen in Eastern Han. In both Western and Eastern Han, the pottery *ding* and *zhong* are the most commonly encountered bronze-derived shapes. Even these, however, were seldom seen from the Wei and Jin periods onward, subsequent to the decline of bronze vessels. In addition to these, there is the *yadanhu*, or "duck-egg jar," a vessel of unusual shape which appeared in the closing years of the Warring States period. It continued to be an important and popular shape in the Qin and early Western Han periods but then disappeared in middle Western Han (fig. 187). The forms of the various other members of the gray pottery facility—such as the *weng*, *guan*, *he*, *zun*, *pen*, and *wan*—also changed through time, never ceasing to evolve. In short, in Han dynasty gray ceramic wares, the types are numerous and the functions varied; their popularity was not restricted to the Yellow

汉墓中发现的一些陶壶和满城汉墓中发现的许多陶壶和陶盆⁴，色彩鲜艳，绘描精致，都是优美的艺术品（图 181、182）。但是，由于花纹是器物烧成以后才绘描的，所以易于脱落，而且除了在坟墓中发现的以外，在居住址里没有发现过这种彩绘的陶器，因而可以肯定它们是专为随葬而作的。此外，汉代还有在灰陶的表面涂漆，以模仿漆器的。山东临沂银雀山汉墓、安徽阜阳双古堆汉墓和湖北云梦大坟头汉墓中的许多灰陶器，涂有浓厚的黑色或褐色漆，很像漆器（图 183—185）。⁵ 大坟头汉墓的一件涂漆陶壶在该墓的"赠方"中被称为"縣画瓦瓷"，便是例证。

在器形方面，上述西汉前期的少数瓮、罐等带有绳纹的器物有时还有系圆底的（图 186）⁶，从西汉中期以后，除了三足器和圈足器以外，几乎所有的陶器都是平底的。从新石器时代到商代和西周一直流行的陶鬲，在汉代之前早已绝迹。战国时代流行的陶豆，在西汉初期还偶有所见，但不久就消失了。陶钫是战国晚期才开始出现的，西汉时很流行，但到东汉也就极少见了。无论是西汉或东汉，陶鼎和陶钟都是最常见的仿铜的陶器，但到了魏晋以后，随着青铜器的衰落，终于近于绝迹了。此外，战国末年出现的一种造型奇特的"鸭蛋壶"，主要流行于秦代和西汉前期，西汉中后期以后也就消失了（图 187）。其他各种属于泥质灰陶系统的器物，如瓮、罐、盒、樽、盆、碗之类，其形态也随着年代的推移而不断演变。总之，汉代的灰陶，种类繁多，用途各异，它们不仅流行于黄河流域

River valley or even to the North in general, but spread to all parts of the country. They were the mainstay of Han ceramics.

Hard Pottery   At the same time, however, to the south of the Yangtze River, in that vast area including Guangdong, Guangxi, Hunan, Jiangxi, Fujian, Zhejiang, and southern Jiangsu, there was another common type of ceramic ware called *ying tao*, or "hard pottery," coexisting with the gray pottery described above. These hard pottery pieces were made from a dense and strongly adhesive clay native to the South. In contrast to gray pottery, hard pottery vessels were fired at a higher temperature and the ceramic paste was much harder. On the surface of the vessels there is often a stamp-impressed checkerboard pattern, or there may be an incised wave or sawtooth pattern, in marked distinction to the plain, undecorated gray pottery vessels discussed above (figs. 188-91). Vessel types include the *weng, guan, hu, he,* and *wan.* But, in comparison with the various types of the gray pottery family, the hard pottery pieces have their distinctive style. In the Guangzhou area, for example, there is a type of *hu,* called the *pao hu,* or "gourd-shaped jar," whose shape resembles a gourd (*pao-gua*)(fig. 192). And in Guangzhou and Changsha there are the *silianguan,* or "four-linked *guan*," and *wulianguan,* or "five-linked *guan*," in which four or five small *guan* vessels are connected (fig. 193). A number of vessels have loop handles at their shoulders or waists for tying cords. And there are also a few small *he* and *guan* with three short legs attached at their bases (fig. 194).[7] In short, the ceramic paste, the firing, the decoration, and the shapes of the vessels all reveal that this hard pottery from the Jiangnan ("South of the Yangtze") area inherited the traditions of the so-called "hard pottery with impressed geometric patterns" which had been developing in that area since late Neolithic times. In the Han dynasty it established itself as a separate tradition.

Glazed Pottery   A new invention of the Han dynasty potters was a ceramic ware with a thick brown or green glaze. This ware began to appear in the late middle Western Han period, especially around

Guanzhong in Shaanxi Province and Luoyang in Henan Province.[8] Afterward it developed rapidly, and by the late Western Han period it was already common, being used throughout a larger area. By Eastern Han not only had it spread throughout the entire Yellow River valley and the North of China in general, it was often seen in the Yangtze River valley as well. Generally speaking, the brown glazed ware appeared earlier, the green glazed ware later. However, the green glazed ware enjoyed great popularity during Eastern Han and became much

和北方地区，而且普及于全国，可以说是当时陶器的主流。

但是，另一方面，必须指出的是，在长江以南，包括广东、广西、湖南、江西、福建、浙江及江苏南部等广大地区，除了上述的灰陶以外，还普遍存在着另一类陶器，称为硬陶。这种硬陶，是用当地的一种密度较大、粘性较强的粘土制成，与灰陶相比，烧制火候更高，陶质更坚硬。器物的表面往往拍印着细密的方格纹，或刻划有水波形纹、锯齿形纹等等，与上述基本上是素面无纹的灰陶迥然相异（图188—191）。器物的种类有瓮、罐、壶、盒、碗等，与灰陶系统的各种陶器相比，它们的器形也别具风格。例如，广州地区有一种壶，称为匏壶，其形状有如匏瓜（图192）；广州、长沙等地有一种"四联罐"或"五联罐"，系由四个或五个小罐互相接合而成（图193）。有许多器物，在肩部或腹部附有系绳用的钮；也有一些小型的盒和罐，在底部附有低矮的三足（图194）。[7]总之，从陶质、火候、纹饰和器形等各个方面看来，可以认为，长江以南广大地区的这种硬陶是继承了当地自新石器时代晚期以来的所谓"几何印纹硬陶"的余绪，在汉代陶器中自成一个系统。

汉代制陶业的一项新的发明，是一种浓厚的棕黄色和绿色的釉陶。它们的开始出现，是在西汉的中后期，地区主要是在陕西省的关中和河南省的洛阳一带[8]，但以后发展很快，到西汉后期即已相当盛行，流行的地区也有所扩大。东汉时，这种釉陶不仅已普及到整个黄河流域和北方地区，甚至在长江流域也颇有所见。一般说来，棕黄色的釉陶出现较早，绿色的釉陶出现较晚，但后者在东汉时大量流行，又远较前者为普遍。这种浓厚的棕黄色和绿色的釉陶，

more widespread than the brown glazed ware. Its glaze contains a large amount of oxidized lead and its firing temperature was relatively low—no more than about 800°C—so it is often called "lead glazed" or "soft glazed" ware. And since it was popular mainly in the Yellow River valley and in the North of China, it can also be termed "Northern glazed ware." The types include the *ding* and *zhong* and a few other bronze-derived shapes. In addition, there are models of granaries, stoves, water wells, and towers, as well as images of such animals as the chicken and dog (figs. 195-97). For several reasons these are considered to have been made for funerary purposes only, not for actual use: first, the red core of this ware is not too hard; second, the glaze readily flakes or deteriorates; and, especially, they were buried in tombs, almost never being found in residential areas.

Although China has had glazed ceramics ever since the Shang and Western Zhou periods, the glazes of those early wares are all light green ones fired at high temperatures, unrelated to the low-fired brown or green lead glazes discussed above. Thus, it was once assumed that the sudden appearance of lead glazes in the late middle Western Han period might be attributable to the influence of glazed wares from Western Asia that were transmitted to China at the time of Han Wu Di, who sent envoys to the West to establish relations and trade. It is widely known that, as early as the Assyrian empire and the Achaemenid empire of Persia, numerous types of glazed ceramic wares had appeared in the area of such modern West Asian countries as Iran and Iraq. By the time of the Parthians, who were contemporaneous with the Han dynasty, vessels with monochrome glazes in green or brown had gained currency; green glazes especially were often used for ceramic coffins. This Parthian glazed ceramic ware was also low-fired, and in appearance it bears a strong resemblance to that of the Han dynasty wares. The "Xiyu Section" of the *Hanshu* relates that after the Han envoys crossed Central Asia and established ties with Parthia, Parthian articles of various types flowed into

China. Thus, the appearance of lead glazes in the late middle Western Han period might be the result of influence from Parthian glazed wares. However, another school of thought believes that the Chinese must have invented lead glazes first, without reference to West Asian glazed wares, even though the latter and the Han dynasty lead wares are both low-fired; this is because the components of the glazes are not identical and the appearance of Chinese lead glazes might date as early as the Warring States period.[9] But, from a great number of Warring States and Western

所用釉药中含有大量的氧化铅，烧制的火候并不高，仅约摄氏 800 度左右，所以被称为"铅釉"或"软釉"，由于主要流行于黄河流域和北方地区，因而在这里也可称为"北方釉陶"。它们在器形上的种类，有鼎、锺等仿铜的容器，也有仓、灶、井、楼阁等模型及鸡、犬等动物偶像（图 195—197）。由于这种釉陶的内胎（一般呈砖红色）并不很坚实，釉也易于脱落或变质，特别是由于它们只是作为随葬品而存在于坟墓中，在居住址里极少发现，所以使人怀疑它们可能是专为随葬而作，不是真正的实用器。

应该指出的是，虽然中国自商代和西周以来即有釉陶，但所施的釉都属浅色的青釉，烧成温度甚高，与上述棕黄色和绿色的低温的铅釉并不相同。因此，曾经有一种看法认为，铅釉在西汉中后期的突然出现可能与汉武帝时通西域，加强了中国与西亚的交通和贸易，从而受到西亚地区釉陶的影响有关。如所周知，在西亚的伊朗、伊拉克等地，早在亚述帝国和波斯的阿契美尼德王朝时期，就盛行各种釉陶制品。到了与汉代同时的安息王朝时，则流行绿、褐等单色的釉陶器，甚至在陶制的棺材上也多施绿色釉。安息的这种釉陶，亦系低温烧成，从外表看来，与汉代的铅釉很相似。据《汉书·西域传》记载，汉通西域以后，与安息的交往频繁，安息的各种事物颇有传入中国的。因此，可以认为，铅釉在西汉中后期的出现，正是由于受到安息釉陶影响的结果。但是，也有不同的意见认为，西亚的釉陶与汉代的铅釉虽然同属低温烧成，但釉的成分有所不同，而中国铅釉出现的年代则又可以上溯到战国，从而认为铅釉为中国所首创，与西亚的釉陶无关。[9] 其实，从新中国成立以来

Han period tombs excavated since the founding of New China, we know that lead glazed vessels may not necessarily have appeared so early as the Warring States period. An answer to the question of whether or not West Asian glazed ceramics and Han dynasty lead glazed wares are physically identical will have to await further research and analysis. Archaeological excavations have revealed that, although lead glazes continued to be used through the Wei, Jin, and succeeding periods, their quality declined significantly. The art of lead glazing was revived in the Tang dynasty, whereupon great progress was made and glorious achievements attained.

Hard pottery pieces coated with a thin layer of glaze have been discovered in many places in the South, but this glaze is quite different from the lead glazes of the Northern glazed wares. Whether yellow or green, the color is always light. The pieces are always very high-fired, and they belong to the family of celadon (or light green) glazed wares. Moreover, *ping*, or bottles with two ears or handles, have been found in late Western Han tombs in such places as Changsha in Hunan Province and Haizhou in Jiangsu Province.[10] The clay body of these is purplish brown in color and extremely hard. The green glaze on the neck and shoulder portions of this *ping* tends to be relatively thick. These pieces also belong to the Southern group of glazed wares (fig. 198). In addition, several identical glazed bottles, perhaps imported from the South, have been discovered in late Western Han tombs in Luoyang (fig. 199).[11] These hard-bodied glazed potteries, which were popular mainly in the South, are most certainly related to celadon glazed stonewares of the Wei and Jin periods. All characteristics considered, however, there is still a great distance between the glazed hard potteries of the South and the celadon glazed stonewares.

Celadon   It was formerly believed that true celadon, or green-glazed stoneware, first appeared in the state of Wu during the Three Kingdoms period and that the various types of green-glazed stoneware vessels unearthed from tombs in the area of Wuchang and Nanjing, the capital area of the state of Wu—dating to A.D. 227, 251, and 265 are standard examples of that ware.[12] From recent investigation, excavation, and research, however, we now believe that green-glazed stoneware vessels had already appeared as early as the late Eastern Han period, first in Zhejiang Province in the region of Shaoxing and Shangyu. Archaeologists have investigated many old kiln sites in the Shangyu area, among which are a number that belong to Eastern Han; their shape and structure are those of the so-called dragon kilns. In this type of kiln, which was built on the side of a small hill, the kiln chamber is low and narrow, but quite long,

对大量的战国和西汉墓葬的发掘来看，铅釉陶器的出现未必能早到战国时代。至于西亚的釉陶与汉代铅釉的性质是否相同，则需要进一步作分析研究。考古发掘工作表明，到了魏晋以后，陶器上施铅釉的工艺虽然继续存在，但和汉代相比，显然是衰落了。

与"北方釉陶"所施的"铅釉"不同，在南方各地发现的各种硬陶上往往有一层薄薄的釉，或黄或绿，颜色都很浅，烧成温度甚高，属于青釉的系统。此外，在湖南长沙、江苏海州等地的西汉后期墓中有一种附有双耳的陶瓶，胎壁呈紫褐色，甚坚硬，颈部和肩部施较厚的绿色釉，亦属南方系统的釉陶（图 198）。[10] 在洛阳的西汉晚期墓中也发现了同样的釉陶瓶（图 199），估计可能是从南方传来的。[11] 这些主要流行于南方地区的硬质釉陶，与魏晋时期的青瓷有一定的渊源关系，但从各方面的条件看来，它们与青瓷器之间还存在着很大的差距。

以往认为，真正的青瓷器是在三国时代的吴地开始出现的，在吴的首都武昌和南京附近发现的有黄武六年（公元 227 年）、赤乌十四年（公元 251 年）、甘露元年（公元 265 年）等纪年的墓中所出土的各种青瓷器便是典型的代表。[12] 但是，经过近年来的调查、发掘和研究，可以认为，早在东汉的后期，首先是在浙江省的绍兴、上虞一带，已经出现了青瓷器。考古工作者在上虞地区调查了许多古窑址，其中有不少是属于东汉时期的，它们的形制和结构属于所谓"龙窑"。这种窑是利用山坡的斜面筑成，窑室较狭、较低，

a shape advantageous in circulating the air, and thus, in elevating the temperature. In the shreds unearthed at the kiln sites, the glaze is light green in color, and after careful scrutiny it shows all the characteristics of standard stoneware. A complete *sixiguan*—that is, a *guan* with four loops for tying a cord—from the late Eastern Han period was obtained near one of the kiln sites, and it is typical of the green-glazed stoneware of the period.[13] Similar *sixiguan* have also been recovered from late Eastern Han tombs in Luoyang, Henan Province, and in Boxian, Anhui Province;[14] their shape implies that they also belong to the Southern group. Preserved in tombs of relatives of Cao Cao discovered in 1977 in Yuanbaokengcun and Dongyuancun, Boxian, are a large number of green-glazed stoneware vessels characterized by the *sixiguan*. Their shiny glaze and the absence of impurities in their bodies indicate that by late Eastern Han the technique of manufacturing green-glazed stoneware vessels was already quite advanced.[15] In summary, the development of green-glazed stoneware must be considered another important mark of the creativity of the Han dynasty potters.

Pottery Types Another distinguishing characteristic of Han dynasty ceramics is the extreme variety of articles produced. In general, pottery containers of the Han dynasty can be divided into two categories. The first category—vessels derived from bronze shapes—includes the *ding*, *dou, zhong, fang*, and other such vessels; in general these shapes gradually declined in importance during the course of the Han dynasty. The second category—articles for daily use—includes the *weng, guan, ping, he, pen, wan*, and other such vessels; the types are varied and the shapes complex. In addition to these, there are a number of pottery articles generally for daily use, but not for food or drink and not for storage, articles such as tables, lamps, censers, and money jars (figs. 200-02). From the middle Western Han period onward, one of the most important characteristics of the potter's art was the prevalence of various types of pottery *mingqi*, or burial articles, for funerary use—a reflection of changes in burial customs. The variety of types and the quantity of objects were staggering. The first to appear were models of granaries and stoves. They were already present in tombs of the early Western Han period, but they gained widespread popularity after middle Western Han. Other models were also made—water wells, millstones, pigsties, towers, buildings for grinding grain, paddy fields, and fish ponds—as well as images of such animals as pigs, sheep, horses, dogs, chickens, and ducks. In short, almost any object that could be named was likely to have been crafted in clay. As time progressed, the types became more numerous, especially after Eastern Han.

但却很长，有利于通风，从而使温度提高。窑址中出土的瓷片，釉呈淡青色，经鉴定，各方面都符合瓷器的标准。在窑址附近采集的一件东汉晚期的完整的"四系罐"，便是当时典型的青瓷器。[13] 类似的"四系罐"，在河南洛阳和安徽亳县的东汉后期的墓中也有发现[14]，从它们的器形看来，似乎也属南方的产品。特别是 1977 年在亳县元宝坑村和董园村发现的曹操的宗族墓中，存在着以四系罐为代表的大量青瓷器，釉色光亮，质地纯净，说明了东汉晚年制造青瓷的技术已经相当成熟。[15] 总之，青瓷器的开始出现，是汉代制陶业的又一重要的创造。

汉代制陶业的特点，还表现在器物种类的极其多样化。汉代作为容器的陶器，大体上可分两类。一类是鼎、豆、锺、钫等模仿铜器的器物，总的说来，它们在汉代是在逐渐趋向衰落。另一类是瓮、罐、瓶、盒、盆、碗等日常用器，种类繁多，器形复杂。除此以外，还有不少陶器，如案、灯、熏炉以及扑满之类，既非饮食器，亦非贮藏器，而是一般的生活用具（图 200—202）。在制陶工艺上最富特色的是，随着丧葬习俗的改变，在西汉中期以后，还盛行制作各种专为随葬用的陶质明器，种类之多，数量之大，达到了惊人的程度。最初出现的是仓和灶，它们在秦和西汉前期的墓中即有所见，但普遍流行则在西汉中期以后。其他诸如井、磨、猪圈、楼阁、碓房、农田和陂塘等模型，以及猪、羊、马、狗、鸡、鸭等动物偶像，应有尽有，不一而足，时代越晚，特别是东汉以后，种类越多。有些地区的汉墓中有一种小型的陶瓶，外形像枭，过去曾被误认为"三代器"，其实是汉代特有的一种随葬陶器。

Pottery figurines were also buried in great numbers. These pottery burial articles were often exquisitely crafted; for example, a number of lively, painted pottery figures on horseback have been unearthed from a Western Han tomb in Yangjiawan in Xianyang, Shaanxi Province. (fig. 203).[16] And pottery dogs and sheep (from an Eastern Han tomb in Baiquancun, Huixian, Henan Province) were sculpted with such verisimilitude that they must be called masterworks of the sculptor's art (figs. 204, 205).[17]

Ceramic Industry The most widely used articles of daily life were pottery. They are comparatively easy to make and most must have been made by small, privately operated workshops. But, during the Han dynasty, many local governments also owned their own workshops and pottery articles from them often have stamped marks. To give some examples: vessels stamped "He ting" and "He shi," unearthed from the site of the Han city of Henanxian in Luoyang (fig. 206); vessels stamped "Shan ting" and "Shan shi," unearthed from Han tombs in Shanxian, Henan Province (figs. 207, 208); vessels marked "Han ting," recovered from Han dynasty sites in Handan, Hebei Province (fig. 209); and vessels stamped "An ting," unearthed from the site of the Han city at Anyi in Xiaxian, Shanxi Province (fig. 210).[18] From excavations at the site of the Han city of Henanxian we have learned that those vessels marked "He ting" are earlier and belong to early Western Han, while those marked "He shi" are later, belonging to late Western Han.[19] The characters "ting" and "shi" in the marks refer respectively to the craft and commercial districts of the cities, which in Han times were under the supervision of the local governments. The marks just discussed indicate that these ceramic vessels were made by workshops belonging to the government agencies which supervised crafts and commerce.[20]

A piece of clay with an impressed seal reading "An cheng tao wei" provides the best insight into the government-controlled workshops (fig. 211).[21] The characters on the seal indicate that at that time Anchengxian in Runan Jun (modern Zhengyang, Henan Province) had an official solely responsible for supervising the ceramic industry.[22] It is important to note that the last character in the seal, "wei," is a military title. That a military official was supervising the ceramic workshops most probably indicates that in the government-operated kilns many workers were convicted criminals who had been organized for work along military lines.

各式各样的陶俑，亦被大量制作以随葬。这些陶质的明器，有时制作得很精致。例如：陕西咸阳杨家湾西汉墓中的大量骑马陶俑，造型生动，并施彩绘（图 203）。[16] 河南辉县百泉村东汉墓中的陶狗和陶羊，塑造得十分逼真，堪称塑像艺术中的杰作（图 204、205）。[17]

陶器是日常生活中最普遍的用品，制作又比较容易，所以应该多为私营的小规模的手工业作坊所制造。但是，在汉代，各地的官府也普遍经营陶器制造业。由各地官府经营的手工业作坊，所制陶器往往印有戳记。例如：洛阳汉河南县城遗址出土的陶器印有"河亭"、"河市"字样（图 206），河南陕县汉墓中出土的陶器印有"陕亭"、"陕市"字样（图 207、208），河北邯郸汉代遗址出土的陶器印有"邯亭"字样（图 209），山西夏县安邑汉城遗址出土的陶器印有"安亭"字样（图 210），等等。[18] 根据汉河南县城遗址的发掘，可以认为，印有"河亭"字样的陶器年代较早，属西汉前期，印有"河市"字样的陶器年代较晚，属西汉晚期。[19] 戳印中的"亭"和"市"的意义是相同的，是指汉代各地城市中的手工业和商业区，它们是由官府来管理的。上述的各种戳印，说明了这些陶器是由各地官府中主管手工业和商业的机构所属的作坊制作的。[20]

最能说明汉代各地存在着官营的制陶手工业的，是一块传世的"安城陶尉"的封泥（图 211）。[21] 它说明了当时汝南郡的安城县（今河南省正阳）设有专门管理制陶业的官吏。[22] 值得注意的是，"尉"是一种武职的职称。由武职的官吏来主管制陶业，可能是由于在官营的制陶手工业作坊中从事劳动的主要是许多被判刑的刑徒，他们大概是按照军事性的编制被组织起来的。

Bricks   The manufacture of bricks and pottery roof tiles was an important aspect of the Han dynasty ceramic industry. In ancient China, the earliest bricks were exceptionally large, most of them measuring more than a meter in length. The interior of these bricks is hollow, so they are called *kongxinzhuan*, that is, "hollow core bricks," or simply "hollow bricks"(fig. 212). They began to appear in the late Warring States period and were limited in area of use to the Central Plains. They were not used in building houses, but rather in constructing tombs. Hollow bricks were most commonly used in the Western Han period. More than half of the many Western Han tombs excavated in such areas as Baisha in Yuxian and Shaogou in Luoyang (both in Henan Province) were constructed with these hollow bricks.[23] Throughout the Western Han, hollow bricks were used in tombs only, their use not being further extended. And the area in which they were commonly used was also still limited to the region including present-day Henan, central Shaanxi, and southern Shanxi. Although the great majority are rectangular, a few of the Western Han hollow bricks are triangular or long and strip-like, convenient shapes for constructing tomb entrances. The decorative motifs on the bricks were designed to enhance the tomb interiors, and they were impressed one by one with a stamp. In addition to geometric patterns, the motifs include numerous varieties of plants and animals as well as human figures, horses and carriages, and buildings.[24] With the coming of Eastern Han, the use of hollow bricks suddenly declined and eventually died out.

True bricks appeared in early Western Han. They were one of the Han dynasty's great contributions to architecture. In contrast to the hollow bricks discussed above, they were all small, solid, and rectangular or square, the length usually ranging between 20 and 30 cm. We call them "small bricks" to distinguish them from the large, hollow bricks discussed above (fig. 213). They were used in all types of buildings, the rectangular bricks predominating over the square ones. Square bricks were used only for paving floors (fig. 214). In order to meet architectural needs, the size of the bricks had to be regularized. The length, width, and thickness of the rectangular bricks followed a standard formula, the width being one-half the length and the thickness one-fourth the width. Once the small bricks appeared, they were used extensively, quickly spreading to all parts of the country. As the findings from excavations at the Han city site at Henanxian in Luoyang reveal, small, rectangular bricks were used in constructing all types of dwellings and granaries and were also used in lining the walls of water wells (fig. 215).[25] At the Han site of Chang'an in

　　制砖和造瓦，是汉代陶业的一个重要的方面。在中国古代，最初的砖是一种体积庞大的特殊的砖，长度一般都在一米以上，内部是空的，所以称为空心砖（图212）。它开始出现于战国晚期，地区限在中原，其用途主要不在于建筑房屋，而在于造墓。西汉是空心砖的极盛时期，在河南禹县白沙和洛阳烧沟等地发掘的大量的西汉墓，几乎有半数是用这种空心砖建筑的。[23] 但是，在汉代，除了筑墓以外，空心砖的用途并未被推广，它的流行地区亦仍限于河南省及陕西省的中部、山西省的南部一带。除了大多数是长方形的以外，西汉的空心砖也有少数是三角形或长条状的，以便砌造墓门。砖面上的花纹是作为墓室的装饰而设计的，系用戳印逐个打印，纹样除几何图案以外，还有各种动物、植物，以及人物、车马和房屋，等等。[24] 到了东汉，空心砖突然衰落，乃至绝迹。

　　在西汉前期，真正的砖出现了。这是汉代在建筑方面的一大发明。与上述的空心砖相比，它们都系小型、实心，长方形或正方形，长度一般从二十多厘米到三十多厘米不等，这里称之为"小型砖"（图213），以区别于上述庞大的空心砖。小型砖用于各种建筑物，大量使用的是长方砖，正方砖只用于铺地（图214）。为了符合建筑上的要求，砖的尺寸必须整齐划一。长方砖的长、宽、厚，都按一定的比例，一般说来，长与宽是二比一，宽与厚多为四比一。小型砖一经出现，就被广泛使用，迅速普及到全国各地。以洛阳的汉河南县城遗址的发掘所见为例，小型长方砖用于建筑各种住房和粮仓，也被用来砌筑水井（图215）。[25] 在西安的汉长安城遗址，

Xi'an, they were used in constructing underground water drain holes.[26] In the Han dynasty, they were not, however, used for building city walls. In the Yellow River valley, small bricks were widely used in constructing tomb chambers as early as middle and late Western Han period. And by Eastern Han, their use in constructing tomb chambers had already spread to all parts of the country. With the introduction of small bricks, arch-building technique also became extensively used. Most rectangular bricks can be used in making arches. But in order to reinforce the top of the arch, Han builders used *xiexingzhuan*, that is, "wedge-shaped bricks" or voussoirs, and *zimuzhuan*, or bricks with mortise and tenon arrangements, both of which were used only in constructing arches (figs. 216, 217).[27] Most of the rectangular bricks are undecorated, but there are some which have decorative motifs stamped on their sides. The patterns are usually geometric, though other patterns do occur. Most of the square bricks used in paving floors have stamped geometric patterns on their tops. In addition, in Eastern Han pictorial bricks, called *huaxiang zhuan*, were also in use. Both square and rectangular bricks sometimes exhibit figural motifs showing scenes of Han social life and daily work. These were mainly used in constructing and decorating tomb chambers, and, in general, their use was limited to Sichuan Province (fig. 218).[28]

Tiles In China, pottery roof tiles, or *wa*, were in use long before bricks. Archaeological excavations have shown that pottery roof tiles had already appeared as early as the early Western Zhou period. A great many were recovered at the site of Kexingzhuang in the vicinity of Xi'an.[29] In the Spring and Autumn and Warring States periods the production and use of roof tiles spread rapidly; furthermore, the tiles were distinguished according to function into flattened ones and cylindrical ones. The flattened ones were placed on the lower level and the cylindrical ones overlapped them on top. In the Warring States period, the faces of the cylindrical tiles (also called eaves tiles, or *wadang*) usually were semicircular. Some of the faces were left plain, but others were decorated.

Each of the seven states of that period had its own distinctive style of decorating eaves tiles.

By the Han dynasty, the manufacture and use of pottery roof tiles had progressed greatly and technical improvements had occurred. Both flattened and cylindrical tiles were becoming regularized in shape as well as in stamped, cord-pattern decor. Finds from the excavations at the Han city site at Henanxian reveal that in early Western Han many eaves tiles were semicircular, but from the middle Western Han period onward semicircular tiles were gradually replaced by ones with full, circular

则可以看到它们被用以砌筑排水的涵洞。[26] 但是，在汉代，它们还没有被用来建筑城墙。在黄河流域，早在西汉中后期，就盛行用小型砖建筑墓室。到了东汉，用它们来筑造的砖室墓已普及到全国各地。随着小型砖的出现，发券的技术也就被广泛使用。一般的长方砖都可以用以发券，但为了增加券顶的强度，也有专门用于发券的"楔形砖"和"子母砖"（图216、217）。[27] 长方砖以素面的为多，但也有不少在侧面印有花纹，纹样以几何图案为主，有时也有其他各种图纹。铺地用的正方砖，则多在正面印几何图案。此外，东汉时还有一种"画像砖"，或为正方形，或为长方形，砖面上印着各种有关社会生活和生产活动的图纹，主要是用于构筑并装饰墓室，流行的地区主要限于四川（图218）。[28]

在中国，瓦的使用比砖早。根据考古发掘，早在西周初期就有了瓦，在西安附近的客省庄遗址中就有大量的发现。[29] 到了春秋战国时期，瓦的制作和使用迅速推广，并已按其用途分为板瓦和筒瓦，前者铺在下面，后者覆在上面。在战国时代，筒瓦前端的瓦当多为半圆形的，有的为素面，有的有花纹。当时的七个主要国家，瓦当上的花纹各有特点，互不相同。

到了汉代，瓦的制作和使用又进一步得到了发展，制瓦的方法也有所改进。无论是筒瓦或板瓦，形状都比较规整，表面上拍印的绳纹也显得比较整齐。根据洛阳汉河南县城的发掘，在西汉前期，除了圆形的瓦当以外，仍有不少瓦当是半圆形的；到了西汉中期以

faces.[30] During the Han dynasty, decoration on the faces of eaves tiles became uniform throughout China. From the great metropolitan cities of Chang'an and Luoyang to the small towns on the distant frontiers, the geometric patterns on the roof tiles all came to follow the *juanyun* or "scrolling cloud" motif, almost without exception (figs. 219-22). Moreover, from the Western Han period onward auspicious phrases such as "Chang le wei yang" ("Profound happiness without end"), "Chang sheng wu ji" ("Long life without limit"), "Qian qiu wan sui" ("A thousand autumns, ten thousand years" or "Everlasting life"), and "Yi nian wu jiang" ("A hundred million years without limit") were impressed on tiles as decoration (figs. 223-26). On eaves tiles found in the towns near the northern frontier other phrases such as "Chanyu tian jiang" ("Heaven-descended khan") and "Chanyu he qin" ("The khan in quest of marriage with Han") were applied (figs. 227, 228).[31] In Xihai Jun (a commandery established by Wang Mang of the Xin dynasty) in the vicinity of Qinghai Lake, eaves tiles have been found with impressed characters reading "Xihai an ding" ("Pacified Xihai") (fig. 229).[32] During the reign of Wang Mang, designs of the so-called *sishen* or Four Deities—the Green Dragon, the White Tiger, the Red Bird, and the Black Turtle—appeared on eaves tiles intended for buildings of a ceremonial nature.[33]

It is important to note that in the Han dynasty eaves tiles with impressed character decoration were used for palaces and government buildings in the capital Chang'an, and in the *san fu*—the three military districts contiguous with and immediately surrounding the capital (namely, Jingzhao, Fengyi, and Fufeng). The characters used in the decoration indicate the names of the buildings. Many examples have been found. In the Shanglinyuan garden complex in the suburbs of Chang'an, for example, eaves tiles were stamped with characters reading "Shang lin" (fig. 230). In the Yidang Hall and Zhefeng Tower of the Jianzhang Palace west to Chang'an, eaves tiles were stamped with characters reading "Yidang wan nian" ("Yidang ten thousand years") and "Zhefengque dang" ("Eaves tile of Zhefengque") respectively (figs. 231, 232). In the Huangshan Palace in Huailixian, You Fufeng, eaves tiles were stamped "Huangshan" (fig. 233). In the Lanchi Palace in Weichengxian, You Fufeng, eaves tiles were stamped "Lanchigong dang" ("Eaves of Lanchigong") (fig. 234). And in the Zongzheng government building, within the city of Chang'an, eaves tiles were stamped with "Zongzhengguan dang" ("Tile of the Zongzheng official [building]") (fig. 235).[34] The examples cited above indicate that at that time the government had established special ceramic workshops to supply bricks and roof tiles for use in palaces and government buildings. In the excavations of the Han capital at Chang'an, there were found a number of eaves tiles impressed with characters reading "Dusikong wa"

后，半圆形的瓦当才逐渐消失。[30] 在汉代，瓦当上的花纹也统一了。从长安、雒阳等大城市到边远地区的小城镇，瓦当上的几何图案几乎都是属于所谓卷云纹，绝少例外（图 219—222）。用"长乐未央"、"长生无极"、"千秋万岁"、"亿年无疆"等吉祥文字作为瓦当上的装饰，也是从西汉开始的（图 223—226）。北方边境城镇所用的瓦当有"单于天降"、"单于和亲"的文字（图 227、228）。[31] 青海湖附近的西海郡（新莽时所置）所用的瓦当则有"西海安定"的字样（图 229）。[32] 在新莽时期，还流行用"青龙"、"白虎"、"朱雀"、"玄武"的所谓"四神"的图纹作为瓦当上的装饰，这种瓦当主要用于礼仪性的建筑物上。[33]

　　值得注意的是，在西汉首都长安城及三辅地区的宫殿、官署所用的瓦当，往往用文字作为装饰，而这些文字正是宫殿和官署的名称。例如：长安郊区上林苑中的各宫观用"上林"瓦当（图 230），长安城西建章宫中的骀荡殿和折风阙分别用"骀荡万年"、"折风阙当"瓦当（图 231、232），右扶风槐里县的黄山宫用"黄山"瓦当（图 233），右扶风渭城县的兰池宫用"兰池宫当"瓦当（图 234），长安城内的宗正署用"宗正官当"瓦当（图 235），等等。[34] 这说明了当时的政府设有专门的制陶作坊，制造专供宫廷和官署使用的砖瓦。在长安城遗址的发掘工作中，发现了许多印有"都司空瓦"文

("Tile of Dusikong") (fig. 236), as well as tiles impressed with characters reading "Dusikong," "Baocheng Dusikong," "Youkong", and "Du Jian Ping sannian" (a date equivalent to 4 B.C.), "Du Yuan Shou ernian" (equivalent to 1 B.C.), and "Du Yuan Shi wunian" (equivalent to A.D. 5) (figs. 237-39). Here, the character *du* is an abbreviation of Dusikong, the name of a government bureau which was changed to "Baocheng dusikong" for a brief period during the reign of Wang Mang. It can be concluded, therefore, that the manufacture of these tiles was supervised by officials from the Dusikong bureau of the Zongzhengqing and by officials from the Zuosikong and Yousikong of the Shaofuqing.[35] According to the *Hanshu*, the Dusikong, Zuosikong, and Yousikong were bureaus in charge of both construction and convicted criminals. Since these bureaus supervised the manufacture of bricks and tiles, the evidence from the *Hanshu* reveals that, in the Han dynasty, numerous prisoners were employed in the government-operated ceramic workshops.

字的瓦当（图236），并发现在大量的瓦片上印着有"都司空"、"保城都司空"、"右空"及"都建平三年"、"都元寿二年"、"都元始五年"等字样（图237—239）（"都"是都司空的简略）的戳记，充分说明了这些瓦的制作是由宗正的属官"都司空令"（新莽时改称"保城都司空"）和少府的属官"左司空令"、"右司空令"所主管。[35]《汉书·百官公卿表》说"（宗正）属官有都司空令丞"。颜师古注引如淳曰："律，司空主水及罪人。贾谊曰，输之司空，编之徒官。"可见"都司空"、"左司空"和"右司空"等管理工程的机构同时也是管理刑徒的机构，由它们主管砖瓦的制造正说明了汉代官营的制陶手工业作坊中使用大量的刑徒作为劳动力。

173. Large pottery urn unearthed from a Han tomb in Luoyang (height: 50 cm)
洛阳汉墓出土的陶瓮 （高 50 cm）

174. Large pottery urn unearthed from a Han tomb in Luoyang (height: 64 cm)
洛阳汉墓出土的陶瓮 （高 64 cm）

175. Pottery kiln of the Han dynasty excavated from the site of the old city of Wuji in Wu'anxian, Hebei 河北武安午汲古城中的汉代陶窑

176. Pottery kiln of the Han dynasty excavated from the site of the old city of Wuji in Wu'anxian, Hebei 河北武安午汲古城中的汉代陶窑

177. Pottery kiln of the Han dynasty excavated from the site of the old city of Wuji in Wu'anxian, Hebei
河北武安午汲古城中的汉代陶窑

178. Gray pottery jar unearthed from a Han tomb in Luoyang
洛阳汉墓出土的灰陶罐

179. Gray pottery jar unearthed from the Han tomb in Luoyang　洛阳汉墓出土的灰陶罐

180. Gray pottery *ding*-tripod unearthed from the Han tomb in Luoyang　洛阳汉墓出土的灰陶鼎

181. Painted pottery jar unearthed from the Han tomb in Luoyang
洛阳汉墓出土的彩绘陶壶

182. Painted pottery basin unearthed from the Han tomb in Mancheng　满城汉墓出土的彩绘陶盆

183. Lacquered pottery jar unearthed from the Han tomb at Yinqueshan in Linyi, Shandong
山东临沂银雀山汉墓出土的涂漆陶壶

184. Lacquered pottery *ding*-tripod unearthed from the Han tomb at Yinqueshan in Linyi, Shandong
山东临沂银雀山汉墓出土的涂漆陶鼎

185. Lacquered pottery box unearthed from the Han tomb at Yinqueshan in Linyi, Shandong
山东临沂银雀山汉墓出土的涂漆陶盒

186. Round-based pottery urn unearthed from the Western Han tomb in Guanghua, Hubei
湖北光化西汉墓出土的圆底陶瓮

187. "Duck-egg jar" unearthed from the Han tomb in Xinxiang, Henan　河南新乡汉墓出土的彩绘"鸭蛋壶"

188. Hard pottery jar with impressed designs, unearthed from the Han tomb in Mawangdui, Changsha
长沙马王堆汉墓出土的印纹硬陶罐

189. Hard pottery jar with impressed designs, unearthed from the Han tomb in Shaoxing, Zhejiang
浙江绍兴汉墓出土的印纹硬陶罐

190. Hard pottery jar with impressed designs, unearthed from the Han tomb in Shaoxing, Zhejiang
浙江绍兴汉墓出土的印纹硬陶罐

191. Hard pottery jar with impressed designs, unearthed from the Han tomb in Shaoxing, Zhejiang
浙江绍兴汉墓出土的印纹硬陶罐

192. Gourd-shaped jar unearthed from the Han tomb in Guangzhou 广州汉墓出土的匏壶

193. Jar with four interconnecting parts, unearthed from the Han tomb in Guangzhou　广州汉墓出土的四联罐

194. Pottery jar with three legs, unearthed from the Han tomb in Guangzhou　广州汉墓出土的三足陶罐

195. Pottery jar with green glaze of the Han dynasty, in the collection of the Palace Museum
汉绿釉陶壶（故宫博物院藏）

196. Pottery model of granary with green glaze, unearthed from the Han tomb
in Lingbao, Henan 河南灵宝汉墓出土的绿釉陶仓

197. Pottery model of storied building with green glaze,
unearthed from the Han tomb in Shaanxi
陕西汉墓出土的绿釉陶楼

198. Hard pottery jar with green glaze and purple core, unearthed from the Han
tomb in Changsha 长沙汉墓出土的绿釉紫胎硬陶壶

199. Same as fig. 198, from Luoyang 洛阳出土的绿釉紫胎硬陶壶

200. Pottery lamp unearthed from the Han tomb in Luoyang
洛阳汉墓出土的陶灯

201. Pottery incense burner unearthed from the Han tomb in Luoyang
洛阳汉墓出土的陶薰炉

202. Pottery money jar unearthed from the Han tomb in Luoyang　洛阳汉墓出土的陶扑满

203. Pottery human figure on horseback, unearthed from the Han tomb at Yangjiawan in Xianyang, Shaanxi
陕西咸阳杨家湾西汉墓中的骑马陶俑

204. Pottery dog unearthed from the Han tomb at Baiquan in Huixian, Henan　河南辉县百泉村汉墓中的陶狗

205. Pottery sheep from the same site as fig. 204　河南辉县百泉村汉墓中的陶羊

206. The names "He ting" and "He shi" stamped on pottery unearthed from the site of the Han town of Henanxian in Luoyang
洛阳河南县汉墓出土陶器上的"河亭"、"河市"戳记

207. The name "Shan ting" stamped on pottery unearthed from the Han tomb in Shanxian, Henan 河南陕县汉墓出土陶器上的"陕亭"戳记

208. The name "Shan shi" stamped on pottery unearthed from the Han tomb in Shanxian, Henan
河南陕县汉墓出土陶器上的"陕市"戳记

209. The name "Han ting" stamped on pottery unearthed from a Han dynasty site in Handan, Hebei
河北邯郸汉代遗址出土陶器上的"邯亭"戳记

210. The name "An ting" stamped on pottery unearthed from a Han dynasty site in Xiaxian, Shanxi
山西夏县汉城遗址出土陶器上的"安亭"戳记

211. Clay seal impressed with the inscription "An cheng tao wei"
"安城陶尉"封泥

212. Hollow bricks of the Han dynasty, unearthed in Henan 河南出土的汉代空心砖

213. Small, rectangular brick of the Han dynasty, unearthed from a
Han tomb in Luoyang　洛阳汉墓出土的小型长方砖

214. Square bricks unearthed at the site of the Han city of Chang'an in Xi'an
汉长安城遗址出土的正方砖

215. Granary built with small, rectangular bricks, excavated at the site of the Han town of Henanxian in Luoyang
洛阳汉河南县城遗址发掘出的小型长方砖砌筑的粮仓

216. Wedge-shaped brick unearthed from a Han tomb in Luoyang　洛阳汉墓的楔形砖

217. Bricks with tenons and mortises, unearthed from the Han tomb in Luoyang　洛阳汉墓的子母砖

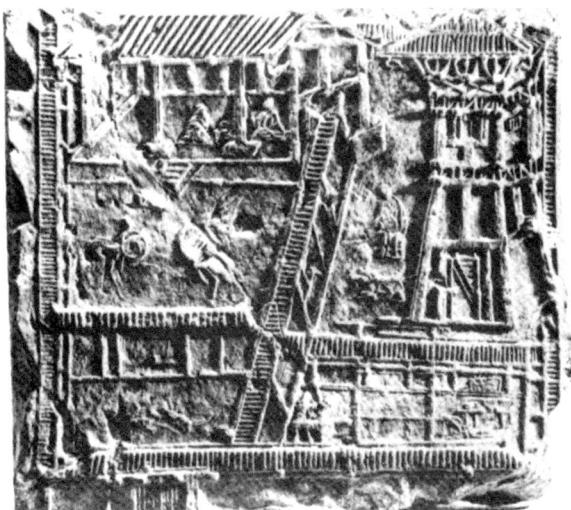

218. Pictorial brick unearthed from the Han tomb in Chengdu, Sichuan　四川成都汉墓出土的画像砖

258

219. Eaves tile with "scrolling cloud" design, unearthed from the site of the Han city of Chang'an in Xi'an
汉长安城遗址出土的卷云纹瓦当

220. Eaves tile with "scrolling cloud" design, unearthed from the site of the Han city of Chang'an in Xi'an
汉长安城遗址出土的卷云纹瓦当

221. Eaves tile with "scrolling cloud" design, unearthed from the site of the Han city of Chang'an in Xi'an
汉长安城遗址出土的卷云纹瓦当

222. Eaves tile with "scrolling cloud" design, unearthed from the site of the Han city of Chang'an in Xi'an 汉长安城遗址出土的卷云纹瓦当

223. Eaves tile with the inscription "Chang le wei yang," unearthed at the site of the Han city of Chang'an in Xi'an
汉长安城遗址出土的"长乐未央"瓦当

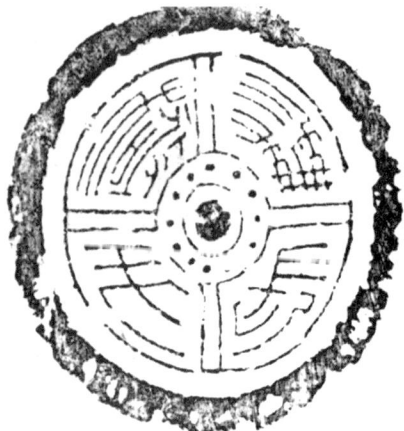

224. Eaves tile from the same site as fig. 223, with the inscription "Chang sheng wu ji" 汉长安城遗址出土的"长生无极"瓦当

225. Eaves tile from the same site as fig. 223, with the inscription "Qian qiu wan sui" 汉长安城遗址出土的 "千秋万岁" 瓦当

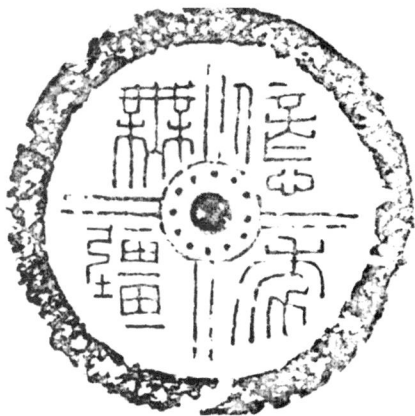

226. Eaves tile from the same site as fig. 223, with the inscription "Yi nian wu jiang" 汉长安城遗址出土的 "亿年无疆" 瓦当

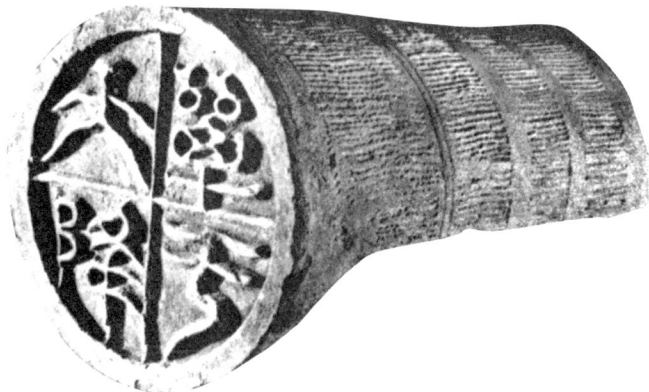

227. Eaves tile with the inscription "Chanyu tian jiang," unearthed from the Han tomb in Baotou, Inner Mongolia 内蒙古包头汉墓出土的 "单十天降" 瓦当

228. Eaves tile with the inscription "Chanyu he qin," unearthed from the Han tomb in Baotou, Inner Mongolia 内蒙古包头汉墓出土的 "单于和亲" 瓦当

259

229. Eaves tile with the inscription "Xihai an ding yuanxing yuan nian zuo dang," unearthed at a Han dynasty site in Haiyan, Qinghai
青海海晏汉代遗址出土的"西海安定"瓦当图

230. Eaves tile inscribed with the name "Shang lin," unearthed at the site of the Han city of Chang'an in Xi'an
长安汉城遗址出土的"上林"瓦当

231. Eaves tile with the inscription "Yidang wan nian" "骀汤万年"瓦当

232. Eaves tile with the inscription "Eaves Tile of Zhefengque"
"折风阙当"瓦当

233. Eaves tile with the inscription "Huangshan" "黄山"瓦当

234. Eaves tile with the inscription "Eaves Tile of Lanchigong"
"兰池宫当"瓦当

235. Eaves tile with the inscription "Eaves Tile of the Zongzheng official," unearthed at the site of the Han city of Chang'an in Xi'an 汉长安城遗址出土的 "宗正官当" 瓦当

236. Eaves tile from the same site as fig. 235, with the inscription "Tile of Dusikong" 汉长安城遗址出土的 "都司空瓦" 瓦当

237. Tile from the same site as fig. 235, with the inscription "Shi Jian Guo sinian Baocheng Dusikong" 汉长安城遗址出土的 "始建国四年保城都司空" 瓦

238. Tile from the same site as fig. 235, with the inscription "Du Jian Ping sannian" 汉长安城遗址出土的 "都建平三年" 瓦

239. Tile from the same site as fig. 235, with the inscription "Du Jian Ping sannian" 汉长安城遗址出土的 "都建平三年" 瓦

CHAPTER 8   TOMBS—I

Han dynasty tombs have been encountered in the course of industrial or agricultural construction as well as during archaeological investigations and excavations with great frequency. This stems from several factors. First, the Western and Eastern Han dynasties lasted for more than four hundred years. During that time China was a unified empire, its political situation relatively stable, its economy relatively prosperous, and its population dense. Han landowners and officials were fond of furnishing their graves richly; consequently, in their graves there are large numbers of many kinds of objects. Burial chambers, furthermore, were often built of brick and stone, which helped to preserve the remains. We estimate that since the founding of New China, at least ten thousand Han dynasty tombs have been found as a result of archaeological work throughout the country. These discoveries have made possible a relatively good understanding of the mortuary institutions and customs of the Han dynasty.

Characteristics of Han Tomb Construction   Compared with tombs of previous periods, Han dynasty tombs have many distinctive features. Prior to the Han, during the Neolithic, Shang, and Zhou periods, tombs were mostly placed in rectangular earthen pits. Of varying sizes and depths, these pits were excavated from the ground downward and are referred to as "vertical pits." Beginning in middle Western Han in the Yellow River valley, the custom originated of digging the burial chamber laterally or horizontally underground, resulting in "horizontal pits." In the Western Han period, large hollow bricks were used to build the burial chamber, mainly in the Central Plains area. In Eastern Han, throughout China, in the Central Plains and in the northern and the southern border regions, small bricks were universally used to build a burial chamber with arches and a domed top. Tombs of stone began in late Western Han. In addition, during both Western and Eastern Han, horizontal burial chambers were excavated into mountain cliffs in some regions. In short, the principal formal and structural features of Han dynasty tombs that distinguish them from those of earlier periods are, first, the use of horizontal pits for burial and, second, the use of bricks and stones for the construction of the tomb chamber. These features came from an effort to imitate the houses of the living.

It should be noted that such changes in tombs began in the middle Western Han period, starting in the Yellow River valley and then

卅 汉代的墓葬（上）

在工农业基本建设的施工动土的过程中，或是在考古学家们的调查发掘工作中，汉墓是最容易遇到的。这是由于西汉和东汉两朝共达四百余年之久，年代很长；也是由于当时中国是统一的大帝国，政治局面比较安定，经济比较发达，因而人口兴旺。此外，汉代地主官僚阶级讲求厚葬，墓中随葬器物种类多，数量大，易于被人发现，而墓室又往往采用砖石结构，不易毁坏，这些也都是重要的原因。新中国成立以来，全国各地考古工作中所发现的汉墓，估计已达万座之多。这使得对于汉代的丧葬制度和习俗能够有比较充分的了解。

和前代比较起来，汉代的墓葬可以说是最富有时代的特色的。汉以前的墓，包括从新石器时代、商代、西周以迄春秋、战国时代的墓，其墓圹主要是长方形的土坑，不论大小深浅如何，都是由地面一直往下掘，所以称为"竖穴"。西汉中期，在黄河流域开始流行在地下横掘土洞，作为墓圹，所以称为"横穴"。西汉时，主要是在中原地区，盛行用庞大的空心砖堆砌墓室。到了东汉，无论是在中原还是在南方和北方的边远地区，都普遍用小型砖来券筑墓室。从西汉末年开始，还流行石室墓。此外，从西汉到东汉，在有些地区，还有一种"崖墓"，其墓圹亦属横穴式。总起来说，用横穴式的洞穴作墓圹，用砖和石料构筑墓室，是汉墓与汉以前的墓在形制和构造上的主要区别，其特点在于模仿现实生活中的房屋。

但是，如上面所指出的，汉代墓制的这种变化，从时代上说，主要是在西汉中期才开始的，从地区上说，首先发生于黄河流域，

spreading throughout the country. Previously, in early Western Han, members of the ruling class were still entombed in the vertical pit graves with wooden encasements that continued from the Warring States period. In fact, this older style of tomb, known as the "vertical pit-wooden chamber grave," continued to be built into late Western Han or even early Eastern Han in the Yangtze River valley and in the southern and northern border regions.

Examples of these vertical pit-wooden chamber graves of early and middle Western Han are the tombs found at Mawangdui (Changsha), Fenghuangshan (Jiangling), and Dabaotai (Beijing). Construction of the coffins and wooden chambers in these graves still followed the older customs of the Zhou dynasty. Both *Zhuangzi* ("Tianxiapian") and *Xunzi* ("Lilunpian") describe burial caskets of varying degrees of elaborateness, as follows: "The caskets of the emperor are of seven layers; of the feudal lords, five layers; of the Da Fu class, three layers; and of the Shi class, two layers." Han tomb number one of Mawangdui was the tomb of the wife of Li Cang, Marquis of Dai, and her caskets consisted of four coffins and one wooden encasement, the prescribed number for a feudal lord (fig. 240). In Han tomb number 168 at Fenghuangshan in Jiangling was buried a certain Sui Shaoyan, a Da Fu of the fifth rank. His rank was the ninth grade on a scale of twenty, corresponding to that of a county magistrate, and his grave contained two coffins and one wooden encasement (fig. 241). Tomb number 1 of Dabaotai in Beijing was probably the tomb of the Prince of Yan. What survives of his caskets appears to be the remains of five coffins and two outer encasements, a burial which corresponds to the grade of emperor, a full grade higher than a feudal lord (fig. 242). It goes without saying that rules for burial according to rank could not have been strictly followed at all times. Li Cang, the Marquis of Dai, who was buried in tomb number 2 of Mawangdui, was himself buried within two coffins and one outer encasement.[1] In the tombs of Dabaotai in Beijing and Xianjiahu in Changsha, a wooden structure named "Huang chang ti cou" was built outside the chamber.[2]

Good examples of the new horizontal pit graves that appeared in the middle Western Han dynasty are the tombs of Prince Jing of Zhongshan, found in Mancheng, Hebei, and of Prince Lu of Qufu in Shandong.[3] In both cases the tomb chambers were caves dug into cliffs, and the caves were divided into several compartments, such as side chambers, frontal hall, and rear hall. In the tomb of Liu Sheng, Prince Jing of Zhongshan, the southern side chamber was for horses and carriages (fig. 243). The northern side chamber was for storage, and large numbers of pottery vessels were placed there (fig. 244). The front hall is of large dimensions,

然后逐渐普及到各地。在西汉前期，统治阶级仍然习惯于沿用战国以来的竖穴式土坑墓，墓中筑木椁。在长江流域以及南方和北方的边远地区，这种竖穴式木椁墓一直延续到西汉晚期，甚至到东汉。

长沙马王堆汉墓、江陵凤凰山汉墓、北京大葆台汉墓，可以作为西汉前期和中期的土坑木椁墓的代表。墓中的棺椁，沿袭着周代以来的礼制。《庄子·天子篇》和《荀子·礼论篇》都说："天子棺椁七重，诸侯五重，大夫三重，士再重。"长沙马王堆一号汉墓所葬为轪侯利苍的夫人，其棺椁按诸侯的规格，是四棺一椁（图240）。江陵凤凰山一六八号汉墓所葬为"五大夫"遂少言，他的爵位在汉代二十等爵中属九等，略高于八等"公乘"以下的所谓"民爵"，身份相当于县令，所以是二棺一椁（图241）。北京大葆台一号墓所葬可能为燕王，墓中棺椁保存不大好，但仍可看出是五棺二椁，比列侯又高了一等，而与天子的"棺椁七重"之制相同（图242）。当然，有的时候也并不严格按礼制的规定办事，如长沙马王堆二号墓所葬为轪侯利苍本人，但却只有二棺一椁。[1]在北京大葆台汉墓和长沙咸家湖汉墓中，还使用了所谓"黄肠题凑"。[2]

在贵族的大墓中，河北满城的中山靖王墓和山东曲阜的鲁王墓可以作为西汉中期新兴的横穴式墓的代表。[3]它们都是在山崖中穿凿巨大的洞穴，作为墓室，所以称为"崖墓"。全墓可分为耳室、前室和后室等部分。以中山靖王刘胜墓为例，墓中的南耳室为车马房，放置车辆和驾车的马匹（图243），北耳室为仓库，贮存大量盛有食物的陶器（图244），前室是宽大的厅堂，陈列着帷帐和各种

and in it were placed drapes and the principal grave goods (fig. 245). The rear hall was an interior room where the coffin was placed. Within the front hall and the side chambers, houses made of timber had been erected, with tiles on the roofs. In the rear hall, stone slabs had been used to build another house which had two stone doors. In short, the form and the structure of the tomb imitated residential architectures above ground: thus the term, "underground palaces" *dixia gongdian* (fig. 246).[4] In this new kind of tomb, the coffins also assumed new settings. In fact, the wooden outer encasements in the tomb of Liu Sheng were basically different from those of Zhou tombs, for they were no longer linings of pits and became in fact outer caskets. It follows also that the number of casket layers is no longer an indication of the status of the master of the grave. Since this new burial custom adopted by Liu Sheng and other nobles is evidently different from the older burial customs continued from the Zhou dynasty as adopted by Li Cang and other nobles, some scholars have maintained that Liu Sheng represented the Legalists, who were progressive and innovative, and that Li Cang represented the Confucians, who were conservative. Actually, tomb customs cannot be related to the Legalist-Confucian struggles; Liu Sheng was not a Legalist, and Li Cang was not necessarily a Confucian.

Another manifestation of the new burial customs of the Han dynasty is the emergence of hollow-brick tombs in the Central Plains area (fig. 247). The Han dynasty hollow-brick tombs differed from the hollow-brick tombs of the Warring States period in that the Han tombs were generally built within horizontal pit caves. These tombs were usually of moderate scale and possibly belonged to members of the middle and small landowner class. In early Western Han, the burial chamber of the hollow-brick tomb was rectangular, shaped like the wooden chamber that it replaced. In middle and late Western Han, the typical hollow-brick tomb was shaped more like a house, with gabled roof and door-shaped front wall (fig. 248).[5] The hollow bricks were often stamped with designs and scenes which constituted the interior decoration of the burial chamber. Polychromic murals begin to appear in some of the tombs. A hollow-brick tomb found in Luoyang has murals with images of sun and moon, of Green Dragon, White Tiger, and Red Bird, and of Fu Xi and Nü Wa (figs. 249-51).[6] Another tomb found in Luoyang not only has sun, moon, and stars depicted in its murals, some of its pictures even depict historical stories such as "Using two peaches to kill three gentlemen," and "The banquet at Hongmen" (figs. 252-54).[7] The mural scenes and stone

主要的随葬器物（图 245），后室是内室，放置棺材。前室和两个耳室，都用木材搭成房屋，屋顶铺瓦；后室也用石板搭成房屋形，并在前方设两扇石门，门上装有铜质镀金的铺首。总之，墓的形制和结构完全模仿地面上的居住建筑，所以称为"地下宫殿"（图 246）。[4]在这种新式的墓中，棺椁也就摆脱了旧的礼制。实际上，刘胜墓中的木椁也与周代以来的木椁不同，它只不过是一种套棺而已。在这里，棺椁的层数多少已经不是衡量墓主人身份的标准了。刘胜等人采用这种新的墓制，与利苍等人沿袭周代以来的旧墓制迥然不同。因此，曾有人从墓制的新旧出发，认为刘胜是代表革新势力的法家，利苍是代表保守势力的儒家。其实，墓制与儒法斗争并没有什么关系。刘胜不是什么法家，利苍也未必是儒家。

汉代的新的墓制，还表现在中原一带盛行"空心砖墓"（图 247）。与战国晚期的空心砖墓不同的是，汉代的空心砖墓往往是在横穴式的土洞内砌筑墓室。空心砖墓的规模，一般并不很大，大概是属于当时的中小地主阶级的。在西汉前期，空心砖墓的墓室呈长方形，形状像木椁，到了西汉中晚期，它的顶部往往搭成两面坡的屋顶状，并将前壁搭成门的样子，更显得像房屋（图 248）。[5]砖面上所印的花纹和图像，成了墓室内的装饰，有的墓里还开始有了彩色的壁画。在洛阳发现的一座空心砖墓，所绘壁画有日、月、青龙、白虎、朱雀及伏羲、女娲的形象（图 249—251）。[6]同地发现的另一座墓，其壁画除了日、月、星辰的天象图以外，还有以"二桃杀三士"、"鸿门宴"等历史故事为题材的（图 252—254）。[7]这种"天象图"、

engravings in tombs of the Eastern Han dynasty developed even further these sky charts and representations of the Four Deities, myths, and historical stories.

Sometime after middle Western Han, tombs with chambers built of small bricks began to appear in the Central Plains and in central Shaanxi; these we refer to as "brick chamber tombs" to distinguish them from the hollow-brick tombs. As soon as it appeared on the scene, the brick chamber tomb became rapidly adopted everywhere, replacing the hollow-brick tombs in the Central Plains and replacing the vertical pit-wooden chamber graves in the Yangtze River valley and the southern and northern border regions. By the Eastern Han dynasty, brick chamber tombs were the prevailing form of burial throughout the country (figs. 255, 256). The brick chamber tombs of high nobles—such as the tomb of the Prince Jing of Pengcheng in Xuzhou, Jiangsu, and the tomb of Prince Jian of Zhongshan, in Dingxian, and the tomb of Taiyuan Taishou in Wangdu, Hebei—are of large scale and complex construction with a layout similar to the mansions these princes inhabited during their lifetimes.[8] Some of the brick chamber tombs also were decorated with frescoes, the well-known ones including those found in the family tomb of the Marquis of Fuyang, in Wangdu, Hebei, and in the family tomb of Hongnong Taishou in Mixian, Henan. The Wangdu tomb has murals depicting the various officials and attendants of the tomb master (fig. 257), causing the chamber to look like his official quarters.[9] The Mixian tomb has murals depicting processions of horses and carriages and scenes of banquets and entertainments, fully attesting to the luxurious life of the tomb master (fig. 258).[10]

A huge brick chamber tomb was excavated in 1972 at Holingor in Inner Mongolia. The master of the grave was a military colonel of the Wuhuan district, and the murals in the tomb mainly illustrate the history of his official career through scenes of horse and carriage processions. From the inscriptions that accompany the various segments of the murals, we know that he was a native of Dingxiang Jun, where he qualified for officialdom by being selected as a Xiaolian candidate. Then he was assigned various administrative positions until he finally reached the military colonelcy of the Wuhuan district. The murals show scenes

"四神图"、神话传说和历史故事图，在以后的东汉墓的壁画和石刻画像中得到了进一步的发展。

大约在西汉中期以后，在中原和关中一带开始出现了用小型砖建筑的墓，这里称为"砖室墓"，以区别于上述的空心砖墓。砖室墓一经出现，便迅速普及，它在中原地区逐渐取代空心砖墓，在长江流域以及南方和北方的边远地区则代替了当时尚在延续的土坑木椁墓。到了东汉，砖室墓在全国各地流行，成为最常见的一种墓（图255、256），大贵族、大官僚的砖室墓，如河北定县的中山简王墓、望都的太原太守墓，规模宏大，结构复杂，其布局有如他们的府第。[8] 有的砖室墓里，有彩色的壁画。比较有名的壁画墓，如河北望都的浮阳侯墓和河南密县的弘农太守家族墓，前者所绘主要是墓主人的属吏和侍从等人物（图257），把墓室布置得像他的官署一样。[9] 后者所绘有车马出行图和宴会百戏图等，表现了墓主人生前的豪奢的生活（图258）。[10]

1972年在内蒙古和林格尔发掘的一座庞大的砖室墓，墓主人官至护乌丸校尉。墓内壁画的内容十分丰富，主要是以车马出行图的形式描绘了墓主人生前的全部仕途经历，这可以从壁画上所书的文字得到说明：首先是在他的家乡襄郡（其治所西汉时在内蒙古和林格尔，东汉时在山西省右玉）被选拔为"孝廉"，取得了做官的资格，不久便按照常例被分配到首都雒阳担任"郎"官。他首次出任地方官是担任西河郡的"长史"，郡的治所在离石（今山西省离石县）；以后又被提升为上郡属国都尉，其治所在土军（今山西省石楼县）。他曾一度被调到中原地区的魏郡繁阳县（今河南省内黄县）任县令，在这里曾受到皇帝的褒奖。最后，他又迅速被提拔，到边境地区的上谷郡宁城（今河北省万全县，或以为在张家口附近）担任护乌丸校尉的大官。结合着上述车马出行图中的仕途经历，

of the various towns in which he had worked—their streets, official buildings, warehouses, and markets—and various activities in which he had engaged in during his career (figs. 259-61). At the time, high officials also were owners of large manors. In the murals is a scene of a manor, depicting such productive activities as cultivating fields, preparing tree nurseries, raising cattle, feeding animals and picking mulberry leaves. Possibly the occupant-to-be of the tomb had retired to his manor, but in any event the manor was in all likelihood his home. The Holingor murals were indeed an unprecedented discovery, fully exemplifying such murals and their objectives and significance.[11]

Beginning in early Eastern Han, a new kind of tomb known as the "stone chamber grave" came upon the scene, and it became even more popular after middle Eastern Han. The burial chamber was constructed with neatly dressed stones on which were engraved designs and scenes— thus the name, the "tomb with pictorial stones" (*hua xiang shi mu*) (fig. 262). Seen mostly in Shandong, northern Jiangsu, Henan, and northern Hubei, these tombs also occur in middle Sichuan, northern Shaanxi and western Shanxi. During the past centuries, many of them were destroyed and the stone reliefs scattered about. Since the founding of New China, a few have been archaeologically excavated. Some of these, such as the Han tombs in Tanghe (Henan) and in Anqiu, Cangshan, and Yi'nan (Shandong), are preserved well enough to show that again the layout of the burial chamber imitated the house of the tomb master in his real life (fig. 263).[12] The most obvious case is the Han tomb in Yi'nan, excavated in 1954. A scene in the tomb depicts the courtyard house in which the master lived during his lifetime, and the layout of the tomb is identical with the layout of the house (fig. 264). Many scenes are depicted in the engravings, all pertaining to scenes of his life and his career history. The master of the Yi'nan tomb was probably a military general. Above the tomb entrance, in a most prominent location, a battle scene was engraved in fine detail. In it a squad of Han dynasty foot soldiers is in the act of defeating mounted and foot soldiers from a northern nomadic group. The occupant of the tomb, standing in a carriage, is seen behind the soldiers supervising the battle. Obviously this must have been the most memorable scene in his career (figs. 265-67).[13] The Yi'nan tomb with stone reliefs and the fresco tomb of Holingor may be called the two best examples of the tomb art of Eastern Han.

还有许多画面绘描着离石城、土军城、繁阳城和宁城的城郭、官府、仓库、市场等等（图 259—261），以及墓主人在任职期间的各种活动场面。当时的大官僚，同时也是大庄园地主，所以壁画中还有一大幅庄园图，描绘着庄园中的耕种、作圃、放牧、饲养、采桑等各种生产活动。不论墓主人晚年是否有一段退职还乡的生活，壁画中的庄园应该是在他的家乡。总之，和林格尔汉墓中的壁画，是一项空前的大发现，它明确地说明了壁画的内容及在墓中绘描壁画的意义和目的。[11]

从西汉末年开始，还新兴一种石室墓，到东汉更为盛行。墓室由许多整齐的石块筑成，石块上雕刻着各种画像，所以称为"画像石墓"（图 262）。它们的分布，以山东省到江苏省的北部、河南省到湖北省的北部为最多，四川省的中部、陕西省的北部和山西省的西部一带也颇不少。长久以来，许多墓都被破坏，只剩下大量的画像石，分散各处。新中国成立以来，在考古发掘工作中发现了一些画像石墓，其中如河南省的唐河汉墓、山东省的安丘汉墓、苍山汉墓、沂南汉墓等，保存甚好，结构完整，可以看出墓室的布局也是仿照现实生活中的住宅（图 263）。[12] 最明显的是 1954 年发掘的沂南汉墓，墓内有一幅画像是刻绘墓主人生前居住的宅院，而墓室的布局正和画像中的宅院一致（图 264）。画像的题材十分广泛，但主要也是表现地主官僚阶级的生活和事迹。沂南汉墓的主人，生前大概是一位将军，所以在墓门的上方以最显著的位置雕刻着一幅精致的攻战图：一队占优势的汉朝步兵，正在战胜北方游牧民族的骑兵和步兵，而墓主则乘车在阵后督战，以表示这是他生前最值得纪念和宣扬的重要事迹（图 265—267）。[13] 沂南画像石墓与和林格尔壁画墓，可以并称为东汉画像石墓和壁画墓中的双绝。

During the Eastern Han period, many of the brick chamber tombs in the Sichuan region had a kind of pictorial brick fitted onto the walls of the burial chamber. The pictorial bricks are square or rectangular; the square ones are found mostly near Chengdu, but the rectangular ones are widely seen. The designs were stamped on the bricks before they were dried and some were also painted after the bricks were fired. They depict such life scenes as lectures, banquets, musicales and dances, and carriage processions. Such productive activities as harvesting, hunting, mulberry-leaf picking, taro digging, pestling of rice, wine making, and salt making are also shown—the latter scenes full of local flavor (figs. 268-72). These pictorial bricks were mass-produced, and identical scenes are often seen at tombs in different places. For this reason, it is clear that the scenes shown on these bricks were not directly related to the individual occupants of tombs.[14] In addition, in various places in Sichuan there were many cliff burials during the Eastern Han period. Excavated into high mountain cliffs, these were of varying scales and sizes. Sometimes several tens of tombs have been found clustered together, forming a large cemetery.[15]

Burial Mounds   All that has been described above pertains to the underground portion of the burial chamber. The portion of the tomb above ground in Han tombs also has distinctive features. During the Shang and Western Zhou periods, even large tombs were not covered with an earthen mound above ground. As *Li ji* ("Tan gong") states, "In the past the tombs were without mounds." Earthen mounds began to be built in the Warring States period, such as the mounds over some of the Chu tombs in Jiangling in Hubei,[16] but they were not yet widely distributed. But during the Han dynasty, earthen mounds became universal. The tombs of the emperors and the upper nobility were, *Yan tie lun* records, covered with accumulated earth as tall as a hill. To build them required a vast outlay of manpower and much time.

Funerary Shrines   In the Warring States period funerary shrines were built atop the tombs of some feudal lords. The Wei tomb at Guweicun in Huixian, Henan, and the tomb of the king of Zhongshan in Pingshan-xian, Hebei, are examples.[17] In the Han dynasty, funerary shrines and monumental towers became very popular, especially in Eastern Han. In his *Shuijingzhu*, Li Daoyuan makes mention of many Han funerary shrines and monumental towers. Since most of these were built of masonry,

东汉时，四川省境内的砖室墓，往往在墓室的砖壁上另嵌一种"画像砖"，作为装饰，故称"画像砖墓"。画像砖有正方形和长方形两种，砖上的画像都是趁泥坯未干时用模子印成，烧成后还有施加彩色的。画像的题材很广泛，既有讲经、宴饮、乐舞、车骑等地主官僚阶级的生活场面，也有收获、射猎、采桑、采芋、舂米、酿酒、煮盐等各种社会生产活动的情景，而后者具有浓厚的地方色彩（图268—272）。这种画像砖是成批制作的，所以常常可以在几个不同地方的墓中发现完全相同的砖。因此，画像的内容并不是直接与墓主人有关的。[14] 此外，在四川各地，东汉时还普遍流行崖墓。它们系在山崖中开凿，规模大小各有不同，往往几十座墓聚集在一处，形成一片很大的墓地。[15]

以上所说，都是关于地下的墓室。在地面上，和前代比较起来，汉墓也有许多新的特点。在殷代和西周，即使是规模很大的墓，地面上也没有坟丘，这就是《礼记·檀弓》所谓的"古者墓而不坟"。春秋晚期和战国时代，有些地区的大墓，已经在地面上筑有坟丘[16]，但从全国来说，还不很普遍。到了汉代，坟丘普遍流行。皇帝、贵族和官僚墓上的坟丘，如《盐铁论》所说，"积土如山"，要集中大量的人力，费很多的时间，才能筑成。坟丘的形状，多为截尖方锥状。据《汉书·卫青霍去病传》记载，卫青墓的坟丘像庐山，霍去病墓的坟丘像祁连山，则是特殊的例子。

战国时代，在诸侯陵墓的地面上，已有建"享堂"的，河南辉县固围村魏王墓和河北平山县中山国王墓便是例证。[17] 到了汉代，地主官僚们则盛行在墓前设祠堂，并在墓域的前方立墓阙。郦道元的《水经注》中，有很多关于汉代祠堂和墓阙的记述。东汉墓前的

some survive to this day. The better-known ones are the Guo lineage shrine at Xiaotangshan in Feicheng, Shandong; the Wu lineage shrine and monumental tower in Jiaxiangxian (now Jining); and the funerary tower at Wang Zhizi's tomb in Xinduxian and that at Gao Yi's tomb in Ya'anxian, both in Sichuan (fig. 273).[18] In front of some of these tombs were erected stone sculptures. Stone animal sculptures occur in front of the Wu family tomb and the Gao Yi tomb mentioned above, and additional finds have been made in recent years.[19]

Steles   Beginning in Eastern Han, a stone stele was sometimes erected in front of the tomb, with inscriptions describing the birth and death dates of the persons buried and their life histories.[20] Tomb inscriptions, the preparation of which became popular in the Wei and Jin dynasties, were a further development of the Han dynasty tomb steles. The earliest tomb inscriptions, such as the inscribed bricks of 287 and the inscribed stone of 297, both found in Luoyang, were very similar to Han tomb steles in shape.[21] The difference was that the Han tomb steles were large and placed on the ground, whereas tomb inscriptions were written on small tablets placed inside the tomb.

Caskets   In ancient China, *guan* and *guo*, or inner and outer caskets, were both used, and this practice continued into early Western Han in the vertical pit-wooden chamber graves of that time. However, as stated earlier, in the horizontal pit graves (after the middle of Western Han), and especially in the brick chamber and the stone chamber tombs (of Eastern Han), the burial chamber itself functioned as an outer casket. It may be referred to as the brick *guo* or the stone *guo* (as against the wooden *guo),* and within the chamber there was only an inner casket but no *guo* or outer casket. The coffins themselves are of wood and are mostly wider and higher in the front than in the rear—except for the coffins found in wooden chambers, which are of equal width and height from front to rear. In the Western Han dynasty, the wooden coffins were put together with tenons and mortises, and the lid was secured onto the coffin by means of hourglass-shaped wooden wedges placed into notches on both lid and coffin, but in the Eastern Han iron nails were universally used. Liu Xi of Eastern Han said, in his *Shiming* ("Shi sang zhi"): "In the past the coffins were not nailed." The coffins for the nobility were beautifully and elaborately made, as illustrated by the two lacquered coffins in tomb number 1 at Mawangdui. *Qianfulun* ("Fuchipian") states that "to make a coffin required the labor of thousands and tens of thousands." This has

祠堂和墓阙多用石材建成，所以有一直保留到今天的，山东肥城孝堂山的"郭巨祠"、嘉祥县（今济宁）的武氏祠和阙，四川新都县的王稚子墓阙和雅安县的高颐墓阙，是其中最有名的（图 273）。[18]有的墓前还置立动物的立体石雕像，除上述武氏墓和高颐墓前的石兽外，近年来在各地还颇有新的发现。[19]墓前置石雕立体人像的，亦颇不乏例。

从东汉开始，还流行在墓前立石碑，碑文记述墓主人的死亡日期和平生的主要事迹，加以宣扬，这就是所谓"树碑立传"。[20]从魏晋时期开始流行的墓志，就是从汉代的墓碑演变而来的。初期的墓志，如在洛阳发现的西晋太康八年（公元 287 年）的砖质墓志和元康七年（公元 297 年）的石质墓志，在形式上就和汉代的墓碑相似。[21]所不同的是，墓碑甚大，立在地面上，墓志较小，放在地下的墓室里。

中国古代，一般是棺椁并称，两者都属葬具。西汉前期的竖穴式木椁墓，仍然如此。但是，如同前面已经说过的那样，西汉中期以后的横穴式墓，特别是东汉的砖室墓和石室墓，墓室本身就起了椁的作用，可称为"砖椁"和"石椁"，而墓室内的葬具则有棺无椁。一般说来，除有的木椁墓里的棺材形状与战国时代的一样，前后两端的宽度、高度相等而外，汉代的木棺多是前端较宽较高，后端较狭较低。西汉时的木棺多用榫卯相接，"细腰"合盖，东汉则普遍使用铁钉，所以东汉刘熙在《释名·释丧制》中说"古者棺不钉也"。贵族们的木棺，采用上好木料，制作得十分精致、美观，极其奢侈。只要看过长沙马王堆一号汉墓的三具彩绘的漆棺，就可以知道《潜夫论·浮侈篇》所说"计一棺之成功将千万夫"之语不虚

indeed been borne out (figs. 274, 275).[22]

Funerary Banners Han practice continued the Zhou custom of using a funerary banner in funerary processions. At the time of burial the banner would be placed over the coffin. The typical banner is over 2 m long, identical with the length of the coffin. These banners have been found at tomb number 1 of Mawangdui, Changsha, Hunan, number 3 of Mawangdui, and number 9 at Jinqueshan in Linyi, Shandong (fig. 276).[23] The Mawangdui banners are slightly wider at the top, forming a T shape, and the Jinqueshan banner is rectangular, with the top and bottom of equal width. They are all of silk and are painted with fine colored pictures. The picture is divided into three sections, depicting, from top to bottom, heaven, man's world, and the underworld. Both heaven and the underworld are represented by mythological images; the heaven picture has sun, moon, and sometimes stars, and the sun has a golden crow and the moon has a toad and a white rabbit, and sometimes a picture of Chang'e, the goddess of the moon (fig. 277). The underworld picture shows various aquatic animals, representing an aquatic palace at the bottom of the sea. As for man's world, the picture depicts scenes from daily life and also a portrait of the master of the tomb (fig. 278). The three banners from Mawangdui and Jinqueshan have elaborate pictures and are valued as art objects. Similar, but much coarser, banners have been found in the Han tombs at Mozuizi in Wuwei, Gansu; some were made of silk, others hemp. All were covering coffins. Some of them have no pictures, others were painted only with the sun and the moon, but all bear inscriptions containing the names and the homeplaces of the masters of the tombs (fig. 279), the inscriptions substituting for the portraits of the silk paintings.[24] Presumably the funerary banners were widely used in Han dynasty funerary rituals, but few of them have survived because they were made of perishable materials such as silk and hemp. They did survive at Mawangdui and Mozuizi because the former tombs had special preservation conditions and the latter tombs were in an especially dry region.

（图 274、275）。²² 满城窦绾墓的漆棺，在棺盖和棺的外壁嵌饰圆形的玉璧二十余块，在棺的内壁更满镶长方形或方形的玉版近二百块，简直像是一具玉棺，其设计可能是出于对玉的迷信，以为可使棺内的尸体不朽。

按照周代以来的丧礼，汉代出殡时张举着的一种旌幡，入葬时被覆盖在棺材上；旌幡长二米余，正与棺材的长度相等。在湖南长沙马王堆一号墓、三号墓和山东临沂金雀山九号墓中，都发现了这种旌幡（图 276）。²³ 长沙马王堆的二幅，上部较宽，全体呈 T 字形；临沂金雀山的一幅，上下等宽，全体成长方条状。它们都系由绢帛制成，绘有精致的彩色图画。图画的内容，自上而下分三段，分别表示天上、人间、地下。天上和地下，都是根据各种神话传说绘描的，前者主要是绘太阳和月亮，有时也有星辰，太阳中有金乌，月亮中有蟾蜍和玉兔，有时还有奔月的嫦娥（图 277）。后者则绘各种怪异的水族动物，实际上是表示海底的"水府"。至于人间，则绘墓主人日常生活的情景，并突出地绘有他本人的肖像（图 278）。上述长沙马王堆和临沂金雀山的三幅旌幡，由于有着细致、精美的彩色图画，所以称为"帛画"，被作为珍贵的艺术品而受到重视。类似的旌幡，在甘肃武威县磨咀子汉墓中也有发现，有的为丝织品，有的为麻织品，都系覆盖在棺上，它们或者完全没有图画，或者只简单地绘太阳和月亮，但都书写着墓主人的姓名和籍贯等，代替了上述帛画中的墓主人肖像，这便是所谓"铭旌"（图 279）。²⁴ 可以认为，在汉代的丧礼中，使用这种旌幡，是相当普遍的，只是由于它们都系丝麻织物，易于腐朽，所以没有被保留下来。长沙马王堆汉墓和临沂金雀山汉墓由于有特殊的防腐设施，武威磨咀子汉墓由于当地气候干燥，所以独能得到保存。

尸体在棺内的放置，一般都采取仰身伸直的方式。战国时代在黄河流域各地流行的屈肢葬，到汉代已经绝迹。大概是为了企图使尸骨不朽，有时使用各种小玉具遮盖或充塞死者的七窍。塞在口中的称"琀"，往往被制成蝉的形状。《汉书·杨王孙传》说，"口含玉石，欲化不得，郁为枯腊"，这当然是不可信的。

Jade Shrouds   The emperor and nobles of Han were buried wearing jade shrouds. Made from small square jade plates, these shrouds had small holes at the corners, through which gold, silver, or copper threads were strung in order to piece them together to form shrouds with gold, silver, or copper threads.[25] Since 1949, more than ten jade shrouds have been discovered from Han dynasty tombs, and five have been completely restored. Of the five, two were found at Mancheng, Hebei; one was worn by Liu Sheng, the Prince Jing of Zhongshan of Western Han, and one by his wife Dou Wan (fig. 280). One was worn by Liu Xing, the Prince Xiao of Zhongshan of Western Han; it was found in Dingxian, Hebei (fig. 281). One was worn by Liu Gong, the Prince Jing of Pengcheng, of Eastern Han; it was found in Xuzhou, Jiangsu (fig. 282). The last was worn by a Mr. Cao of late Eastern Han, a lineage relative of Cao Cao; it was found in Boxian, Anhui.[26]

The two Mancheng shrouds are excellent examples. The Liu Sheng shroud consisted of 2,498 jade plates and used 1,100 grams of golden threads, and the Dou Wan shroud used 2,160 jade plates and 700 grams of golden threads. The manpower and wealth represented by these figures are astonishing. Combining evidence from archaeological finds and historical records, we believe that Western Han jade shrouds used golden threads, and Eastern Han jade shrouds used golden, silver, or copper threads. According to *Xu Hanshu* ("Li Yi zhi"), for the emperor golden threads were used, for imperial princes and first-generation feudal lords, silver threads, and for others, copper threads. The Dingxian shroud used copper threads gilded in gold,[27] which probably corresponded to silver in quality. So far the earliest complete jade shrouds to be discovered are the two from Mancheng, but shroud fragments have occurred in tomb number 5 at Yangjiawan, in Xianyang, Shaanxi, which dates from Wen Di or Jing Di.[28] It appears that jade shrouds began to be used in early Western Han, and their use continued until the end of Eastern Han. The latest shroud is the one found in Boxian, worn by Mr. Cao. It is recorded in *Sanguozhi* ("Wei zhi") that Cao Pi, Emperor Wen Di of Wei, banned the use of jade shrouds in A.D. 222. Archaeological excavations have failed to uncover any shroud remains from Wei or Jin sites. The use of the jade shroud seems clearly confined to the Han dynasty. The Eastern Han court occasionally presented jade shrouds as gifts to the chiefs of minority groups. It is stated in "Biography of Fu Yu" in "Wei Zhi" of *Sanguozhi* that the king of Fu Yu was buried in a jade shroud and that the

汉代皇帝和贵族，死时穿"玉衣"（又称"玉匣"）入葬，它们是用许多四角穿有小孔的玉片，用金丝、银丝或铜丝编缀起来的，分别称为"金缕玉衣"、"银缕玉衣"、"铜缕玉衣"。[25] 新中国成立以来，汉墓中所发现的玉衣已在十件以上，其中河北省满城西汉中山靖王刘胜及其妻窦绾的二件（图 280）、定县西汉中山孝王刘兴的一件（图 281）、江苏省徐州东汉彭城靖王刘恭的一件（图 282）、安徽省亳县东汉末年曹操的宗族曹某的一件，共五件，已经完全复原。[26] 以满城汉墓的二件为例，刘胜的玉衣共用玉片 2498 片，金丝重 1100 克，窦绾的玉衣共用玉片 2160 片，金丝重 700 克，其制作所费的人力和物力是十分惊人的。从出土的实物，并结合文献的记载来看，西汉的玉衣似乎多属金缕，东汉的玉衣则有金缕、银缕、铜缕之分。据《续汉书·礼仪志》记载，皇帝用金缕，诸侯王和始封的列侯用银缕，其他多用铜缕，估计袭爵的列侯也在用铜缕之列。河北定县东汉中山简王刘焉的玉衣是鎏金的铜缕[27]，其等级可能与银缕的相当。迄今发现的完整的玉衣，以满城汉墓（武帝时期）的二件为最早。由于在陕西咸阳杨家湾五号墓（其年代在文帝或景帝时）中也发现了玉衣上的玉片[28]，可见西汉前期即已开始使用玉衣，以后一直沿袭到东汉。亳县董园村东汉末年曹氏墓中出土的玉衣，应该是年代最晚的。据《三国志·魏志》记载，魏文帝曹丕于黄初三年（公元 222 年）下令禁止用玉衣，而在实际的考古发掘工作中也没有发现过魏晋以后的玉衣，可见它的使用限于汉代。东汉的政府还以玉衣赠送给少数民族的首领。据《魏志·扶余传》记载，扶余国王葬时用玉衣，汉朝政府将玉衣存放在玄菟郡（其治所在

Han court stored a jade shroud at Xuantu Jun, where it would be picked up when the king of Fu Yu died. When Sima Yi exterminated Gongsun Yuan of Liaodong, a jade shroud was found in the warehouse at Xuantu Jun. This incident happened after the ban by Cao Pi. Perhaps this was an exceptional situation involving policy toward minority groups. The purpose of using jade for funerary shrouds was to preserve the body. *Hou Hanshu* (the "Biography of Liu Penzi") claimed that the bodies in jade shrouds in the imperial mausoleums of the Western Han were all so well preserved that they looked like living people. This is, of course, not true. Cao Pi was perhaps more on the mark when he said, in banning the practice, that the use of jade shrouds was a "stupid and vulgar act."

Inventories of Grave Goods   Many early Western Han tombs, such as the Han tombs at Mawangdui in Changsha and at Fenghuangshan in Jiangling, have yielded books of bamboo slips that give an inventory of the grave goods—their names and quantities.

These are called *qian ce*, or inventory slips, from the phrase, "inscribe the grave goods on slips," in *Yi li* ("Ji xi li") (fig. 283).[29] Within some other Han tombs, such as the ones at Dafentou in Yunmeng, Hubei, and the tombs of Huo He and Shi Qi Yao in Haizhou, Jiangsu, rectangular wooden tablets were found, on which are inscribed the names and quantities of the grave goods.[30] These were called *feng fang*, or inventory tablets, following the statement, "inscribe grave goods on tablets" in *Yi li* ("Ji xi li") (fig. 284). By consulting these inventories, archaeologists may be able to achieve an understanding of the names and uses of a variety of objects from the Han era.

今辽宁省沈阳附近），等扶余王死时派人前来领取。司马懿消灭割据辽东的公孙渊时，玄菟郡库房中尚存留玉衣一件。这时已在曹丕下禁令之后，但大概由于事关对少数民族的政策，所以是一种例外。以玉衣为葬服，其目的是企图保存尸骨不朽。《后汉书·刘盆子传》说，西汉诸帝陵墓内凡穿有玉衣的尸体都完好如生人，这当然是无稽之谈，不足为信。曹丕在下禁令时就说，用玉衣之类随葬是"愚俗之所为"。

长沙马王堆汉墓、江陵凤凰山汉墓等许多西汉前期的墓，和战国时代的许多墓一样，墓中存放着用竹简编成的簿册，记录着各种随葬品的名称和数量，根据《仪礼·既夕礼》"书遣于册"的记载，可以称之为"遣策"（图283）。[29] 考古学家们按照"遣策"中的记录，可以了解当时各种器物的名称和用途。湖北云梦大坟头汉墓、江苏海川霍贺墓和侍其繇墓中则有长方形的木版，书写着随葬器物的名称和数量[30]，根据《仪礼·既夕礼》"书赗于方"的记载，可称之为"赗方"，其性质与"遣策"相似。发掘工作证明，直到三国和晋代仍然流行这种"赗方"。

240. Top view of wooden chamber of Han tomb number 1 at Mawangdui, Changsha
长沙马王堆一号汉墓棺椁俯视

241. Top view of wooden chamber of Han tomb number 168 at Fenghuangshan, Jiangling
江陵凤凰山一六八号汉墓棺椁俯视

242. View of the entire burial chamber of the Han tomb at Dabaotai, Beijing　北京大葆台汉墓

243. The southern side chamber and remains of carriages and horses in the tomb of Liu Sheng in Mancheng　满城刘胜墓的南耳室及车辆马匹遗址

244. The northern side chamber with its furnished pottery vessels, in the tomb of Liu Sheng in Mancheng　满城刘胜墓北耳室及陶器

245. The anterior chamber of Liu Sheng's tomb in Mancheng　满城刘胜墓前室

246. Reconstruction of Liu Sheng's tomb in Mancheng 满城刘胜墓复原图

247. Hollow-brick tomb of Western Han, excavated at Shaogou, Luoyang 洛阳烧沟的西汉空心砖墓

248. Structure of the top of the hollow-brick tomb of Western Han, excavated at Shaogou, Luoyang
洛阳烧沟空心砖墓顶部结构

249. Green Dragon and White Tiger in the murals of a Han tomb (tomb of Bu Qianqiu) in Luoyang
洛阳汉墓（卜千秋墓）壁画中的青龙、白虎像

250. Portrait of Fu Xi in the mural of a Han tomb (tomb of Bu Qianqiu) in Luoyang
洛阳汉墓（卜千秋墓）壁画中的伏羲像

251. Portrait of Nü Wa in the mural of a Han tomb (tomb of Bu Qianqiu) in Luoyang
洛阳汉墓（卜千秋墓）壁画中的女娲像

252. Mural scene depicting the story "Using two peaches to kill three gentlemen" in a Han tomb in Luoyang　洛阳汉墓壁画"二桃杀三士"

253. "The Banquet at Hongmen" (right half) in the mural of a Han tomb in Luoyang　洛阳汉墓壁画"鸿门宴"（右半部分）

254. "The Banquet at Hongmen" (left half) in the mural of a Han tomb in Luoyang　洛阳汉墓壁画"鸿门宴"（左半部分）

255. Brick chamber tomb of Eastern Han, excavated in Luoyang 洛阳发掘的东汉砖室墓

256. Structure of the top of a brick chamber tomb of Eastern Han, excavated in Luoyang
洛阳发掘的东汉砖室墓顶部结构

257. Subordinates, servants, and other human figures in the wall painting of a Han tomb in Wangdu, Hebei
河北望都汉墓壁画中的 "辟车伍佰"

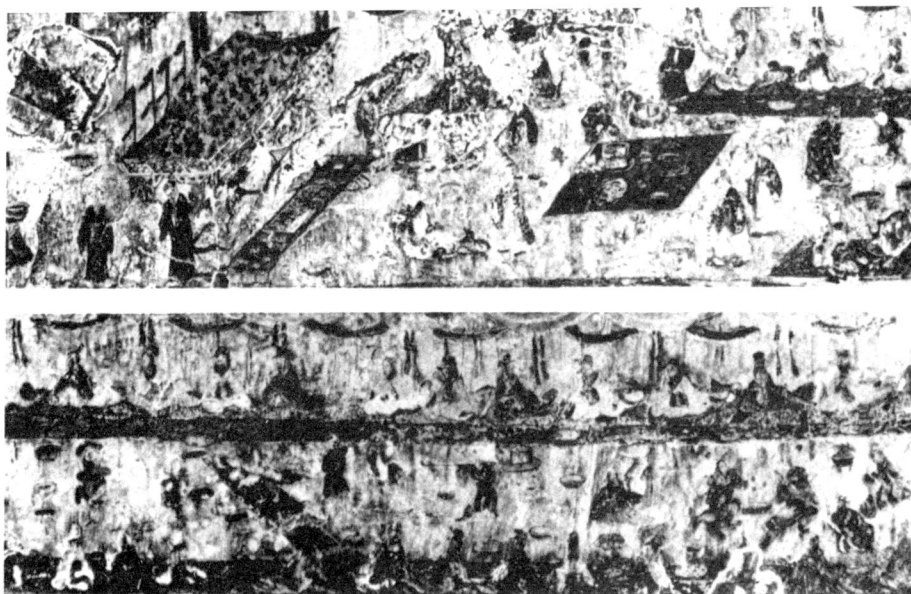

258. A feast and a performance in wall painting of a Han tomb at Dahuting in Mixian, Henan
河南密县打虎亭汉墓壁画中的宴会百戏图

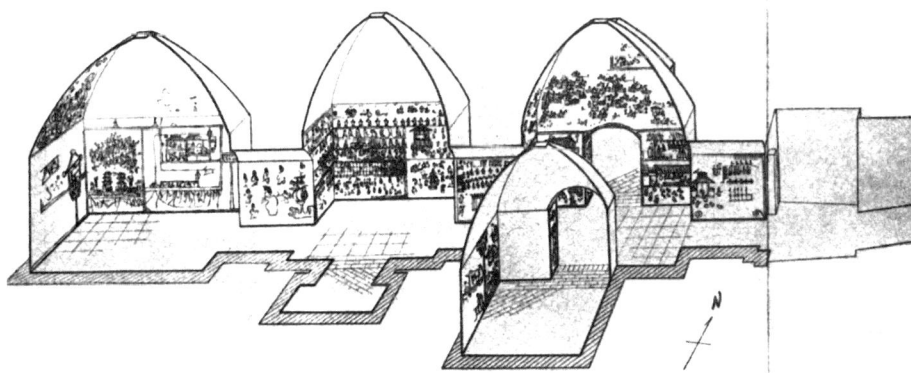

259. Diagram of the chamber of the Han tomb in Holingor, Inner Mongolia　内蒙古和林格尔汉墓墓室透视图

260. Scene of Ningcheng (partial) in the wall painting of the Han tomb in Holingor, Inner Mongolia
内蒙古和林格尔汉墓壁画中的宁城 （部分）

261. Scene of Ningcheng (partial) in the wall painting of the Han tomb in Holingor, Inner Mongolia
内蒙古和林格尔汉墓壁画中的宁城 （部分）

262. Structure of the burial chamber of the Han tomb in Anqiu, Shandong　山东安丘汉墓墓室结构

263. The doors of the Han tomb in Yi'nan, Shandong　山东沂南汉墓墓门

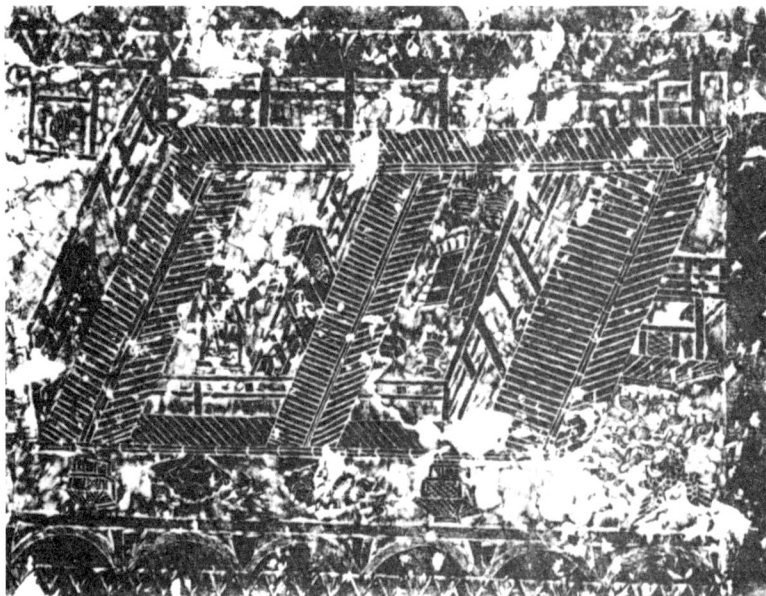

264. Rubbing of the courtyard scene in the stone engravings in the Han tomb in Yi'nan, Shandong　山东沂南汉墓石刻画像中的宅院（拓片）

265. Rubbing of the right third of the battle scene in the stone engravings in the Han tomb in Yi'nan, Shandong
山东沂南汉墓石刻画像中的攻战图（右侧三分之一，拓片）

266. Rubbing of the middle third of the battle scene in fig. 265　沂南汉墓石刻画像中的攻战图（中间三分之一，拓片）

267. Rubbing of the left third of the battle scene in fig. 265　沂南汉墓石刻画像中的攻战图（左侧三分之一，拓片）

268. Pictorial brick depicting a lecture scene, unearthed in Deyang, Sichuan　四川德阳出土的讲经画像砖

269. Pictorial brick depicting a feast scene, unearthed in Chengdu, Sichuan　四川成都出土的宴饮画像砖

270. Pictorial brick depicting music and dance, unearthed from the Han tomb in Chengdu, Sichuan
　　　四川成都汉墓出土的乐舞画像砖

271. Pictorial brick depicting carriages and horseback riding, unearthed from the Han tomb in Chengdu, Sichuan
四川成都汉墓出土的车骑画像砖

272. Pictorial brick depicting salt making, unearthed in Chengdu, Sichuan 四川成都出土的煮盐画像砖

273. Monumental tower (*que*) in front of the grave of Gao Yi in Ya'an, Sichuan　四川雅安高颐墓阙

274. Painted lacquered coffin from Han tomb number 1 at Mawangdui, Changsha　长沙马王堆一号汉墓中的黑地彩绘漆棺

275. Second painted lacquered coffin from Mawangdui　马王堆一号汉墓中的朱地彩绘漆棺

276. Funerary banner unearthed from Han tomb number 1 at Mawangdui, Changsha
长沙马王堆一号汉墓出土的旌幡

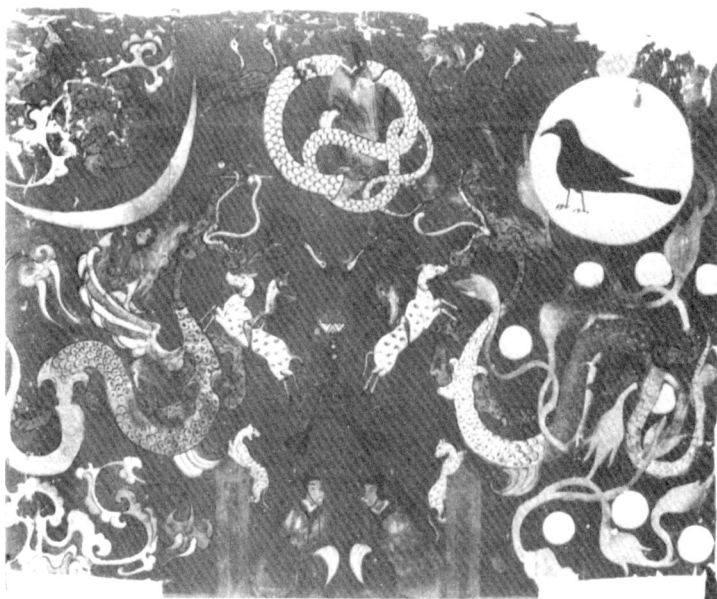

277. The heaven scene in the funerary banner unearthed from Han tomb number 1 at Mawangdui, Changsha
长沙马王堆一号汉墓中旌幡上的"天上"部分

278. Portrait of the tomb master in the funerary banner unearthed from Han tomb number 1 at
Mawangdui, Changsha 长沙马王堆一号汉墓中旌幡上的"人间"部分

279. Funerary banner unearthed from the Han tomb
at Mozuizi in Wuwei, Gansu
甘肃武威磨咀子汉墓出土的旌幡

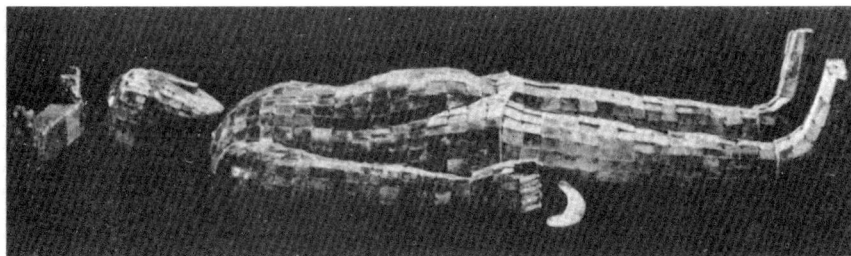

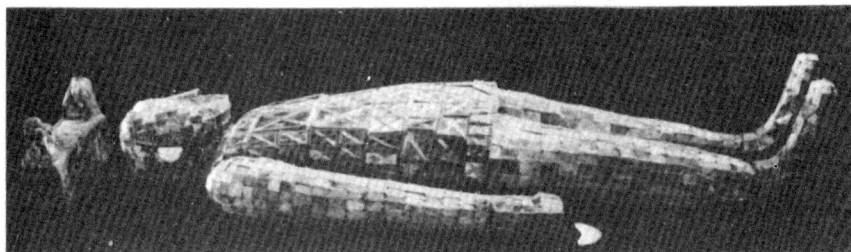

280. Jade mortuary shrouds with gold threads, unearthed from the Han tomb in Mancheng (upper: Liu Sheng's; lower: Dou Wan's)
满城汉墓出土的金缕玉衣 （上：刘胜、下：窦绾）

281. Jade shroud with gold threads, unearthed from Han tomb number 40 in Dingxian, Hebei 河北定县四十号汉墓出土的金缕玉衣

282. Jade shroud with silver threads, unearthed from the Han tomb in Xuzhou, Jiangsu 江苏徐州汉墓出土的银缕玉衣

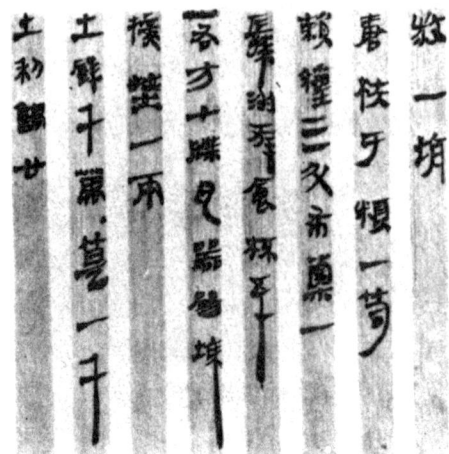

283. Details of *qian ce*, or inventory slips, unearthed from Han tomb number 1 at Mawangdui, Changsha
长沙马王堆一号汉墓出土的遣策

284. *Feng fang*, or inventory tablet, unearthed from the tomb
of Shi Qi Yao of Western Han in Haizhou, Jiangsu
江苏海州西汉侍其繇墓出土的赗方

CHAPTER 9 TOMBS—II

Grave Goods One of the central ideas of the funerary rites prevailing among the landowners and bureaucrats of the Han dynasty was that the dead should be treated in the same way as the living. As stated in "Bo zang pian," *Lun heng*, "treat death as life." Consequently, not only did the form and the structure of the burial chamber imitate a real-life house, the grave was also provided with as complete a complement of furnishings and provisions as possible. No utensils and objects that were used by the living were barred from the tomb.

First off, in order that the dead person be able to continue a comfortable life in the other world, foods of various sorts were supplied as the principal grave goods (figs. 285-86). Take tomb number 1 of Mawangdui as an example. The following food items were discovered in the tomb: cereals and legumes including rice, wheat, barley, panic millet, foxtail millet, soybeans, and red beans; fruits and vegetables including melons, jujubes (Chinese dates), pears, plums, Chinese strawberries, malva, mustard greens, lotus roots, and bamboo shoots; animals including pigs, cattle, sheep, dogs, deer, and rabbits; birds including chickens, ducks, cranes, turtledoves, owls, wild geese, magpies, sparrows, mandarin ducks, bamboo pheasants, and ringed pheasants; fish including carp, crucian carp, two other kinds of carp, perch, and bream.[1] These foodstuffs were prepared into cooked cereals, cakes, and various other dishes, with the addition of condiments such as sweetener, honey, soy sauce, salt, and several kinds of wine. The names of the dishes were listed on *qian ce*, or inventory slips in the tomb; the classes were complex and the names numerous.[2] Liu Sheng, the Prince Jing of Zhongshan, buried in the Han dynasty tomb of Mancheng, was famous for his fondness of drinking. In the tombs in which he and his wife were buried there were more than thirty large pottery urns, each 70 cm tall. Some of the urns were inscribed in red on the outside: "15 piculs of Grade A panic millet wine"; "15 piculs of sweet liqueur"; "11 piculs of rice wine"; and the like.

Traces of wine were still visible inside the urns at the time of excavation. It is estimated that more than 5,000 kg of wine—a remarkable amount—were contained in these urns (fig. 287).[3]

Another major part of the grave goods of that time consisted of various garments and fabrics. The clothing from tomb number 1 of

玖 汉代的墓葬（下）

在汉代地主官僚阶级中流行的丧礼和葬俗，其中心思想之一，是把死人当作生人看待，即《论衡·薄葬篇》所说的"谓死如生"。所以，不仅在墓室的形制和结构上模仿现实生活中的房屋，而且在随葬品方面也尽量做到应有尽有，凡是生人所用的器具、物品，无不可以纳入墓中。《盐铁论·散不足》所谓"厚资多藏，器用如生人"，也正说明了这一事实。

首先，为了使死者能在另一世界继续过着美好的生活，各种各样的食物就成为主要的随葬品（图285、286）。以长沙马王堆一号汉墓为例，墓中发现的食物，包括稻米、小麦、大麦、黍、粟、大豆、赤豆等粮食，甜瓜、枣、梨、梅、杨梅、葵（冬苋菜）、芥菜、藕、笋等瓜果和蔬菜，猪、牛、羊、狗、鹿、兔等兽类，鸡、鸭、鹤、斑鸠、鸮、雁、喜鹊、麻雀、鸳鸯、竹鸡、雉等禽类，鲤鱼、鲫鱼、鳜鱼、银鲴、鳡鱼等鱼类[1]，它们多被制成饭、饼，烹调成各种羹肴，加上糖、蜜、酱、盐等调味品和各种酒类，其名称见于墓中的"遣策"，品类之繁，名目之多，举不胜举。[2]满城汉墓所葬中山靖王刘胜是以嗜酒出名的，在他和他的妻子窦绾的墓中有着三十余个高达七十厘米的大陶缸，有的缸上写着朱红色的文字，如云"黍上尊酒十五石"、"甘醪十五石"、"黍酒十一石"、"稻酒十一石"、"甘醪十石"等，出土时缸内都清楚地遗留着酒的痕迹，估计当时所装的酒共达五千多公斤，达到了惊人的程度（图287）。[3]《论衡·死伪篇》说，汉元帝傅后墓内多藏食物，腐朽猥发，改葬时发棺，臭气熏天，以致身临现场的洛阳丞闻臭而死，这是对当时统治阶级厚葬的莫大讽刺。

各种衣物和衣料，也是当时主要的随葬品。马王堆一号汉墓中

Mawangdui included padded robes, double-layered robes, single-layered robes, single-layered skirts, shoes, socks, and mittens—most of them made of silk (figs. 288, 289). In addition, many silk fabrics were placed in large bamboo-matted suitcases, including warp-patterned fabric and embroidery, common silk, damask and brocade, the leno (or gauze) weave—their quality excellent, their colors bright, and their designs beautiful (figs. 290, 291).[4] Presumably clothing and fabrics were placed in many other Han dynasty tombs, but elsewhere the conditions for preservation have not been as favorable and they have not survived. But inventory tablets (*feng fang*) in some of these tombs, such as the tombs of Huo He and Shi Qi Yao, in Haizhou, Jiangsu, listed names and quantities of clothing, although very little of the clothing itself has survived.

Bronze, lacquer, and pottery items were the most common Han grave goods. Most of these were containers in which food and drink were originally placed. Utensils such as lamps, incense burners, irons (for ironing clothes), toilet article boxes, mirrors, as well as weapons such as knives and swords, were also commonly found in tombs. Ornaments were found also: various beads and pendants of such materials as jade, opal, amber, quartz, gold, and silver. In short, so numerous were the grave goods that they cannot be exhaustively listed. They varied in quality and quantity from grave to grave, depending upon the status and wealth of the grave's occupant; on the other hand, their characteristics changed along with changes in social conditions and manners and customs. In general, in early and middle Western Han, what the nobility and the bureaucrats would place in tombs were the real thing—various valuable objects that they would use in real life. But after middle Western Han fashions changed, and mortuary pottery made specifically for burial purposes increased in quantity. The earliest to appear were pottery granaries and pottery stoves; they had appeared in early Western Han and became popular in middle Western Han (figs. 292, 293). After that, pottery models of wells, querns, pigsties, multistoried buildings, pestling

shops, and farm fields, along with pottery images of domestic animals
and fowl such as pigs, dogs, sheep, chickens, and ducks, made a gradual
appearance. The later the grave (especially after Eastern Han), the more
numerous were these pottery models. In Eastern Han tombs, the grave
goods consisted mostly of pottery vessels and such pottery mortuary
models as described above. There was a decrease in the more valuable
utilitarian vessels of bronze and lacquerware. Even the large graves of

的衣物，计有棉袍、夹袍、单衣、单裙、鞋、袜和手套等类，多系
用丝绸制成（图 288、289），并有大量成幅的丝绸放置在大型的竹
笥中，其种类包括绢、纱、罗、绮、锦和刺绣，质地精致，颜色鲜
艳，花纹美丽（图 290、291）。[4] 可以认为，各地许多汉墓中都有不
少衣物和衣料随葬，只是由于缺乏保存的条件，年久朽坏，没有能
够遗留下来而已。有些汉墓，如江苏省海州的霍贺墓和侍其繇墓，
虽然没有发现较多的衣物，但在它们的"赗方"中却记录着各种衣
物的名称和数量，便是例证。

　　各种铜器、漆器和陶器，是汉墓中最常见的随葬品，它们主要
是容器，当时应该是装有食物和饮料的。灯、熏炉、熨斗、奁、镜
等生活用具及刀、剑等武器，也在墓中普遍地存在。装饰品方面，
则有各种珠佩等类，其质料包括玉石、玛瑙、琥珀、水晶及金银
等。总之，墓中随葬品的种类极多，不胜枚举。它们往往视墓主人
的身份和财富的不同而有厚薄、多寡之分。但是，另一方面，随着
时代的推移，社会情况和风俗的改变，随葬品的种类和性质也有所
变化。总的说来，西汉前期和中期，贵族、官僚们往往主要是将生
前实用的各种珍贵器物纳入墓中。值得注意的是，西汉中期以后，
风气为之一变，专为随葬而作的陶质明器开始显著地增多。最初出
现的是陶仓和陶灶，它们在秦和西汉前期即已存在，但普遍流行则
在西汉的中期（图 292、293）。以后，诸如井、磨、猪圈、楼阁、
碓房、田地等模型，以及猪、狗、羊、鸡、鸭等家畜和家禽的偶
像，陆续出现，应有尽有，时代愈晚，特别是东汉以后，种类和
数量愈多。在东汉的墓中，大量的随葬品主要是各种陶制容器和
上述的各种陶质明器，而比较贵重的实用品如铜器和漆器等则反而

bureaucrats and nobility are no exception. What is indicated is that, with the development of the manorial economy, the ideology pertaining to grave goods among the members of the landowning class underwent a significant change. They may have felt that, rather than placing valuable objects of limited quantity underground, it might be better to make symbolic pottery models of everything in the manor and to place them in the tomb.

What is amply reflected in the grave goods is that landowners of the Han dynasty paid special attention to the possession of land. In tomb number 167 at Fenghuangshan in Jiangling, which is dated to early Western Han, was found a piece of hardened clay wrapped in dark red silk. This was referred to as *bu tu* on the *qian ce* found in the same grave, meaning that it was a legally owned piece of land that had been officially registered. This piece of clay is rectangular, 20 by 14 by 12 cm. Placed in the tomb, it probably symbolized the continued possession of this piece of land by the master of the tomb.[5] The use of pottery models of farm fields in Eastern Han probably carried the same implication (fig. 294).

During the Shang, Western Zhou, and Eastern Zhou dynasties, graves of rulers were often accompanied by nearby pit burials of horses and chariots or of carriages. Real carriages and horses were still used in some tombs of the nobility in middle Western Han, examples being the tombs of the Prince Jing of Zhongshan in Mancheng and the Prince Lu in Qufu.[6] Special pits containing chariot and horses were placed in front of the burial chamber of the tomb of the Prince of Yan at Dabaotai in Beijing, a continuation of the traditional Shang and Zhou custom (fig. 295).[7] But in late Western Han and Eastern Han, wooden and pottery models of carriages and horses replaced real ones. The burial of human victims as part of grave furnishings was by then legally banned, as recorded in *Hanshu* ("Biography of the Prince Jingsu of Zhao") and other texts. Therefore, with a few exceptions, human victims no longer are found in Han tombs, and wooden or pottery figurines take the place of servants and maids (fig. 296).

Tombs number 4 and 5 found at Yangjiawan, in Xianyang city of Shaanxi, are dated to emperors Wen Di and Jing Di of Western Han; their occupants probably were important military generals. Some archaeologists speculate that these were the tombs of Zhou Bo and his son Zhou Yafu, based on the descriptions of their tombs in *Shuijingzhu*,

逐渐减少，即使是官僚、贵族们的大墓亦不在例外。这说明随着庄园经济的发展，地主阶级对随葬品的观念已经有了改变。他们可能觉得，与其将一些有限的珍贵器物带到地下，还不如将庄园中的全部动产和不动产都制作成象征性的陶质明器，纳入墓中。

汉代的地主阶级，对土地的占有特别重视，这在随葬品方面也得到充分的反映。在属于西汉前期的江陵凤凰山一六七号墓中，发现了一块用绛红色绢布包裹着的土块，对照该墓的遣策，可知它的名称为"簿土"，意即在官府的簿册中经过登记的合法的土地；土块呈长方形，长二十、宽十四、厚十二厘米，它被放在墓中随葬，象征着墓主人对土地的占有权。[5] 凤凰山八号墓和一六八号墓，据遣策的记录，也有同样的簿土；八号墓的竹笥中有泥土一堆，应该便是它的实物。到了东汉，则又盛行用陶质的田地模型随葬，其含意正与上述用"簿土"随葬相同（图 294）。

自商代、西周以来，直至战国时代，在统治阶级的陵墓附近，往往另设坑穴，埋置车马。在西汉中期的贵族墓中，仍然有用真车、真马随葬的，满城的中山靖王墓、曲阜的鲁王墓[6] 和北京大葆台的燕王墓（图 295）[7] 便是例证。但是，到了西汉晚期，特别是东汉，一般也都用木制或陶制的车的模型和马的偶像来代替了。杀人殉葬在法律上已被禁止，这可以从《汉书·赵敬肃王传》等记载得到说明。所以，除了个别例外，汉墓中已没有人殉的现象，一般也是用木俑或陶俑随葬，作为奴婢的替身（图 296）。

陕西省咸阳市杨家湾四号墓和五号墓，年代相当于西汉的文帝和景帝时期，墓主人可能是当时重要的将领。有人根据《水经注》的记述，认为它们也许是周勃、周亚夫父子二人的墓，但不能

but this hypothesis is by no means a certainty. Ten pits to the south of the graves contain a large number of pottery figurines. Altogether there are more than 1,800 figurines of foot soldiers and more than 580 figurines of mounted soldiers. The soldiers are holding weapons in their hands and wearing armor and are arranged in neat formations.[8] It is recorded that in the Han dynasty when important military officials died the imperial court would give them elaborate funerals and use military formations in the funerary processions. The large group of pottery figurines at Yangjiawan could be a model of such a funeral formation (fig. 297).

Although most of the models of carriages, people, and horses were wooden or ceramic in Han dynasty tombs, there are exceptions. A remarkable example of bronze models of carriages, horses, soldiers, and servants has been found in the Han tombs at Leitai in Wuwei, Gansu (figs. 298-300).[9] As I described in a previous chapter, processions of carriages and horses constituted an important motif in Eastern Han murals found in brick chamber tombs. The Han tomb of Leitai does not have such murals, but instead used bronze models. In the front of the procession were soldiers mounted on horses and holding spears and *ji*-halberds. The rear of the procession was made up of various carriages and attendants who were either handling the carriages and the horses or were simply in attendance. Altogether in the procession were seventeen soldiers, twenty-eight servants and attendants, thirty-nine horses, and fourteen carriages, forming a remarkable and unique sight. To acquire such furnishings obviously required vast sums of manpower and money. In late Eastern Han, officials and generals in border regions very often were wealthy and powerful and were capable of indulging in anything they wanted. The Han tomb of Leitai is a true indication of this fact.

Perhaps because money was becoming increasingly important in the Han dynasty, the use of coins in graves became quite fashionable. Even in the large graves of nobility and bureaucrats, where there were already many valuable goods, some coins would be included to symbolize their wealth. In Western Han, although coins were used in tombs, the number used was often small. It increased in Eastern Han. In the Han tomb of Leitai, mentioned earlier, which dates from late Eastern Han, there were

肯定。在墓的南面附近，附设有十个坑穴，埋藏着大量的陶俑，其中步兵俑共一千八百余，骑兵俑共五百八十余，士兵们手执武器，身被铠甲，行列整齐有序。[8]在汉代，重要的将领死后，朝廷给以隆重的礼遇，用军阵送葬。杨家湾汉墓的庞大的陶俑群，正是这种军阵的模拟（图297）。

虽然在大多数汉墓里用以随葬的车的模型和人、马的偶像是木制或陶制的，但也不无例外。在甘肃省武威县雷台汉墓中，随葬着一批铜质的车马模型和兵士、奴婢的铸像，便是最突出的一例（图298—300）。[9]如前所述，在东汉砖室墓的壁画中，常有车马出行图。雷台汉墓中没有这种壁画，却用铜质的车的模型和人、马的偶像来模拟出行时的行列，前面是手执矛、戟的骑马武士，后面则是各种车辆以及御车、牵马和随从的奴婢，共计武士十七人、奴婢二十八人、马三十九匹、车十四辆，排列起来，颇为壮观，可以说是别出心裁。当然，这要耗费很大的人力和物力。东汉后期，边郡的大吏和将领们往往拥有很大的财富和权力，可以在当地为所欲为，雷台汉墓正反映了这种情形。

在长江流域和南方地区，水上交通发达，所以除了车马之外，船的模型也成为墓中的随葬品。在江陵的西汉前期墓、长沙和广州的西汉后期墓中，都曾发现木船的模型，在广州的东汉墓中还曾发现陶船的模型。这些木船和陶船模型，都制作得相当细致，形状和结构逼真。有的模型显示了是用于运输的船，它们在墓中随葬，可能与墓主人从事商业活动有关。

大概是由于对货币的重视在汉代已日益加深，所以在墓中用铜钱随葬已成为风气。即使是贵族、官僚们的大墓，墓中有着各种各样贵重的随葬品，也免不了要再添上一些铜钱，作为财富的象征。西汉时，虽然已盛行用铜钱随葬，但所用铜钱的数量往往并不很多，到了东汉，才逐渐增多。上述东汉后期的雷台汉墓，随葬铜钱

more than 28,000 coins.[10] In some regions, such as Changsha of Hunan, clay (mortuary) coins were used in addition to bronze coins. These are not a reflection of the frugality of the tomb master but of prevailing custom. In the Han tomb of Mawangdui, for example, with its quantities of valuable grave goods, clay coins were still used instead of bronze coins (fig. 301).[11]

The nobles, bureaucrats, and landowners of the Han dynasty were fond of burying books as grave goods. Books at the time were often on silk or on slips of bamboo or wood. Such written materials have been unearthed in large quantities from Han tombs since 1949. At the Western Han tomb at Mawangdui were found silk books of *Laozi*, *Yi jing*, *Zhan guo ce* (figs. 302, 303) and in the Western Han tomb at Shuanggudui were found bamboo books of *Shi jing* and *Cang Jie pian*.[12] From a Western Han tomb at Yinqueshan in Linyi, Shandong, came *Sunzi bing fa*, *Sun Bin bing fa*, *Yanzi chun qiu* and other bamboo books (fig. 304).[13] A wooden slip book of *Yi li* was found in an early Eastern Han tomb at Mozuizi, Wuwei, in Gansu (fig. 305), and wooden slips of medicinal texts were found from an early Eastern Han tomb at Hantanpo in Wuwei.[14] These books have been preserved because either special, effective preservation measures were taken, or the tombs were submerged in water, or they were preserved by extremely dry conditions. Presumably books were a common grave furnishing in Han dynasty tombs, but in most cases they have not survived.

Seals were another object that was used by landowners and bureaucrats of the Han dynasty for burial. Some of the seals were private seals, others official seals. Almost a hundred have been found in the Han tombs in the Changsha area alone in the last two decades or so.[15] From tomb number 2 at Mawangdui came three seals, the inscriptions being "Seal of Marquis Dai," "The Chengxiang [Chancellor] of Changsha," and "Li Cang." The first two are of gilded bronze, and the third is of jade. They helped determine the name and identity of the master of the tomb (fig. 306).[16] Most of the seals of the

Han dynasty belonged to men, but there were exceptions. Tomb number 2 of Mancheng was the tomb of Dou Wan, the wife of Liu Sheng, the Prince Jing of Zhongshan. From her tomb came seals inscribed with the characters "Dou Wan" and "Dou Jun Xu" (fig. 307).[17]

竟达二万八千余枚之多。[10] 有的地区，例如在湖南省的长沙一带，除了铜钱以外，还盛行用泥质的冥钱随葬。必须指出，这并不是出于墓主人的节约，而是一种风俗。马王堆汉墓随葬着大量珍贵的器物，但却用泥钱来代替铜钱，便是最好的说明（图 301 ）。[11]

汉代的贵族、官僚和地主们，往往喜欢用书籍随葬。当时的书籍，有的是书写在丝织品上，称为帛书，有的书写在竹简和木牍上，可称之为竹书和木书。新中国成立以来，在汉墓中发现的帛书、竹书和木书，已经达到相当大的数量。例如，湖南长沙马王堆西汉墓中发现了《老子》、《易经》、《战国策》等帛书（图 302、303 ），安徽阜阳双古堆西汉墓中发现了《诗经》、《苍颉篇》等竹书[12]，山东临沂银雀山西汉墓中发现了《孙子兵法》、《孙膑兵法》、《晏子春秋》等竹书（图 304 ）[13]，甘肃武威磨咀子东汉初期墓中发现了《仪礼》的木书（图 305 ），武威旱滩坡东汉初期墓中发现了有关医药的木书[14]，它们都是十分珍贵的文物。上述这些西汉和东汉的墓，有的由于有特殊的防腐设施，有的由于墓穴较深而使棺椁被长期浸泡在地下水中，有的则由于当地气候干燥，所以墓中的书籍能够得到保存，可以认为，汉代用书籍随葬的风气是相当普遍的，只是由于大多数的墓不具备保存书籍的条件，所以没有能够遗留下来而已。

汉代的地主官僚阶级，还流行用印章随葬，有的为私印，有的为官印。仅就湖南省长沙一地而言，近二十余年来，汉墓中出土的各种印章已有近百枚之多，可见当时用印章随葬的风气之盛。[15] 在长沙马王堆二号汉墓中，发现了三枚印章，印文分别为"轪侯之印"、"长沙丞相"和"利苍"，前二者为铜质鎏金，后者为玉质，它们的发现确定了墓主人的姓名和身份（图 306 ）。[16] 在汉代，使用印章的虽多为男子，但亦颇有例外。满城二号汉墓所葬为中山靖王刘胜之妻，墓中出土的铜印刻有"窦绾"、"窦君须"字样，便是一例（图 307 ）。[17]

In Eastern Han tombs were sometimes found sales contracts for the purchase of the tomb plot, in the form of elongated lead plates called *mai di quan*.[18] They were probably symbolic contracts, placed in the tomb for the security of the deceased, testifying to his right of possession. Sometimes the inscription included the admonition that all persons who were buried within the plot area should become his servants. Although such sales contracts were for the use in the afterlife, they also reflect the fierceness of the struggles for land in real life and some of the situations which led peasants to become bond servants.

Tombs of the middle and, especially, the late Eastern Han period often contained what are called "tomb security jars." These bottles were inscribed in red on the outside; the inscriptions often began with a notation on the year, month, and date, and always end with the phrase *ru lü ling* ("as ordered by the spell") (fig. 308).[19] As suggested by the red inscriptions, the function of these jars was to assure the tranquility of the remaining members of the family, to assure the security of the tomb of the dead, and in the name of "the angels of the god" to eliminate the guilt of the living and seek blessing for the dead. In late Eastern Han Taoism became quite popular, and these bottles were probably indicative of Taoist concepts. Their use was by this time quite common and they even found their way into the tombs of famous upper-class people among the bureaucrats and landowners, such as those of the Yang lineage at Hongnong in Huayin, Shaanxi.[20]

Family and Lineage Graves There were literary records pertaining to the burial of husband and wife in the same tomb before Han, but such burials have not yet been found in the archaeological record at such an early date. Excavations have shown that the husband-and-wife burials of the Warring States period were in fact two separate burials in two grave pits next to each other. The same custom was followed even in early and middle Western Han. After middle Western Han, however, husband-and-wife burials in the same pit became popular; in late Western Han and throughout Eastern Han such burials were the rule (figs. 309, 310).

The manorial economy of the Han dynasty caused the family members among the landowning class to be very close, especially in Eastern Han. This intimacy was reflected in mortuary practices in long-continuing family tombs. Members of the same family of several

在东汉的墓中，有时还随葬着一种买卖墓地的契约，多数是刻在长条状的铅板上，称为"买地券"。[18]它是作为一种象征性的证券，放在墓里，使得死者有所凭持，以保证对墓地的所有权不被侵犯，券上所刻文字还往往强调要墓地范围内所埋葬的其他死者都成为他的奴婢。这种买地券虽专供"阴间"使用，但也反映了现实生活中土地兼并的激烈，以及广大农民因破产而沦为奴婢的情况。

此外，在墓中随葬的还有一种所谓"镇墓瓶"，流行于东汉中期，特别是东汉的后期。陶瓶上的文字多为朱书，有的冠以年月日，最后都以"如律令"的字样结束（图308）。[19]如朱书文字本身所表明的那样，"镇墓瓶"的作用在于使生人的家宅安宁，使死者的冢墓稳定，以"天帝使者"之类的名义为生人解罪，为死者求福，安慰并约束亡灵，使其认识死生有别，勿事纠缠。东汉后期，巫道流行。从"镇墓瓶"上的文字看来，当与巫术有关。应该指出的是，"镇墓瓶"的用意虽十分荒诞，但它的使用却相当普遍，即使是官僚地主阶级中极有名望的士大夫亦不能免俗，陕西华阴的弘农杨氏墓中也有这种"镇墓瓶"的存在，便是证明。[20]

汉代以前，文献上虽有关于夫妇合葬的记载，但在考古发掘工作中迄今极少发现同墓合葬的情形。发掘工作证明，汉以前的合葬，一般是夫妇分别葬于两个并排紧靠的墓坑中，可称为"异穴合葬"。直到西汉前期和中期，夫妇合葬仍然多采用这种方式，长沙马王堆汉墓和满城汉墓即如此。西汉中期以后，制度为之一变，除帝陵以外，逐渐流行夫妇同墓合葬，从此以迄东汉，遂成为定制，绝少例外（图309、310）。横穴式的、砖石结构的墓室，为同墓合葬提了方便。

汉代的庄园经济，使地主阶级的家族关系十分紧密，东汉时尤其如此。表现在丧葬制度上，家族的墓地往往被长期延续，一家数世，

generations were often buried together. Persons who died away from home, no matter how far away, had to be brought back home to be interred in the family tomb, the so-called "return to the old cemetery." An example is the Yang lineage cemetery at Hongnong in Huayin, Shaanxi. The Hongnong Yang lineage was a famous lineage during Han, and their cemetery in Huayin was the center of much attention. The monuments erected at the cemetery have often been mentioned in books since the Tang and Song dynasties. Archaeological excavations in 1959 disclosed seven tombs in orderly arrangement; namely, the bodies were buried from east to west according to generation. Those who were buried here were Yang Zhen, Yang Mu, Yang Rang, Yang Tong, Yang Zhuo, Yang Fu, and Yang Biao. They belonged to four generations and succeeded each other over a period of a whole century.[21]

Imperial Mausoleums   The tombs of the highest rank among all noble burials were, of course, those of the emperors. The scale of the imperial mausoleums was not to be compared to the tombs of mere nobles and officials. Aside from Ba Ling, the tomb of Wen Di, and Du Ling, the tomb of Xuan Di, which are located in the southeastern suburbs of Chang'an, all the other imperial tombs of Western Han, nine mausoleums in all, were constructed on the high ground northwest of Chang'an and north of the Weishui River.[22] The imperial tombs of Eastern Han, other than the Yuan Ling of Guang Wu Di, which is at Mengjin north of Luoyang, are all thought to be situated on Mang Shan north and west of Luoyang.[23] In general, Western Han imperial tombs were modeled on the Qin Shi Huang tomb, and Eastern Han imperial tombs followed the Western Han tradition. No archaeological excavations have yet taken place at any of the Han imperial mausoleums, and our understanding of them is confined to the structures above ground. The Ba Ling of the Western Han emperor Wen Di was built on a natural hill, but all the others had large mounds of rammed earth built over them; the mounds were mostly rectangular, similar to the Egyptian pyramids. Each of the mounds was then surrounded by a large, square enclosure, with a door on each of the four sides. Sleeping and working halls were built inside the enclosure, and temples were built for ritual purposes. Mao Ling, Emperor Wu Di's tomb, is the largest example. According to investigations in 1962, the enclosure was 430 m east to west and 414 m north to south, about one *li* square according to the Han system. The walls of the enclosure were about 6 m thick. The earthen mound at the center of the enclosure was 67,600 m^2 and 46 m tall, truly a

父子兄弟并葬。死在异乡的人，即使是千里迢迢，也必须归葬于故乡的家族墓地，即所谓"归旧茔"。在这方面，陕西华阴的弘农杨氏家族墓地是一个典型的例子。汉代弘农杨氏是一个有名的家族，其在华阴的墓地也长期受到世人的重视，墓地上树立的石碑还曾经在唐宋以来的书籍中被著录。1959 年的发掘工作证明，杨氏墓地中共有七座墓，排列整齐，自东而西按辈分定次序，分别埋葬着杨震、杨牧、杨让、杨统、杨著、杨馥和杨彪，祖孙四代，前后相继，竟达百年之久。[21]

汉代统治阶级的坟墓，以帝陵为最高级，其规模之大则又远非一般贵族、官僚的坟墓所能比。西汉的帝陵，除文帝的"霸陵"和宣帝的"杜陵"在长安城的东南郊，其余九陵都在长安西北方渭水北岸的高原上。[22] 东汉的帝陵，除光武帝的"原陵"多认为是在洛阳北面的孟津以外，其余诸陵的位置尚难确定，但估计有不少是在洛阳北面和西面的邙山。[23] 大概西汉帝陵的形制系模仿秦始皇陵，而东汉的帝陵则又系承袭西汉的制度。由于未经发掘，所以对汉代帝陵的了解只限于地面上的建筑。除西汉文帝的"霸陵"系依山为陵以外，其余的帝陵都有用夯土筑成的截尖方锥状的巨大坟丘，有些像埃及的"金字塔"。陵园的范围很大，平面呈正方形，以坟丘为中心，四面筑围墙，每面围墙的正中设一门，四面共四门。陵园建寝殿和便殿，陵旁立庙，以供奉、祭祀。以规模最大的汉武帝的"茂陵"为例，据 1962 年的勘察所知，陵园东西长 430 米，南北宽 414 米，大约为当时的一里见方，围墙厚约 6 米；陵园正中的坟丘，每边长 260 米，高 46 米，

majestic sight (fig. 311).[24] In the neighborhood of imperial mausoleums, there were often satellite graves in which were buried meritorious officials and imperial relatives. Near Mao Ling are the graves of Wei Qing and Huo Qubing nearby, and of Huo Guang, a little farther away.[25] To the northeast of Chang Ling, the tomb of Han Gao Zu, more than seventy satellite tombs have been located. The two tombs at Yangjiawan mentioned earlier are among them and are the only ones that have been excavated.[26] In the Han dynasty, as soon as an emperor was enthroned he began to build his own grave, calling it his Shou Ling, or "longevity grave." It is said that probably a third of all national income in taxes and tributes was spent on the construction of this longevity grave and its furnishings. In addition, under the Internal Revenue Department there was an office called the Dong Yuan Jiang; it along with the Kao Gong Shi and the You Gong Shi were known as the Three Construction Offices. The Dong Yuan Jiang specialized in the preparation of imperial funerary articles such as caskets, jade shrouds with gold threads, and various mortuary objects. These treasures, collectively called the Dong Yuan Mi Qi, cost in the tens of millions annually.

Graves of Prisoner-Laborers and of the Poor　Exploited by the ruling class, Han dynasty peasants often became bankrupt and turned into bond servants, or they were found guilty of crimes and turned into prisoner-laborers. Prisoner-laborers engaged in heavy work in handicraft shops managed by the state. They were also sent into the labor force for construction projects, such as road and bridge construction, opening of mountain passes, irrigation and canal work, building of city walls, and construction of palaces and imperial mausoleums. The imperial mausoleums, like the Qin Shi Huang tomb, were often built using prisoner-laborers in the tens of thousands brought in from all over the country. In 1972, in an area about 1.5 km northwest of Yang Ling (the imperial tomb of the Han emperor Jing Di) in Xianyang of Shaanxi, a satellite cemetery was excavated, in which, in an area of about

80,000 m^2, were buried an estimated number of ten thousand plus prisoner-laborers.[27] The tomb pits were irregularly arranged, some rectangular, some amorphous. In each pit was buried either a single person or many persons. Some of the skeletons had iron shackles on their necks and some on their feet, indicating that these mausoleum builders were the category of prisoner-laborers called *kun qian*, those who labored with their shackles on. *Shiji* ("Jing Di ben ji") states that "those prisoner-laborers who participated in the construction of Yang Ling were given an amnesty." *Hanshu* ("Jing Di ji") also states that "prisoner-laborers who

可称宏伟之极（图 311）。[24] 在皇帝陵园的附近，往往有许多功臣、贵戚陪葬，称为陪陵。汉武帝"茂陵"的附近有卫青、霍去病墓，稍远处则有霍光的墓，它们都系陪葬墓。[25] 在汉高祖"长陵"的东北方，已发现的陪葬墓达七十余座之多，前面说过的杨家湾四号墓和五号墓便是其中已经发掘的两座。[26] 汉代皇帝即位之后，就开始经营自己的陵墓，称为寿陵。为了建筑寿陵和筹备各种珍贵的随葬器物，据说要耗费全国贡赋收入的三分之一，达到了惊人的程度。少府属官中有东园匠，它与考工室、右工室并称为三工官；东园匠专门为皇帝制作丧葬用品，诸如棺椁、金缕玉衣及各种明器之类，称为"东园秘器"，每年所费达数千万。

　　在统治阶级的残酷剥削和压迫下，汉代的农民往往因破产而沦为奴婢，或被判罪而成为刑徒。刑徒们被强迫从事各种繁重的体力劳动，除了在官营的手工业作坊中充当各种粗杂工以外，还被大批地投入诸如修路架桥、开凿栈道、治水挖河、筑城、建宫殿和造陵墓等工程中。两汉的帝陵，和秦始皇陵一样，往往是从全国各地集中数以万计的刑徒来营建的。1972 年，在陕西省咸阳市汉景帝"阳陵"西北约一公里半处，发现了一片丛葬的墓地，经勘探，面积达八万平方米，埋葬着筑陵的刑徒，估计人数在万人以上。[27] 墓坑排列无序，有的呈长方形，有的不成形状，坑内或埋一人，或埋多人。发掘出来的尸骨，有在颈上带铁钳的，有在脚上带铁钛的，证明他们是刑徒无疑，刑罚的性质属于所谓"髡钳"。可以肯定，这些刑徒是带着刑具参加劳动的。《史记·景帝本纪》说"免徒隶作阳陵

constructed Yang Ling were pardoned from the death penalty." These passages suggest that the construction of Yang Ling was mainly done by prisoner-laborers, a hypothesis that has been confirmed by archaeological excavations. The magnificent imperial mausoleums were built on top of the bodies of thousands of slaves!

Another cemetery of prisoner-laborers was found in Xidajiaocun, in Yanshixian, Henan, at a spot about 2.5 km from the Eastern Han capital city of Luoyang. For a long time farmers in that area have turned up skeletons during farm work, and they call that area the "Ditch of the Skeletons." In the early years of the twentieth century, many inscribed bricks were found here. Referred to as "prisoner-laborer bricks," they have been noted in scholarly works, bringing this area to the attention of archaeologists. The whole area of the cemetery was over 50,000 m². In 1964, about 2,000 m² of this cemetery were excavated, bringing to light in excess of five hundred graves of prisoner-laborers (fig. 312).[28] The graves were rectangular pits, about 2 m long and half a meter wide, less than 1 m deep. The pits were placed one alongside another, with little room in between (figs. 313, 314). Among the skeletons that were found, 96 percent were men and 4 percent were women. Most of them were in their youth and early adulthood and many showed signs of wear on their bones. A few graves contained one or two coins, but the overwhelming majority of the graves were empty of any furnishings. One or two broken bricks were found in each grave, with incised inscriptions on them recording the name of the supervising unit, the skill if any of the prisoner, the presence of shackles, the original prison, the organizational unit to which the prisoner belonged, and the date of death and the name of the penalty. On the last point, there are such terms as "Kun qian", "Wan cheng dan," "Gui xin," "Si kou," and so forth, with the first two the most common (figs. 315-18). From studies of these inscriptions it is clear that the overwhelming majority of the prisoners were laboring people; very few of them were nobles or officials. They came to Luoyang from prisons all over the country to engage in forced labor. The 500-plus graves date from A.D. 107 to 121, namely, a brief interval of less than fourteen years. Obviously the prisoner-laborers died continually, probably from heavy labor and extremely poor living conditions, and when they died they were buried in shallow, small graves. Sometimes, after only a few years their graves would be turned over to make room for new dead prisoners.

者"，《汉书·景帝纪》说"赦徒作阳陵者死罪"，都说明了在"阳陵"的营建工程中所用的劳动力主要是刑徒。考古发掘工作的结果，正与文献的记载相合。规模宏伟的帝陵，正是建筑在成千上万的奴隶们的尸骨之上，生动而形象地说明了统治阶级的残酷！

　　在河南省偃师县西大郊村，离东汉的首都雒阳城遗址约 2.5 公里处，存在着另一处属于东汉中期的埋葬刑徒的墓地。长期以来，附近的农民们在掘地翻土时，常常发现尸骨，因而称其地为"骷髅沟"。早在 20 世纪初期，这里出土的一些称为"刑徒砖"的刻有文字的砖块已被作为一种古物，著录在有关的书籍中，引起研究者的注意。墓地的面积，在五万平方米以上。1964 年，发掘了其中约二千平方米，发现了刑徒墓五百余座（图 312）。[28] 刑徒们的墓是一个长方形的土坑，长约二米，宽约半米，深不足一米，仅能容身。它们被紧紧地排列在一起，相互之间没有什么余地（图 313、314）。刑徒们的性别，男的占 96%，女的占 4%，绝大多数是青壮年，尸骨上往往有明显的劳损痕迹。除少数墓内有一二枚铜钱之外，绝大多数的墓没有任何随葬品。墓中放置一二块残缺的砖，砖面上刻文字，记明刑徒所属的监管机构、有无技能、是否戴刑具、来自何处监狱、编制组织、死亡日期，刑罚的名称有"髡钳"、"完城旦"、"鬼薪"、"司寇"等，而以前二者为绝大多数（图 315—318）。对砖文的研究说明，刑徒中绝大多数是劳动人民，贵族、官吏被判罪而成为刑徒的极少。他们从全国各地的监狱被押送到雒阳，被强制从事各种劳役。发掘出来的五百余座墓，年代自东汉安帝永初元年（公元 107 年）至永宁二年（公元 121 年），前后不到十四年。这说明了繁重的劳动、极端低劣的生活条件，使刑徒们不断死亡，而被草率埋葬在一个仅能容身的浅坑中。过不了几年，他们的尸骨往往又从墓坑中被掘了出来，以便另葬新死的刑徒。

Other aspects of Han tombs also illustrate the opposition between rich and poor during the Han dynasty. In 1955 a group of poor people's graves were excavated in Luoyang, Henan; they date from late Western Han to late Eastern Han. The cemetery was quite far from the Henanxian seat of the time and was located in a low, depressed area. The caskets were extremely simple: some bodies were buried in pottery, some pits were lined with brick fragments, some pits were covered with tiles, and other pits were bare. The grave furnishings were also extremely simple, usually consisting of a few coarse pottery vessels or a few coins (figs. 319, 320).[29] These stand in sharp contrast to the large graves described earlier of the emperors, nobility, bureaucrats, and landowners.

除了上述的刑徒墓以外，汉代贫富悬殊、阶级对立的情形也可以在其他的墓葬方面得到生动的说明。例如，1955 年在河南省洛阳市发掘了一批西汉后期至东汉后期的贫民墓。墓地离当时的河南县城甚远，处在低洼地带。死者的葬具都很简陋，有的使用陶棺，有的用砖块稍加垒砌，有的则用瓦片覆盖，甚至也有根本没葬具，以身亲土的。随葬品极为贫乏，往往仅有几件粗陋的陶器或几枚铜钱（图 319、320），[29] 这与以上所说的皇帝、贵族、官僚、地主们的陵墓形成了鲜明的对比。

285. Various foods furnished in Han tomb number 1 at Mawangdui, Changsha
长沙马王堆一号汉墓中随葬的食物

286. Bamboo basket containing food in Han tomb number 1 at Mawangdui, Changsha 长沙马王堆一号汉墓竹笥中的食物

287. Large wine urns from the Han tomb in Mancheng 满城汉墓中的大酒缸

288. Silk robe buried in Han tomb number 1 at Mawangdui in Changsha 长沙马王堆一号汉墓出土的锦袍

289. Another silk robe found in the same tomb as fig. 288 长沙马王堆一号汉墓出土的又一锦袍

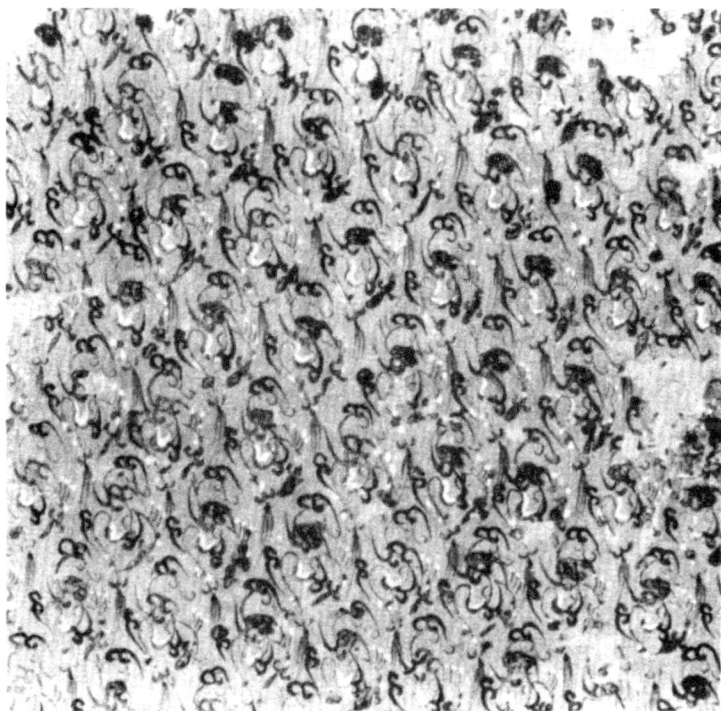

290. Silk gauze with printed patterns and painted colors, buried in Han tomb number 1 at Mawangdui in Changsha
长沙马王堆一号汉墓出土的彩绘印花纱

291. Silk brocade with attached feathers and embroidery, buried in Han tomb number 1 at Mawangdui in Changsha　长沙马王堆一号汉墓出土的羽毛贴花绢

292. Pottery model of stove, unearthed from the Han tomb in Luoyang　洛阳汉墓出土的陶灶

293. Pottery model of multistoried granary, unearthed from the Han tomb in Xingyang, Henan　河南荥阳汉墓出土的陶仓

294. Pottery model of farm field, unearthed from the Han tomb in Lianxian, Guangdong　广东连县汉墓出土的陶水田模型

295. Horse-and-chariot pit burial in the Han tomb at Dabaotai, Beijing
北京大葆台汉墓随葬的车马

296. Wooden human figures buried in Han tomb number 1 at Mawangdui, Changsha　长沙马王堆一号汉墓出土的木俑

297. Pottery figures of warriors on horseback, unearthed from the Han tomb at Yangjiawan in Xianyang, Shaanxi　陕西咸阳杨家湾汉墓出土的骑马陶俑

298. Bronze carriage and horse buried in the Han tomb at Leitai in Wuwei, Gansu　甘肃武威雷台汉墓中的铜质车马模型

299. Bronze carriage and horse buried in the Han tomb at Leitai in Wuwei, Gansu　甘肃武威雷台汉墓中的铜质车马模型

300. Bronze horses buried in the Han tomb at Leitai in Wuwei, Gansu　甘肃武威雷台汉墓中的铜马

301. Clay coins unearthed from Han tomb number 1 at Mawangdui, Changsha
长沙马王堆一号汉墓出土的泥钱

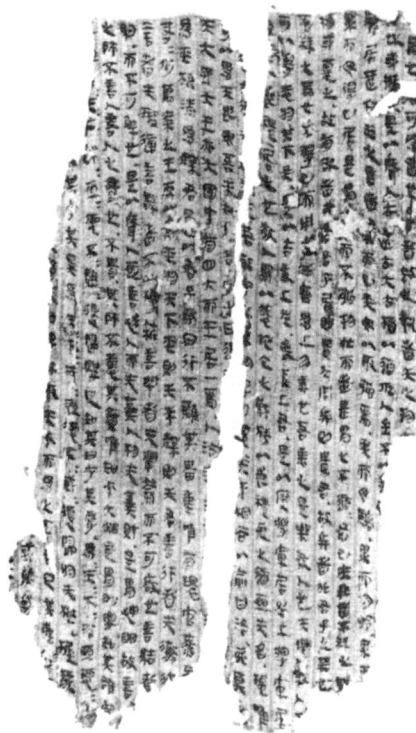

302. Silk book unearthed from Han tomb number 1 at Mawangdui, Changsha (*Laozi*, version A, in part)
长沙马王堆一号汉墓出土的帛书 (《老子》，甲本，部分)

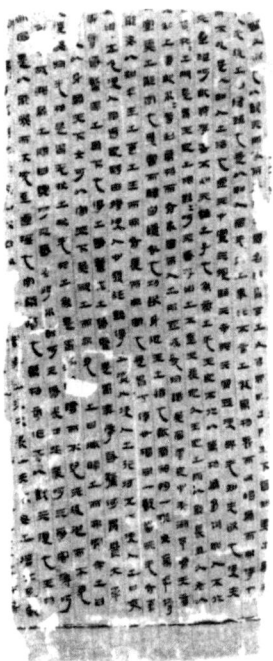

303. Silk book unearthed from Han tomb number 3 at Mawangdui, Changsha (*Laozi*, version B, in part) 长沙马王堆三号墓出土的帛书（《老子》，乙本，部分）

304. Bamboo slips of *Sun Bin bing fa* (in part), unearthed from the Han tomb at Yinqueshan, Linyi, Shandong 山东临沂银雀山汉墓出土的竹书（《孙膑兵法》，部分）

305. Wooden slips of *Yi li*, unearthed from the Han tomb at Mozuizi, Wuwei, Gansu (reproductions)
甘肃武威磨咀子汉墓中木书（《仪礼》，复制品）

306. Seals with the inscriptions "Seal of Marquis Dai," "The Chengxiang of Changsha," and "Li Cang," unearthed from the Han tomb number 2 at Mawangdui, Changsha 长沙马王堆二号墓出土的印有"轪侯之印"、"长沙丞相"和"利苍"的印章

307. Bronze seals with the inscriptions "Don Wan" and "Dou Jun Xu," unearthed from Han tomb number 2 in Mancheng
满城二号汉墓出土的刻有"窦绾"、"窦君须"字样的铜印

308. "Tomb security jar" (dated the third year of Chu Ping), unearthed from a Han tomb in Luoyang
洛阳汉墓出土的初平三年镇墓瓶

309. Husband-and-wife burial in a Western Han tomb in Luoyang　洛阳西汉墓中的夫妇合葬

310. Husband-and-wife burial in an Eastern Han tomb in Luoyang　洛阳东汉墓中的夫妇合葬

311. Earthen mound of the mausoleum of Emperor Wu Di ("Mao Ling") in Xingpingxian, Shaanxi 陕西兴平的汉武帝陵（茂陵）

312. Cemetery of prisoner-laborers of Eastern Han, excavated at Xidajiaocun, Yanshixian, Henan 河南偃师西大郊村出土的东汉刑徒墓地

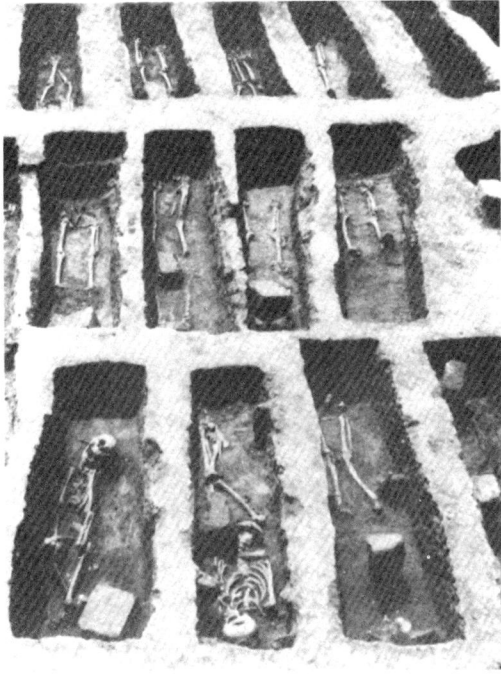

313. Tombs of prisoner-laborers of Eastern Han, excavated at Xidajiaocun, Yanshixian, Henan
河南偃师西大郊村的东汉刑徒墓地

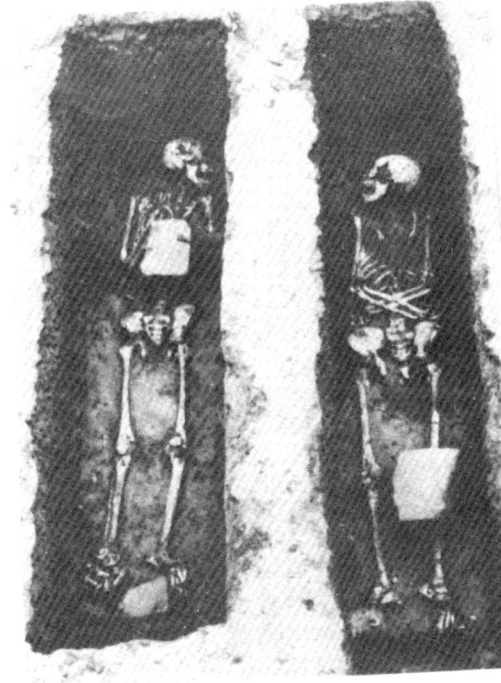

314. Skeletons and inscribed bricks in the tombs of prisoner-laborers of Eastern Han, excavated at Xidajiaocun, Yanshixian, Henan
河南偃师西大郊村的东汉刑徒墓地中的尸骨和刻有文字的砖

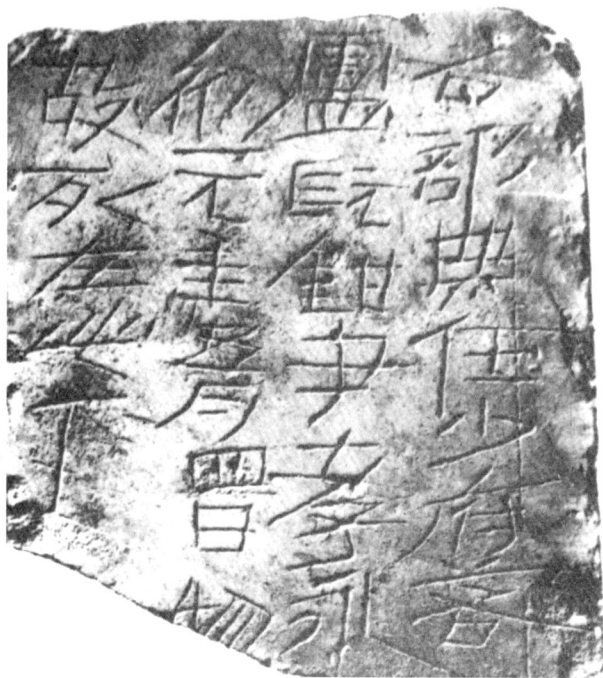

315. Prisoner-laborer brick inscribed with the designation "Kun qian," unearthed from a prisoner-laborer
tomb at Xidajiaocun, Yanshixian, Henan
河南偃师西大郊村刑徒墓地中刻有"髡钳"字样的砖

316. Prisoner-laborer brick inscribed with "Wan cheng dan," unearthed from prisoner-laborer grave at Xidajiaocun, Yanshixian, Henan
河南偃师西大郊村刑徒墓地中刻有"完城旦"字样的砖

317. Prisoner-laborer brick inscribed with "Gui xin," unearthed from prisoner-laborer grave at Xidajiaocun, Yanshixian, Henan
河南偃师西大郊村刑徒墓地中刻有"鬼薪"字样的砖

318. Prisoner-laborer brick inscribed with "Si kou," unearthed from prisoner- laborer grave at Xidajiaocun, Yanshixian, Henan
河南偃师西大郊村刑徒墓地中刻有"司寇"字样的砖

319. Commoner's grave of the Han dynasty, unearthed in Luoyang
洛阳汉代平民墓

320. Commoner's grave of the Han dynasty, unearthed in Luoyang 洛阳汉代平民墓

❶

* Editor's note: It might be useful to note here that in the Han system of measurement a *chi* is divided into 10 *cun*, 6 *chi* make a *bu*, and 300 *bu* make a *li*. Most scholars agree that a Han *chi* is approximately 0.23 m.

1 Wang Zhongshu, "Han Chang'an cheng kaogu gongzuo de chubu shouhuo" [Preliminary results of the archaeological investigation of the Han dynasty city of Chang'an], *Kaogu Tongxun*, 1957, no. 5, pp. 102-04.

王仲殊:《汉长安城考古工作的初步收获》,《考古通讯》, 1957 年, 5 期, 102—104 页。

2 Institute of Archaeology, Chinese Academy of Social Sciences, *Han Chang'an cheng yizhi fajue baogao* [Report of the excavation of the ruins of the Han dynasty city of Chang'an]. In preparation.

中国社会科学院考古研究所:《汉长安城遗址发掘报告》,待刊。

3 The Han text *San fu jue lu* is said to contain the phrase, "san tu dong kai," or "the three roads [or the three-laned road] opened wide." The *Xi jing fu* contains the line, "san tu yi ting, fang gui shi'er," or "the three roads are level and straight, and they have twelve parallel tracks." Xue Zong's commentary explains this line thus: "Each side has three gates, and each gate has three lanes; therefore, it refers to the three roads. Each road contains four wheel tracks; therefore, it refers to having twelve tracks."

4 Wang Zhongshu (see n. 1 above), pp. 104, 105.

同注 1, 104、105 页。

5 See n. 2 above.

同注 2。

6 Wang Zhongshu (n. 1 above), pp. 106-08.

同注 1, 106—108 页。

7 See n. 2 above.

同注 2。

8 See n. 2 above.

同注 2。

9 See n. 2 above.

同注 2。

10 Han City Work Team, Institute of Archaeology, Chinese Academy of Social Sciences, "Han Chang'an cheng wuku yizhi fajue de chubu shouhuo" [Preliminary results of the excavation of the site of the armory in the Han dynasty city of Chang'an], *Kaogu*, 1978, no. 4, pp. 261-69, pls. 9-11.

中国社会科学院考古研究所汉城工作队：《汉长安城武库遗址发掘的初步收获》，《考古》，1978 年，4 期，261—269 页，图版玖——拾壹。

11 See n. 2 above.

同注 2。

12 Hei Guang, "Xi'an Han Taiyechi chutu yijian juxing shi yu" [A gigantic stone fish unearthed near Han dynasty Taiyechi in Xi'an], *Wenwu*, 1975, no. 6, pp. 91, 92.

黑光：《西安汉太液池出土一件巨形石鱼》，《文物》，1975 年，6 期，91、92 页。

13 Yu Weichao, "Han Chang'an cheng xibeibu kancha ji" [Notes on the investigations in the northwestern part of the Han dynasty city of Chang'an], *Kaogu Tongxun*, 1966, no. 5, pp. 20-26, pl. 7.

俞伟超：《汉长安城西北部勘查记》，《考古通讯》，1956 年，5 期，20—26 页，图版柒。

14 Wang Zhongshu, "Han Chang'an cheng kaogu gongzuo shouhuo xuji" [Further notes on the results of archaeological work at the Han city of Chang'an], *Kaogu Tongxun*, 1958, no. 4, p. 25, pl. 4.

王仲殊：《汉长安城考古工作收获续记》，《考古通讯》，1958 年，4 期，25 页，图版肆。

15 In *Hou Hanshu* ("Annals of Emperor Xian Di"), it is recorded that in the third moon of 191, "houses outside the Xuanpingmen Gate were destroyed without cause." Biographies of Dong Zhuo in both *Weizhi* and *Hou Hanshu* refer to an event in which Wang Yun took Emperor Xian Di up to the gate tower atop the Xuanpingmen Gate.

16 See n. 14 above; pp. 25-27, pls. 1-4.

同注 14，25—27 页，图版壹——肆。

17 Both *Jinshu* and *Shiliuguo chunqiu* record that in A.D. 345 Shi Hu conscripted 160,000 people to reconstruct the Weiyanggong Palace in Chang'an. See pp. 27-29 of my article cited in n. 14 above.

同注 14，27—29 页。

18 See pp. 31, 32, pl. 4 of my article cited in n. 14 above.

同注 14，31、32 页，图版肆。

19 Xi'an City Cultural Relics Commission, "Xi'an Sanqiaozhen Gaoyaocun chutu de Xi Han tongqi qun" [A group of Western Han bronzes unearthed in Gaoyaocun, Sanqiaozhen, Xi'an], *Kaogu*, 1963, no. 2, pp. 62-70, pls. 3, 4.

西安市文物管理委员会:《西安三桥镇高窑村出土的西汉铜器群》,《考古》, 1963 年, 2 期, 62—70 页, 图版叁、肆。

20 Chen Zhi, "Gu qiwu wenzi congkao" [Miscellaneous notes on ancient vessel inscriptions], *Kaogu*, 1963, no. 2, pp. 80-82.

陈直:《古器物文字丛考》,《考古》, 1963 年, 2 期, 80—82 页。

21 Gu Tiefu, "Xi'an fujin suojian de Xi Han shidiao yishu" [Stone sculptures seen near Xi'an], *Wenwu Cankao Ziliao*, 1955, no. 11, pp. 3-5.

顾铁符:《西安附近所见的西汉石雕艺术》,《文物参考资料》, 1955 年, 11 期, 3—5 页。

22 Yu Weichao, "Yingdang shenzhong yinyong gudai wenxian" [Ancient texts should be quoted with care], *Kaogu Tongxun*, 1957, no. 2, p. 76.

俞伟超:《应当慎重引用古代文献》,《考古通讯》, 1957 年, 2 期, 76 页。

23 Hu Qianying, "Fenghao diqu zhu shuidao de tacha" [A walking survey of the various water courses in the Fenghao area], *Kaogu*, 1963, no. 4, pp. 189, 190, 194.

胡谦盈:《丰镐地区诸水道的踏察》,《考古》, 1963 年, 4 期, 189、190、194 页。

24 Huang Zhanyue, "Han Chang'an cheng nanjiao lizhi jianzhu de weizhi jiqi youguan wenti" [The location of the ritual structures to the south of the Han city of Chang'an and related problems], *Kaogu*, 1960, no. 9, pp. 53-58.

黄展岳:《汉长安城南郊礼制建筑的位置及其有关问题》,《考古》, 1960 年, 9 期, 53—58 页。

25 Tang Jinyu, "Xi'an xijiao Handai jianzhu yizhi fajue baogao" [Report on the excavations of Han dynasty architectural sites in the western suburbs of Xi'an], *Kaogu Xuebao*, 1959, no. 2, pp. 45-54, pls. 1-9.

唐金裕:《西安西郊汉代建筑遗址发掘报告》,《考古学报》, 1959 年, 2 期, 45—54 页, 图版壹——玖。

26 Han City Excavation Team, Institute of Archaeology, "Han Chang'an cheng nanjiao lizhi jianzhu yizhi qun fajue jianbao" [Brief report on the group of ritual structures to the south of the Han city of Chang'an], *Kaogu*, 1960, no. 7, p. 38.

考古研究所汉城发掘队:《汉长安城南郊礼制建筑遗址群发掘简报》,《考古》, 1960 年, 7 期, 38 页。

Luo Zhongru, "Xi'an xijiao faxian Handai jianzhu yizhi" [Han dynasty architectural remains found in the western suburb of Xi'an], *Kaogu Tongxun*, 1957, no. 6, pp. 26-30, pl. 8.

雒忠如：《西安西郊发现汉代建筑遗址》，《考古通讯》，1957 年，6 期，26—30 页，图版捌。

❷

1　Umehara Sueji, (Zōtei) *Rakuyō Kinson kobo shūei* [Treasures from the ancient tomb of Jincun, Luoyang] (Kyoto: Kobayashi, 1944), pp. 1, 2.

梅原末治：《洛阳金村古墓聚英》（增订版），小林出版部，1944 年，1、2 页。

2　Luoyang Archaeology Team, Institute of Archaeology, Chinese Academy of Sciences, "Han Wei Luoyang cheng chubu kancha" [Preliminary surveys of the Han and Wei cities of Luoyang], *Kaogu*, 1973, no. 4, pp. 198-99, pl. 2.

中国科学院考古研究所洛阳工作队：《汉魏洛阳城初步勘查》，《考古》，1973 年，4 期，198、199 页，图版贰。

3　Ibid., pp. 198-201.

同上，198—201 页。

4　Ibid., p. 200.

同上，200 页。

5　Ibid., pp. 199, 202, 203.

同上，199、202、203 页。

6　Wang Zhongshu, "Han Chang'an cheng kaogu gongzuo shouhuo xuji" [Further notes on the results of archaeological work at the Han city of Chang'an], *Kaogu Tongxun*, 1958, no. 4, p. 24.

王仲殊：《汉长安城考古工作收获续记》，《考古通讯》，1958 年，4 期，24 页。

7　Xi'an City Cultural Relics Commission, "Xi'an Sanqiaozhen Gaoyaocun chutu de Xi Han tongqi qun" [A group of Western Han bronzes unearthed in Gaoyaocun, Sanqiaozhen, Xi'an], *Kaogu*, 1963, no. 2, p. 68, pl. 4.

西安市文物管理委员会：《西安三桥镇高窑村出土的西汉铜器群》，《考古》，1963 年，2 期，68 页，图版肆。

8　Huang Zhanyue, "Xi'an Sanqiao Gaoyaocun Xi Han tongqi mingwen bushi" [Supplementary explanations of the inscriptions on Western Han bronzes from Gaoyaocun, Sanqiao, Xi'an], *Kaogu*, 1963, no. 4, pp. 199, 200.

黄展岳：《西安三桥高窑村西汉铜器铭文补释》，《考古》，1963 年，4 期，199、200 页。

9　Pp. 199, 202, 203 of article cited in n. 2 above.

同注 2，199、202、203 页。

10　Zuo Ming, "Yongledadian juan 9561 yin Yuan Henanzhi de gudai Luoyang tu shisi fu" [Fourteen ancient maps of Luoyang in the *Henanzhi* of the Yuan dynasty quoted in volume 9561 of *Yongledadian*], *Kaogu Xuebao*, 1959, no. 2, p. 39, fig. 2.

作铭：《永乐大典卷 9561 引元河南志的古代洛阳图十四幅》，《考古学报》，1959 年，2 期，39 页，图二。

[11] Pp. 207, 208 of article cited in n. 2 above.

同注 2，207、208 页。

[12] Ibid., pp. 202, 208, pl. 2.

同上，202、208 页，图版贰。

[13] Ibid., pp. 203, 204.

同上，203、204 页。

[14] Ibid., p. 200, pl. 3.

同上，200 页，图版叁。

[15] Ibid., pp. 199, 202, 203.

同上，199、202、203 页。

[16] Luoyang Archaeology Team, Institute of Archaeology, Chinese Academy of Sciences, "Han Wei Luoyang cheng yihao fangzhi he chutu de wa wen" [House floor no. 1 and unearthed tile inscriptions in the city of Luoyang of the Han and Wei dynasties], *Kaogu*, 1973, no. 4, pp. 209-14, pl. 1.

中国科学院考古研究所洛阳工作队：《汉魏洛阳城一号房址和出土的瓦文》，《考古》，1973 年，4 期，209—214 页，图版壹。

[17] Pp. 204-06, pl. 3 of article cited in n. 2 above.

同注 2，204—206 页，图版叁。

[18] Su Bai, "Bei Wei Luoyang cheng he Bei Mang lingmu" [The city of Luoyang of the Northern Wei and the imperial tombs of the Northern Mang], *Wenwu*, 1978, no. 7, pp. 42-46, pl. 4.

宿白：《北魏洛阳城和北邙陵墓》，《文物》，1978 年，7 期，42—46 页，图版肆。

[19] P. 198 of article cited in n. 2 above.

同注 2，198 页。

[20] Institute of Archaeology, Chinese Academy of Social Sciences, "Han Wei Luoyang cheng yizhi fajue baogao" [Report on the excavations of the Luoyang city of the Han and Wei dynasties]. In preparation.

中国社会科学院考古研究所：《汉魏洛阳城遗址发掘报告》，待刊。

21 Yan Wenru, "Luoyang Han Wei Sui Tang chengzhi kancha ji" [Notes on the investigation of Luoyang city sites of the Han, Wei, Sui, and Tang dynasties], *Kaogu Xuebao*, 1955, no. 9, p. 121, pl. 4.

阎文儒:《洛阳汉魏隋唐城址勘查记》,《考古学报》, 1955 年, 9 期, 121 页, 图版肆。

22 See n. 20 above.

同注 20。

23 Luoyang Archaeology Team, Institute of Archaeology, Chinese Academy of Social Sciences, "Han Wei Luoyang cheng nanjiao de Ling Tai yizhi" [The site of Ling Tai in the southern suburb of Luoyang city of the Han and Wei dynasties], *Kaogu*, 1978, no. 1, pp. 54-57, pls. 1-3.

中国社会科学院考古研究所洛阳工作队:《汉魏洛阳城南郊的灵台遗址》,《考古》, 1978 年, 1 期, 54—57 页, 图版壹——叁。

24 See n. 20 above.

同注 20。

❸

1 Xianyang Museum, "Shaanxi Xianyang Maquan Xi Han mu" [Western Han tombs at Maquan, Xianyang, Shaanxi], *Kaogu*, 1979, no. 2, pp. 127, 128.

咸阳市博物馆:《陕西咸阳马泉西汉墓》,《考古》, 1979 年, 2 期, 127、128 页。

Archaeological Excavation Team of Luoyang District, *Luoyang Shaogou Han mu* [Han tombs at Shaogou, Luoyang] (Beijing: Kexue Press, 1959), pp. 112, 113, 156-58, pl. 20.

洛阳区考古发掘队:《洛阳烧沟汉墓》, 科学出版社, 1959 年, 112、113、156—158 页, 图版贰拾。

Yangtze Valley Archaeological Workers' Training Institute, Second Class, "Hubei Jiangling Fenghuangshan Xi Han mu fajue jianbao" [Brief report on the excavation of Western Han tombs at Fenghuangshan, Jiangling, Hubei], *Wenwu*, 1974, no. 6, p. 51.

长江流域第二期文物考古工作人员训练班:《湖北江陵凤凰山西汉墓发掘简报》,《文物》, 1974 年, 6 期, 51 页。

Hubei Provincial Museum, "Guanghua Wuzuofen Xi Han mu" [Western Han tombs at Wuzuofen, Guanghua], *Kaogu Xuebao*, 1976, no. 2, p. 168, pl. 6.

湖北省博物馆:《光化五座坟西汉墓》,《考古学报》, 1976 年, 2 期, 168 页, 图版陆。

Hunan Provincial Museum et al., *Changsha Mawangdui yihao Han mu fajue jianbao* [Brief report on the excavation of Han tomb number 1 at Mawangdui, Changsha] (Beijing: Wenwu Press, 1972), pp. 35-37, pls. 257-64.

湖南省博物馆等:《长沙马王堆一号汉墓发掘简报》, 文物出版社, 1972 年, 35—37 页, 图版二五七——二六四。

Xuzhou Museum, "Jiangsu Xuzhou Kuishan Xi Han mu" [Western Han tombs at Kuishan, Xuzhou], *Kaogu*, 1974, no. 2, p. 120.

徐州博物馆:《江苏徐州奎山西汉墓》,《考古》, 1974 年, 2 期, 120 页。

Nanjing Museum et al., "Haizhou Xi Han Huo He mu qingli jianbao" [Brief report on the clearance of the tomb of Huo He of Western Han in Haizhou], *Kaogu*, 1974, no. 3, pp. 185, 186.

南京博物院等:《海州西汉霍贺墓清理简报》,《考古》, 1974 年, 3 期, 185、186 页。

Liu Liang, "Guanyu Xi Han Huo He mu chutu ji de jianding" [On the identification of the millet unearthed from the Huo He tomb of Western Han], *Kaogu*, 1978, no. 2, p. 90.

刘亮:《关于西汉霍贺墓出土稷的鉴定》,《考古》, 1978 年, 2 期, 90 页。

Nan Bo, "Jiangsu Lianyungangshi Haizhou Xi Han Shi Qi Yao mu" [Tomb of Shi Qi Yao of Western Han at Haizhou, Lianyungang city, Jiangsu], *Kaogu*, 1975, no. 3, p. 176.

南波:《江苏连云港市海州西汉侍其繇墓》,《考古》, 1975 年, 3 期, 176 页。

Archaeology Team of Guangxi Zhuang Autonomous Region, "Guangxi Guixian Luobowan yihao mu fajue jianbao" [Brief report on tomb number 1 at Luobowan, Guixian, Guangxi], *Wenwu*, 1978, no. 9, p. 32.

广西壮族自治区文物工作队:《广西贵县罗泊湾一号墓发掘简报》,《文物》, 1978 年, 9 期, 32 页。

Guangzhou City Cultural Relics Commission, "Guangzhou Xicun Huangdigang 42-hao Dong Han muguomu fajue jianbao" [Brief report on the excavation of Eastern Han wooden-chambered tomb number 42 at Huangdigang in Xicun, Guangzhou], *Kaogu*, 1958, no. 8, pp. 42, 43.

广州市文物管理委员会:《广州西村皇帝冈 42 号东汉木椁墓发掘简报》,《考古》, 1958 年, 8 期, 42、43 页。

[2] Shaanxi Provincial Museum Writing Team et al., "Mizhi Dong Han huaxiangshi mu fajue jianbao" [Brief report on the Eastern Han tomb with painted stones in Mizhi], *Wenwu*, 1972, no. 3, pp. 71-73.

陕西省博物馆写作小组等:《米脂东汉画象石墓发掘简报》,《文物》, 1972 年, 3 期, 71—73 页。

[3] Nakao Sasuke et al., "Henan sheng Luoyang Han mu chutu de daomi" [Rice unearthed from Han tomb in Luoyang, Henan], *Kaogu Xuebao*, 1957, no. 4, pp. 79-82.

中尾佐助等：《河南省洛阳汉墓出土的稻米》，《考古学报》，1957 年，4 期，79—82 页。

4 Institute of Archaeology, Chinese Academy of Sciences, *Xin Zhongguo de kaogu shouhuo* [Archaeological results in the New China] (Beijing: Wenwu Press, 1961), p. 77.

中国科学院考古研究所：《新中国的考古收获》，文物出版社，1961 年，77 页。

5 Yang Shiting, "Tantan Shixia faxian de zaipeidao yiji" [On the remains of cultivated rice found in Shixia], *Wenwu*, 1978, no. 7, p. 28.

杨式挺：《谈谈石峡发现的栽培稻遗迹》，《文物》，1978 年，7 期，28 页。

Hunan Provincial College of Agronomy et al., *Changsha Mawangdui yihao Han mu chutu dong zhi wu biaoben de yanjiu* [Studies of animal and plant remains from Han tomb number 1 at Mawangdui, Changsha] (Beijing: Wenwu Press, 1978), pp. 1-3.

湖南省农学院等：《长沙马王堆一号汉墓出土动植物标本的研究》，文物出版社，1978 年，1—3 页。

6 Fenghuangshan Han Tomb Number 167 Excavation and Reporting Team, "Jiangling Fenghuangshan 167-hao Han mu fajue jianbao" [Brief report on the excavation of Han tomb number 167 at Fenghuangshan in Jiangling], *Wenwu*, 1976, no. 10, p. 34, pl. 2.

凤凰山一六七号汉墓发掘整理小组：《江陵凤凰山一六七号汉墓发掘简报》，《文物》，1976 年，10 期，34 页，图版贰。

7 He Guanbao, "Luoyang Laocheng xibeijiao 81-hao Han mu" [Han tomb number 81 in the northwest suburb of the old city of Luoyang], *Kaogu*, 1964, no. 8, p. 406.

贺官保：《洛阳老城西北郊 81 号汉墓》，《考古》，1964 年，8 期，406 页。

Yang Shiting, "Guanyu Guangdong zaoqi tieqi de ruogan wenti" [Some problems relating to early iron implements in Guangdong], *Kaogu*, 1977, no. 2, p. 104.

杨式挺：《关于广东早期铁器的若干问题》，《考古》，1977 年，2 期，104 页。

Northeast Museum, "Liaoyang Sandaohao Xi Han cunluo yizhi" [Village remains of Western Han at Sandaohao in Liaoyang], *Kaogu Xuebao*, 1957, no. 1, p. 121, pl. 5.

东北博物馆：《辽阳三道壕西汉村落遗址》，《考古学报》，1957 年，1 期，121 页，图版伍。

8 Zhang Zengqi, "Cong chutu wenwu kan Zhanguo zhi Xi Han shiqi Yunnan he Zhongyuan diqu de miqie lianxi" [The close interrelationship of Yunnan and the Central Plains area during the Warring States period and the Western Han dynasty as seen from archaeological relics], *Wenwu*, 1978, no. 10, pp. 32, 33.

张增祺：《从出土文物看战国至西汉时期云南和中原地区的密切联系》，《文物》，

1978 年，10 期，32、33 页。

The Archaeological Section, Institute of Dunhuang Relics et al., "Dunhuang Tianshuijing Handai yizhi de diaocha [The investigation of the Han dynasty site at Tianshuijing in Dunhuang], *Kaogu*, 1975, no. 2, pp. 112-14.

敦煌文物研究所考古组等：《敦煌甜水井汉代遗址的调查》，《考古》，1975 年，2 期，112—114 页。

[9] Tang Yunming, "Baoding Dongbiyangcheng diaocha" [The investigation of Dongbiyangcheng in Baoding], *Wenwu*, 1959, no. 9, p. 82.

唐云明：《保定东壁阳城调查》，《文物》，1959 年，9 期，82 页。

Nanjing Museum, "Liguoyi gudai liantielu de diaocha ji qingli" [Investigation and clearance of ancient iron-smelting furnaces at Liguoyi], *Wenwu*, 1960, no. 4, pp. 46, 47.

南京博物院：《利国驿古代炼铁炉的调查及清理》，《文物》，1960 年，4 期，46、47 页。

[10] Zhang Zhenxin, "Handai de niu geng" [The use of cattle in plowing in the Han dynasty], *Wenwu*, 1977, no. 8, p. 60.

张振新：《汉代的牛耕》，《文物》，1977 年，8 期，60 页。

Zhuang Dongming, "Tengxian Changchengcun faxian Handai tie nongju shi yu jian" [More than ten iron agricultural implements of the Han dynasty discovered at Changchengcun in Tengxian], *Wenwu Cankao Ziliao*, 1958, no. 3, p. 82.

庄冬明：《滕县长城村发现汉代铁农具十余件》，《文物参考资料》，1958 年，3 期，82 页。

[11] Institute of Archaeology, Chinese Academy of Social Sciences et al., *Mancheng Han mu* [Han tombs in Mancheng] (Beijing: Wenwu Press, 1978), pp. 59, 60.

中国社会科学院考古研究所等：《满城汉墓》，文物出版社，1978 年，59、60 页。

[12] Shaanxi Provincial Museum et al., "Shaanxi sheng faxian de Handai tie hua he bi tu" [Han dynasty iron plowshares and moldboards discovered in Shaanxi Province], *Wenwu*, 1966, no. 1, p. 23, pls. 3, 4.

陕西省博物馆等：《陕西省发现的汉代铁铧和镣土》，《文物》，1966 年，1 期，23 页，图版叁、肆。

[13] P. 60 of "Haidai de niu geng," n. 10 above.

同注 10 《汉代的牛耕》，60 页。

[14] P. 23, pl. 3 of article cited in n. 12 above.

同注 12，23 页，图版叁。

15 Gansu Provincial Museum, "Wuwei Mozuizi san zuo Han mu fajue jianbao" [Brief report on the excavations of three Han dynasty tombs at Mozuizi, Wuwei], *Wenwu*, 1972, no. 12, pp. 13, 14, fig. 23.

甘肃省博物馆:《武威磨咀子三座汉墓发掘简报》,《文物》, 1972 年, 12 期, 13、14 页, 图二十三。

Shanxi Provincial Cultural Relics Commission, "Shanxi Pinglu Zaoyuancun bihua Han mu" [The Han dynasty tomb with murals at Zaoyuancun in Pinglu, Shanxi], *Kaogu*, 1959, no. 9, p. 463.

山西省文物管理委员会:《山西平陆枣园村壁画汉墓》,《考古》, 1959 年, 9 期, 463 页。

Jiangsu Provincial Cultural Relics Commission, *Jiangsu Xuzhou Han huaxiang shi* [Pictorial stones of the Han dynasty in Xuzhou, Jiangsu] (Beijing: Kexue Press, 1959), p. 12, pl. 63.

江苏省文物管理委员会:《江苏徐州汉画象石》, 科学出版社, 1959 年, 12 页, 图版陆叁。

Fu Xihua, *Handai huaxiang quan ji (chubian)* [A complete collection of the pictorial art of the Han dynasty (preliminary volume)] (Shanghai: Commercial Press, 1950), pl. 96.

傅惜华:《汉代画象全集》(初编), 上海商务印书馆, 1950 年, 图版九十六。

Pp. 70, 71, 73 of reference cited in n. 2 above.

同注 2, 70、71、73 页。

Inner Mongolia Autonomous Region Museum Archaeological Team, *Holingor Han mu bihua* [Mural paintings in the Han dynasty tomb at Holingor] (Beijing: Wenwu Press, 1978), pp. 20, 123, 145, 146.

内蒙古自治区博物馆文物工作队:《和林格尔汉墓壁画》, 文物出版社, 1978 年, 20、123、145、146 页。

16 Gansu Provincial Museum et al. "Jiayuguan Wei Jin mu bihua de ticai he yishu jiazhi" [Subject matter and artistic value of the mural paintings in the Wei and Jin dynasty tombs at Jiayuguan], *Wenwu*, 1974, no. 9, p. 76, pl. 1.

甘肃省博物馆等:《嘉峪关魏晋墓壁画的题材和艺术价值》,《文物》, 1974 年, 9 期, 76 页, 图版壹。

17 P. 463, pl. 1 of "Shanxi Pinglu Zaoyuancun bihua Han mu" in n. 15 above.

同注 15 引《山西平陆枣园村壁画汉墓》, 463 页, 图版壹。

18 P. 23, fig. 11 of reference cited in n. 12 above.

同注 12, 23 页, 图十一。

19 P. 67, pls. 1 and 3 of reference cited in n. 16 above.

同注 16，67 页，图版壹、叁。

20 Xu Hengbin, "Jiantan Guangdong Lianxian chutu de Xi Jin litian batian moxing" [A brief discussion of clay models showing soil turning and soil raking of Western Jin unearthed in Lianxian, Guangdong], *Wenwu*, 1976, no. 3, pp. 75, 76.

徐恒彬：《简谈广东连县出土的西晋犁田耙田模型》，《文物》，1976 年，3 期，75、76 页。

21 Qin Zhongxing, "Qin Zhengguoqu qushou yizhi diaocha ji" [On the investigation of the canal head of the Zhengguoqu canal of Qin], *Wenwu*, 1974, no. 7, p. 35.

秦中行：《秦郑国渠渠首遗址调查记》，《文物》，1974 年，7 期，35 页。

22 Sichuan Guanxian Cultural and Educational Bureau, "Dujiangyan chutu Dong Han Li Bing shixiang" [Stone statue of Li Bing of Eastern Han unearthed in the Dujiang Weir], *Wenwu*, 1974, no. 7, pp. 27, 28, pl. 18.

四川省灌县文教局：《都江堰出土东汉李冰石像》，《文物》，1974 年，7 期，27、28 页，图版拾捌。

Wang Wencai, "Dong Han Li Bing shixiang yu Dujiangyan shui ze" [Stone statue of Li Bing of Eastern Han and the water gauge for the Dujiang Weir], *Wenwu*, 1974, no. 7, pp. 29, 30.

王文才：《东汉李冰石像与都江堰"水则"》，《文物》，1974 年，7 期，29、30 页。

23 Pls. 1 and 3 of *Handai huaxiang quan ji (chubian)* (n. 15 above).

同注 15 引《汉代画象全集》（初编），图版一、三。

24 Pp. 125-27, pls. 29 and 30 of *Luoyang Shaogou Han mu* (n. 1 above).

同注 1 引《洛阳烧沟汉墓》，125—127 页，图版贰玖、叁拾。

Qin Zhongxing, "Ji Hanzhong chutu de Handai beichi moxing" [Models of water ponds of the Han dynasty unearthed in Hanzhong], *Wenwu*, 1976, no. 3, pp. 77, 78.

秦中行：《记汉中出土的汉代陂池模型》，《文物》，1976 年，3 期，77、78 页。

Liu Zhiyuan, "Chengdu Tianhuishan ya mu qingli ji" [Notes on the clearance of cliff burials at Tianhuishan in Chengdu], *Kaogu Xuebao*, 1958, no. 1, p. 97, pl. 4.

刘志远：《成都天廻山崖墓清理记》，《考古学报》，1958 年，1 期，97 页，图版肆。

Pp. 33, 34 of article cited by Zhang Zengqi in n. 8 above.

同注 8 引张增祺文，33、34 页。

25 Yin Difei, "Anhui sheng Shouxian Anfengtang faxian Handai zhaba gongcheng yizhi" [Site of a Han dynasty sluice-gate and dam construction found in the Anfeng pond in Shouxian, Anhui], *Wenwu*, 1960, no. 1, pp. 61-62.

殷涤非:《安徽省寿县安丰塘发现汉代闸坝工程遗址》,《文物》,1960 年, 1 期, 61—62 页。

26 Liu Zhiyuan, "Sichuan Handai huaxiang zhuan fanying de shehui shenghuo" [Social life reflected in pictorial bricks of the Han dynasty in Sichuan], *Wenwu*, 1975, no. 4, p. 46, pl. 1.

刘志远:《四川汉代画像砖反映的社会生活》,《文物》,1975 年, 4 期, 46 页, 图版壹。

27 Yu Fuwei et al., "Luoyang Dongguan Dong Han xunren mu" [Eastern Han tomb with human sacrificial victims at Dongguan, Luoyang], *Wenwu*, 1973, no. 2, p. 57.

余扶危等:《洛阳东关东汉殉人墓》,《文物》,1973 年, 2 期, 57 页。

Henan Provincial Museum, "Jiyuan Sijiangou sanzuo Han mu de fajue" [Excavation of three Han dynasty tombs at Sijiangou in Jiyuan], *Wenwu*, 1973, no. 2, pp. 50-52.

河南省博物馆:《济源泗涧沟三座汉墓的发掘》,《文物》,1973 年, 2 期, 50—52 页。

28 Mancheng Excavation Team, Institute of Archaeology, Chinese Academy of Sciences, "Mancheng Han mu fajue jiyao" [Major results of the excavation of the Han tombs in Mancheng], *Kaogu*, 1972, no. 1, p. 9.

中国科学院考古研究所满城发掘队:《满城汉墓发掘纪要》,《考古》,1972 年, 1 期, 9 页。

29 Shandong Provincial Museum et al., "Linyi Yinqueshan sizuo Xi Han muzang" [Four Western Han tombs at Yinqueshan in Linyi], *Kaogu*, 1975, no. 6, p. 367, pl. 9.

山东省博物馆等:《临沂银雀山四座西汉墓葬》,《考古》,1975 年, 6 期, 367 页, 图版玖。

30 Dingxian Museum, "Hebei Dingxian 43-hao Han mu fajue jianbao" [Brief report on the excavation of Han tomb number 43 in Dingxian, Hebei], *Wenwu*, 1973, no. 11, p. 12, fig. 26.

定县博物馆:《河北定县 43 号汉墓发掘简报》,《文物》,1973 年, 11 期, 12 页, 图二十六。

Sichuan Provincial Museum, "Sichuan Xinduxian faxian yi pi huaxiang zhuan" [A group of pictorial bricks found in Xinduxian, Sichuan], *Wenwu*, 1980, no. 2, p. 56, pl. 7.

四川省博物馆:《四川新都县发现一批画像砖》,《文物》,1980 年, 2 期, 56 页, 图版柒。

31 Pp. 47, 48, 52-55, 68-73 of *Changsha Mawangdui yihao Han mu chutu dong zhi wu biaoben de yanjiu* in n. 5 above.

同注 5 引《长沙马王堆一号汉墓出土动植物标本的研究》，47、48、52—55、68—73 页。

³² P. 46, pl. 1 of article by Liu Zhiyuan cited in n. 26 above.

同注 26 引刘志远文，46 页，图版壹。

³³ Pp. 77, 78 of "Ji Hanzhong chutu de Handai beichi moxing" (n. 24 above).

同注 24 引秦中行文，77、78 页。

³⁴ Xia Nai, "Wo guo gudai can sang si chou de lishi" [History of silkworm raising and silk in ancient China], *Kaogu*, 1972, no. 2, pp. 14, 15.

夏鼐：《我国古代蚕、桑、丝、绸的历史》，《考古》，1972 年，2 期，14、15 页。

³⁵ Pp. 20, 21 of *Holingor Han mu bihua* (n. 15 above).

同注 15 引《和林格尔汉墓壁画》，20、21 页

³⁶ Pp. 44, 45, pls. 7, 8 of "Hubei Jiangling Fenghuangshan Xi Han mu fajue jianbao" (n. 1 above).

同注 1 引《湖北江陵凤凰山西汉墓发掘简报》，44、45 页，图版柒、捌。

³⁷ Qiu Xigui, "Hubei Jiangling Fenghuangshan shihao Han mu chutu jiandu kaoshi" [An interpretation of some written slips unearthed from Han tomb number 10 at Fenghuangshan in Jiangling, Hubei], *Wenwu*, 1974, no. 7, pp. 56, 57.

裘锡圭：《湖北江陵凤凰山十号汉墓出土简牍考释》，《文物》，1974 年，7 期，56、57 页。

³⁸ Pp. 20, 21, 101, 102, 146, 147 of *Holingor Han mu bihua* (n. 15 above).

同注 15 引《和林格尔汉墓壁画》，20、21、101、102、146、147 页。

³⁹ Ibid., pp. 79, 121-27.

同上，79、121—127 页。

⁴⁰ P. 99, pl. 8 of "Chengdu Tianhuishan ya mu qingli ji" (n. 24 above).

同注 24 引《成都天迴山崖墓清理记》，99 页，图版捌。

⁴¹ Cultural Relics Rescue Team, Jiayuguan City, "Jiayuguan Han huaxiang zhuan mu" [Han tomb with pictorial bricks in Jiayuguan], *Wenwu*, 1972, no. 12, p. 27, pl. 6.

嘉峪关市文物清理小组：《嘉峪关汉画像砖墓》，《文物》，1972 年，12 期，27 页，图版陆。

❹

¹ Hemudu Site Excavation Team, "Zhejiang Hemudu yizhi dierqi fajue de zhuyao shouhuo" [Major results of the second season of excavations of the Hemudu site in Zhejiang], *Wenwu*, 1980, no. 5, p. 5, pl. 3.

河姆渡遗址考古队：《浙江河姆渡遗址第二期发掘的主要收获》，《文物》，1980 年，
5 期，5 页，图版叁。

[2] Hebei Provincial Museum et al., "Hebei Gaochengxian Taixicun Shangdai yizhi 1973 nian de zhongyao faxian" [Important discoveries at the Shang site at Taixicun, Gaochengxian, Hebei, in 1973], *Wenwu*, 1974, no. 8, pp. 47, 48, pl. 1.

河北省博物馆等：《河北藁城县台西村商代遗址 1973 年的重要发现》，《文物》，1974 年，8 期，47、48 页，图版壹。

Taixi Archaeology Team, Hebei Provincial Cultural Relics Department, "Hebei Gaocheng Taixicun Shangdai yizhi fajue jianbao" [Brief report on the excavation of the Shang dynasty site at Taixicun, Gaocheng, Hebei], *Wenwu*, 1979, no. 6, pp. 37, 43.

河北省文物管理处台西考古队：《河北藁城台西村商代遗址发掘简报》，《文物》，1979 年，6 期，37、43 页。

Anyang Excavation Team, Institute of Archaeology, Chinese Academy of Sciences, "1958-1959 nian Yinxu fajue jianbao" [Brief report on the excavations at Yinxu in 1958-1959], *Kaogu*, 1961, no. 2, p. 70.

中国科学院考古研究所安阳发掘队：《1958—1959 年殷墟发掘简报》，《考古》，1961 年，2 期，70 页。

[3] Wang Shixiang, "Zhongguo gudai qigong zashu" [Miscellaneous notes on the lacquer craft of ancient China], *Wenwu*, 1979, no. 3, p. 49.

王世襄：《中国古代漆工杂述》，《文物》，1979 年，3 期，49 页。

[4] Luoyang Museum, "Luoyang Pangjiagou wuzuo Xi Zhou mu de qingli" [Clearance of five Western Zhou tombs at Pangjiagou, Luoyang], *Wenwu*, 1972, no. 10, p. 22.

洛阳博物馆：《洛阳庞家沟五座西周墓的清理》，《文物》，1972 年，10 期，22 页。

Institute of Archaeology, Chinese Academy of Sciences, *Shangcunling Guoguo mudi* [Cemetery of the state of Guo at Shangcunling] (Beijing: Kexue Press, 1959), p. 19, pl. 41.

中国科学院考古研究所：《上村岭虢国墓地》，科学出版社，1959 年，19 页，图版肆壹。

Shi Xingbang, "Chang'an Puducun Xi Zhou muzang fajue ji" [A note on the excavation of Western Zhou burials at Puducun in Chang'an], *Kaogu Xuebao*, 1954, no. 2, p. 124, pl. 4.

石兴邦：《长安普渡村西周墓葬发掘记》，《考古学报》，1954 年，2 期，124 页，图版肆。

[5] Shang Chengzuo, *Changsha chutu Chu qiqi tulu* [Illustrated catalogue of

lacquerware of Chu unearthed in Changsha] (Shanghai: Shanghai Press, 1955).

商承祚：《长沙出土楚漆器图录》，上海出版公司，1955 年。

Umehara Sueji, (Zōtei) *Rakuyō Kinson kobo shūei* [Treasures from the ancient tomb of Jincun, Luoyang] (Kyoto: Kobayashi, 1944), pp. 25-27, pls. 30-35.

梅原末治：《洛阳金村古墓聚英》（增订版），小林出版部，1944 年，25—27 页，图版三十——三十五。

Hunan Provincial Cultural Relics Commission, "Changsha chutu de sanzuo daxing muguomu" [Three large wooden-chambered graves unearthed in Changsha], *Kaogu Xuebao*, 1957, no. 1, pp. 93-101, pls. 1, 2.

湖南省文物管理委员会：《长沙出土的三座大型木椁墓》，《考古学报》，1957 年，1 期，93—101 页，图版壹、贰。

Archaeology Team, Hubei Provincial Bureau of Culture, "Hubei Jiangling sanzuo Chu mu chutu dapi zhongyao wenwu" [A large quantity of important cultural relics unearthed from three Chu tombs in Jiangling, Hubei], *Wenwu*, 1966, no. 5, pp. 33-39, 54, 55.

湖北省文化局文物工作队：《湖北江陵三座楚墓出土大批重要文物》，《文物》，1966 年，5 期，33—39、54、55 页。

Jingzhou District Museum, "Hubei Jiangling Tengdian yihao mu fajue jianbao" [Brief report on tomb number 1 at Tengdian in Jiangling, Hubei], *Wenwu*, 1973, no. 9, p. 11.

荆州地区博物馆：《湖北江陵藤店一号墓发掘简报》，《文物》，1973 年，9 期，11 页。

Suixian Leigudun Tomb Number 1 Archaeological Excavation Team, "Hubei Suixian Zeng Hou Yi mu fajue jianbao" [Brief report on the excavation of the tomb of Zeng Hou Yi in Suixian, Hubei], *Wenwu*, 1979, no. 7, pp. 10, 11.

随县擂鼓墩一号墓考古发掘队：《湖北随县曾侯乙墓发掘简报》，《文物》，1979 年，7 期，10、11 页。

Archaeology Team Number 1, Henan Provincial Bureau of Culture, "Wo guo kaogu shi shang de kongqian faxian: Xinyang Changtaiguan fajue yizuo Zhanguo damu" [An unprecedented discovery in Chinese history of archaeology: A large grave of the Warring States period excavated at Changtaiguan, Xinyang], *Wenwu Cankao Ziliao*, 1957, no. 9, pp. 21, 22.

河南省文化局文物工作队第一队：《我国考古史上的空前发现：阳长台关发掘一座战国大墓》，《文物参考资料》，1957 年，9 期，21、22 页。

Archaeology Team, Henan Provincial Bureau of Culture, "Xinyang Changtaiguan dierhao Chu mu de fajue" [The excavation of Chu tomb number 2 at Changtaiguan, Xinyang], *Kaogu Tongxun*, 1958, no. 11, pp. 79, 80.

河南省文化局文物工作队：《信阳长台关第 2 号楚墓的发掘》，《考古通讯》，1958 年，11 期，79、80 页。

Idem, *Henan Xinyang Chu mu chutu wenwu tulu* [An illustrated catalogue of the cultural relics unearthed from the Chu tombs in Xinyang, Henan] (Henan Renmin Press, 1959).

河南省文化局文物工作队：《河南信阳楚墓出土文物图录》，河南人民出版社，1959 年。

Sichuan Provincial Cultural Relics Commission, "Chengdu Yangzishan di 172-hao mu fajue baogao" [Report on the excavation of tomb number 172 at Yangzishan in Chengdu], *Kaogu Xuebao*, 1956, no. 4, pp. 14-16, pls. 7, 8.

四川省文物管理委员会：《成都羊子山第 172 号墓发掘报告》，《考古学报》，1956 年，4 期，14—16 页，图版柒、捌。

6 Harada Yoshito et al., *Rakurō* [Lolang] (Tokyo: Tōkō Shoin, 1930), pp. 36-49, pls. 43-81.

原田淑人等：《乐浪》，刀江书院，1930 年，36—49 页，图版四十三——八十一。

Oba Tsunekichi et al., *Rakurō Kanbo* [Han Tombs in Lolang], vol. 1 (Nara-ken: Rakurō Kanbo Kankōkai, 1974).

小场恒吉等：《乐浪汉墓》（第一册），乐浪汉墓刊行会，1974 年。

Umehara Sueji, *Mōko Noin-Ula hakken no ibutsu* [Remains found in Noin-Ula, Mongolia], in *Tōyō Bunko Ronsō*, vol. 27, 1960, 28-34, pls. 59-65.

梅原末治：《蒙古诺音乌拉发现的遗物》，东洋文库论丛，第 27 册，1960 年，28—34 页，图版五十九——六十五。

7 Archaeological Excavation Team of Luoyang District, *Luoyang Shaogou Han mu* [Han tombs at Shaogou, Luoyang] (Beijing: Kexue Press, 1959), pp. 203-05, pls. 60, 61.

洛阳区考古发掘队：《洛阳烧沟汉墓》，科学出版社，1959 年，203—205 页，图版陆拾、陆壹。

Shandong Provincial Department of Cultural Relics, "Shandong Wendengxian de Han muguomu ji qiqi" [Han dynasty wooden-chambered tomb and lacquerware in Wendeng, Shandong], *Kaogu Xuebao*, 1957, no. 1, pp. 129, 130, pls. 1, 2.

山东省文物管理处：《山东文登县的汉木椁墓及漆器》，《考古学报》，1957 年，1 期，129、130 页，图版壹、贰。

Jiangsu Provincial Cultural Relics Commission et al., "Jiangsu Yancheng Sanyangdun Han mu qingli baogao" [Report on the clearance of Han tombs at Sanyangdun in Yancheng, Jiangsu], *Kaogu*, 1964, no. 8, pp. 397, 398, pl. 5.

江苏省文物管理委员会等：《江苏盐城三羊墩汉墓清理报告》，《考古》，1964 年，8 期，

397、398 页，图版伍。

Nanjing Museum, "Jiangsu Lianyungangshi Haizhou Wangtongzhuang Han muguomu" [Han wooden-chambered tomb at Wangtongzhuang, Haizhou, Lianyungang city, Jiangsu], *Kaogu*, 1963, no. 6, pp. 287, 288, color plate 1.

南京博物院：《江苏连云港市海州网疃庄汉木椁墓》，《考古》，1963 年，6 期，287、288 页，彩色图版壹。

Zhao Renjun, "Ningbo diqu fajue de gu muzang he guwenhua yizhi" [Ancient graves and ancient cultural sites excavated in the Ningbo district], *Wenwu Cankao Ziliao*, 1956, no. 4, pp. 81, 82.

赵人俊：《宁波地区发掘的古墓葬和古文化遗址》，《文物参考资料》，1956 年，4 期，81、82 页。

Institute of Archaeology, Chinese Academy of Sciences, *Changsha fajue baogao* [Report on the excavations in Changsha] (Beijing: Kexue Press, 1957), pp. 120-23, pls. 74-82.

中国科学院考古研究所：《长沙发掘报告》，科学出版社，1957 年，120—123 页，图版柒肆——捌贰。

Guangzhou City Cultural Relics Commission, "Guangzhoushi Longshenggang 43-hao Dong Han muguomu" [Wooden-chambered tomb number 43 of Eastern Han at Longshenggang in Guangzhou], *Kaogu Xuebao*, 1957, no. 1, pp. 150-52, pls. 4-6.

广州市文物管理委员会：《广州市龙生冈 43 号东汉木椁墓》，《考古学报》，1957 年，1 期，150—152 页，图版肆——陆。

Idem, "Guangzhou Huanghuagang 003-hao Xi Han muguomu fajue jianbao" [Brief report on the excavation of wooden-chambered tomb number 003 of Western Han at Huanghuagang in Guangzhou], *Kaogu Tongxun*, 1958, no. 4, pp. 39, 40, pls. 7, 8.

广州市文物管理委员会：《广州黄花冈 003 号西汉木椁墓发掘简报》，《考古通讯》，1958 年，4 期，39、40 页，图版柒、捌。

Guizhou Provincial Museum, "Guizhou Qingzhen Pingba Han mu fajue baogao" [Report on the excavation of a Han tomb at Pingba, Qingzhen, Guizhou], *Kaogu Xuebao*, 1959, no. 1, pp. 99, 100, pl. 6.

贵州省博物馆：《贵州清镇平坝汉墓发掘报告》，《考古学报》，1959 年，1 期，99、100 页，图版陆。

Idem, "Guizhou Qingzhen Pingba Han zhi Song mu fajue jianbao" [Brief report on the excavations of Han-to-Song-period tombs at Pingba, Qingzhen, Guizhou], *Kaogu*, 1961, no. 4, p. 209, pl. 1.

贵州省博物馆:《贵州清镇平坝汉至宋墓发掘简报》,《考古》,1961 年,4 期,209 页,图版壹。

Gansu Provincial Museum, "Wuwei Mozuizi san zuo Han mu fajue jianbao" [Brief report on the excavations of three Han tombs at Mozuizi, Wuwei], *Wenwu*, 1972, no. 12, pp. 14, 15, pl. 4.

甘肃省博物馆:《武威磨咀子三座汉墓发掘简报》,《文物》,1972 年,12 期,14、15 页,图版肆。

[8] Archaeological Reporting Team, Guangxi Zhuang Autonomous Region, "Guangxi Hepu Xi Han muguomu" [Wooden-chambered tomb of Western Han in Hepu, Guangxi], *Kaogu*, 1972, no. 5, pp. 27, 28.

广西壮族自治区文物考古写作小组:《广西合浦西汉木椁墓》,《考古》,1972 年,5 期,27、28 页。

Archaeology Team of Guangxi Zhuang Autonomous Region, "Guangxi Guixian Luobowan yihao mu fajue jianbao" [Brief report on tomb number 1 at Luobowan, Guixian, Guangxi], *Wenwu*, 1978, no. 9, pp. 31, 32.

广西壮族自治区文物工作队:《广西贵县罗泊湾一号墓发掘简报》,《文物》,1978 年,9 期,31、32 页。

Nanjing Museum et al., "Haizhou Xi Han Huo He mu qingli jianbao" [Brief report on the clearance of the tomb of Huo He of Western Han in Haizhou], *Kaogu*, 1974, no. 3, pp. 181-83, pls. 4, 5.

南京博物院等:《海州西汉霍贺墓清理简报》,《考古》,1974 年,3 期,181—183 页,图版肆、伍。

Shandong Provincial Museum et al., "Linyi Yinqueshan sizuo Xi Han muzang" [Four Western Han tombs at Yinqueshan, Linyi], *Kaogu*, 1975, no. 6, p. 369, pls. 7, 8.

山东省博物馆等:《临沂银雀山四座西汉墓葬》,《考古》,1975 年,6 期,369 页,图版柒、捌。

Mancheng Excavation Team, Institute of Archaeology, Chinese Academy of Sciences, "Mancheng Han mu fajue jiyao" [Major results of the excavation of the Han tombs in Mancheng], *Kaogu*, 1972, no. 1, p. 14.

中国科学院考古研究所满城发掘队:《满城汉墓发掘纪要》,《考古》,1972 年,1 期,14 页。

Anhui Provincial Archaeology Team et al., "Fuyang Shuanggudui Xi Han Ruyinhou mu fajue jianbao" [Brief report on the excavation of the tomb of Marquis Ruyin of Western Han at Shuanggudui in Fuyang], *Wenwu*, 1978, no. 8, pp. 15-17, 20, 21.

安徽省文物工作队等:《阜阳双古堆西汉汝阴侯墓发掘简报》,《文物》,1978 年,8 期,15—17、20、21 页。

9 Hunan Provincial Museum et al., *Changsha Mawangdui yihao Han mu fajue jianbao* [Brief report on the excavation of Han tomb number 1 at Mawangdui, Changsha] (Beijing: Wenwu Press, 1972), pp. 76-96, pls. 154-77.

湖南省博物馆等:《长沙马王堆一号汉墓发掘简报》,文物出版社,1972 年,76—96 页,图版一五四———一七七。

Yangtze Valley Archaeological Workers' Training Institute, Second Class, "Hubei Jiangling Fenghuangshan Xi Han mu fajue jianbao" [Brief report on the excavation of Western Han tombs at Fenghuangshan, Jiangling, Hubei], *Wenwu*, 1974, no. 6, pp. 46-48, 59, 60, pls. 1, 9.

长江流域第二期文物考古工作人员训练班:《湖北江陵凤凰山西汉墓发掘简报》,《文物》,1974 年,6 期,46—48、59、60 页,图版壹、玖。

Ji'nancheng Fenghuangshan Han Tomb Number 168 Excavation and Reporting Team, "Hubei Jiangling Fenghuangshan 168-hao Han mu fajue jianbao" [Brief report on the excavation of Han tomb number 168 at Fenghuangshan, Jiangling, Hubei], *Wenwu*, 1975, no. 9, pp. 4, 5, pls. 5-8.

纪南城凤凰山一六八号汉墓发掘整理组:《湖北江陵凤凰山一六八号汉墓发掘简报》,《文物》,1975 年,9 期,4、5 页,图版伍———捌。

Fenghuangshan Han Tomb Number 167 Excavation and Reporting Team, "Jiangling Fenghuangshan 167-hao Han mu fajue jianbao" [Brief report on the excavation of Han tomb number 167 at Fenghuangshan in Jiangling], *Wenwu*, 1976, no. 10, pp. 32, 33.

凤凰山一六七号汉墓发掘整理小组:《江陵凤凰山一六七号汉墓发掘简报》,《文物》,1976 年,10 期,32、33 页。

Hubei Provincial Museum et al., "Hubei Yunmeng Xi Han mu fajue jianbao" [Brief report on Western Han tombs in Yunmeng, Hubei], *Wenwu*, 1973, no. 9, pp. 24, 25, pl. 1.

湖北省博物馆等:《湖北云梦西汉墓发掘简报》,《文物》,1973 年,9 期,24、25 页,图版壹。

10 P. 76 of *Changsha Mawangdui yihao Han mu fajue jianbao* (n. 9 above).

同注 9 引《长沙马王堆一号汉墓发掘简报》,76 页。

11 Ibid., pp. 76, 77.

同上,76、77 页。

12 Institute of Archaeology, Chinese Academy of Sciences et al., "Mawangdui er san hao Han mu fajue de zhuyao shouhuo" [Major results of the excavation of Han tombs number 2 and 3 at Mawangdui], *Kaogu*, 1975, no. 1, p. 57.

中国科学院考古研究所等:《马王堆二、三号汉墓发掘的主要收获》,《考古》,1975 年,1 期,57 页。

13 P. 53 of article cited in n. 3 above.

同注 3,53 页。

14 Pp. 122, 123, pl. 83 of *Changsha fajue baogao* (n. 7 above).

同注 7 引《长沙发掘报告》,122、123 页,图版捌叁。

15 Harada Yoshito et al., *Rakurō* [Lolang] (Tokyo: Tōkō Shoin, 1930), pp. 42, 43, pls. 56-58.

原田淑人等:《乐浪》,刀江书院,1930 年,42、43 页,图版五十六——五十八。

Koizumi Akio et al., *Rakurō Saikyōzuka* [Mound with painted baskets] (Tokyo: Chōsen Koseki Kenkyūkai, 1934), pp. 41-43, pls. 41-50.

小泉显夫等:《乐浪彩箧冢》,朝鲜古迹研究会,1934 年,41—43 页,图版四十一——五十。

16 Nan Bo, "Jiangsu Lianyungangshi Haizhou Xi Han Shi Qi Yao mu" [Tomb of Shi Qi Yao of the Western Han at Haizhou, Lianyungang city, Jiangsu], *Kaogu*, 1975, no. 3, pp. 172-74, pl. 6.

南波:《江苏连云港市海州西汉侍其繇墓》,《考古》,1975 年,3 期,172—174 页,图版陆。

17 P. 228, color plate, pl. 1, in Nanjing Museum, "Jiangsu Lianyungangshi Haizhou Wangtongzhuang Han muguomu" (see n. 7 above).

同注 7 引南京博物院文,228 页,彩色版,图版壹。

18 P. 203, pl. 60 of *Luoyang Shaogou Han mu* (n. 7 above).

同注 7 引《洛阳烧沟汉墓》,203 页,图版陆拾。

P. 47, pl. 60 of Koizumi (n. 15 above).

同注 15 引小泉显夫书,47 页,图版六十。

19 Oba Tsunekichi et al., *Rakurō Kanbo* [Han tombs in Lolang], vol. 1 (Nara-ken: Rakurō Kanbo Kankōkai, 1974), pp. 35-38.

小场恒吉等:《乐浪汉墓》(第一册),乐浪汉墓刊行会,1974 年,35—38 页。

20 Himoto Kamejiro et al., *Rakurō Ō Kō no haka* [Tomb of Wang Guang in Lolang] (Tokyo: Chōsen Koseki Kenkyūkai, 1935), p. 36, pl. 50.

榧本龟次郎等：《乐浪王光墓》，朝鲜古迹研究会，1935 年，36 页，图版伍拾。

21 Mizuno Seiichi et al., *Mōkyō Yokōken Kanbo josa rakuhō* [Preliminary report of the investigation of Han tombs in Yanggaoxian in Inner Mongolia] (Osaka: Yamato Shoin, 1943), p. 23.

水野清一等：《蒙疆阳高县汉墓调查略报》，大和书院，1943 年，23 页。

22 Pp. 120, 121, pl. 78 of *Changsha fajue baogao* (n. 7 above).

同注 7 引《长沙发掘报告》，120、121 页，图版柒捌。

23 Hunan Provincial Museum, *Hunan Handai qiqi tulu* [Illustrated catalog of Han dynasty lacquerware in Hunan] (Hunan Renmin Press, 1965), p. 27.

湖南省博物馆：《湖南汉代漆器图录》，湖南人民出版社，1965 年，27 页。

24 Pp. 77, 78, pl. 167 of *Changsha Mawangdui yihao Han mu fajue jianbao* (n. 9 above).

同注 9 引《长沙马王堆一号汉墓发掘简报》，77、78 页，图版一六七。

25 Pp. 28-30, pl. 59 of Umehara, *Mōko Noin-Ula hakken no ibutsu* (n. 6 above).

同注 6 引梅原末治书，28—30 页，图版五十九。

26 P. 397 of "Jiangsu Yancheng Sanyangdun Han mu qingli baogao" (n. 7 above).

同注 7 引《江苏盐城三羊墩汉墓清理报告》，397 页。

27 Umehara Sueji, *Shina Kandai kinen mei-shikki zusetsu* [Illustrated catalogue of lacquer wares with dated inscriptions from the Han dynasty in China] (Kyoto: Bunseido, 1943), pp. 40, 41, pl. 35.

梅原末治：《支那汉代纪年铭漆器图说》，桑名文星堂，1943 年，40、41 页，图版三十五。

28 Himoto Tojin et al., "Handai jinian ming qiqi jicheng" [Collection of Han dynasty lacquerware with dated inscriptions], in *Rakurō Kanbo*, vol. 1 (Nara-ken: Rakurō Kanbo Kankōkai, 1974), p. 96.

榧本杜人等：《汉代纪年铭漆器集成》，《乐浪汉墓》第一册，乐浪汉墓刊行会，1974 年，96 页。

29 Mai Yinghao et al., "Qin Shi Huang tongyi Lingnan diqu de lishi zuoyong" [Historical role of the unification of the Lingnan area under Qin Shi Huang], *Kaogu*, 1975, no. 4, p. 208.

麦英豪等：《秦始皇统一岭南地区的历史作用》，《考古》，1975 年，4 期，208 页。

30 Pp. 31, 40 of "Guangxi Guixian Luobowan yihao mu fajue jianbao" (n. 8 above).

同注 8 引《广西贵县罗泊湾一号墓发掘简报》，31、40 页。

31 Jiang Yingju, "Linyi Yinqueshan Xi Han mu qiqi mingwen kaoshi" [Interpretation of the inscriptions on lacquerware in the Western Han tomb at Yinqueshan, Linyi], *Kaogu*, 1975, no. 6, pp. 349-51.

蒋英炬:《临沂银雀山西汉墓漆器铭文考释》,《考古》, 1975 年, 6 期, 349—351 页。

32 Yu Weichao et al., "Mawangdui yihao Han mu chutu qiqi zhidi zhu wenti" [Problems relating to the place of manufacture of the lacquerware unearthed in Han tomb number 1 at Mawangdui], *Kaogu*, 1975, no. 6, pp. 344-48.

俞伟超等:《马王堆一号汉墓出土漆器制地诸问题》,《考古》, 1975 年, 6 期, 344 —348 页。

33 Pp. 20, 21 of "Fuyang Shuanggudui Xi Han Ruyinhou mu fajue jianbao" (n. 8 above).

同注 8 引《阜阳双古堆西汉汝阴侯墓发掘简报》, 20、21 页。

34 Pp. 41-44, pls. 36-38, 47 of book cited in n. 27 above.

同注 27, 41—44 页, 图版三十六——三十八、四十七。

35 Pp. 24-26, 35, 36 of "Hubei Yunmeng Xi Han mu fajue jian bao" (n. 9 above).

同注 9 引《湖北云梦西汉墓发掘简报》, 24—26、35、36 页。

36 Pp. 110-11 of article cited in n. 28 above.

同注 28, 110—111 页。

37 Song Zhimin, "Handai mingke suojian zhiguan xiaoji" [Notes on offices seen in Han dynasty inscriptions], *Kaogu*, 1979, no. 5.

宋治民:《汉代铭刻所见职官小记》,《考古》, 1979 年, 5 期。

❺

1 Mancheng Excavation Team, Institute of Archaeology, Chinese Academy of Sciences, "Mancheng Han mu fajue jiyao" [Major results of the excavation of the Han tombs in Mancheng], *Kaogu*, 1972, no. 1, pp. 10, 11, pls. 4-6.

中国科学院考古研究所满城发掘队:《满城汉墓发掘纪要》,《考古》, 1972 年, 1 期, 10、11 页, 图版肆——陆。

Institute of Archaeology, Chinese Academy of Social Sciences et al., *Mancheng Han mu* [Han tombs in Mancheng] (Beijing: Wenwu Press, 1978), pp. 36-38, 45-50, pls. 8-10, 16.

中国社会科学院考古研究所等:《满城汉墓》, 文物出版社, 1978 年, 36—38、45—50 页, 图版八——十、十六。

2 Xiao Yun, "Mancheng Han mu chutu de cuo jin yin niao chong shu tong hu" [Bronze *hu*-vessel with gold- and silver-inlaid bird-and-worm inscription unearthed in the Han tomb in Mancheng], *Kaogu*, 1972, no. 5, pp. 49-52, pl. 12.

肖蕴：《满城汉墓出土的错金银鸟虫书铜壶》，《考古》，1972 年，5 期，49—52 页，图版拾贰。

Zhang Zhenlin et al., "Guanyu Mancheng Han mu tong hu niao zhuan shiwen de taolun" [Discussion of the transcription of the bird-seal-inscription on the bronze *hu*-vessel from the Han tomb in Mancheng], *Kaogu*, 1979, no. 4, pp. 356-59.

张振林等：《关于满城汉墓铜壶鸟篆释文的讨论》（三篇），《考古》，1979 年，4 期，356—359 页。

Zhang Zhenglang, "Mancheng Han mu chutu cuo jin yin niao chong shu tong hu (jia) shiwen" [Transcription of the bronze *hu*-vessel A with gold- and silver-inlaid bird-and-worm inscription unearthed from the Han tomb in Mancheng], *Zhonghua Wenshi Luncong*, 1979, no. 3, pp. 1-6.

张政烺：《满城汉墓出土错金银鸟虫书铜壶（甲）释文》，《中华文史论丛》，1979 年，第 3 辑，1—6 页。

3 Mancheng Excavation Team, "Mancheng Han mu fajue jiyao" (see n. 1 above), p. 11.

同注 1 引《满城汉墓发掘纪要》，11 页。

4 Umehara Sueji, (Zōtei) *Rakuyō Kinson kobo shūei* [Treasures from the ancient tomb of Jincun, Luoyang] (Kyoto: Kobayashi, 1944), pp. 21, 22, pl. 18.

梅原末治：《洛阳金村古墓聚英》（增订版），小林出版部，1944 年，21、22 页，图版十八。

5 Xi'an City Cultural Relics Commission, "Xi'an Sanqiaozhen Gaoyaocun chutu de Xi Han tongqi qun" [A group of Western Han bronzes unearthed in Gaoyaocun, Sanqiaozhen, Xi'an], *Kaogu*, 1963, no. 2, pp. 62-70, pls. 3, 4.

西安市文物管理委员会：《西安三桥镇高窑村出土的西汉铜器群》，《考古》，1963 年，2 期，62—70 页，图版叁、肆。

6 Chen Zhi, "Gu qiwu wenzi congkao" [Miscellaneous notes on ancient vessel inscriptions], *Kaogu*, 1963, no. 2, pp. 80-82.

陈直：《古器物文字丛考》，《考古》，1963 年，2 期，80—82 页。

Huang Zhanyue, "Xi'an Sanqiao Gaoyaocun Xi Han tongqi qun mingwen bushi" [Supplementary explanations of the inscriptions on Western Han bronzes from Gaoyaocun, Sanqiao, Xi'an], *Kaogu*, 1963, no. 4, pp. 198-200.

黄展岳：《西安三桥高窑村西汉铜器群铭文补释》，《考古》，1963 年，4 期，198—200 页。

7   P. 82 of Chen Zhi, "Gu qiwu wenzi congkao" (n. 6 above).

同注 6 引陈直文，82 页。

8   Mancheng Excavation Team, "Mancheng Han mu fajue jiyao," pp. 11-12, pl. 6 (n. 1 above).

同注 1 引《满城汉墓发掘纪要》，11—12 页，图版陆。

Archaeology Reporting Team, Guangxi Zhuang Autonomous Region, "Guangxi Hepu Xi Han muguomu" [Wooden-chambered tomb of Western Han in Hepu, Guangxi], *Kaogu*, 1972, no. 5, p. 20, pl. 7.

广西壮族自治区文物考古写作小组：《广西合浦西汉木椁墓》，《考古》，1972 年，5 期，20 页，图版柒。

Gansu Provincial Museum, "Wuwei Leitai Han mu" [Han tomb at Leitai in Wuwei], *Kaogu Xuebao*, 1974, no. 2, pp. 100-01, pl. 13.

甘肃省博物馆：《武威雷台汉墓》，《考古学报》，1974 年，2 期，100—101 页，图版拾叁。

9   Institute of Archaeology, Chinese Academy of Sciences, *Changsha fajue baogao* [Report on the excavations in Changsha] (Beijing: Kexue Press, 1957), p. 112.

中国科学院考古研究所：《长沙发掘报告》，科学出版社，1957 年，112 页。

10   Pp. 23-25 of "Guangxi Hepu Xi Han muguomu" (n. 8 above).

同注 8 引《广西合浦西汉木椁墓》，23—25 页。

11   Wuzhou City Museum, "Guangxi Wuzhoushi jin nian lai chutu de yipi Handai wenwu" [Han dynasty relics unearthed recently in Wuzhou city, Guangxi], *Wenwu*, 1977, no. 2, pp. 70-71.

梧州市博物馆：《广西梧州市近年来出土的一批汉代文物》，《文物》，1977 年，2 期，70—71 页。

12   Guo Yong, "Shanxi sheng Youyuxian chutu de Xi Han tongqi" [Bronze vessels unearthed in Youyu county, Shanxi], *Wenwu*, 1963, no. 11, pp. 4-12.

郭勇：《山西省右玉县出土的西汉铜器》，《文物》，1963 年，11 期，4—12 页。

13   Xia Nai, "Wuchanjieji wenhua da geming zhong de kaogu xin faxian" [New archaeological discoveries during the Great Proletarian Cultural Revolution], *Kaogu*, 1972, no. 1, p. 33.

夏鼐：《无产阶级"文化大革命"中的考古新发现》，《考古》，1972 年，1 期，33 页。

14   Pp. 98-100, pl. 11 of "Wuwei Leitai Han mu" (n. 8 above).

同注 8 引《武威雷台汉墓》，98—100 页，图版拾壹。

15   Ibid., pp. 90-103, pls. 3-12.

同上，90—103 页，图版叁——拾贰。

16   Hunan Provincial Museum et al., *Changsha Mawangdui yihao Han mu fajue jianbao* [Brief report on the excavation of Han tomb number 1 at Mawangdui, Changsha] (Beijing: Wenwu Press, 1972), p. 128, pl. 178.

湖南省博物馆等：《长沙马王堆一号汉墓发掘简报》，文物出版社，1972 年，128 页，图版一七八。

17   Mancheng Excavation Team, "Mancheng Han mu fajue jiyao" (n. 1 above), p. 17.

同注 1 引《满城汉墓发掘纪要》，17 页。

18   Wang Shilun, *Zhejiang sheng chutu tongjing xuan ji* [Selected bronze mirrors unearthed in Zhejiang] (Beijing: Chinese Classic Art Press, 1957).

王士伦：《浙江省出土铜镜选集》，中国古典艺术出版社，1957 年。

19   Northeast Museum, "Liaoyang Sandaohao liangzuo bihua mu de qingli gongzuo jianbao" [Brief report on the clearance of two tombs with murals at Sandaohao, Liaoyang], *Wenwu Cankao Ziliao*, 1955, no. 12, pp. 51, 52.

东北博物馆：《辽阳三道壕两座壁画墓的清理工作简报》，《文物参考资料》，1955 年，12 期，51、52 页。

20   Luo Ping, "Hebei Chengde zhuanqu Handai kuangye yizhi de diaocha" [The investigation of a Han dynasty mining and smelting site in Chengde district, Hebei], *Kaogu Tongxun*, 1957, no. 1, pp. 22-27.

罗平：《河北承德专区汉代矿冶遗址的调查》，《考古通讯》，1957 年，1 期，22—27 页。

21   He Zicheng, "Xi'an Han cheng yizhi fujin faxian Handai tongding shi kuai" [Ten copper ingots of the Han dynasty discovered in the Han city ruins in Xi'an], *Wenwu Cankao Ziliao*, 1956, no. 3, p. 82.

贺梓城：《西安汉城遗址附近发现汉代铜锭十块》，《文物参考资料》，1956 年，3 期，82 页。

22   Fang Guojin, "Liu jin tong hu" [The gilded bronze *hu*], *Wenwu Cankao Ziliao*, 1958, no. 9, pp. 69, 70.

方国锦：《鎏金铜斛》，《文物参考资料》，1958 年，9 期，69、70 页。

23   Harada Yoshito et al., *Rakurō* [Lolang] (Tokyo: Tōkō Shoin, 1930), p. 39, pls. 44, 45.

原田淑人等：《乐浪》，刀江书院，1930 年，39 页，图版四十四、四十五。

24   Mancheng Excavation Team, "Mancheng Han mu fajue jiyao" (see n. 1 above), p. 77.

同注 1 引《满城汉墓发掘纪要》，77 页。

❻

1   Fan Wenlan, *Zhongguo Tongshi (Di'erce)* [General history of China], 5th ed. (Beijing: Renmin Press, 1978), vol. 2, p. 59.

范文澜：《中国通史》（第二册），人民出版社，第五版，1978 年，59 页。

2   Guangzhou City Cultural Relics Department et al., "Guangzhou Qin Han zaochuan gongchang yizhi shijue" [Test excavation of a shipyard site of the Qin-Han period in Guangzhou], *Wenwu*, 1977, no. 4, pp. 1-16, pls. 2-5.

广州市文物管理处等：《广州秦汉造船工场遗址试掘》，《文物》，1977 年，4 期，1—16 页，图版贰——伍。

3   Xia Nai, "Kaoguxue he kejishi" [Archaeology and the history of science and technology], *Kaogu*, 1977, no. 2, p. 84.

夏鼐：《考古学和科技史》，《考古》，1977 年，2 期，84 页。

Shanghai Jiaotong University Shipbuilding History Team, "Qin Han shiqi de chuanbo" [Ships of the Qin-Han period], *Wenwu*, 1977, no. 4, p. 21.

上海交通大学"造船史话"组：《秦汉时期的船舶》，《文物》，1977 年，4 期，21 页。

4   Zhejiang Province Cultural Relics Commission, "Hangzhou Gudang Handai Zhu Lechang mu qingli jianbao" [Brief report on the clearance of the tomb of Zhu Lechang of the Han dynasty at Gudang, Hangzhou], *Kaogu*, 1959, no. 3, pp. 150-52.

浙江省文物管理委员会：《杭州古荡汉代朱乐昌墓清理简报》，《考古》，1959 年，3 期，150—152 页。

5   Inner Mongolia Autonomous Region Archaeology Team, "Huhehaote Ershijiazi gucheng chutu de Xi Han tiejia" [Iron armor of Western Han unearthed at an ancient town site at Ershijiazi in Huhehaote], *Kaogu*, 1975, no. 4, pp. 249-53, pl. 9.

内蒙古自治区文物工作队：《呼和浩特二十家子古城出土的西汉铁甲》，《考古》，1975 年，4 期，249—253 页，图版玖。

Institute of Archaeology, Chinese Academy of Social Sciences et al., *Mancheng Han mu* [Han tombs in Mancheng] (Beijing: Wenwu Press, 1978), pp. 66-68.

中国社会科学院考古研究所等：《满城汉墓》，文物出版社，1978 年，66—68 页。

6   Institute of Archaeology, Chinese Academy of Social Sciences, *Han Chang'an cheng yizhi fajue baogao* [Report of the excavation of the ruins of the Han dynasty city of Chang'an]. In preparation.

中国社会科学院考古研究所：《汉长安城遗址发掘报告》，待刊。

7   Henan Provincial Museum et al., "Henan Handai yetie jishu chu tan"

[Preliminary discussion of iron technology of the Han dynasty in Henan], *Kaogu Xuebao*, 1978, no. 1, p. 13.

河南省博物馆等:《河南汉代冶铁技术初探》,《考古学报》, 1978 年, 1 期, 13 页。

8 Fenghuangshan Han Tomb Number 167 Excavation and Reporting Team, "Jiangling Fenghuangshan 167-hao Han mu fajue jianbao" [Brief report on the excavation of Han tomb number 167 at Fenghuangshan in Jiangling], *Wenwu*, 1976, no. 10, p. 34.

凤凰山一六七号汉墓发掘整理小组:《江陵凤凰山一六七号汉墓发掘简报》,《文物》, 1976 年, 10 期, 34 页。

9 Institute of Archaeology, Chinese Academy of Social Sciences et al., *Mancheng Han mu fajue baogao* [Report on the excavation of the Han dynasty tombs in Mancheng] (Beijing: Wenwu Press, 1980).

中国社会科学院考古研究所等:《满城汉墓发掘报告》, 文物出版社, 1980 年。

10 Archaeological Excavation Team of Luoyang District, *Luoyang Shaogou Han mu* [Han tombs at Shaogou, Luoyang] (Beijing: Kexue Press, 1959), pp. 196, 197, pl. 58.

洛阳区考古发掘队:《洛阳烧沟汉墓》, 科学出版社, 1959 年, 196、197 页, 图版伍捌。

11 Gansu Provincial Museum, "Wuiwei Leitai Han mu" [Han tomb at Leitai in Wuwei], *Kaogu Xuebao*, 1974, no. 2, p. 103, pls. 16, 17.

甘肃省博物馆:《武威雷台汉墓》,《考古学报》, 1974 年, 2 期, 103 页, 图版拾陆、拾柒。

12 Luo Zhenyu, *Qi Lu fengni jicun* [Catalogue of seal clays from Qi and Lu] (1912), pp. 10, 11, 45.

罗振玉:《齐鲁封泥集存》, 1912 年, 10、11、45 页。

13 Li Jinghua, "Handai tie nongqi mingwen shishi" [A tentative interpretation of some inscriptions on iron agricultural implements of the Han dynasty], *Kaogu*, 1974, no. 1, pp. 61-66.

李京华:《汉代铁农器铭文试释》,《考古》, 1974 年, 1 期, 61—66 页。

14 Su Tianjun, "Shi nian lai Beijing shi suo faxian de zhongyao gudai muzang he yizhi" [Important ancient burials and sites found in Beijing in the last decade], *Kaogu*, 1959, no. 3, p. 136.

苏天钧:《十年来北京市所发现的重要古代墓葬遗址》,《考古》, 1959 年, 3 期, 136 页。

Li Buqing, "Shandong Tengxian faxian tie fan" [Iron molds discovered in Tengxian, Shandong], *Kaogu*, 1960, no. 7, p. 72.

李步青:《山东滕县发现铁范》,《考古》, 1960 年, 7 期, 72 页。

Nanjing Museum, "Liguoyi gudai liantielu de diaocha ji qingli" [Investigation and clearance of ancient iron-smelting furnaces at Liguoyi], *Wenwu*, 1960, no. 4, pp. 46, 47.

南京博物院：《利国驿古代炼铁炉的调查及清理》，《文物》，1960 年，4 期，46、47 页。

15 Pp. 1-4 of article cited in n. 7 above.

同注 7，1—4 页。

16 Archaeology Team, Henan Provincial Bureau of Culture, *Gongxian Tieshenggou* (Beijing: Wenwu Press, 1962), pp. 5-26, pls. 4-13.

河南省文化局文物工作队：《巩县铁生沟》，文物出版社，1962 年，5—26 页，图版肆——拾叁。

17 P. 4 of article cited in n. 7 above.

同注 7，4 页。

18 Archaeology Team, Henan Provincial Bureau of Culture, "Nanyang Handai tie gongchang fajue jianbao" [Brief report on the Han dynasty iron foundry in Nanyang], *Wenwu*, 1960, no. 1, pp. 58-60.

河南省文化局文物工作队：《南阳汉代铁工厂发掘简报》，《文物》，1960 年，1 期，58—60 页。

19 Pp. 11-13, pl. 1 of article cited in n. 7 above.

同注 7，11—13 页，图版壹。

20 Li Zhong, "Zhongguo fengjian shehui qianqi gangtie yelian jishu fazhan de tantao" [An exploration of the development of steel and iron manufacturing techniques in the early period of Chinese feudal society], *Kaogu Xuebao*, 1975, no. 2, pp. 1-20.

李众：《中国封建社会前期钢铁冶炼技术发展的探讨》，《考古学报》，1975 年，2 期，1—20 页。

The Writing Team of *Zhongguo yejin jianshi*, Beijing Steel and Iron College, *Zhongguo yejin jianshi* [A short history of metallurgy in China] (Beijing: Kexue Press, 1978), pp. 40-136.

北京钢铁学院《中国冶金简史》编写小组：《中国冶金简史》，科学出版社，1978 年，40—136 页。

21 Nanjing Museum, "Jiangsu Liuhe Chengqiao erhao Dong Zhou mu" [Eastern Zhou tomb number 2 at Chengqiao in Liuhe, Jiangsu], *Kaogu*, 1974, no. 2, p. 120, pl. 6.

南京博物院：《江苏六合程桥二号东周墓》，《考古》，1974 年，2 期，120 页，图版陆。

22 Hebei Provincial Cultural Relics Department, "Hebei Yixian Yanxiadu 44-hao mu fajue baogao" [Report on the excavation of tomb number 44 at Yanxiadu in Yixian, Hebei], *Kaogu*, 1975, no. 4, pp. 231, 232.

河北省文物管理处：《河北易县燕下都 44 号墓发掘报告》，《考古》，1975 年，4 期，231、232 页。

Pressure Processing Program, Beijing Steel and Iron College, "Yixian Yanxiadu 44-hao muzang tieqi jinxiang kaocha chubu baogao" [Preliminary report on the metallographical examination of the iron implements from tomb number 44 at Yanxiadu in Yixian], *Kaogu*, 1975, no. 4, pp. 241, 242.

北京钢铁学院压力加工专业：《易县燕下都 44 号墓葬铁器金相考察初步报告》，《考古》，1975 年，4 期，241、242 页。

23　Li Zhong (see n. 20 above), pp. 11-13.

同注 20 引李众文，11—13 页。

Pp. 54-57 of *Mancheng Han mu* (n. 5 above).

同注 5 引《满城汉墓》，54—57 页。

24　Li Zhong (see n. 20 above), p. 5, pl. 1.

同注 20 引李众文，5 页，图版壹。

25　Ibid., pp. 6, 7.

同上，6、7 页。

26　P. 57 of *Mancheng Han mu* (n. 5 above).

同注 5 引《满城汉墓》，57 页。

27　Pp. 20, 21 of article cited in n. 7 above.

同注 7，20、21 页。

28　See n. 9 above.

同注 9。

29　Liu Xinjian et al., "Shandong Cangshan faxian Dong Han Yongchu jinian tie dao" [An Eastern Han iron knife with a Yongchu date discovered in Cangshan, Shandong], *Wenwu*, 1974, no. 12, p. 61, pl. 5.

刘心健等：《山东苍山发现东汉永初纪年铁刀》，《文物》，1974 年，12 期，61 页，图版伍。

30　Li Zhong (see n. 20 above), p. 14, pl. 6.

同注 20 引李众文，14 页，图版陆。

31　Shandong Provincial Museum, "Han huaxiang yetie tu shuoming" [Explanation of the Han iron foundry picture], *Wenwu*, 1959, no. 1, p. 2.

山东省博物馆:《汉画象冶铁图说明》,《文物》, 1959 年, 1 期, 2 页。

[32] Fu Xihua, *Handai huaxiang quan ji (chubian)* [A complete collection of the pictorial art of the Han dynasty (preliminary volume)] (Shanghai: Commercial Press, 1950), pl. 73.

傅惜华:《汉代画象全集》(初编), 上海商务印书馆, 1950 年, 图版七十三。

❼

[1] Archaeological Excavation Team of Luoyang District, *Luoyang Shaogou Han mu* [Han tombs at Shaogou, Luoyang] (Beijing: Kexue Press, 1959), pp. 109-12, pls. 1, 22.

洛阳区考古发掘队:《洛阳烧沟汉墓》, 科学出版社, 1959 年, 109—112 页, 图版壹、贰贰。

Institute of Archaeology, Chinese Academy of Social Sciences et al., *Mancheng Han mu* [Han tombs in Mancheng] (Beijing: Wenwu Press, 1978), p. 40, pl. 5.

中国社会科学院考古研究所等:《满城汉墓》, 文物出版社, 1978 年, 40 页, 图版五。

[2] Hebei Provincial Cultural Relics Commission, "Hebei Wu'anxian Wuji gucheng zhong de yao zhi" [Kiln remains in the city of Wuji in Wuanxian, Hebei], *Kaogu*, 1959, no. 7, pp. 339-42, pl. 8.

河北省文物管理委员会:《河北武安县午汲古城中的窑址》,《考古》, 1959 年, 7 期, 339—342 页, 图版捌。

[3] Yellow River Reservoir Archaeology Team, "1957 nian Henan Shanxian fajue jianbao" [Brief report on the excavation in Shanxian, Henan, in 1957], *Kaogu Tongxun*, 1958, no. 11, p. 76.

黄河水库考古工作队:《1957 年河南陕县发掘简报》,《考古通讯》, 1958 年, 11 期, 76 页。

Archaeology Team, Henan Provincial Bureau of Culture, "Henan Tongbo Wangang Han mu de fajue" [Excavation of Han tombs in Wangang, Tongbo, Henan], *Kaogu*, 1964, no. 8, pp. 386-88.

河南省文化局文物工作队:《河南桐柏万冈汉墓的发掘》,《考古》, 1964 年, 8 期, 386—388 页。

[4] *Luoyang Shaogou Han mu* (see n. 1 above), pp. 103-06, color plates 1-3.

同注 1 引《洛阳烧沟汉墓》, 103—106 页, 彩版壹——叁。

Mancheng Excavation Team, Institute of Archaeology, Chinese Academy of Sciences, "Mancheng Han mu fajue jiyao" [Major results of the excavation of the Han tombs in Mancheng], *Kaogu*, 1972, no. 1, pp. 13-14.

中国科学院考古研究所满城发掘队：《满城汉墓发掘纪要》，《考古》，1972 年，1 期，13、14 页。

5 Shandong Provincial Museum et al., "Linyi Yinqueshan sizuo Xi Han muzang" [Four Western Han tombs at Yinqueshan, Linyi], *Kaogu*, 1975, no. 6, p. 364, pl. 6.

山东省博物馆等：《临沂银雀山四座西汉墓葬》，《考古》，1975 年，6 期，364 页，图版陆。

Anhui Provincial Archaeology Team et al., "Fuyang Shuanggudui Xi Han Ruyinhou mu fajue jianbao" [Brief report on the excavation of the tomb of Marquis Ruyin of Western Han at Shuanggudui in Fuyang], *Wenwu*, 1978, no. 8, pp. 17, 23.

安徽省文物工作队等：《阜阳双古堆西汉汝阴侯墓发掘简报》，《文物》，1978 年，8 期，17、23 页。

Hubei Provincial Museum et al., "Hubei Yunmeng Xi Han mu fajue jianbao" [Brief report on Western Han tombs in Yunmeng, Hubei], *Wenwu*, 1973, no. 9, pp. 24, 27.

湖北省博物馆等：《湖北云梦西汉墓发掘简报》，《文物》，1973 年，9 期，24、27 页。

6 Archaeology Team, Henan Provincial Bureau of Culture, "Henan Tongbo Wangang Han mu de fajue" (see n. 3 above), pp. 386, 387.

同注 3 引《河南桐柏万冈汉墓的发掘》，386、387 页。

7 Institute of Archaeology, Chinese Academy of Sciences, *Changsha fajue baogao* [Report on the excavations in Changsha] (Beijing: Kexue Press, 1957), pp. 104-06, pls. 57-61.

中国科学院考古研究所：《长沙发掘报告》，科学出版社，1957 年，104—106 页，图版伍柒——陆壹。

Mai Yinghao, "Guangzhou Huaqiaoxincun de Xi Han mu" [Western Han Tombs at Huaqiaoxincun in Guangzhou], *Kaogu Xuebao*, 1958, no. 2, pp. 52-64, pls. 4-9.

麦英豪：《广州华侨新村的西汉墓》，《考古学报》，1958 年，2 期，52—64 页，图版肆——玖。

8 Su Bingqi, *Doujitai Goudongqu muzang* [Burials in Goudongqu, Doujitai] (Beijing: Beijing University Press, 1948), pp. 143-46, 170-89.

苏秉琦：《斗鸡台沟东区墓葬》，国立北京大学出版部，1948 年，143—146、170—189 页。

Archaeological Excavation Team of Luoyang District, *Luoyang Shaogou Han mu* (n. 1 above), pp. 100-05, pl. 21.

同注 1 引《洛阳烧沟汉墓》，100—105 页，图版贰壹。

9 Mizuno Seiichi, "Ryoku yūto ni tsuite" [On green-glazed porcelain], in *Sekai Toji Zenshū* (Tokyo: Kowaide Shobō, 1955) 8:236-38.

水野清一:《绿釉陶について》,《世界陶磁全集》,河出书房,1955 年,第八卷,236—238 页。

10 Institute of Archaeology, *Changsha fajue baogao* (see n. 7 above), pp. 107-09, pl. 61.

同注 7 引《长沙发掘报告》,107—109 页,图版陆壹。

Nanjing Museum et al., "Haizhou Xi Han Huo He mu qingli jianbao" [Brief report on the clearance of the tomb of Huo He of Western Han in Haizhou], *Kaogu*, 1974, no. 3, p. 185, pl. 5.

南京博物院等:《海州西汉霍贺墓清理简报》,《考古》,1974 年,3 期,185 页,图版伍。

11 Pp. 107, 108, pl. 21 of *Luoyang Shaogou Han mu* (n. 1 above).

同注 1 引《洛阳烧沟汉墓》,107、108 页,图版贰壹。

12 Wuhan City Cultural Relics Commission, "Wuchang Renjiawan Liuchao chuqi muzang qingli jianbao" [Brief report on the clearance of tombs of early Six Dynasties period at Renjiawan, Wuchang], *Wenwu Cankao Ziliao*, 1955, no. 12, pp. 68-70.

武汉市文物管理委员会:《武昌任家湾六朝初期墓葬清理简报》,《文物参考资料》,1955 年,12 期,68—70 页。

Cheng Xinren, "Wuhan chutu de liangkuai Dong Wu qianquan shiwen" [Annotated transcription of two lead documents of the Eastern Wu dynasty unearthed in Wuhan], *Kaogu*, 1965, no. 10, p. 529.

程欣人:《武汉出土的两块东吴铅券释文》,《考古》,1965 年,10 期,529 页。

Ni Zhenkui et al., "Nanjing Zhaoshigang faxian Sanguo shidai Sun Wu you ming ciqi" [Inscribed porcelain of Sun Wu of the Three Kingdoms period discovered at Zhaoshigang, Nanjing], *Wenwu Cankao Ziliao*, 1955, no. 8, pp. 156-57.

倪振逵等:《南京赵士冈发现三国时代孙吴有铭瓷器》,《文物参考资料》,1955 年,8 期,156、157 页。

Nanjing Museum et al., *Jiangsu sheng chutu wenwu xuanji* [Selected cultural relics unearthed in Jiangsu province] (Beijing: Wenwu Press, 1963), figs. 127, 128.

南京博物院等:《江苏省出土文物选集》,文物出版社,1963 年,图 127、128。

13 Ye Hongming et al., "Guanyu wo guo ciqi qiyuan de kanfa" [A view of the origin of porcelain in China], *Wenwu*, 1978, no. 10, pp. 86, 87.

叶宏明等:《关于我国瓷器起源的看法》,《文物》,1978 年,10 期,86、87 页。

14 Institute of Archaeology, Chinese Academy of Sciences, *Luoyang Zhongzhoulu* [Zhongzhou Road in Luoyang] (Beijing: Kexue Press, 1959), p. 134, pl. 85.

中国科学院考古研究所:《洛阳中州路》,科学出版社,1959 年,134 页,图版捌伍。

Boxian Museum, "Boxian Fenghuangtai yihao Han mu qingli jianbao" [Brief report on the clearance of Han tomb number 1 at Fenghuangtai in Boxian], *Kaogu*, 1974, no. 3, pp. 187, 188, pl. 6.

亳县博物馆:《亳县凤凰台一号汉墓清理简报》,《考古》,1974 年,3 期,187、188 页,图版陆。

15 Boxian Museum of Anhui Province, "Boxian Cao Cao zongzu muzang" [Tombs of lineage members of Cao Cao in Boxian], *Wenwu*, 1978, no. 8, pp. 33, 34, 39.

安徽省亳县博物馆:《亳县曹操宗族墓葬》,《文物》,1978 年,8 期,33、34、39 页。

16 Shaanxi Provincial Cultural Relics Commission et al., "Xianyang Yangjiawan Han mu fajue jianbao" [Brief report on the excavation of the Han tomb at Yangjiawan in Xianyang], *Wenwu*, 1977, no. 10, pp. 10-16, pls. 1, 3.

陕西省文管会等:《咸阳杨家湾汉墓发掘简报》,《文物》,1977 年,10 期,10—16 页,图版壹、叁。

17 Institute of Archaeology, Chinese Academy of Sciences, *Huixian fajue baogao* [Report on excavations in Huixian] (Beijing: Kexue Press, 1956), p. 141, pls. 101, 102.

中国科学院考古研究所:《辉县发掘报告》,科学出版社,1956 年,141 页,图版壹零壹、壹零贰。

18 Yu Weichao, "Handai de ting shi tao wen" [Han dynasty pottery inscriptions with the characters "ting" and "shi"], *Wenwu*, 1963, no. 2, pp. 34-38.

俞伟超:《汉代的"亭""市"陶文》,《文物》,1963 年,2 期,34—38 页。

19 P. 37 of *Luoyang Zhongzhoulu* (n. 14 above).

同注 14 引《洛阳中州路》,37 页。

20 See n. 18 above.

同注 18。

21 Luo Zhenyu, *Qi Lu fengni jicun* [Catalogue of seal clays from Qi and Lu] (1912), p. 48.

罗振玉:《齐鲁封泥集存》,1912 年,48 页。

22 Chen Zhi, *Liang Han jingji shi liao luncong* [Discussion of data on the economic history of the two Han dynasties] (Xi'an: Shaanxi Renmin Press, 1958), pp. 169, 170.

陈直:《两汉经济史料论丛》,陕西人民出版社,1958 年,169、170 页。

23 Archaeology Team, Henan Provincial Bureau of Culture, "Henan Yuxian Baisha Han mu fajue baogao" [Report on the excavation of Han tombs at Baisha in Yuxian, Henan], *Kaogu Xuebao*, 1959, no. 1, pp. 62-70, pl. 1.

河南省文化局文物工作队：《河南禹县白沙汉墓发掘报告》，《考古学报》，1959 年，1 期，62—70 页，图版壹。

Pp. 8-22, pls. 1-3, 6 of *Luoyang Shaogou Han mu* (n. 1 above).

同注 1 引《洛阳烧沟汉墓》，8—22 页，图版壹——叁、陆。

24 Archaeology Teams Number 1 and 2, Henan Provincial Bureau of Culture, *Henan chutu kongxinzhuan tapian ji* [Catalogue of rubbings of hollow bricks unearthed in Henan] (Beijing: Renmin Art Press, 1963).

河南省文化局文物工作队第一、二队：《河南出土空心砖拓片集》，人民美术出版社，1963 年。

25 Guo Baojun, "Luoyang xijiao Handai juzhu yiji" [Han dynasty dwelling site in the western suburb of Luoyang], *Kaogu Tongxun*, 1956, no. 1, pp. 19-23, pls. 1-4.

郭宝钧：《洛阳西郊汉代居住遗迹》，《考古通讯》，1956 年，1 期，19—23 页，图版壹——肆。

26 Institute of Archaeology, Chinese Academy of Social Sciences, *Han Chang'an cheng yizhi fajue baogao* [Report of the excavation of the ruins of the Han dynasty city of Chang'an]. In preparation.

中国社会科学院考古研究所：《汉长安城遗址发掘报告》，待刊。

27 Pp. 91, 92, pl. 13 of *Luoyang Shaogou Han mu* (n. 1 above).

同注 1 引《洛阳烧沟汉墓》，91、92 页，图版拾叁。

28 Liu Zhiyuan, *Sichuan Handai huaxiangzhuan yishu* [The pictorial brick art of the Han dynasty in Sichuan] (Beijing: Chinese Classic Art Press, 1958).

刘志远：《四川汉代画象砖艺术》，中国古典艺术出版社，1958 年。

29 Institute of Archaeology, Chinese Academy of Sciences, *Fengxi fajue baogao* [Report on archaeological excavations on the west bank of the Feng river] (Beijing: Wenwu Press, 1963), pp. 26, 27, pl. 11.

中国科学院考古研究所：《沣西发掘报告》，文物出版社，1963 年，26、27 页，图版拾壹。

30 Pp. 46-49, pls. 30-34 of *Luoyang Zhongzhoulu* (n. 14 above).

同注 14 引《洛阳中州路》，46—49 页，图版叁拾——叁肆。

31 Inner Mongolia Autonomous Region Archaeology Team, *Neimenggu chutu wenwu xuan ji* [Selected cultural relics unearthed in Inner Mongolia] (Beijing: Wenwu

Press, 1963), p. 7, figs. 71, 72.

内蒙古自治区文物工作队：《内蒙古出土文物选集》，文物出版社，1963 年，7 页，图 71、72。

32 An Zhimin, "Qinghai de gudai wenhua" [Ancient cultures in Qinghai], *Kaogu*, 1959, no. 7, p. 381.

安志敏：《青海的古代文化》，《考古》，1959 年，7 期，381 页。

An Zhimin, "Yuanxing yuan nian wadang buzheng" [Supplement and correction concerning the "Yuanxing First Year" eaves tile), *Kaogu*, 1959, no. 11, pp. 626-28.

安志敏：《元兴元年瓦当补正》，《考古》，1959 年，11 期，626—628 页。

33 Han City Excavation Team, Institute of Archaeology, "Han Chang'an cheng nanjiao lizhi jianzhu yizhi qun fajue jianbao" [Brief report on the group of ritual structures to the south of the Han city of Chang'an], *Kaogu*, 1960, no. 7, p. 38.

考古研究所汉城发掘队：《汉长安城南郊礼制建筑遗址群发掘简报》，《考古》，1960 年，7 期，38 页。

Luo Zhongru, "Xi'an xijiao faxian Handai jianzhu yizhi" [Han dynasty architectural remains found in the western suburb of Xi'an], *Kaogu Tongxun*, 1957, no. 6, pp. 26-30, pl. 8.

雒忠如：《西安西郊发现汉代建筑遗址》，《考古通讯》，1957 年，6 期，26—30 页，图版捌。

34 Chen Zhi, "Qin Han wadang gaishu" [A general description of the eaves tiles of Qin and Han], *Wenwu*, 1963, no. 11, pp. 20-24.

陈直：《秦汉瓦当概述》，《文物》，1963 年，11 期，20—24 页。

35 Pp. 170-71 of reference cited in n. 22 above.

同注 22，170、171 页。

❽

1 Shi Wei, "Changsha Mawangdui yihao Han mu de guan guo zhidu" [The coffin and wooden chamber in the Han tomb number 1 at Mawangdui in Changsha], *Kaogu*, 1972, no. 6, pp. 49-52.

史为：《长沙马王堆一号汉墓的棺椁制度》，《考古》，1972 年，6 期，49—52 页，

Ji'nancheng Fenghuangshan Han Tomb Number 168 Excavation and Reporting Team, "Hubei Jiangling Fenghuangshan 168-hao Han mu fajue jianbao" [Brief report on the excavation of Han tomb number 168 at Fenghuangshan, Jiangling, Hubei], *Wenwu*, 1975, no. 9, p. 2, pl. 1.

纪南城凤凰山一六八号汉墓发掘整理组：《湖北江陵凤凰山一六八号汉墓发掘简

报》，《文物》，1975 年，9 期，2 页，图版壹。

Beijing Municipality Ancient Tombs Excavation Office, "Dabaotai Xi Han muguomu fajue jianbao" [Brief report on the excavation of the wooden-chambered tomb of Western Han at Dabaotai], *Wenwu*, 1977, no. 6, pp. 23-29, pl. 4.

北京市古墓发掘办公室：《大葆台西汉木椁墓发掘简报》，《文物》，1977 年，6 期，23—29 页，图版肆。

Institute of Archaeology, Chinese Academy of Sciences et al., "Mawangdui er san hao Han mu fajue de zhuyao shouhuo" [Major results of the excavation of Han tombs number 2 and 3 at Mawangdui], *Kaogu*, 1975, no. 1, p. 48.

中国科学院考古研究所等：《马王堆二、三号汉墓发掘的主要收获》，《考古》，1975 年，1 期，48 页。

2 Cultural Relics Team, Changsha City Bureau of Culture, "Changsha Xianjiahu Xi Han Cao Zhuan mu" [The tomb of Cao Zhuan of Western Han at Xianjiahu, Changsha], *Wenwu*, 1979, no. 3, pp. 1-4.

长沙市文化局文物组：《长沙咸家湖西汉曹㜏墓》，《文物》，1979 年，3 期，1—4 页。

3 Shandong Provincial Museum, "Qufu Jiulongshan Han mu fajue jianbao" [Brief report on the excavation of the Han tomb at Jiulongshan in Qufu], *Wenwu*, 1972, no. 5, pp. 39-41.

山东省博物馆：《曲阜九龙山汉墓发掘简报》，《文物》，1972 年，5 期，39—41 页。

4 Institute of Archaeology, Chinese Academy of Social Sciences, et al., *Mancheng Han mu* [Han tombs in Mancheng] (Beijing: Wenwu Press, 1978), pp. 14-17, pl. 3.

中国社会科学院考古研究所等：《满城汉墓》，文物出版社，1978 年，14—17 页，图版三。

5 Archaeological Excavation Team of Luoyang District, *Luoyang Shaogou Han mu* [Han tombs at Shaogou, Luoyang] (Beijing: Kexue Press, 1959), p. 30, pl. 6.

洛阳区考古发掘队：《洛阳烧沟汉墓》，科学出版社，1959 年，30 页，图版陆。

6 Luoyang Museum, "Luoyang Xi Han Bu Qianqiu bihua mu fajue jianbao" [Brief report on the excavation of the frescoed tomb of Bu Qianqiu of Western Han in Luoyang], *Wenwu*, 1977, no. 6, pp. 8-12, pls. 1-3.

洛阳博物馆：《洛阳西汉卜千秋壁画墓发掘简报》，《文物》，1977 年，6 期，8—12 页，图版壹——叁。

7 Guo Moruo, "Luoyang Han mu bihua shitan" [An exploratory study of the murals in the Han tomb in Luoyang], *Kaogu Xuebao*, 1964, no. 2, pp. 1-5.

郭沫若：《洛阳汉墓壁画试探》，《考古学报》，1964 年，2 期，1—5 页。

8 Xia Nai, "Wuchanjieji wenhua da geming zhong de kaogu xin faxian" [New archaeological discoveries during the "Great Proletarian Cultural Revolution"], *Kaogu*, 1972, no. 1, p. 33.

夏鼐：《无产阶级 "文化大革命" 中的考古新发现》，《考古》，1972 年，1 期，33 页。

Archaeology Team, Hebei Provincial Bureau of Culture, "Hebei Dingxian Beizhuang Han mu fajue baogao" [Report on the excavation of the Han tomb at Beizhuang in Dingxian, Hebei], *Kaogu Xuebao*, 1964, no. 2, pp. 127-33.

河北省文化局文物工作队：《河北定县北庄汉墓发掘报告》，《考古学报》，1964 年，2 期，127—133 页。

Idem, *Wangdu erhao Han mu* [Han tomb number 2 at Wangdu] (Beijing: Wenwu press, 1959), pp. 2-5.

河北省文化局文物工作队：《望都二号汉墓》，文物出版社，1959 年，2—5 页。

9 Beijing History Museum et al., *Wangdu Han mu bihua* [Han tomb wall pictures in Wangdu] (Beijing: Chinese Classic Art Press, 1955), pp. 3-14, pls. 8, 9.

北京历史博物馆等：《望都汉墓壁画》，中国古典艺术出版社，1955 年，3—14 页，图版捌、玖。

10 An Jinhuai et al., "Mixian Dahuting Handai huaxiangshi mu he bihua mu" [Han dynasty tombs with pictorial stones and murals at Dahuting, Mixian], *Wenwu*, 1972, no. 10, p. 52, pl. 1.

安金槐等：《密县打虎亭汉代画象石墓和壁画墓》，《文物》，1972 年，10 期，52 页，图版壹。

11 Inner Mongolia Autonomous Region Museum Archaeology Team, *Holingor Han mu bihua* [Mural paintings in the Han dynasty tomb at Holingor] (Beijing: Wenwu Press, 1978).

内蒙古自治区博物馆文物工作队：《和林格尔汉墓壁画》，文物出版社，1978 年。

12 Zhou Dao et al., "Tanghe Zhenzhichang Han huaxiangshi mu de fajue" [Excavation of the Han tomb with pictorial stones at the needlework factory at Tanghe], *Wenwu*, 1973, no. 6, pp. 26, 27, 33-36.

周到等：《唐河针织厂汉画像石墓的发掘》，《文物》，1973 年，6 期，26、27、33—36 页。

Yin Ruzhang, "Shandong Anqiu Moushan shuiku faxian daxing shike Han mu" [A large Han tomb with engraved stones discovered at the Moushan reservoir in Anqiu in Shandong], *Wenwu*, 1960, no. 5, pp. 55-59.

殷汝章：《山东安邱牟山水库发现大型石刻汉墓》，《文物》，1960 年，5 期，55—59 页。

Shandong Provincial Museum, "Shandong Anqiu Han huaxiangshi mu fajue jianbao" [Brief report on the excavation of the Han tomb with pictorial stones in Anqiu, Shandong], *Wenwu*, 1964, no. 4, pp. 30-35.

山东省博物馆:《山东安丘汉画象石墓发掘简报》,《文物》,1964 年, 4 期, 30—35 页。

Shandong Provincial Museum et al., "Shandong Cangshan Yuanjia yuan nian huaxiangshi mu" [Tomb with pictorial stones dated to the first year of Yuanjia in Cangshan, Shandong], *Kaogu*, 1975, no. 2, pp. 124, 125.

山东省博物馆等:《山东苍山元嘉元年画象石墓》,《考古》,1975 年, 2 期, 124、125 页。

Zeng Zhaoyu et al., *Yi'nan gu huaxiangshi mu fajue baogao* [Report on the excavation of the ancient tomb with pictorial stones in Yi'nan] (Beijing: Bureau of Cultural Relics, Ministry of Culture, 1956), pp. 3-11, pls. 5-7, 9-16.

曾昭燏等:《沂南古画像石墓发掘报告》, 文化部文物管理局, 1956 年, 3—11 页, 图版五——七、九——十六。

13 Pp. 12, 21, pls. 24, 49 of the article by Zeng Zhaoyu (see n. 12 above).

同注 12 引曾昭燏书, 12、21 页, 图版二十四、四十九。

14 Liu Zhiyuan, *Sichuan Handai huaxiangzhuan yishu* [The pictorial brick art of the Han dynasty in Sichuan] (Beijing: Chinese Classical Art Press, 1958).

刘志远:《四川汉代画象砖艺术》, 中国古典艺术出版社, 1958 年。

15 Liu Zhiyuan, "Chengdu Tianhuishan ya mu qingli ji" [Notes on the clearance of cliff burials at Tianhuishan in Chengdu], *Kaogu Xuebao*, 1958, no. 1, pp. 88-93, pls. 1-2.

刘志远:《成都天廻山崖墓清理记》,《考古学报》, 1958 年, 1 期, 88—93 页, 图版 壹、贰。

16 Archaeology Team, Hubei Provincial Bureau of Culture, "Hubei Jiangling sanzuo Chu mu chutu dapi zhongyao wenwu" [A large quantity of important cultural relics unearthed from three Chu tombs in Jiangling, Hubei], *Wenwu*, 1966, no. 5, p. 33.

湖北省文化局文物工作队:《湖北江陵三座楚墓出土大批重要文物》,《文物》, 1966 年, 5 期, 33 页。

17 Fu Xinian, "Zhanguo Zhongshan wang Xi mu chutu de *Zhaoyu tu* jiqi lingyuan guizhi de yanjiu" [The mausoleum plan unearthed in the tomb of Xi, the king of Zhongshan of the Warring States period, and the study of the tomb plan], *Kaogu Xuebao*, 1980, no. 1, pp. 113-15, pl. 1.

傅熹年:《战国中山王罃墓出土的〈兆域图〉及其陵园规制的研究》,《考古学报》, 1980 年, 1 期, 113—115 页, 图版壹。

Yang Hongxun, "Zhanguo Zhongshan wang ling ji zhaoyu tu yanjiu" [Study of the mausoleum of the king of Zhongshan in the Warring States period and the mausoleum plan], *Kaogu Xuebao*, 1980, no. 1, pp. 127-32.

杨鸿勋：《战国中山王陵及兆域图研究》，《考古学报》，1980 年，1 期，127—132 页。

18 Chen Mingda, "Handai de shi que" [Stone monumental towers of the Han dynasty], *Wenwu*, 1961, no. 12, pp. 9-23.

陈明达：《汉代的石阙》，《文物》，1961 年，12 期，9—23 页。

19 Kong Ciqing, "Shandong Qufu Konglin faxian Handai shi shou" [Han dynasty stone animals discovered in the Konglin in Qufu, Shandong], *Kaogu*, 1964, no. 4, p. 209.

孔次青：《山东曲阜孔林发现汉代石兽》，《考古》，1964 年，4 期，209 页。

Tao Mingkuan et al, "Lushanxian de Dong Han shike" [Eastern Han stone sculptures in Lushanxian], *Wenwu Cankao Ziliao*, 1957, no. 10, pp. 41, 42.

陶鸣宽等：《芦山县的东汉石刻》，《文物参考资料》，1957 年，10 期，41、42 页。

20 Tianjin Municipality Cultural Relics Department et al., "Wuqingxian faxian Dong Han Xianyu Huang mu bei" [Tomb stele of Xianyu Huang of Eastern Han discovered in Wuqingxian], *Wenwu*, 1974, no. 8, pp. 68-70.

天津市文物管理处等：《武清县发现东汉鲜于璜墓碑》，《文物》，1974 年，8 期，68—70 页。

21 Archaeology Team Number 2, Henan Provincial Bureau of Culture, "Luoyang Jin mu de fajue" [Excavation of Jin tombs in Luoyang], *Kaogu Xuebao*, 1957, no. 1, pp. 181-84.

河南省文化局文物工作队第二队：《洛阳晋墓的发掘》，《考古学报》，1957 年，1 期，181—184 页。

22 Hunan Provincial Museum et al., *Changsha Mawangdui yihao Han mu fajue jianbao* [Brief report on the excavation of Han tomb number 1 at Mawangdui, Changsha] (Beijing: Wenwu Press, 1972), pp. 13-27, pl. 26.

湖南省博物馆等：《长沙马王堆一号汉墓发掘简报》，文物出版社，1972 年，13—27 页，图版二十六。

23 Pp. 39-43, pl. 71 of the book cited in n. 22.

同注 22 引书，39—43 页，图版七十一。

P. 57, pl. 6 of "Mawangdui er san hao Han mu fajue de zhuyao shouhuo" (see n. 1 above).

同注 1 引《马王堆二、三号汉墓发掘的主要收获》，57 页，图版陆。

Linyi Jinqueshan Han Tomb Excavation Team, "Shandong Linyi Jinqueshan jiuhao Han mu fajue jianbao" [Brief report on the excavation of Han tomb number 9 at Jinqueshan in Linyi, Shandong], *Wenwu*, 1977, no. 11, pp. 25, 26, pl. 1.

临沂金雀山汉墓发掘组：《山东临沂金雀山九号汉墓发掘简报》，《文物》，1977 年，11 期，25、26 页，图版壹。

24 Gansu Provincial Museum et al, *Wuwei Han jian* [Han slips from Wuwei] (Beijing: Wenwu Press, 1964), pp. 148-49, pl. 23.

甘肃省博物馆等：《武威汉简》，文物出版社，1964 年，148、149 页，图版二十三。

25 Shi Wei, "Guanyu 'jinlü yuyi' de ziliao jianjie" [A short introduction to the materials on the gold-threaded jade shroud], *Kaogu*, 1972, no. 2, pp. 48-50.

史为：《关于"金缕玉衣"的资料简介》，《考古》，1972 年，2 期，48—50 页。

26 Technical Laboratory, Institute of Archaeology, Chinese Academy of Sciences, "Mancheng Han mu 'jinlü yuyi' de qingli he fuyuan" [Study and restoration of the gold-threaded jade shroud in the Han tomb in Mancheng], *Kaogu*, 1972, no. 2, pp. 39-47.

中国科学院考古研究所技术室：《满城汉墓"金缕玉衣"的清理和复原》，《考古》，1972 年，2 期，39—47 页。

Hebei Provincial Museum et al., "Dingxian 40-hao Han mu chutu de jinlü yuyi" [Gold-threaded jade shroud unearthed from Han tomb number 40 in Dingxian], *Wenwu*, 1976, no. 7, pp. 57-59, pl. 4.

河北省博物馆等：《定县 40 号汉墓出土的金缕玉衣》，《文物》，1976 年，7 期，57—59 页，图版肆。

Fujita Kunio et al., *Chūka Jinmin Kyōwakoku shutsudo bumbutsu ten zushū* [A catalogue of the exhibition of archaeological finds in the People's Republic of China] (Tokyo: Asahi Shinbunshya, 1973), pl. 95.

藤田国雄等：《中华人民共和国出土文物展图录》，朝日新闻东京本社企画部，1973 年，图版 95。

Boxian Museum of Anhui Province, "Boxian Cao Cao zongzu muzang" [Tombs of lineage members of Cao Cao in Boxian], *Wenwu*, 1978, no. 8, p. 36, fig. 19.

安徽省亳县博物馆：《亳县曹操宗族墓葬》，《文物》，1978 年，8 期，36 页，图十九。

27 Pp. 149-51 of "Hebei Dingxian Beizhuang Han mu fajue baogao" (see n. 8 above).

同注 8 引《河北定县北庄汉墓发掘报告》，149—151 页。

28 Shaanxi Provincial Cultural Relics Commission et al., "Xianyang Yangjiawan Han mu fajue jianbao" [Brief report on the excavation of the Han tomb at Yangjiawan in Xianyang], *Wenwu*, 1977, no. 10, p. 16.

陕西省文管会等：《咸阳杨家湾汉墓发掘简报》，《文物》，1977 年，10 期，16 页。

29 Institute of Archaeology, Chinese Academy of Sciences, *Changsha fajue baogao* [Report on the excavations in Changsha] (Beijing: Kexue Press, 1957), p. 55.

中国科学院考古研究所：《长沙发掘报告》，科学出版社，1957 年，55 页。

30 Hubei Provincial Museum et al., "Hubei Yunmeng Xi Han mu fajue jianbao" [Brief report on Western Han tombs in Yunmeng, Hubei], *Wenwu*, 1973, no. 9, p. 24, fig. 44, 45.

湖北省博物馆等：《湖北云梦西汉墓发掘简报》，《文物》，1973 年，9 期，24 页，图 44、45。

Nanjing Museum et al., "Haizhou Xi Han Huo He mu qingli jianbao" [Brief report on the clearance of the tomb of Huo He of Western Han in Haizhou], *Kaogu*, 1974, no. 3, pp. 183, 184, fig. 5.

南京博物院等：《海州西汉霍贺墓清理简报》，《考古》，1974 年，3 期，183、184 页，图五。

Nan Po, "Jiangsu Lianyungangshi Haizhou Xi Han Shi Qi Yao mu" [Tomb of Shi Qi Yao of Western Han at Haizhou, Lianyungang city, Jiangsu], *Kaogu*, 1975, no. 3, p. 175, fig. 6.

南波：《江苏连云港市海州西汉侍其繇墓》，《考古》，1975 年，3 期，175 页，图六。

❾

1 Hunan Provincial College of Agronomy et al., *Changsha Mawangdui yihao Han mu chutu dong zhi wu biaoben de yanjiu* [Studies of animal and plant remains from Han tomb number 1 at Mawangdui, Changsha] (Beijing: Wenwu Press, 1978).

湖南省农学院等：《长沙马王堆一号汉墓出土动植物标本的研究》，文物出版社，1978 年。

2 Hunan Provincial Museum et al., *Changsha Mawangdui yihao Han mu fajue jianbao* [Brief report on the excavation of Han tomb number 1 at Mawangdui, Changsha] (Beijing: Wenwu Press, 1972), pp. 130-42, 154, 155, pls. 11, 219-22.

湖南省博物馆等：《长沙马王堆 号汉墓发掘简报》，文物出版社，1972 年，130—142、154、155 页，图版十一、二一九——二二二。

3 Institute of Archaeology, Chinese Academy of Social Sciences et al., *Mancheng Han mu* [Han tombs in Mancheng] (Beijing: Wenwu Press, 1978), pp. 40, 41, pl. 5.

中国社会科学院考古研究所等：《满城汉墓》，文物出版社，1978 年，40、41 页，图版五。

4 Pp. 46-75, pls. 78-152 of work cited in n. 2 above.

同注 2，46—75 页，图版七八——一五二。

5 Fenghuangshan Han Tomb Number 167 Excavation and Reporting Team, "Jiangling Fenghuangshan 167-hao Han mu fajue jianbao" [Brief report on the excavation of Han tomb number 167 at Fenghuangshan in Jiangling], *Wenwu*, 1976, no. 10, p. 35.

凤凰山一六七号汉墓发掘整理小组：《江陵凤凰山一六七号汉墓发掘简报》，《文物》，1976 年，10 期，35 页。

6 Shandong Provincial Museum, "Qufu Jiulongshan Han mu fajue jianbao" [Brief report on the excavation of the Han tomb at Jiulongshan in Qufu], *Wenwu*, 1972, no. 5, pp. 41, 42.

山东省博物馆：《曲阜九龙山汉墓发掘简报》，《文物》，1972 年，5 期，41、42 页。

7 Beijing Municipality Ancient Tombs Excavation Office, "Dabaotai Xi Han muguomu fajue jianbao" [Brief report on the excavation of the wooden-chambered tomb of Western Han at Dabaotai], *Wenwu*, 1977, no. 6, p. 23, pl. 4.

北京市古墓发掘办公室：《大葆台西汉木椁墓发掘简报》，《文物》，1977 年，6 期，23 页，图版肆。

8 Zhan Li et al., "Shi tan Yangjiawan Han mu qibing yong" [A tentative discussion of the figurines of mounted soldiers from the Han tomb of Yangjiawan], *Wenwu*, 1977, no. 10, pp. 22-26.

展力等：《试谈杨家湾汉墓骑兵俑》，《文物》，1977 年，10 期，22—26 页。

9 Gansu Provincial Museum, "Wuwei Leitai Han mu" [Han tomb at Leitai in Wuwei], *Kaogu Xuebao*, 1974, no. 2, pp. 90-97, pls. 3-9.

甘肃省博物馆：《武威雷台汉墓》，《考古学报》，1974 年，2 期，90—97 页，图版叁——玖。

10 Ibid., pp. 104, 105.

同上，104、105 页。

11 P. 126, pls. 226, 227 of work cited in n. 2 above.

同注 2，126 页，图版二二六、二二七。

12 Institute of Archaeology, Chinese Academy of Sciences et al., "Mawangdui er san hao Han mu fajue de zhuyao shouhuo" [Major results of the excavation of Han tombs number 2 and 3 at Mawangdui], *Kaogu*, 1975, no. 1, pp. 48-55.

中国科学院考古研究所等：《马王堆二、三号汉墓发掘的主要收获》，《考古》，1975 年，1 期，48—55 页。

Mawangdui Han Silk Books Study Group, *Mawangdui Han mu boshu* [Silk books from Han tombs at Mawangdui], vols. 1-3 (Beijing: Wenwu Press, 1974).

马王堆汉墓帛书整理小组：《马王堆汉墓帛书》（壹）、（贰）、（叁），文物出版社，1974 年。

Anhui Provincial Archaeology Team et al., "Fuyang Shuanggudui Xi Han Ruyinhou mu fajue jianbao" [Brief report on the excavation of the tomb of Marquis Ruyin of Western Han at Shuanggudui in Fuyang], *Wenwu*, 1978, no. 8, p. 15, pl. 2.

安徽省文物工作队等：《阜阳双古堆西汉汝阴侯墓发掘简报》，《文物》，1978 年，8 期，15 页，图版贰。

13 Shandong Provincial Museum et al., "Shandong Linyi Xi Han mu faxian Sunzi bing fa he Sun Bin bing fa deng zhujian de jianbao" [Brief report on the discovery of *Sunzi bing fa*, *Sun Bin bing fa*, and other bamboo slips from a Western Han tomb in Linyi, Shandong], *Wenwu*, 1974, no. 2, pp. 16-18, pls. 1-8.

山东省博物馆等：《山东临沂西汉墓发现＜孙子兵法＞和＜孙膑兵法＞等竹简的简报》，《文物》，1974 年，2 期，16—18 页，图版壹——捌。

Yinqueshan Han mu zhujian Study Group, *Yinqueshan Han mu zhujian* [Bamboo slips from the Han tomb at Yinqueshan], vol. 1 (Beijing: Wenwu Press, 1975).

《银雀山汉墓竹简》整理小组：《银雀山汉墓竹简》（壹），文物出版社，1975 年。

14 Gansu Provincial Museum et al., *Wuwei Han jian* [Han slips from Wuwei] (Beijing: Wenwu Press, 1964).

甘肃省博物馆等：《武威汉简》，文物出版社，1964 年。

Gansu Provincial Museum et al., "Wuwei Hantanpo Han mu fajue jianbao" [Brief report on the excavation of Han tomb at Hantanpo in Wuwei], *Wenwu*, 1973, no. 12, pp. 18-21, pls. 1-4.

甘肃省博物馆等：《武威旱滩坡汉墓发掘简报》，《文物》，1973 年，12 期，18—21 页，图版壹——肆。

Idem, *Wuwei Handai yi jian* [Medical tablets of the Han dynasty in Wuwei] (Beijing: Wenwu Press, 1975).

甘肃省博物馆等：《武威汉代医简》，文物出版社，1975 年。

15 Zhou Shirong, "Changsha chutu Xi Han yinzhang jiqi youguan wenti yanjiu" [Western Han seals from Changsha and related problems], *Kaogu*, 1978, no. 4, pp. 271-79.

周世荣：《长沙出土西汉印章及其有关问题研究》，《考古》，1978 年，4 期，271—279 页。

16 Hunan Provincial Museum et al., "Changsha Mawangdui er san hao Han mu

fajue jianbao" [Brief report on Han tombs number 2 and 3 at Mawangdui, Changsha], *Wenwu*, 1974, no. 7, p. 40, pl. 15.

湖南省博物馆等:《长沙马王堆二、三号汉墓发掘简报》,《文物》, 1974 年, 7 期, 40 页, 图版拾伍。

17 Mancheng Excavation Team, Institute of Archaeology, Chinese Academy of Sciences, "Mancheng Han mu fajue jiyao" [Major results of the excavation of the Han tombs in Mancheng], *Kaogu*, 1972, no. 1, p. 17.

中国科学院考古研究所满城发掘队:《满城汉墓发掘纪要》,《考古》, 1972 年, 1 期, 17 页。

18 Lu Bo, "Handai Xu Sheng mai di qian quan jianjie" [A short introduction to the lead document concerning a sale of land by Xu Sheng of the Han dynasty], *Wenwu*, 1972, no. 5, pp. 60-62.

鲁波:《汉代徐胜买地铅券简介》,《文物》, 1972 年, 5 期, 60—62 页。

19 Institute of Archaeology, Chinese Academy of Sciences, *Luoyang Zhongzhoulu* [Zhongzhou Road in Luoyang] (Beijing: Kexue Press, 1959), p. 134, pl. 88.

中国科学院考古研究所:《洛阳中州路》, 科学出版社, 1959 年, 134 页, 图版捌捌。

20 Shaanxi Provincial Cultural Relics Commission, "Tongguan Diaoqiao Handai Yang shi mu qun fajue jianji" [A brief note on the excavation of the Yang lineage graves of the Han dynasty at Diaoqiao, Tongguan], *Wenwu*, 1961, no. 1, p. 59.

陕西省文物管理委员会:《潼关吊桥汉代杨氏墓群发掘简记》,《文物》, 1961 年, 1 期, 59 页。

21 Wang Zhongshu, "Han Tongting Hongnong Yangshi zhongying kaolüe" [A short examination of the Yang lineage graves at Hongnong in the Han era in Tongting], *Kaogu*, 1963, no. 1, pp. 33-38.

王仲殊:《汉潼亭弘农杨氏冢茔考略》,《考古》, 1963 年, 1 期, 33—38 页。

22 Du Baoren, "Xi Han zhu ling weizhi kao" [A study of the locations of the imperial mausoleums of Western Han], *Kaogu yu Wenwu*, 1980, no. 1, pp. 29-33.

杜葆仁,《西汉诸陵位置考》,《考古与文物》, 1980 年, 1 期, 29—33 页。

Adachi Kiroku, *Chōan shiseki kō* [A study of historical monuments in Chang'an] (Chinese translation, Shanghai: Commercial Press, 1935), pp. 63-86.

足立喜六:《长安史迹考》(中译本), 商务印书馆, 1935 年, 63—86 页。

23 Li Jianren, *Luoyang gu jin tan* [Talks on Luoyang's past and present] (Historical Studies Society, 1936), pp. 309-10.

李健人:《洛阳古今谈》, 史学研究社, 1936 年, 309、310 页。

24 Shaanxi Provincial Cultural Relics Commission, "Shaanxi Xingpingxian Mao Ling kancha" [Investigation of Mao Ling in Xingpingxian, Shaanxi], *Kaogu*, 1964, no. 2, pp. 86-89.

陕西省文物管理委员会:《陕西兴平县茂陵勘查》,《考古》,1964 年,2 期,86—89 页。

25 Mao Ling Relics Preservation Office et al., "Mao Ling he Huo Qubing mu" [Mao Ling and the tomb of Huo Qubing], *Wenwu*, 1976, no. 7, pp. 87-89, pl. 3.

茂陵文物保管所等:《茂陵和霍去病墓》,《文物》,1976 年,7 期,87—89 页,图版叁。

26 Shaanxi Provincial Cultural Relics Commission et al., "Xianyang Yangjiawan Han mu fajue jianbao" [Brief report on the excavation of the Han tomb at Yangjiawan in Xianyang], *Wenwu*, 1977, no. 10, p. 10.

陕西省文管会等:《咸阳杨家湾汉墓发掘简报》,《文物》,1977 年,10 期,10 页。

27 Qin Zhongxing, "Han Yang Ling fujin qiantu mu de faxian" [Discovery of tombs of shackled convict-laborers near Yang Ling of Han], *Wenwu*, 1972, no. 7, pp. 51-53.

秦中行:《汉阳陵附近钳徒墓的发现》,《文物》,1972 年,7 期,51—53 页。

28 Luoyang Archaeology Team, Institute of Archaeology, Chinese Academy of Sciences, "Dong Han Luoyang cheng nanjiao de xingtu mudi" [Cemetery of prisoner-laborers in the southern suburb of Luoyang city of Eastern Han], *Kaogu*, 1972, no. 4, pp. 2—17, pls. 4, 5.

中国科学院考古研究所洛阳工作队:《东汉洛阳城南郊的刑徒墓地》,《考古》,1972 年,4 期,2—17 页,图版肆、伍。

29 Archaeology Team, Henan Provincial Bureau of Culture, "1955 nian Luoyang Jianxiqu xiaoxing Han mu fajue baogao" [Report of the excavations of small tombs of Han Dynasty in the area west of the Jian river in Luoyang in 1955], *Kaogu Xuebao*, 1959, no. 2, pp. 75-89, pls. 1, 2.

河南省文化局文物工作队:《一九五五年洛阳涧西区小型汉墓发掘报告》,《考古学报》,1959 年,2 期,75—89 页,图版壹、贰。

APPENDIX: A SUPPLEMENTARY BIBLIOGRAPHY OF WESTERN SOURCES

The following is a highly selective list of major works in the Western languages on Han archaeology, prepared by the editor, which is meant to supplement the original sources in Chinese and Japanese given in the footnotes. It includes only works wherein important archaeological material is reported or studied.

Ayscough, Florence. 1939. "An Uncommon Aspect of Han Sculpture: Figures from Nan-yang." *Monumenta Serica* 4: 334–44.

Bergman, Folke. 1939. *Archaeological Researches in Sinkiang, Especially the Lop-nor Region.* Stockholm: Bokförlags Aktiebolaget Thule.

Bielenstein, Hans. 1976. "Lo-yang in Later Han Times." *Bulletin of the Museum of Far Eastern Antiquities* 48: 1–142.

Buck, David D. 1975. "Three Han Dynasty Tombs at Ma-wang-tui." *World Archaeology* 7: 30–45.

Bulling, A. 1960. *The Decoration of Mirrors of the Han Period: A Chronology* (Artibus Asiae Supplementum). Ascona: Artibus Asiae Publishers.

Cammann, S. 1948. "The 'TLV' Pattern on Cosmic Mirrors of the Han Dynasty." *Journal of America Oriental Society* 68, no. 4: 159–67.

Chang, K. C. 1981. "Archaeology," in *Early Chinese History in the People's Republic of China: The Report of the Han Dynasty Studies Delegation.* Y. S. Yu, ed. Seattle: School of International Studies University of Washington.

Chavannes, Édouard. 1893. *La sculpture sur pierre en Chine au temps des deux dynasties Han.* Paris: E. Leroux.

———. 1909. "La Sculpture à l'époque des Hans." *Mission archéologique dans la Chine septentrionale.* Vol. 1, part 1. Paris: E. Leroux.

Chaves, Jonathan. 1968. "A Han Painted Tomb at Loyang." *Artibus Asiae* 30: 5–27.

Cheng, Te-k'un. 1978. "Ch'in-Han Architectural Remains." *Journal of the Insitute of Chinese Studies, The Chinese University of Hong Kong.* Vol. 9, no. 2: 503–83.

Croissant, Doris. 1964. "Funktion und Wanddekor der opferschreine von Wu Liang Tz'u: Typologische und Iconographische Untersuchungen." *Monumenta Serica* 23: 88–162.

Drake, F. S. 1943. "Sculptured Stones of the Han Dynasty." *Monumenta Serica* 8: 280–318.

Dubs, H. H. 1964. "Han 'Hill Censers,'" in *Studia Serica B. Karlgren Dedicata.* Glahn, E. and S. Egerod, eds. Copenhagen: E. Munksgaard.

Fairbank, Wilma. 1941. "The Offering Shrines of 'Wu Liang Tz'u.'" *Harvard Journal of Asiatic Studies* 6: 1–36.

—— 1942. "A Structural Key to Han Mural Art." *Harvard Journal of Asiatic Studies* 7: 52–88.

—— and M. Kitano. 1954. "Han Mural Paintings in the Pei-yuan Tomb at Liao-yang, South Manchuria." *Artibus Asiae.* Vol. 17, nos. 3-4: 238–64.

Finsterbusch, K. 1966, 1971. *Verzeichnis und Motivindex der Han Darstellungen.* 2 vols. Weisbaden: Otto Harrassowitz.

Fischer, Otto. 1931. *Die Chinesische Malerei der Han-Dynastie.* Berlin: Neff Verlag.

Franke, Wolfgang. 1948. "Die Han-Zeitlichen Felsengraeber bei Chia-ting." *Studia Serica* 7: 19–39.

Hotaling, Stephen James. 1978. "The City Walls of Han Ch'ang-an." *T'oung Pao* 64: 1–46.

Janse, O. R. T. 1947. *Archaeological Research in Indo-China.* 3 vols. Cambridge: Harvard University Press.

Karlgren, B. 1941. "Huai and Han." *Bulletin of the Museum of Far Eastern Antiquities* 13.

Laufer, B. 1909. *Chinese Pottery of the Han Dynasty.* Leiden: E. J. Brill.

——. 1911. *Chinese Grave Sculptures of the Han Period.* London: E. L. Morice.

Loewe, Michael. 1961. "The Measurement of Grain during the Han Period." *T'oung Pao* 49: 64–95.

——. 1965. "The Wooden and Bamboo Strips Found at Mon-chü-tzu." *Journal of the Royal Asiatic Society of Great Britain and Ireland,* nos. 1-2: 13–26.

——. 1977. "Manuscripts Found Recently in China: A Preliminary Survey." *T'oung Pao* 63, no. 2/3: 99–136.

——. 1979. *Ways to Paradise—The Chinese Quest for Immortality.* London: Allen & Unwin.

Rawson, Jessica. 1973. "A Group of Han Dynasty Bronzes with Chased Decoration and Some Related Ceramics." *Oriental Art* 19, no. 4: 1–16.

Riboud, Krishna. 1973. "Some Remarks on Strikingly Similar Han Figured Silks Found in Recent Years in Diverse Sites." *Archives of Asian Art* 26: 12–25.

Rostovtzeff, M. 1927. *Inlaid Bronzes of the Han Dynasty in the Collection of C. T. Loo.* Paris/Brussels: G. Vanoest.

Rudolph, Richard C. 1965. "Notes on the Han Dynasty Reliefs at Nanyang." *Symposium in Honor of Dr. Li Chi on His Seventieth Birthday.* Part 1, pp. 97–104, The Tsing Hua Journal.

———. 1965. "Newly Discovered Chinese Painted Tombs." *Archaeology* 18: 171–80.

———. 1973. "Two Recently Discovered Han Tombs." *Archaeology* 26, no. 2: 106–15.

———, and Wen Yu. 1951. *Han Tomb Art of West China*. Berkeley and Los Angeles: University of California Press.

Schloss, Ezekiel. 1979. *Art of the Han*. New York: China House Gallery.

Segalen, V. et al. 1935. *L'art funéraire à l'époque des Han*. Paris: P. Geuthner.

Shih, Hsio-yen. 1959. "I-nan and Related Tombs." *Artibus Asiae* 22: 277–312.

———. 1968. "Review of *Chinese Pottery of the Han Dynasty* by Berthold Laufer." *Artibus Asiae* 30: 347–51.

Tomita, Kojito. 1938. *Portfolio of Chinese Paintings in the Museum (Han to Sung Periods)*. Boston: Museum of Fine Arts.

Trubner, H. 1961. *Arts of the Han Dynasty*. New York: Chinese Art Society of America, Asia House.

Tsiang, K. R. 1978. "Glazed Stonewares of the Han Dynasty. Part One: The Eastern Group." *Artibus Asiae* 40, nos. 2/3: 143–76.

Watt, J. C. Y. 1970. *A Han Tomb in Lei Cheng UK*. Hong Kong: City Museum and Art Gallery.

White, W. C. 1939. *Tomb Tile Pictures of Ancient China*. Toronto: University of Toronto Press.

Yang, Lien-sheng. 1947. "A Note on the So-called TLV Mirrors and the Game Liu-po." *Harvard Journal of Asiatic Studies* 9: 202–06.